AI-Driven Cybersecurity for Autonomous Systems

Toufik Mzili
https://orcid.org/0000-0002-5733-3119
Chouaib Doukkali University, Morocco

Zahra Oughannou
Ibn Zohr University, Morocco

Nebojsa Bacanin
https://orcid.org/0000-0002-2062-924X
Singidunum University, Serbia

Mohamed Hanine
Chouaib Doukkali University, Morocco

Widi Aribowo
https://orcid.org/0000-0002-4059-1293
Surabaya State University, Indonesia

IGI Global
Scientific Publishing
Publishing Tomorrow's Research Today

Vice President of Editorial — Melissa Wagner
Director of Acquisitions — Mikaela Felty
Director of Book Development — Jocelynn Hessler
Production Manager — Mike Brehm
Cover Design — Jose Rosado

Published in the United States of America by
IGI Global Scientific Publishing
701 East Chocolate Avenue
Hershey, PA, 17033, USA
Tel: 717-533-8845 | Fax: 717-533-7115
Website: https://www.igi-global.com E-mail: cust@igi-global.com

Library of Congress Cataloging-in-Publication Data

Names: Mzili, Toufik, 1995- editor | Oughannou, Zahra, 1992- editor | Bacanin, Nebojsa, 1983- editor | Hanine, Mohamed, 1987- editor | Aribowo, Widi, 1980- editor
Title: AI-driven cybersecurity for autonomous systems / edited by Toufik Mzili, Zahra Oughannou, Nebojsa Bacanin, Mohamed Hanine, and Widi Aribowo.
Description: Hershey, PA : IGI Global Scientific Publishing, [2026] | Includes bibliographical references and index. | Summary: "This publication seeks to bridge gaps between AI, robotics, cybersecurity, and IA domain by providing actionable insights on mitigating AI bias, defending against adversarial attacks, and securing autonomous systems"-- Provided by publisher.
Identifiers: LCCN 2025011170 (print) | LCCN 2025011171 (ebook) | ISBN 9798337329222 h/c | ISBN 9798337329239 s/c | ISBN 9798337329246 ebook
Subjects: LCSH: System safety--Data processing | Autonomous distributed systems--Security measures--Data processing | Computational intelligence--Industrial applications | Artificial intelligence--Security measures | Artificial intelligence--Industrial applications | Robotics--Security measures | Computer security | Computer networks--Security measures
Classification: LCC TA169.7 .A43 2025 (print) | LCC TA169.7 (ebook)
LC record available at https://lccn.loc.gov/2025011170
LC ebook record available at https://lccn.loc.gov/2025011171

British Cataloguing in Publication Data
A Cataloguing in Publication record for this book is available from the British Library.

Detailed Table of Contents

AI-powered biometric security. Through industry insights and real-world applications, this chapter highlights the transformative impact of biometrics and AI in shaping the future of autonomous transportation.

Sherly Alphonse, Vellore Institute of Technology, Chennai, India
Neha Khadeeja, Vellore Institute of Technology, Chennai, India
Azra Q. Fathima, Vellore Institute of Technology, Chennai, India
Manasa Balaji, Vellore Institute of Technology, Chennai, India

The social problem of deepfake videos is becoming a critical issue. A rising social problem is the manipulation of these recordings by artificial intelligence (AI) techniques, particularly deep learning. Malicious people employ deepfake technologies to disseminate bogus content, including phony audio, video, and image files. The creation of convincing fake information poses a threat to privacy, security, and politics. Most deepfake video detection techniques rely on data. In-depth analysis of deepfake video production and detection is the goal of this chapter. Identifying the many difficulties in identifying deepfake films is the primary contribution of the chapter. This chapter describes about the science behind the deepfake, detection and mitigation of deepfake etc. This chapter also describes about the applications of deepfake and also the policies and technologies to combat deepfake. This chapter describes in detail about the ethical, legal and social implications.

M. Bhavana, Dayananda Sagar College of Engineering, India
U. Roopa, Dayananda Sagar College of Engineering, India

Vision Transformers (ViTs) offer significant potential for vision tasks in autonomous systems, but their susceptibility to adversarial attacks and real-time deployment challenges pose critical issues. This study analyzes ViTs' security, highlighting patch-based and backdoor attacks as primary threats, with ViT-S/16's robust accuracy declining to 40.4% and an 85% misclassification rate, respectively. Defense strategies, including adversarial training and SEViT ensembles, improve robustness by 13.1% and achieve a 0.93 AUC for adversarial detection, while denoised smoothing ensures a 59.44% certified robust accuracy. Deployment obstacles emerge with ViT-L/16's 120 ms latency, twice that of CNNs, impacting safety-critical performance. Through empirical assessments and simulations, this research emphasizes the necessity of scalable defenses and lightweight ViT designs to optimize robustness, efficiency, and safety, providing a framework to enhance ViT reliability in autonomous applications.

In recent years, the rapid proliferation of Internet of Things devices has expanded the attack surface for cyber threats, with Command-and-Control (C&C) attacks emerging as a particularly critical and stealthy threat vector. Traditional intrusion detection systems often fail to detect these low-frequency events due to severe class imbalance, where benign traffic dominates network logs. This study evaluates the effectiveness of the Synthetic Minority Over-sampling Technique (SMOTE) in enhancing C&C attack detection using a Random Forest classifier trained on flow-level data from the IoT-23 dataset. Two experimental setups were implemented: one trained on the original imbalanced dataset and the other on a SMOTE-balanced version. Without SMOTE, the model achieved a high overall accuracy of 93%, but with a low recall of 14% and F1-score of 22% for the C&C class, misclassifying over 2,600 C&C flows. The SMOTE-enhanced model lowered overall accuracy to 81%, but significantly improved C&C detection with a recall of 94% and F1-score of 83%, correctly identifying nearly 37,000 C&C instances.

Preface

INTRODUCTION

The rapid evolution of autonomous systems, ranging from self-driving vehicles and smart healthcare infrastructures to industrial automation and Internet of Things (IoT) ecosystems, has ushered in unprecedented opportunities for innovation and efficiency. However, this transformation has also significantly expanded the cybersecurity threat landscape. As these systems increasingly rely on real-time data processing, interconnected networks, and intelligent decision-making, traditional security mechanisms are proving inadequate against sophisticated, adaptive, and often AI-driven cyber threats.

This book, *AI-Driven Cybersecurity for Autonomous Systems*, brings together a diverse group of researchers and practitioners from across the globe to explore how artificial intelligence can be leveraged to secure next-generation autonomous environments. The chapters collectively address the dual role of AI as both a powerful defensive tool and a potential attack vector, offering a comprehensive examination of emerging techniques, challenges, and solutions in this critical domain.

The primary objective of this volume is to bridge the gap between theoretical advancements and practical implementations of AI-driven cybersecurity. It highlights the importance of adaptive, intelligent, and explainable security frameworks capable of responding to dynamic threats in real time. Furthermore, the book explores ethical, privacy, and performance considerations that must be addressed to ensure trustworthy and resilient autonomous systems.

CHAPTER OVERVIEWS

Chapter 1 introduces AI-based Intrusion Detection and Response Systems (IDRS), emphasizing their role in identifying anomalies and mitigating cyber risks in autonomous systems. It provides foundational knowledge on how AI enhances detection accuracy and enables rapid response mechanisms, while also discussing implementation challenges and future research directions.

Chapter 2 expands on intrusion detection by integrating privacy-preserving AI techniques. It explores adversarial machine learning, highlighting vulnerabilities within AI systems and the necessity of explainable AI to ensure transparency and trust in cybersecurity operations.

Chapter 3 presents a broader perspective on AI-powered cybersecurity, detailing how machine learning, deep learning, and predictive analytics contribute to proactive threat detection and automated responses. It also addresses critical challenges such as bias, ethical concerns, and adversarial misuse of AI.

Chapter 4 revisits intrusion detection systems with a comparative lens, analyzing traditional versus AI-enabled approaches. It delves into system design, adaptive response mechanisms, and the operational complexities associated with deploying AI-driven IDS in real-world environments.

Chapter 5 focuses on the healthcare sector, proposing an AI-powered cybersecurity model tailored to protect sensitive medical data and interconnected healthcare systems. It highlights the importance of predictive analysis, threat detection, and vulnerability management in safeguarding healthcare infrastructures.

Chapter 6 presents a case study on biometric security in autonomous vehicles, examining how AI-driven authentication methods such as facial, voice, and fingerprint recognition enhance both security and user experience. It also discusses challenges related to privacy, reliability, and system integration.

Chapter 7 addresses the growing threat of deepfake technologies, providing an in-depth analysis of their creation, detection, and societal implications. The chapter explores technical countermeasures alongside ethical and legal considerations in combating misinformation and digital manipulation.

Chapter 8 investigates the security of Vision Transformers (ViTs) in autonomous systems, focusing on their vulnerability to adversarial attacks. It evaluates advanced defense strategies and discusses the trade-offs between robustness, efficiency, and real-time deployment constraints.

Chapter 9 examines cybersecurity in IoT networks through the lens of data imbalance and attack detection. It evaluates the effectiveness of the SMOTE technique in improving the detection of Command-and-Control (C&C) attacks, demonstrating the importance of data preprocessing in enhancing AI model performance.

Together, these chapters provide a holistic view of AI-driven cybersecurity, addressing both foundational principles and cutting-edge research. This book is intended for academics, researchers, industry professionals, and policymakers seeking to understand and develop secure, intelligent systems in an increasingly autonomous world.

We hope this volume serves as a valuable resource and inspires further innovation in the pursuit of resilient and trustworthy autonomous technologies.

Chapter 1
AI-Based Intrusion Detection and Response Mechanisms:
Enhancing Cybersecurity in Autonomous Systems

Mayur Jariwala
http://orcid.org/0009-0008-1686-8791
University of the Cumberlands, USA

ABSTRACT

Autonomous systems, including self-driving vehicles and industrial robots, face escalating cybersecurity threats due to their reliance on interconnected networks and real-time data processing. Traditional security measures often fail to detect advanced attacks, necessitating AI-driven intrusion detection and response systems (IDRS). AI enhances security by identifying anomalies, adapting to evolving threats, and executing rapid countermeasures. This chapter explores AI-based IDRS, highlighting their role in mitigating cyber risks. It examines technical challenges, implementation strategies, and future advancements. By integrating theoretical insights with practical applications, this work contributes to strengthening cybersecurity in autonomous environments.

DOI: 10.4018/979-8-3373-2922-2.ch001

1. INTRODUCTION

1.1 Overview of Cybersecurity Challenges in Autonomous Systems

Autonomous systems have evolved at a rapid pace. Self-driving vehicles, industrial robots, and unmanned aerial systems now operate in our everyday environments. These systems rely on sensors, control algorithms, and networked communications. They face unique cybersecurity challenges. Digital threats target every link in the chain. A single vulnerability may compromise an entire system. Cyber attackers seek weak spots in firmware and communication protocols (Imamverdiyev & Abdullayeva, 2020). One breach can trigger cascading failures. Security in autonomous systems is not merely a technical issue. It touches on safety, privacy, and even public trust.

Security challenges manifest in many forms. Data streams from sensors can be intercepted or altered. Communication channels may be jammed or spoofed. Software flaws may let hackers inject malicious code. Outdated protocols or misconfigured networks widen the attack surface. Each element of an autonomous system represents a potential door for cyber intrusions. These systems must process data in real time. They cannot afford delays caused by traditional security checks. Their dynamic nature demands equally agile defenses.

Systems operating in public spaces face additional hazards. A compromised vehicle or drone poses risks to human life and property. The interconnection of devices creates vulnerabilities similar to those in large-scale IoT networks. Every node in the network is a possible entry point for attackers. The convergence of cyber and physical realms amplifies the potential damage. This challenge calls for a new mindset. Stakeholders must consider security from the design stage. Resilience needs to be built into every system component. The field is evolving, and threats grow more sophisticated with time.

This overview invites a careful examination of risks. It highlights the urgency for protective measures. Security must be robust yet flexible. The stakes are high in autonomous environments. The field demands vigilance and innovation.

1.2 The Importance of AI-Based Intrusion Detection and Response Mechanisms

AI-based intrusion detection systems are reshaping the defense against cyber threats. They use algorithms that learn from data. This dynamic process spotlights unusual patterns in network traffic. AI identifies subtle deviations that may signal an attack. Traditional rule-based systems lag behind sophisticated adversaries. AI

Table of Contents

mechanisms operate at speeds that keep pace with emerging threats. Their rapid decision-making is vital in dynamic, interconnected environments.

AI models benefit from continuous learning. They adapt to novel tactics used by hackers. Simple thresholds no longer suffice. Instead, these systems harness machine learning to detect even the smallest anomalies. They integrate vast data streams from sensors and logs. The approach reduces false alarms and sharpens the accuracy of alerts. In many cases, the systems act as a first line of defense. They initiate countermeasures before human operators can intervene. Fast, precise responses are crucial in mitigating potential damage.

Acar et al. (2019) discussed the role of AI extends beyond detection. It orchestrates an immediate response. Systems isolate affected components and cut off the spread of intrusions. This automated reaction helps preserve system integrity. It lightens the burden on cybersecurity teams. AI-based responses provide a safety net when manual intervention may be too slow. The use of deep learning has added layers of complexity. Neural networks capture intricate relationships in data. They enhance the ability to foresee and neutralize threats.

The evolution of cyber-attacks necessitates such adaptive systems. New attack vectors emerge almost daily. AI offers the adaptability needed to counter these threats. The technology is akin to a vigilant guardian, continuously learning and evolving. Its benefits extend to saving resources and preventing large-scale disruptions.

1.3 Scope, Objectives, and Key Contributions of This Chapter

This chapter embarks on a journey through the intricate nexus of AI and cybersecurity in autonomous systems. It spans theoretical insights and practical implementations. The scope is broad and multifaceted. The text examines technical challenges, emerging methodologies, and real-world applications. It highlights the vulnerabilities inherent in systems that merge digital and physical realms. The chapter scrutinizes the use of artificial intelligence in strengthening intrusion detection and response. It provides a framework that is accessible to scholars, industry professionals, and policy makers alike.

The objectives are clear and well defined. The chapter seeks to explain the fundamental principles behind intrusion detection systems. It aims to clarify the benefits of using AI over traditional methods. It also outlines the risks that come with rapid technological evolution. By presenting case studies and technical analyses, the chapter paints a comprehensive picture. It bridges gaps between academic theory and operational practices. The work offers a platform for future research. It encourages the exploration of new defenses against cyber threats.

The contributions of this chapter are significant. It establishes a structured approach to understanding and deploying AI-based cybersecurity measures in autonomous systems. It presents original insights into advanced threat detection, including behavioral analysis and adversarial learning. The narrative does not limit itself to current trends. It delves into future prospects like federated learning and quantum computing's impact on cyber defense. The chapter is a call to action. It invites readers to rethink established paradigms and explore innovative solutions. The text serves as a beacon for those navigating the evolving landscape of digital security.

The discussion blends academic rigor with practical relevance. It provides a thorough analysis without losing sight of real-world implications. The insights aim to empower stakeholders to build safer systems in an era of rapid digital transformation.

2. FUNDAMENTALS OF INTRUSION DETECTION AND RESPONSE IN AUTONOMOUS SYSTEMS

2.1 Defining Intrusion Detection and Response Systems (IDRS)

Intrusion Detection and Response Systems, or IDRS, are safeguards for digital networks (Farzaan et al., 2024). They watch over systems and flag odd behavior. Imagine them as a security guard on patrol. They scan network traffic, check logs, and compare current activity to known patterns. Suspicious events trigger alerts. These systems work much like our body's immune response. A small signal of trouble can start a cascade of protective measures. Simple rules or statistical checks may set off alarms. AI may step in to learn from every encounter. This learning makes the system a bit like a well-trained detective. It improves with each investigation.

IDRS carry two main duties. One duty is to detect intrusions. They sift through data and monitor communication channels. Each anomaly or deviation is noted and flagged (Cheng et al., 2021). The detection part works fast. It spots intrusions before they can escalate. The system might use signatures of known attacks or notice patterns that stray from normal behavior. It is like having multiple sensors alerting you to potential dangers.

The other duty is to respond. When an alert fires, the system reacts. It may cut off suspicious traffic or isolate parts of the network. Imagine a valve that shuts when pressure builds. The system takes swift action to reduce harm. It can block access or send alerts to security staff. This quick response often saves the day. Each measure is meant to stop an attack from spreading further. The response mechanism is not static. It adjusts with new threats. It evolves much like a seasoned firefighter learning new techniques on the job.

The combination of detection and response forms a robust defense. IDRS are not one-size-fits-all. They combine various methods to suit specific needs. They are built for flexibility and speed. New threats keep emerging. IDRS must adapt and update. In many ways, they are the frontline in the fight against cyber crime. Can any system be perfect? Not really. But a well-designed IDRS comes close to a reliable shield against intrusions.

2.2 Challenges in Implementing IDS for AI-Driven Autonomous Systems

Implementing intrusion detection systems in AI-driven autonomous systems poses many hurdles. Autonomous systems run on rapid sensor data and real-time processing (Jawhar et al., 2024). IDS must watch every data stream. They scan network packets and monitor system logs. Suspicious behavior triggers alerts. The systems live in a fast-paced digital arena. They face threats that shift like sand in the wind. One challenge is the high volume of data. Sensors produce data in torrents. Processing this information in real time taxes even advanced systems. The load can slow detection and response. It is like trying to catch raindrops in a storm.

Data accuracy forms another hurdle. False alarms raise stress. False negatives hide real dangers. An IDS must balance detection with precision. Small mistakes can disrupt operations. One missed alert might allow a breach. A wrong flag might freeze crucial tasks. Striking the right balance feels like walking on a narrow beam. It requires continuous fine-tuning and testing.

Adaptability also creates difficulties. Threat actors invent new attack methods daily. AI models learn from historical data. They may not catch something entirely new. The dynamic nature of cyber threats keeps developers on their toes. It is a game of cat and mouse. The system must update its defenses continuously. Sometimes updates lag behind the latest attack trends. That gap can be exploited.

Computational demands add to the complexity. Real-time processing needs speedy algorithms. AI-driven IDS combine multiple detection methods. They integrate signature checks with anomaly detection. Running these algorithms simultaneously stresses hardware. Energy consumption and latency become real issues. Systems sometimes struggle to keep pace with the flood of data.

Trust is yet another challenge. Users demand reliable, steady performance. Inconsistent alerts make operators wary. The system's credibility is fragile. Regular testing and recalibration are essential. Each tweak is like tuning a musical instrument. The wrong note can break the harmony. The challenge is as technical as it is human.

The field is evolving. New threats emerge every day. Implementing IDS in autonomous systems remains a work in progress. Developers must adapt, learn, and overcome. It is an ongoing battle that tests both technology and human ingenuity.

2.3 AI's Role in Real-Time Threat Detection and Mitigation

AI plays a vital part in watching over networks and systems as threats evolve in real time. It works like a vigilant sentry that never sleeps. The technology scans streams of data at lightning speed. It detects tiny deviations that might escape a human eye. Sensors feed a torrent of information to the system. AI parses this data with rapid precision. It learns from every anomaly it encounters. Patterns are recognized and logged. Unusual behaviors prompt immediate alerts.

The process is dynamic. A deep learning model sifts through data continuously. It uses layers of neural networks to spot subtle hints of danger. The model may flag a slight fluctuation in network traffic. It might also pick up on an odd sequence of system calls. The system does not wait for a clear-cut signature of an attack. It adapts on the fly. It evolves its understanding with every tick of the clock. This speed is crucial in preventing breaches from growing.

Real-time threat detection relies on speed and accuracy (Humayed et al., 2017). An AI system can weigh multiple factors at once. It uses algorithms that check for known vulnerabilities. It simultaneously searches for new patterns. Its strength lies in constant learning. It becomes smarter with each incident. Picture a chess player who improves by reviewing every move. The system refines its strategies based on past encounters. Every anomaly, every misstep, adds to its experience.

Response actions are triggered instantly. The AI may isolate a compromised node or cut off suspicious traffic. These actions are swift and calculated. They serve as a digital counterpunch to an unfolding attack. The real-time mitigation process saves resources and limits damage. The approach brings a fresh perspective to traditional cybersecurity. It combines creativity with data-driven decision-making. The field is a mix of art and science, where each alert tells a story of adaptation and resilience.

3. AI AND MACHINE LEARNING IN INTRUSION DETECTION AND RESPONSE

3.1 AI's Role in Real-Time Threat Detection and Mitigation

AI plays a vital part in watching over networks and systems as threats evolve in real time. It works like a vigilant sentry that never sleeps. The technology scans streams of data at lightning speed (Humayed et al., 2017). It detects tiny deviations that might escape a human eye. Sensors feed a torrent of information to the system.

AI parses this data with rapid precision. It learns from every anomaly it encounters. Patterns are recognized and logged. Unusual behaviors prompt immediate alerts.

The process is dynamic. A deep learning model sifts through data continuously. It uses layers of neural networks to spot subtle hints of danger. The model may flag a slight fluctuation in network traffic. It might also pick up on an odd sequence of system calls. The system does not wait for a clear-cut signature of an attack. It adapts on the fly. It evolves its understanding with every tick of the clock. This speed is crucial in preventing breaches from growing.

Real-time threat detection relies on speed and accuracy. An AI system can weigh multiple factors at once. It uses algorithms that check for known vulnerabilities. It simultaneously searches for new patterns. Its strength lies in constant learning. It becomes smarter with each incident. Picture a chess player who improves by reviewing every move. The system refines its strategies based on past encounters. Every anomaly, every misstep, adds to its experience.

Response actions are triggered instantly. The AI may isolate a compromised node or cut off suspicious traffic. These actions are swift and calculated. They serve as a digital counterpunch to an unfolding attack. The real-time mitigation process saves resources and limits damage. The approach brings a fresh perspective to traditional cybersecurity. It combines creativity with data-driven decision-making. The field is a mix of art and science, where each alert tells a story of adaptation and resilience.

3.2 Supervised vs. Unsupervised Learning Models for Cyber Threat Detection

Supervised and unsupervised learning models lie at the heart of cyber threat detection (Atzori, Iera, & Morabito, 2010). These approaches help systems recognize patterns in vast data streams. Supervised models use labeled data. Each sample comes with a clear tag. The data shows whether an event is normal or malicious. The model learns as if a teacher guides a student. It builds a map from past examples. It works best when historical data is clean and complete. Labeled records act as stepping stones. The algorithm finds familiar patterns quickly. Accuracy rises when the input is well defined. Yet, the method struggles with new, unseen threats. Data labeling demands time and expertise. Human bias can seep in. This can lead to blind spots. The model may not catch emerging attack vectors. It is like reading an old map in a changing terrain.

Unsupervised models take another path. They do not need pre-assigned labels. Instead, they search for hidden structures in data. They cluster similar events together. They flag anomalies that do not fit any cluster. Picture an explorer charting unknown lands. The model spots outliers without prior hints. It uncovers irregular behavior that might signal a novel threat. This method thrives in environments where patterns evolve fast. It adapts to changes on its own. The system can signal alerts for suspicious events. Sometimes, it might cry wolf. Yet, its flexibility proves useful when new attacks emerge. The approach is a journey into uncharted territory. It shines when past records are sparse or outdated.

Choosing between these models depends on context. One must assess data availability and threat dynamics. Many systems blend both techniques. They use known patterns and explore unknown risks simultaneously. This mix builds a defense that learns from history and stays alert to surprises. The challenge is to design a system that remains sharp yet open to new signals. The field is a constant battle between order and chaos. Research continues to push the limits of these models. The quest for better detection is a race against evolving cyber threats.

3.3 Deep Learning and Neural Networks for Advanced Threat Modeling

Deep learning has reshaped cybersecurity (Dehghantanha & Choo, 2019). Neural networks process data in layers. They detect subtle hints of danger. These models work with raw data. They learn from patterns that repeat. This approach is both clever and adaptive. It spots signals that traditional methods might miss. The system learns on its own. It evolves with each new piece of information. The process is similar to learning a language through immersion.

The network begins with simple tasks. Early layers recognize basic features. Later layers capture more abstract traits. Each layer adds a new dimension to the analysis. This design helps the system understand complex patterns. Think of it like stacking transparent sheets with images. The final view reveals hidden details. Threat modeling benefits greatly from this method. Neural networks detect anomalies that lie deep within data. They catch signals that are almost invisible. The method adapts to changes in the threat landscape. The system continuously updates its knowledge. It adjusts as new threats emerge. It learns like a seasoned detective collecting clues.

The technique offers a proactive shield against cyber attacks. It learns to differentiate between benign and harmful patterns. The network refines its understanding over time. It can flag subtle deviations before they escalate. The method works in real time. It can spot irregular behavior almost instantly. This speed is crucial in high-stakes environments. The approach does not rely solely on pre-defined rules. Instead, it discovers new indicators of compromise through continuous learning. The result is a dynamic model that grows smarter with each challenge.

The promise of deep learning in threat modeling is vast. It bridges the gap between static defenses and evolving attacks. The method provides insights that were once hidden. It empowers security teams to act quickly and decisively. This journey is not without challenges. Tuning neural networks requires expertise. Misconfigurations can lead to false alarms. Yet, the potential for improved security is immense. The field is ripe for innovation and discovery. Cybersecurity now has a tool that learns, adapts, and protects with remarkable agility.

3.4 Advantages of AI-Driven IDRS over Traditional Security Frameworks

AI-driven IDRS have reshaped the cybersecurity landscape. They learn from vast amounts of data. They adjust quickly to new threats. Traditional frameworks rely on static rules. They struggle with novel attack vectors. AI-driven systems act like smart guardians. They study patterns and flag deviations. They work with speed and flexibility. This technology learns on the fly. It improves with every incident. Static systems often depend on predefined signatures (Chiriac et al., 2025). They miss subtle shifts in behavior. AI systems see nuances that older models ignore. They operate as both detector and responder.

The benefits of AI-driven IDRS are numerous. They process real-time data without tiring. They sift through network traffic like a finely tuned filter. They catch anomalies that standard tools may overlook. Imagine a seasoned detective who picks up on minute clues. That is how AI-driven systems operate. They balance precision with rapid response. They reduce false alarms by learning from past mistakes. They adapt their models with each new input. This ongoing evolution is a game changer. It transforms reactive defense into proactive protection.

Users feel a sense of reassurance with AI-driven IDRS. The systems work silently in the background. They adapt to shifting threat landscapes. They detect patterns that emerge in unpredictable ways. The digital world is in constant flux. AI-driven systems evolve alongside attackers. They are agile and responsive. Traditional methods feel static in comparison. They work like an old lock versus a modern biometric system. One is rigid, the other dynamic. This flexibility is critical in today's fast-paced cyber environment.

Cyber defenders appreciate the ability of AI to reduce manual oversight. The systems automate routine tasks. They allow security teams to focus on complex problems. The enhanced efficiency saves both time and resources. The outcome is a more robust defense. AI-driven IDRS offer a resilient shield that evolves with the threat landscape.

4. AI-BASED INTRUSION DETECTION TECHNIQUES FOR AUTONOMOUS SYSTEMS

4.1 Behavioral Analysis and Anomaly Detection in Cybersecurity

Behavioral analysis and anomaly detection are core techniques in cybersecurity. They watch over user actions and system events. They build a baseline of normal activity. They spot deviations that signal potential threats (Dehghantanha & Choo, 2019). These methods work like a finely tuned radar. They catch subtle changes that static systems might miss. Patterns form a digital fingerprint of routine operations. An unexpected pattern stands out. It can reveal suspicious behavior in real time.

Data gathers over time. The system learns what is normal. It records activity like footsteps on a path. Each step forms a part of the bigger picture. Unusual steps alert the system. A sudden surge in network traffic may hint at data exfiltration. Strange login times might flag unauthorized access. The process is akin to noticing a familiar face acting oddly in a crowd. It triggers curiosity and caution. The system adapts with each new event. It updates its understanding continuously. This dynamic learning builds a resilient defense.

The method thrives on simplicity and depth. Simple rules give way to complex insights. It is like watching a river change its course after a heavy rain. The anomaly detection engine senses the shift. It signals when data drifts from its usual flow. Cyber defenders benefit from this insight. They receive alerts that prompt further investigation. The technique works hand-in-hand with other detection methods. It offers an extra layer of security by focusing on behavior rather than static signatures. This approach captures both known attacks and novel intrusions.

The technique has a human touch. It is comparable to a seasoned security guard noticing a subtle twitch in a visitor's demeanor. The method complements signature-based systems and enhances overall security. It adapts as networks evolve. It reduces false alarms and zeroes in on real threats. The result is a system that learns, reacts, and safeguards digital assets with remarkable agility.

4.2 AI-Powered Threat Intelligence for Proactive Security

AI-powered threat intelligence redefines our approach to digital defense. It collects data from logs, sensors, and online chatter. It scours vast information streams to spot early warning signs of danger. Imagine a vigilant scout on a busy frontier. This technology searches for faint clues that reveal emerging cyber threats. It works with rapid precision. Its algorithms learn from past attacks and adapt to new tactics.

A proactive mindset replaces reactive measures. The result is a system that predicts and prevents breaches.

Data pours in from many channels. The system gathers details from network traffic, security feeds, and even social media (Biamonte et al., 2017). It transforms raw figures into clear patterns. It compares current trends with historical records. An unusual spike or shift in behavior immediately raises an alert. This process mirrors how a meteorologist predicts storms. The system becomes a digital weather forecast, warning of potential cyber tempests. Security teams then prepare defenses before an incident escalates. This foresight cuts the window for attackers.

The intelligence engine learns continuously. Each new data point adds depth to its understanding. It works much like a seasoned detective who refines their intuition over time. Minor anomalies grow into significant indicators through persistent learning. The technology makes sense of chaos by spotting trends that others might miss. It adapts on the fly. Each update improves its accuracy and response speed. The system becomes not only a guardian but a strategic advisor. It offers insights that guide risk management decisions and bolster resilience.

The integration of AI-powered intelligence means security is no longer reactive. It provides a constant pulse on the evolving threat landscape. Alerts are generated swiftly, and actions can be taken in near real time. This approach minimizes damage and curbs potential disruptions. Its predictive capacity turns data into a proactive shield that fortifies defenses. It is a transformative step in cybersecurity. The promise lies in its ability to learn, adapt, and ultimately outsmart adversaries.

4.3 Adversarial Machine Learning in Cybersecurity and Countermeasures

Adversarial machine learning shakes up the digital defense arena. It pits clever attackers against robust systems. Attackers craft subtle inputs that mislead models. They exploit tiny weaknesses in algorithms. A small tweak in data can fool a model. The process is like sneaking past a guard by imitating a friend. Systems built on machine learning face a constant threat. Their decision boundaries become targets for deception. Imagine a chess game where one move changes the whole board. That is the risk here.

Attackers use adversarial examples to bypass defenses (Bhuyan et al., 2014). They add slight noise to images or modify network packets. The changes are nearly invisible. Yet, the impact is huge. The system may misclassify or ignore a threat. Security teams feel the pressure. The stakes are high when life-critical systems are involved. Autonomous vehicles, industrial controls, and health devices run on these models. A single misstep can lead to disastrous consequences.

Countermeasures exist to fight back. Adversarial training stands out as a common defense. Systems learn to recognize manipulated inputs. They see the trickery and adjust their response. Defensive distillation smooths decision boundaries. This makes it harder for attackers to find weak spots. Hybrid methods mix traditional rules with adaptive learning. They bring the best of both worlds. Some defenses incorporate human oversight. This helps catch anomalies that machines might miss. The battle is never one-sided. Every defense spurs new attack strategies.

Research in this field feels like an arms race. Each breakthrough in defense triggers fresh ideas on offense. The landscape evolves fast. One day, a method seems foolproof; the next, it is outsmarted. This constant tug-of-war drives innovation. Systems must stay agile and learn continuously. Cyber defenders need to balance speed with caution. The dynamic nature of the challenge makes it a fascinating study in adaptation. Can we build models that truly anticipate every trick? The quest continues with each new experiment and test.

5. RESPONSE MECHANISMS IN AI-DRIVEN CYBERSECURITY

5.1 Automated Incident Response Systems for Mitigating Cyber Threats

Automated incident response systems act as a rapid shield against cyber threats. They watch network traffic, log events, and flag suspicious behavior (Ahmad, Maynard, & Shanks, 2015). They work like a well-drilled team of firefighters who rush to a blaze. The system spots a threat and moves fast. It isolates affected devices. It blocks harmful connections. It sends alerts to security teams. This speed can stop an attack before it spreads.

The system uses playbooks that guide its actions. It follows pre-set instructions when a threat appears. It might cut off an IP address or disable a compromised user account. The system learns from past incidents. It adjusts its rules to fit new challenges. Its algorithms update without waiting for human intervention. It is always on duty, tirelessly scanning data. The process is not clumsy. Each decision is measured and precise.

Imagine a security team with super-fast reflexes. The automated system provides that power. It minimizes the window of opportunity for attackers. It lowers the risk of data breaches. It protects sensitive information and maintains network stability. The system works in real time. It takes seconds to react. This speed matters when every moment counts. It is like having a digital lifeguard who never sleeps.

The system also reduces human error. Manual response can be slow and inconsistent. Automated incident response keeps operations smooth. It allows security professionals to focus on strategic tasks. It builds a bridge between technology and human oversight. The human team monitors alerts and refines the playbooks. The two work in tandem to fight cybercrime. The system learns from each incident. It becomes more resilient and robust. Its efficiency grows with every challenge it meets.

The benefits of this automation stretch beyond speed. It scales with the network and adapts to new threats. It helps organizations save time and money. It reinforces a proactive security posture. The system is a crucial ally in a world of evolving cyber risks.

5.2 Reinforcement Learning (RL) for Cybersecurity Adaptation

Reinforcement learning stands as a dynamic force in cybersecurity. It mirrors a trial-and-error process. The algorithm tries an action and checks the result. It learns from each move. Picture training a pet. Each good step earns praise. A misstep gets a correction. The system improves with every trial.

Ahmed et al. (2016) discussed security landscapes are in constant flux. Threats shift like wind. Attackers keep changing their tactics. RL adapts quickly. It learns which defenses work best in a live setting. The algorithm explores various moves. It tests simple rules and novel ideas alike. It tracks rewards when actions protect the system. It notes penalties when defenses fail. The result is an evolving strategy that fits a changing threat environment. The method works in real time. It does not wait for updates from a human operator. Instead, it adjusts as soon as conditions change.

The process uses rewards and penalties. Actions that thwart an attack earn rewards. Flawed moves incur penalties. This feedback loop fine-tunes decisions. The system finds the balance between caution and openness. It optimizes its actions continuously. Think of it as a digital athlete that trains every day. Each session builds resilience. The system can adjust firewall settings, manage network access, or trigger alerts. It makes decisions based on its accumulated experience. It acts with a speed that manual processes cannot match.

The approach reduces human load. It takes on routine adjustments and adapts to new threats. It transforms cybersecurity from reactive to proactive. Every incident becomes a lesson for future defense. The technique brings an innovative edge to digital protection. It learns from mistakes and builds on successes. The result is a robust defense that evolves with every challenge.

5.3 Reinforcement Learning (RL) for Cybersecurity Adaptation

Reinforcement learning stands as a dynamic force in cybersecurity. It mirrors a trial-and-error process. The algorithm tries an action and checks the result. It learns from each move. Picture training a pet. Each good step earns praise. A misstep gets a correction. The system improves with every trial.

Security landscapes are in constant flux. Threats shift like wind. Attackers keep changing their tactics. RL adapts quickly. It learns which defenses work best in a live setting. The algorithm explores various moves. It tests simple rules and novel ideas alike. It tracks rewards when actions protect the system. It notes penalties when defenses fail. The result is an evolving strategy that fits a changing threat environment. The method works in real time. It does not wait for updates from a human operator. Instead, it adjusts as soon as conditions change.

The process uses rewards and penalties. Actions that thwart an attack earn rewards. Flawed moves incur penalties. This feedback loop fine-tunes decisions. The system finds the balance between caution and openness. It optimizes its actions continuously. Think of it as a digital athlete that trains every day. Each session builds resilience. The system can adjust firewall settings, manage network access, or trigger alerts. It makes decisions based on its accumulated experience. It acts with a speed that manual processes cannot match.

The approach reduces human load. It takes on routine adjustments and adapts to new threats (Keerthi et al., 2017). It transforms cybersecurity from reactive to proactive. Every incident becomes a lesson for future defense. The technique brings an innovative edge to digital protection. It learns from mistakes and builds on successes. The result is a robust defense that evolves with every challenge.

5.4 Self-Healing and Adaptive Cyber Defense Frameworks

Self-healing frameworks act like an immune system for networks (Dam et al., 2023). They detect faults and fix them on the fly. They watch over every packet and user action. They sense a disruption and jump into action. The system isolates the faulty area. It repairs or reroutes traffic as needed. The defense resets compromised components. It works automatically without waiting for human input. The process is much like a body healing a wound.

These frameworks combine sensors, analysis modules, and repair tools. They track data across the network. They build a baseline of normal behavior. They spot even small deviations from this norm. When a threat appears, the system reconfigures itself. It might block dangerous ports or reset affected nodes. The design minimizes the exposure time. The network bounces back swiftly. It learns from every incident and adjusts its rules accordingly. New threats shape its evolving defense.

The approach uses artificial intelligence to drive decisions. The system gathers evidence from every corner. It evaluates risk and acts accordingly. Think of it as a vigilant caretaker who adapts based on experience. It records past events and refines its detection models. This constant learning means the framework improves with each encounter. It grows more resilient over time. The process is dynamic. It adapts to new types of attacks as they surface.

The framework reduces the workload on security teams. It prevents minor issues from escalating into major breaches. It brings a proactive edge to cybersecurity. Organizations benefit from faster recovery and continuous monitoring. The system acts like a digital mechanic. It repairs, adapts, and shields the network with minimal delay. This self-healing ability is vital in today's fast-changing digital world. It fosters resilience and ensures stability in critical infrastructures.

5.5 AI-driven Security Orchestration, Automation, and Response (SOAR) Solutions

AI-driven SOAR solutions blend smart algorithms with automated workflows (Dwork & Roth, 2014). They link firewalls, intrusion detection systems, and threat intelligence feeds. They act as a digital conductor, directing each security tool in harmony. The system watches incoming alerts and sorts them by risk. It connects data from network sensors, endpoint monitors, and cloud logs. It brings together scattered information into one clear picture. The solution then triggers pre-defined responses. It can block a malicious IP or quarantine a compromised device. It sends real-time notifications to security teams. It reduces the need for manual intervention. Speed matters. The system works around the clock.

The technology learns from each incident. It studies past responses and refines its playbooks. It adapts to new threats with each alert. The AI improves its decisions as it gathers more data. It updates rules automatically. It adjusts to the evolving threat landscape. Think of it as a digital strategist that gets sharper with every move. Its agility bridges the gap between detection and mitigation. The system ensures all parts of the security apparatus work in sync.

The solution transforms chaotic data into clear action. It can process huge volumes of information in seconds. It uncovers hidden patterns and flags unusual behavior. The result is a proactive defense that stops breaches before they spread. It unifies disparate tools into one streamlined process. This unification boosts overall efficiency. It lightens the load on security analysts who no longer need to chase every alert manually. It is like having a tireless assistant who never sleeps.

The benefits are tangible. Response times drop significantly. Risk exposure shortens. Organizations save time and resources. The system becomes a key player in protecting critical assets. It turns reactive security into a proactive shield. Its orchestration capability enhances both detection and response. This innovative solution marks a new era in cybersecurity, where speed and intelligence work hand in hand.

6. PRIVACY, ETHICS, AND COMPLIANCE IN AI-BASED IDRS

6.1 Privacy-Preserving AI for Secure Data Handling

Privacy-preserving AI shields sensitive data during analysis. It works like a lock on a treasure chest. The system extracts insights without exposing personal details. Researchers build models that respect privacy. They use techniques such as differential privacy, homomorphic encryption, and federated learning. Each method offers a unique way to protect data. The goal remains clear: secure data handling while enabling smart analysis.

Data moves from user devices to centralized servers (Elovici et al., 2009). Privacy-preserving AI keeps raw data hidden. It transforms information into abstract patterns. This method ensures that individual records remain confidential. It acts as a digital veil over personal details. Organizations can mine valuable insights without risking data leaks. The balance between utility and privacy is delicate. The system must learn without revealing secrets. It is like reading a story without showing the pages.

The approach draws on advanced mathematics. Differential privacy adds small amounts of noise. It prevents any one record from standing out. Homomorphic encryption lets algorithms run on encrypted data. The content stays locked even as computations occur. Federated learning gathers updates from many devices. Data never leaves its source. The system learns from trends while keeping identities secure. These techniques work in tandem to build trust.

The promise of privacy-preserving AI extends beyond technical merit. It supports compliance with laws like GDPR and HIPAA. Users feel safer when their data remains confidential. The approach nurtures a culture of ethical data use. Companies that adopt these methods signal responsibility. They show that innovation and privacy can coexist. The challenge is constant. Cyber threats evolve daily. Security measures must grow alongside new risks (Buczak & Guven, 2016).

The field thrives on collaboration. Researchers and practitioners exchange ideas and improve algorithms. Each breakthrough paves the way for stronger protections. The digital world demands both progress and prudence. Privacy-preserving AI stands as a bulwark against misuse. Its techniques create a safe space for data to be useful. Can innovation survive without trust? In today's environment, the answer is clear. Secure data handling is not just a feature—it is a necessity.

6.2 Ethical Concerns in AI-Driven Cybersecurity and Bias Mitigation

Ethical concerns in AI-driven cybersecurity are a major challenge (Jobin et al., 2019). The technology protects systems and data but also risks embedding bias.

Algorithms may favor one group over another. This outcome can lead to unfair treatment. The stakes are high. Trust and safety hang in the balance. It is like using a tool that sometimes cuts off the wrong branch. Mistakes matter.

Bias often starts with data. Training sets can contain historical prejudices. These flaws transfer to models. The system may misjudge threats or flag harmless activity. Errors can have serious consequences. Users may face unwarranted scrutiny. Some groups might see more false positives. Others might get overlooked in critical situations. This imbalance undermines fairness and erodes trust.

Ethical AI must be transparent (Ahmad, Maynard, & Shanks, 2015). Developers need to reveal how models make decisions. They must regularly audit systems for bias. Fairness-aware algorithms help reduce disparities. The process involves careful testing and adjustments. It is like tuning an instrument to play in harmony. The outcome can be a system that is both secure and just.

Organizations must set clear standards. They need guidelines that enforce fairness and accountability. Legal frameworks play a role. They ensure that AI respects individual rights. Collaboration between public and private sectors is vital. Standards guide developers and build public trust. Bias mitigation is not a one-time fix. It demands ongoing attention and refinement. The goal is to create systems that protect without prejudice.

The discussion extends to ethical responsibilities. Stakeholders must balance security and individual privacy. They must consider the human impact of automated decisions. The debate is both technical and moral. Societies demand that technology be used responsibly. Continuous monitoring, clear policies, and open dialogue are key. This ensures that cybersecurity measures do not inadvertently harm vulnerable groups. The path forward requires vigilance, empathy, and sustained effort.

6.3 Regulatory Compliance and Security Standards (NIST, GDPR, ISO/IEC 27001)

Regulatory compliance guides organizations through complex security landscapes (NIST, 2018). NIST, GDPR, and ISO/IEC 27001 act as blueprints for building strong defenses. These standards help shape policies and procedures that protect sensitive data. They serve as maps that lead businesses through a maze of cyber risks. Organizations follow these guides to earn trust and avoid legal pitfalls.

NIST creates a framework that many turn to for guidance. It lays out clear steps to identify risks and protect assets. Its guidelines feel like a checklist for security. Companies use it to evaluate their current posture (NIST, 2018). The framework helps them plan for the unexpected. It works like a roadmap in uncertain weather. The system demands continuous review and updates. This keeps defenses ready against new threats.

GDPR changes how companies treat personal data. It insists on clear consent and transparency. Businesses must report data breaches quickly. Individuals gain more control over their digital footprints. The regulation pushes organizations to rethink data collection. It sets rules that are hard to ignore. Companies learn to balance innovation with privacy rights. The rules foster a culture of respect for personal information. They build confidence among users and partners alike.

ISO/IEC 27001 focuses on information security management systems (Kairouz et al., 2021). It lays out requirements for a risk-based approach. Companies go through rigorous audits to gain certification. This standard feels like a quality seal in a crowded market. It proves that an organization takes security seriously. The process builds trust with customers and investors. It offers a continuous cycle of planning, doing, checking, and acting. This cycle keeps the security system robust and evolving.

Together, these standards form a powerful trio. They help organizations manage risks and protect digital assets. Compliance is more than a box to check. It is a commitment to ethical practices and ongoing vigilance. In today's digital world, adhering to these standards is both a strategic and moral choice.

7. CASE STUDIES AND REAL-WORLD APPLICATIONS

7.1 AI-Powered IDRS in Autonomous Vehicles

AI-powered IDRS secure autonomous vehicles from hidden threats (Petit & Shladover, 2015). Self-driving cars depend on sensors and communication channels. They gather data from cameras, radars, and LiDAR. The system learns what is normal. It flags anomalies that could signal cyber intrusions. An attack may aim to misguide navigation or disrupt control systems. Quick detection matters. The AI system studies data in real time. It spots deviations that a human might miss. A sudden change in sensor readings can trigger an alert. The system then isolates the affected module. It may block harmful commands and alert operators. The response happens fast. Every millisecond counts on the road.

The technology rests on deep learning models. It trains on vast driving datasets. It adapts with each journey. The system grows smarter as it learns from each incident. Field tests show that these systems catch sensor spoofing. They notice when a LiDAR beam reports unusual reflections (Huang et al., 2011). They see if vehicle-to-vehicle messages stray from expected patterns. The AI model checks data consistency. When it finds a mismatch, it steps in. This proactive measure prevents dangerous missteps. The vehicle can switch to a safe mode. Passengers remain secure while the system investigates.

Some tests reveal fewer false alarms when the model is fine-tuned. Developers adjust the system to avoid overreactions. The outcome is a balanced defense that filters genuine threats from noise. The approach builds trust in autonomous technology. Road trials prove that AI-driven IDRS boost overall vehicle security. They cut down response times and reduce risk exposure. Operators and manufacturers embrace these systems. They act as the digital guardians of our highways. Such case studies illustrate the promise of integrating AI with cybersecurity in mobility. The lessons learned help shape next-generation safety features across the industry.

7.2 Intrusion Detection in Smart Cities and IoT Networks

Smart cities thrive on interconnected devices. IoT networks drive urban innovations. Sensors track environmental conditions. Cameras monitor public spaces. Smart meters report energy consumption. These devices create streams of data (Bhuyan et al., 2014). They support efficient management of city services. They also widen the attack surface. Every device may become a vulnerability. Hackers seek weak points. They may exploit a single insecure sensor. They can disrupt traffic systems or compromise public safety. Intrusion detection systems act as vigilant guardians. They watch network flows. They search for irregularities. They alert operators when something seems off.

Urban IoT networks face unique challenges. Devices are often resource-constrained. They run on basic hardware. Security updates lag behind. Attackers take advantage of these gaps. Intrusion detection must work in real time. It scans data continuously. It differentiates between normal and anomalous behavior. It is like a digital sniffer, catching the faintest whiff of danger. The system learns from patterns. It adapts to new threats quickly. It protects critical infrastructures from potential breaches.

City services depend on reliable data. Intrusion detection preserves data integrity. It ensures that information remains trustworthy. It supports decision-making in emergency responses. A single breach may compromise multiple systems. Smart cities risk not only data loss but also public harm. The system must be swift and precise. It processes enormous volumes of data every second. It adapts to shifting cyber threats. What if a device suddenly misbehaves? The detection mechanism isolates the culprit. It blocks malicious traffic. It prevents further damage, acting like a digital firewall.

The digital pulse of a city must remain strong. Intrusion detection transforms chaos into order. It secures interconnected systems and builds trust. Urban cybersecurity is a constant battle. It demands vigilance, innovation, and resilience. The journey is challenging but essential for maintaining safe and smart environments.

7.3 Cyber Threats and AI Security in Industrial Robotics

Industrial robotics drive modern manufacturing and process automation. They operate in environments where precision matters. These systems integrate sensors, actuators, and control units. They communicate with each other in real time. This connectivity opens new avenues for cyber threats. Hackers may target communication links (Kairouz et al., 2021). They may exploit weak points in network protocols. A breach can lead to malfunctioning robots. This risk poses significant hazards to production lines and human safety.

Cyber attackers use various methods. They launch malware to disrupt robotic processes. They manipulate data to alter machine behavior. They can steal intellectual property from design blueprints. An attacker may cause a robotic arm to deviate from its programmed path. The result is equipment damage or injury. Vulnerabilities lie in outdated software and insecure interfaces. Many industrial robots run on legacy systems. These older systems often lack modern security features. They become soft targets for skilled adversaries.

AI security measures work as a protective shield. AI algorithms monitor data streams from industrial systems. They flag abnormal behavior in real time. The system learns from normal operating conditions. It adapts quickly when anomalies appear. Think of it as an ever-watchful guardian. The AI model detects subtle deviations that may signal an intrusion. It sends alerts and initiates countermeasures. This fast reaction limits the damage caused by cyber attacks.

Cybersecurity experts design layers of defense around industrial robotics. They secure networks with firewalls and encryption. They update firmware and patch vulnerabilities frequently. AI-driven security tools help refine these defenses. They identify risks before they escalate. The focus remains on maintaining both safety and operational continuity. Researchers and engineers work together to create resilient systems. Their goal is to blend advanced AI techniques with robust industrial practices.

7.4 AI-driven IDRS in Healthcare and Critical Infrastructure

AI-driven IDRS protect healthcare systems and critical infrastructure from digital intrusions (Sigma Solve INC., 2024). Hospitals use electronic records and connected devices. They face risks from ransomware and unauthorized access. These systems guard patient data and medical devices. Critical infrastructure such as power grids, water supplies, and transportation networks rely on secure communications. A breach in these sectors can disrupt lives and endanger public safety. The stakes are very high.

The system monitors network traffic and device behavior in real time. It learns patterns from historical data. The AI model spots anomalies that may signal an attack. It acts fast to isolate compromised nodes. This response resembles a quick reflex in a high-stakes game. The technology adapts continuously. It evolves as new threats emerge. The model adjusts itself by studying prior incidents and outcomes. This self-improving quality is essential for environments that change rapidly.

Healthcare facilities require strict confidentiality and uninterrupted service. The system ensures that patient records stay secure. It stops malicious commands from reaching connected medical devices. Such interference could harm patients or lead to diagnostic errors. Similarly, in critical infrastructure, the system safeguards vital operations. It stops unauthorized access that might lead to cascading failures. Think of it as a digital firewall that learns and defends continuously.

The integration of multiple sensors, cloud analytics, and edge computing enhances the defense. Data flows from different sources are fused into a unified picture. The system is like a vigilant guardian that scans every corner of a facility. It triggers alerts and automatically applies countermeasures. This minimizes downtime and protects essential services. The challenges are complex, yet the promise of AI-driven IDRS lies in their speed, adaptability, and proactive response.

8. FUTURE DIRECTIONS AND EMERGING TECHNOLOGIES

8.1 The Impact of Quantum Computing on AI-driven Cybersecurity

Quantum computing brings a radical change. It uses qubits that can be 0 and 1 at once. This ability speeds up computations beyond classical limits. It shakes up our current cryptographic systems. Encryption that protects sensitive data may fall to quantum attacks. AI-driven cybersecurity must evolve in response. Defenders face a race against time and technology.

Quantum computers can break traditional encryption methods. They may unravel RSA and ECC schemes with ease. This risk forces a search for quantum-safe cryptography. Researchers are busy developing new algorithms. They aim for secure systems that stand the test of quantum power. The challenge is formidable. It is like trying to outsmart a master chess player who learns every move instantly.

At the same time, quantum computing opens exciting doors. It speeds up machine learning algorithms. It processes massive datasets in a flash. AI systems may detect anomalies faster than ever before. They learn complex patterns quickly. Imagine a security system that anticipates threats before they occur. This is no longer science fiction. The merging of quantum power with AI could create unprecedented defenses. The promise is immense. It may transform threat detection into a proactive science.

Defenders and attackers both eye quantum technology. The dual nature of quantum computing makes it a double-edged sword. Its potential for harm and protection exists side by side. Cybersecurity experts must build quantum-resistant measures. They have to rethink risk management from the ground up. This transition requires new skills and updated protocols. The field stands at the brink of a revolution. A careful blend of quantum and classical methods seems necessary.

Innovation in this area demands collaboration. Quantum physicists and cybersecurity experts must work hand in hand. Their combined expertise will shape the future of digital defense. The journey will be challenging, but progress is inevitable. The race to secure information in a quantum era is on.

8.2 Edge AI for Real-Time Intrusion Detection in Distributed Systems

Edge AI brings intelligence close to where data is generated (Liao et al., 2013). It processes information at the network's edge. Devices such as sensors and gateways analyze data locally. They detect intrusions almost instantly. The approach reduces latency and improves response time. The system works like a vigilant guard at a busy checkpoint. It scans traffic continuously. It spots irregular behavior with keen eyes.

Local processing is key in distributed systems. Data flows from many devices spread across a large area. Centralized systems may lag. Edge AI shortens this delay by acting on the spot. It learns normal patterns from nearby devices. It flags deviations that might indicate an attack. The process is quick and agile. It resembles the human immune system, which fights infections at the entry point. The method minimizes the impact of threats.

Computational power at the edge is limited. The algorithms must be efficient and lightweight. They perform tasks without draining resources. The challenge is to balance speed and accuracy. The model adapts continuously. It updates itself based on fresh data from its surroundings. This self-improvement boosts detection rates over time. Operators can trust the system to act before an intrusion spreads.

Edge AI also reduces network load. Data is filtered locally, and only critical information moves to the cloud. This design supports scalability in vast networks. It is like filtering water at the source to ensure only the cleanest reaches the main reservoir. The decentralized approach improves resilience. Even if one node is compromised, others remain secure. The result is a robust defense across distributed systems.

The integration of edge AI with intrusion detection changes the security landscape. It makes real-time analysis possible on a grand scale. This approach benefits smart cities, industrial plants, and IoT networks alike. It protects sensitive data and ensures system reliability. The future of cybersecurity lies in blending edge intelligence with proactive threat detection.

8.3 Federated Learning for Decentralized AI Security

Federated learning gathers insights without centralizing data. It trains models at each device or site. Devices keep data on local servers. The system learns from local patterns. It sends only model updates to a central hub. This keeps raw data private. The approach mimics a roundtable discussion. Each node contributes its own piece. The central model then improves from many voices. The process protects sensitive information. It reduces risks associated with data breaches.

The method suits decentralized systems well. In distributed networks, data comes from many locations. Centralizing it creates a single point of failure. Federated learning avoids this trap. It lets each unit keep control of its data. The system learns collectively yet remains distributed. Think of it as a chorus singing in harmony. Each singer maintains their unique voice. The overall melody stays robust and resilient.

Security improves with decentralization. Data never leaves its source. This minimizes the risk of interception. Model updates are aggregated without revealing details. It is like sharing secret recipes without disclosing ingredients. The system builds defenses from diverse perspectives. It adapts to local threats and broad trends alike. The network learns to recognize unusual patterns quickly. It can flag potential attacks before they spread. The decentralized approach builds trust across all nodes.

Challenges remain in communication efficiency and consistency. Devices may have varying computing power. Synchronization issues can occur. Developers work on algorithms that handle these differences gracefully. The focus is on both speed and reliability. The approach must ensure that updates are accurate. Each node plays its part in building a stronger model. The result is a robust defense that learns over time.

Federated learning transforms decentralized AI security. It marries privacy with performance. It offers a path to secure, collaborative intelligence. In a world where data is everywhere, this method sets a high standard for safe innovation.

8.4 Zero Trust Architecture (ZTA) in AI-driven Cyber Defense

Zero Trust Architecture challenges the old notion of inherent trust (Patcha & Park, 2007). Every access request is treated with caution. The model insists that no user or device is trusted by default. It asks for verification at every step. In AI-driven environments, this philosophy becomes critical. The system continuously checks identities and validates data requests. It acts like a vigilant gatekeeper. Each incoming packet earns its right to pass through. The approach minimizes opportunities for lateral movement in a network.

The concept is straightforward. Trust is never assumed. Every interaction is examined. The system uses real-time analytics to evaluate risk. AI tools assess behavioral patterns and context. They flag suspicious activity with speed. The model learns from repeated interactions. It adapts to evolving threats and refines its decisions. This constant evaluation strengthens the defense. It creates a dynamic shield that protects sensitive assets.

The integration of AI elevates Zero Trust capabilities. AI models process enormous amounts of data in seconds. They compare each request against learned patterns. They detect deviations that might signal an attack. The process resembles an immune system that identifies harmful invaders. The system isolates potential threats immediately. It prevents unauthorized access from spreading. This blend of Zero Trust principles and AI intelligence forms a robust security framework.

Organizations benefit from granular control. Each segment of the network is secured independently. No single breach compromises the entire system. The approach supports continuous monitoring and micro-segmentation. It acts like a collection of mini-guardians placed throughout the network. Each one is responsible for its own area. This design reduces the attack surface significantly.

Adopting Zero Trust Architecture requires cultural and technical shifts. Companies must rethink legacy systems and embrace agile security practices. The benefits include enhanced data protection and improved regulatory compliance. AI-driven Zero Trust offers a proactive stance against sophisticated attacks. The framework not only detects threats but also learns from them. The evolving nature of cyber threats calls for a defense that is equally dynamic and responsive.

9. CONCLUSION AND RECOMMENDATIONS

9.1 Summary of Key Takeaways from AI-based Intrusion Detection Research

AI-based intrusion detection systems (IDRS) show great promise in protecting digital assets. Research has shown these systems learn quickly from vast data streams. They pick up unusual patterns and flag potential threats. The models adapt to evolving attack methods. The research highlights that deep learning models enhance both detection speed and accuracy. These models catch subtle anomalies that traditional systems might miss. The findings suggest that AI-driven IDRS reduce false alarms and improve overall system resilience.

The studies reveal that AI-based approaches scale well with growing data volumes. They process information in real time. They work tirelessly, much like a vigilant guard who never sleeps. The technology leverages historical data to predict new attack vectors. It refines its criteria through continuous feedback. Experiments indicate that the models adjust to fresh threats. The research points out that constant updates and rigorous testing are essential. This adaptability is vital in today's rapidly shifting cyber landscape.

Field experiments and case studies demonstrate that AI-based systems lighten the load on human analysts. They free up resources for strategic decision-making. The systems operate on a hybrid approach that merges signature-based detection with anomaly spotting. This combination creates a more comprehensive defense. Early detection of attacks not only prevents damage but also reduces recovery costs. The studies underscore that real-time response is critical. They also note that balancing computational cost with performance remains a central challenge.

Ethical and operational considerations emerge from the research. Transparency and accountability in model decisions are important for trust. The work calls for clear guidelines and continuous evaluations. The collective insights guide future innovations in cybersecurity. Each breakthrough sets the stage for more robust, adaptive, and secure networks. The journey to a safer digital world continues, driven by the lessons learned in AI-based intrusion detection research.

9.2 Best Practices for Securing Autonomous Systems Using AI-driven IDRS

Autonomous systems operate in dynamic environments. They require fast, accurate protection. AI-driven IDRS offer promising security. The systems learn from real-time data. They spot anomalies with precision. Best practices emerge from blending technology with sound security policies.

Organizations must adopt layered defenses. They secure network endpoints and control systems alike. Regular software updates are vital. Engineers must patch vulnerabilities swiftly. Automated monitoring detects unusual activity. These systems work like constant sentinels. They review every network transaction. They flag unusual patterns as potential threats.

Collaboration between IT and operational technology teams is essential. Teams share insights and streamline responses. Trust is built on transparency and accountability. Strict access controls help reduce risks. Segmentation of networks prevents threats from spreading. The strategy resembles compartmentalization in a ship. If one area fails, others remain safe.

Robust encryption is critical for data exchange. The systems use secure protocols to protect communications. AI models continuously learn from fresh data. They adjust thresholds based on new insights. Security experts test the models against simulated attacks. This ensures that defenses remain sharp. Training data must be diverse. It reduces biases and improves detection accuracy. Regular audits help verify the system's integrity. They provide feedback to refine the models further.

User awareness also plays a role. Employees must learn safe practices and report suspicious behavior. A culture of security strengthens the overall defense. Best practices call for regular drills and simulations. These exercises prepare teams for real incidents. The integration of human expertise and AI defense creates a resilient posture. The system is proactive rather than reactive. It anticipates threats and takes preemptive actions.

Best practices for autonomous systems security combine technology, policy, and human factors. AI-driven IDRS are at the heart of this approach. They provide real-time, adaptive defense in complex environments.

9.3 Future Research Opportunities and Challenges in AI Cybersecurity

The future of AI cybersecurity is ripe with opportunities and challenges. Researchers face an exciting frontier. New algorithms promise faster threat detection. Systems learn from enormous data streams. They spot subtle anomalies with impressive speed. Every breakthrough nudges defenses toward greater resilience. The landscape is dynamic. Attackers evolve continuously. Defenders must innovate just as quickly. It is like a never-ending chess match where each move matters.

Emerging research focuses on adversarial robustness. Models often struggle with small perturbations in data. Studies show that even minor input changes can fool systems. Research now seeks methods to harden models. This work aims to build systems that learn from attacks. It strives to turn weaknesses into strengths. The process is iterative. Every discovered vulnerability paves the way for improved defenses. The research community is exploring innovative techniques that blend machine learning with rigorous statistical testing. The result may be systems that not only detect but also anticipate attacks.

Opportunities exist in distributed learning and federated architectures. These methods help safeguard privacy and improve collaboration across networks. They enable decentralized security. Systems can learn collectively while keeping data local. This approach is particularly promising for industries with sensitive information. It builds trust and fortifies defenses. Researchers are also examining the role of quantum computing in both attacking and defending digital infrastructures. Quantum advances promise significant speedups in processing power. They challenge existing encryption methods. In turn, they open avenues for quantum-resistant techniques.

Yet challenges remain. Model interpretability is still a pressing issue. Understanding why an AI makes a decision is crucial for trust and accountability. Ethical concerns, such as bias and fairness, call for clear guidelines and transparency. Future research must balance technical advancement with ethical practices. These challenges invite a multidisciplinary approach. The journey ahead requires collaboration between computer scientists, statisticians, and ethicists alike. The dynamic nature of cyber threats ensures that research in this area will remain vibrant and essential.

REFERENCES

Acar, A., Aksu, H., Uluagac, A. S., & Conti, M. (2019). A survey on homomorphic encryption schemes: Theory and implementation. ACM Computing Surveys, 51(4). *ACM Computing Surveys*, *79*(4), 1–35. DOI: 10.1145/3214303

Ahmad, A., Maynard, S. B., & Shanks, G. (2015). A case analysis of information systems and security incident responses. *International Journal of Information Management*, *35*(6), 717–723. DOI: 10.1016/j.ijinfomgt.2015.08.001

Ahmed, M., Mahmood, A. N., & Hu, J. (2016). A survey of network anomaly detection techniques. *Journal of Network and Computer Applications*, *60*, 19–31. DOI: 10.1016/j.jnca.2015.11.016

Atzori, L., Iera, A., & Morabito, G. (2010). The Internet of Things: A survey. *Computer Networks*, *54*(15), 2787–2805. DOI: 10.1016/j.comnet.2010.05.010

Bhuyan, M. H., Bhattacharyya, D. K., & Kalita, J. K. (2014). Network anomaly detection: Methods, systems, and tools. *IEEE Communications Surveys and Tutorials*, *16*(1), 303–336. DOI: 10.1109/SURV.2013.052213.00046

Biamonte, J., Wittek, P., Pancotti, N., Rebentrost, P., Wiebe, N., & Lloyd, S. (2017). Quantum machine learning. *Nature*, *549*(7671), 195–202. DOI: 10.1038/nature23474 PMID: 28905917

Buczak, A. L., & Guven, E. (2016). A survey of data mining and machine learning methods for cyber security intrusion detection. *IEEE Communications Surveys and Tutorials*, *18*(2), 1153–1176. DOI: 10.1109/COMST.2015.2494502

Cheng, L., Liu, F., & Zhang, Y. (2021). A survey of zero trust security architecture in emerging networks. *IEEE Communications Surveys and Tutorials*, *23*(2), 165–190. DOI: 10.1109/COMST.2021.3051049

Chiriac, B.-N., Anton, F.-D., Ioni ă, A.-D., & Vasilică, B.-V. (2025). A modular AI-driven intrusion detection system for network traffic monitoring in Industry 4.0, using Nvidia Morpheus and generative adversarial networks. *Sensors (Basel)*, *25*(1), 130. DOI: 10.3390/s25010130 PMID: 39796921

Dam, D. T., Tran, T. H., Hoang, V. P., Pham, C. K., & Hoang, T. T. (2023). A survey of post-quantum cryptography: Start of a new race. *Cryptography*, *7*(3), 40. DOI: 10.3390/cryptography7030040

Dehghantanha, A., & Choo, K.-K. R. (2019). *Handbook of big data and IoT security*. Springer., DOI: 10.1007/978-3-030-10543-3

Dwork, C., & Roth, A. (2014). The algorithmic foundations of differential privacy. *Foundations and Trends in Theoretical Computer Science*, *9*(3–4), 211–407. DOI: 10.1561/0400000042

Elovici, Y., Shabtai, A., Rokach, L., & Braha, D. (2009). Collaborative attack on Internet users' anonymity. *Internet Research*, *19*(1), 60–77. DOI: 10.1108/10662240910927821

Farzaan, M. A. M., Ghanem, M. C., El-Hajjar, A., & Ratnayake, D. N. (2024). AI-enabled system for efficient and effective cyber incident detection and response in cloud environments. arXiv preprint arXiv:2404.05602. https://arxiv.org/abs/2404.05602

Huang, L., Joseph, A. D., Nelson, B., Rubinstein, B. I. P., & Tygar, J. D. (2011). Adversarial machine learning. In *Proceedings of the 4th ACM Workshop on Security and Artificial Intelligence (AISec '11)* (pp. 43–58). Association for Computing Machinery. DOI: 10.1145/2046684.2046692

Humayed, A., Lin, J., Li, F., & Luo, B. (2017). Cyber-physical systems security—A survey. *IEEE Internet of Things Journal*, *4*(6), 1802–1831. DOI: 10.1109/JIOT.2017.2703172

Imamverdiyev, Y. N., & Abdullayeva, F. J. (2020). Deep learning in cybersecurity: Challenges and approaches. International Journal of Cyber Warfare and Terrorism (IJCWT, 10(2), 82–105.

Jawhar, S., Miller, J., & Bitar, Z. (2024, February). AI-based cybersecurity policies and procedures. In 2024 IEEE 3rd International Conference on AI in Cybersecurity (ICAIC) (pp. 1-5). IEEE.

Jobin, A., Ienca, M., & Vayena, E. (2019). The global landscape of AI ethics guidelines. *Nature Machine Intelligence*, *1*(9), 389–399. DOI: 10.1038/s42256-019-0088-2

Kairouz, P., McMahan, H. B., Avent, B., Bellet, A., Bennis, M., Bhagoji, A. N., Bonawitz, K., Charles, Z., Cormode, G., Cummings, R., D'Oliveira, R. G. L., Eichner, H., El Rouayheb, S., Evans, D., Gardner, J., Garrett, Z., Gascón, A., Ghazi, B., Gibbons, P. B., & Zhao, S. (2021). Advances and open problems in federated learning. *Foundations and Trends in Machine Learning*, *14*(1–2), 1–210. DOI: 10.1561/2200000083

Keerthi, C. K., Jabbar, M. A., & Seetharamulu, B. (2017). Cyber-physical systems (CPS): Security issues, challenges, and solutions. In *2017 IEEE International Conference on Computational Intelligence and Computing Research (ICCIC)* (pp. 1–4). IEEE. DOI: 10.1109/ICCIC.2017.8524312

Liao, H.-J., Lin, C.-H. R., Lin, Y.-C., & Tung, K.-Y. (2013). Intrusion detection system: A comprehensive review. *Journal of Network and Computer Applications*, *36*(1), 16–24. DOI: 10.1016/j.jnca.2012.09.004

National Institute of Standards and Technology. (2018). *Framework for Improving Critical Infrastructure Cybersecurity, Version 1.1*. DOI: 10.6028/NIST.CSWP.04162018

Patcha, A., & Park, J.-M. (2007). An overview of anomaly detection techniques: Existing solutions and latest technological trends. *Computer Networks*, *51*(12), 3448–3470. DOI: 10.1016/j.comnet.2007.02.001

Petit, J., & Shladover, S. E. (2015). Potential cyberattacks on automated vehicles. *IEEE Transactions on Intelligent Transportation Systems*, *16*(2), 546–556. DOI: 10.1109/TITS.2014.2342271

Sigma Solve, I. N. C. (2024, September 12). Future of AI in cybersecurity: Key technologies and trends. Sigma Solve INC. https://www.sigmasolve.com/blog/the-future-of-ai-in-cybersecurity-emerging-technologies-and-trends/

KEY TERMS AND DEFINITIONS

Adversarial Machine Learning: A security concern where attackers manipulate input data to deceive AI models, causing incorrect threat assessments or bypassing security measures.

AI-driven IDRS in Healthcare and Critical Infrastructure: The use of artificial intelligence to secure medical devices, electronic health records, and vital national infrastructure from cyber threats.

AI-Powered Threat Intelligence for Proactive Security: The application of artificial intelligence to gather, analyze, and apply real-time threat intelligence to predict and prevent cyber attacks.

Anomaly Detection: A technique that analyzes normal system behavior and flags deviations that may indicate potential security breaches or cyber attacks.

Automated Incident Response Systems: AI-driven tools that detect, analyze, and mitigate cyber threats in real-time without requiring human intervention.

Behavioral Analysis for Cyber Defense: A method of monitoring user activities and system behavior to identify suspicious deviations that could signal malicious intent.

Best Practices for Securing Autonomous Systems Using AI-driven IDRS: Guidelines for implementing AI-powered intrusion detection and response systems to protect self-driving vehicles, drones, and other autonomous technologies.

Cloud Security in AI Systems: The application of AI-driven security techniques to protect cloud-based services, preventing unauthorized access and data breaches.

Cyber-Physical Systems (CPS) Security: The protection of integrated computing and physical systems, such as automated factories and smart transportation, from cyber attacks.

Cyber Threats and AI Security in Industrial Robotics: The application of AI-powered security solutions to protect robotic manufacturing systems from cyber attacks and operational disruptions.

Deep Learning in Cybersecurity: A branch of machine learning that employs neural networks to process vast amounts of data, identifying complex patterns that enhance threat detection.

Edge AI for Real-Time Intrusion Detection: The deployment of AI models on edge devices, enabling immediate threat detection and response without relying on cloud computing.

Federated Learning for Decentralized AI Security: A machine learning approach that allows multiple devices or organizations to train AI models collaboratively while keeping sensitive data localized.

Future Research Opportunities and Challenges in AI Cybersecurity: Emerging trends and unresolved issues in AI-driven security, including adversarial AI defenses, quantum-safe encryption, and ethical considerations in automated decision-making.

Hybrid Intrusion Detection Systems (HIDS): A combination of signature-based and anomaly-based intrusion detection techniques to enhance cybersecurity defenses.

Insider Threat Detection in AI-Driven Security: The identification and prevention of security risks posed by individuals within an organization who have access to critical systems.

Intrusion Detection and Response System (IDRS): A security mechanism that continuously monitors network traffic, detects anomalies, and initiates automated or manual countermeasures to mitigate cyber threats.

Intrusion Detection in Smart Cities and IoT Networks: AI-driven security mechanisms designed to protect interconnected urban infrastructure, including traffic control systems, power grids, and surveillance networks.

Machine Learning (ML) for Threat Detection: A subset of artificial intelligence that enables cybersecurity systems to recognize patterns in data, adapt to emerging threats, and improve response times.

Next-Generation Firewalls (NGFW) with AI Integration: Advanced firewalls equipped with artificial intelligence, deep packet inspection, and behavioral analysis to detect and neutralize cyber threats in real time.

Privacy-Preserving AI for Secure Data Handling: Techniques such as differential privacy and homomorphic encryption that enable AI systems to process sensitive information without exposing user data.

Quantum Computing and AI Cybersecurity: The study of quantum technologies and their impact on cybersecurity, including both defensive advancements and potential encryption-breaking threats.

Reinforcement Learning (RL) for Cybersecurity Adaptation: A self-learning approach where AI models improve security decisions by interacting with the environment and learning from feedback.

Regulatory Compliance and Security Standards (NIST, GDPR, ISO/IEC 27001): A set of cybersecurity regulations that organizations must follow to ensure data protection, privacy, and security governance.

Security Orchestration, Automation, and Response (SOAR) Solutions: A cybersecurity framework that integrates multiple security tools, automates workflows, and enhances response efficiency.

Self-Healing Cyber Defense Frameworks:AI-based security systems that automatically detect vulnerabilities and apply corrective actions to restore system integrity.:

Zero Trust Architecture (ZTA) in AI-Driven Cyber Defense: A security model that continuously verifies users, devices, and applications, ensuring no entity is trusted by default.

Chapter 2

AI-Powered Intrusion Detection and Privacy-Preserving Mechanisms in Cybersecurity

Vikas Sharma
http://orcid.org/0000-0001-8173-4548
Department of Computer Applications, SRM Institute of Science and Technology, Delhi NCR, India

Puneet Chauhan
http://orcid.org/0009-0000-1652-8764
Department of Computer Application, Swami Vivekanand Subharti University, Meerut, India

Tarun Kumar Vashishth
http://orcid.org/0000-0001-9916-9575
Deparment of Computer Applications, Vidya University, Meerut, India

Pushpendra Kumar Verma
http://orcid.org/0000-0003-2777-5626
IIMT University, Meerut, India

Shashiraj Teotia
http://orcid.org/0000-0002-0849-3642
Department of Computer Application, Swami Vivekanand Subharti University, Meerut, India

DOI: 10.4018/979-8-3373-2922-2.ch002

ABSTRACT

The integration of Artificial Intelligence (AI) in cybersecurity has revolutionized intrusion detection and response mechanisms. This chapter explores AI-driven intrusion detection systems (IDS) and the role of adversarial machine learning in cybersecurity, highlighting both opportunities and vulnerabilities. It delves into privacy-preserving AI techniques that enhance data security while mitigating risks posed by sophisticated cyber threats. Additionally, the chapter examines the challenges of securing AI-driven systems against adversarial attacks, emphasizing the need for explainable AI in ensuring transparency. The discussion includes case studies on AI-driven cyberattacks and privacy-enhancing strategies for securing sensitive data. Future directions for AI-powered cybersecurity solutions are also explored to establish robust defense mechanisms against evolving threats.

1. INTRODUCTION

1.1 Overview of AI in Cybersecurity

The rapid evolution of cyber threats, ranging from sophisticated malware to advanced persistent threats (APTs), has necessitated the adoption of Artificial Intelligence (AI) in cybersecurity. Traditional security mechanisms, which rely heavily on rule-based systems and signature detection, struggle to keep pace with the dynamic and ever-changing nature of cyberattacks. AI, particularly machine learning (ML) and deep learning (DL), has revolutionized cybersecurity by providing intelligent, adaptive, and automated threat detection capabilities. AI-powered systems can analyze vast amounts of network traffic data, identify anomalies, and detect malicious activities in real time, significantly improving the accuracy and efficiency of cybersecurity defences. One of the primary applications of AI in cybersecurity is Intrusion Detection Systems (IDS), where AI-driven models can recognize patterns indicative of cyber intrusions with minimal human intervention. Unlike traditional IDS that rely on pre-defined signatures, AI-based systems employ behavioural analysis and predictive modeling to detect unknown and zero-day threats. Additionally, AI enhances Security Information and Event Management (SIEM) systems by automating log analysis and correlating security incidents across various data sources, reducing response times and mitigating threats proactively. Beyond detection, AI is also transforming cybersecurity through automated response mechanisms. AI-driven Security Orchestration, Automation, and Response (SOAR) platforms enable rapid incident containment and mitigation by automating repetitive tasks, allowing cybersecurity professionals to focus on more complex security challenges. Furthermore, AI plays a crucial role in phishing detection, fraud prevention, and endpoint security, leveraging Natural Language Processing (NLP) and anomaly detection techniques to identify suspicious activities across multiple channels, including emails, websites, and financial transactions (Chukwunweike et al., 2024). However, the integration of AI into cybersecurity is not without challenges. AI models themselves can become targets for adversarial attacks, where attackers manipulate data inputs to deceive AI-based security systems. Moreover, privacy concerns arise as AI-powered security solutions often require access to vast amounts of sensitive data to function effectively. As a result, researchers and industry leaders are increasingly exploring privacy-preserving AI techniques, such as federated learning and homomorphic encryption, to ensure robust security without compromising user data confidentiality (Vashishth et al., 2025).

1.2 Evolution of Intrusion Detection Systems (IDS)

Intrusion Detection Systems (IDS) have evolved significantly over the past few decades in response to the increasing complexity and sophistication of cyber threats. Initially, cybersecurity relied on basic access controls and manual monitoring to detect malicious activities, but as cyberattacks became more frequent and advanced, automated detection mechanisms were required.

1. **First-Generation IDS: Rule-Based and Signature-Based Detection:** The earliest forms of IDS, developed in the 1980s and 1990s, were rule-based and signature-based systems. These IDS operated by maintaining a database of known attack patterns (signatures) and comparing incoming traffic against these predefined signatures. Tools-like Snort and Bro (now Zeek) became popular for their ability to detect well-documented threats with high accuracy. While signature-based IDS provided a reliable defense against known attacks, they had significant limitations. They were ineffective against zero-day attacks (new and unknown threats) because they could only detect attacks that were already documented in their databases. Additionally, they required frequent updates to their rule sets, making them reactive rather than proactive in addressing evolving cyber threats.
2. **Second-Generation IDS: Anomaly-Based Detection:** To overcome the limitations of signature-based IDS, anomaly-based IDS emerged in the early 2000s. Instead of relying on predefined attack patterns, anomaly-based IDS established a baseline of normal system behavior and flagged any deviations as potential threats. These systems used statistical analysis, heuristics, and behavioural modeling to detect unusual patterns in network traffic, making them more effective against unknown threats and zero-day attacks. Anomaly-based

IDS offered greater flexibility and adaptability compared to signature-based systems, but they also had drawbacks. One major issue was the high rate of false positives—legitimate activities that deviated from normal patterns were often mistakenly classified as threats. Moreover, defining what constitutes "normal" behavior in a dynamic network environment proved to be a challenging task.

3. **Third-Generation IDS: AI and Machine Learning-Based Detection:** With the rise of Artificial Intelligence (AI) and machine learning (ML) in the 2010s, intrusion detection systems became significantly more sophisticated. AI-powered IDS leverage advanced data analytics, deep learning, and real-time pattern recognition to identify cyber threats with greater accuracy and efficiency. Unlike traditional rule-based and anomaly-based IDS, AI-driven systems continuously learn and adapt to emerging attack techniques. Machine learning-based IDS can analyze large volumes of network data, identify correlations, and detect previously unknown attack vectors without relying on predefined signatures. These systems utilize techniques such as supervised learning (training models on labelled attack data), unsupervised learning (clustering anomalies without prior knowledge), and reinforcement learning (adaptive security responses based on attack patterns). Deep learning models, particularly neural networks and autoencoders, further enhance IDS by detecting sophisticated attacks like Advanced Persistent Threats (APTs) and insider threats, which may not exhibit obvious anomalies in network traffic. AI-driven IDS also integrate with Security Information and Event Management (SIEM) systems to provide automated threat intelligence and faster incident response (Adeyeye et al., 2024).
4. **Modern IDS: Hybrid Approaches and Explainable AI (XAI):** As cyber threats continue to evolve, modern IDS are adopting hybrid approaches that combine the strengths of signature-based, anomaly-based, and AI-powered detection mechanisms. Hybrid IDS improve detection accuracy by using multiple techniques simultaneously, minimizing the risk of false positives while ensuring comprehensive threat coverage. Another critical advancement in IDS is the incorporation of Explainable AI (XAI) to address the "black-box" problem associated with deep learning models. Traditional AI-based IDS often lack transparency, making it difficult for cybersecurity professionals to understand why a particular activity is flagged as malicious. XAI techniques aim to make AI-driven IDS more interpretable by providing human-readable explanations for threat detection decisions. This transparency is crucial for gaining trust in AI-based security solutions and ensuring compliance with regulatory frameworks (Sadaram et al., 2024). There has been significant growth of research in explainable AI (XAI), federated intrusion detection systems (FIDS), and privacy-enhancing technologies to improve cybersecurity with transparent, decentralized, and collaborative AI models with a focus on privacy and data

protection. One aspect being researched regards explainable AI models (e.g. SHAP and LIME). More explainable AI approaches like SHAP and LIME are being used to tackle the interpretability issue that exists with IDS based on deep learning, which helps to ameliorate trust and accountability for analysts (Nadella et al., 2025).

5. **Future Directions of IDS:** The future of IDS is likely to be shaped by advancements in quantum computing, blockchain technology, and federated learning. Quantum-enhanced IDS may leverage quantum machine learning for faster and more accurate anomaly detection. Blockchain-based IDS can offer decentralized and tamper-proof logging of security incidents, enhance data integrity, and reduce false alarms. Federated learning will enable organizations to train AI-driven IDS models collaboratively without sharing sensitive data, improving privacy-preserving cybersecurity measures. As cyber threats become more sophisticated, IDS will continue to evolve, integrating new technologies to provide real-time, proactive, and adaptive defense mechanisms. The convergence of AI, big data analytics, and automation is setting the stage for next-generation IDS that can effectively combat the ever-growing cybersecurity challenges of the digital age (Emehin et al., 2024).

1.3 Importance of Privacy-Preserving Mechanisms

In today's digital era, data privacy has become a critical concern due to the increasing reliance on Artificial Intelligence (AI) and cybersecurity mechanisms that process vast amounts of sensitive information. Privacy-preserving mechanisms play a crucial role in ensuring that personal, corporate, and government data remain secure while enabling AI-driven systems to function effectively. As cyber threats continue to evolve, protecting confidential data from unauthorized access, breaches, and misuse has become a top priority for individuals, businesses, and regulatory authorities. The significance of privacy-preserving mechanisms in cybersecurity extends beyond just compliance with data protection laws; it directly impacts user trust, system reliability, and the overall security posture of organizations. Traditional security measures such as firewalls and encryption are no longer sufficient in preventing sophisticated cyberattacks. AI-powered cybersecurity solutions, while effective in detecting and mitigating threats, often require access to extensive datasets, raising concerns about data exposure, unauthorized surveillance, and potential misuse. This is where privacy-preserving techniques become essential in maintaining a balance between security and confidentiality (Rangaraju, 2023).

1. **Addressing Data Sensitivity in AI-Powered Cybersecurity:** AI-powered cybersecurity systems rely on continuous data collection and analysis to detect

and mitigate threats effectively. However, this reliance on large datasets, which often include sensitive personal, corporate, and governmental information, raises significant privacy concerns. Sensitive data such as personally identifiable information (PII), financial transactions, medical records, and confidential business strategies must be protected from unauthorized access, breaches, and misuse (Vashishth et al., 2024). If such data falls into the wrong hands, it can lead to identity theft, financial fraud, corporate espionage, or even national security threats. Privacy-preserving mechanisms play a crucial role in ensuring that AI models can process and analyze data while maintaining confidentiality. By implementing encryption, anonymization, and secure data-sharing protocols, cybersecurity systems can safeguard sensitive information without compromising their effectiveness in detecting cyber threats (Al-Mukhtar, 2024).

2. **Privacy Challenges in AI-Driven Cybersecurity:** While AI enhances cybersecurity by automating threat detection, incident response, and predictive analysis, it also introduces unique privacy challenges. One major concern is the exposure of sensitive data in cloud and edge computing environments, where AI models process vast amounts of data remotely. Without adequate encryption and access controls, malicious actors may intercept or exploit this data. Another challenge is adversarial attacks, where cybercriminals manipulate input data to mislead AI models, causing false classifications or system failures. Additionally, insider threats pose a risk when employees or administrators misuse their access privileges to extract confidential information. These privacy challenges require organizations to adopt robust security measures, such as access control mechanisms, encrypted communications, and privacy-enhancing AI techniques, to ensure the integrity and confidentiality of sensitive data (Nacheva and Azeroual, 2024).
3. **Key Privacy-Preserving Mechanisms:** To mitigate privacy risks in AI-driven cybersecurity, various privacy-preserving mechanisms have been developed to protect data while maintaining system efficiency. Differential privacy is one such technique that introduces controlled noise to datasets, ensuring that AI models can analyze trends without exposing individual records. This approach is widely used in sectors like healthcare and finance to share valuable insights while preserving user anonymity. Homomorphic encryption enables computations on encrypted data without decrypting it, allowing cybersecurity systems to analyze network traffic securely. Federated learning decentralizes AI training, keeping data localized on user devices while allowing collaborative model improvements. This reduces the risk of data leaks associated with centralized data storage. Secure Multi-Party Computation (SMPC) allows multiple organizations to jointly analyze security threats without revealing their private data to one another. Additionally, Zero-Knowledge Proofs (ZKP) help authenticate

users and validate transactions without disclosing any sensitive information, enhancing the security of authentication and blockchain-based cybersecurity solutions (Vashishth et al., 2024).

4. **Regulatory and Ethical Considerations:** The growing concerns over data privacy have led to the establishment of strict regulatory frameworks that organizations must adhere to when implementing AI-driven cybersecurity solutions. The General Data Protection Regulation (GDPR) in the European Union enforces stringent guidelines on data collection, processing, and storage, requiring organizations to prioritize user consent and privacy protection. Similarly, the California Consumer Privacy Act (CCPA) grants California residents' greater control over their personal data, mandating transparency in data collection practices. In the healthcare sector, HIPAA (Health Insurance Portability and Accountability Act) ensures that patient information remains confidential and protected from unauthorized access. Additionally, the NIST Privacy Framework provides guidelines for integrating privacy measures into AI-powered cybersecurity systems. Failing to comply with these regulations can lead to severe legal penalties, financial losses, and reputational damage. Therefore, organizations must implement privacy-preserving AI mechanisms to maintain compliance while securing their digital assets (Vashishth et al., 2025).
5. **Future Directions of Privacy-Preserving AI in Cybersecurity:** As cyber threats evolve, the future of privacy-preserving AI in cybersecurity will focus on advanced cryptographic techniques, decentralized security models, and explainable AI (XAI). Quantum cryptography is expected to revolutionize data protection by making encryption virtually unbreakable, ensuring highly secure communications. By providing clear explanations for threat detection and decision-making, XAI will build trust in AI-based security solutions while ensuring compliance with privacy regulations. Moving forward, organizations must adopt a privacy-by-design approach, embedding privacy measures into AI model development and cybersecurity frameworks to create a safer digital ecosystem (Nadella et al., 2024).

2. AI-DRIVEN INTRUSION DETECTION SYSTEMS (IDS)

2.1 Fundamentals of IDS and Their Role in Cybersecurity

Intrusion Detection Systems (IDS) play a crucial role in cybersecurity by monitoring network traffic, system activities, and user behavior to detect potential security breaches, unauthorized access, and malicious activities. These systems serve as an early warning mechanism, alerting security teams to possible cyber threats before they cause significant damage. IDS can be deployed in various environments, including enterprise networks, cloud-based infrastructures, and critical systems such as banking, healthcare, and government databases. The primary function of IDS is to analyze incoming and outgoing network traffic for patterns that indicate suspicious activity. This is achieved through signature-based detection, which compares observed behavior with known attack signatures, and anomaly-based detection, which uses machine learning algorithms to identify deviations from normal behavior. While signature-based IDS are effective against well-documented threats, anomaly-based systems are more adept at detecting new and evolving cyber threats, including zero-day attacks. Traditional IDS solutions, such as Snort and Suricata, rely on predefined rules and human expertise to identify threats. However, the increasing complexity and sophistication of cyberattacks have led to the integration of Artificial Intelligence (AI) in IDS to enhance their accuracy and adaptability. AI-driven IDS utilize machine learning, deep learning, and natural language processing (NLP) to automatically analyze vast amounts of network data, identify hidden attack patterns, and respond to security incidents in real time. Figure 1. illustrates architectural structure of intrusion detection system. These intelligent systems not only detect intrusions more efficiently but also help in automating threat response mechanisms, reducing false positives, and improving overall network resilience. By leveraging AI-driven IDS, cybersecurity teams can detect, analyze, and neutralize threats more effectively, ensuring the protection of sensitive data, business operations, and critical infrastructure (Ejeofobiri et al., 2024).

Figure 1. Intrusion Detection Architecture

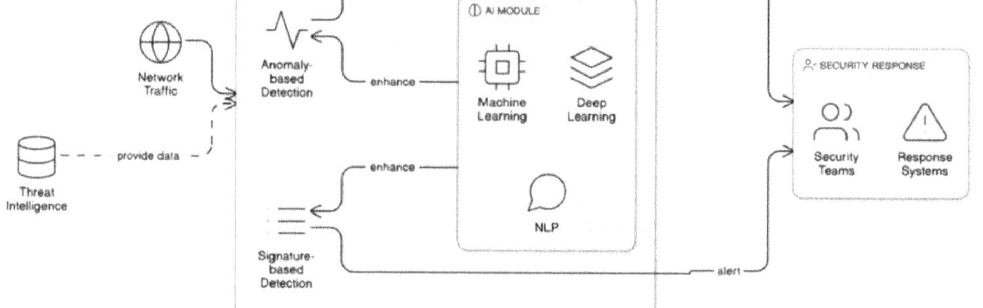

2.2 AI techniques in IDS: Machine Learning (ML) and Deep Learning (DL)

The integration of Artificial Intelligence (AI) into Intrusion Detection Systems (IDS) has significantly enhanced their ability to detect, analyze, and respond to cyber threats in real-time. Traditional IDS rely on static rule-based and signature-based approaches, which struggle to keep up with the rapidly evolving threat landscape. AI-driven IDS leverage Machine Learning (ML) and Deep Learning (DL) techniques to automate threat detection, improve accuracy, and reduce false positives. These techniques enable IDS to analyze vast amounts of network traffic, identify patterns, and detect anomalies that could indicate malicious activities.

2.2.1 Machine Learning (ML) in IDS

Machine learning plays a vital role in modern IDS by enabling systems to learn from historical data and improve their threat detection capabilities over time. ML models in IDS can be broadly categorized into supervised, unsupervised, and reinforcement learning approaches.

1. **Supervised Learning**: This approach involves training an ML model on labelled datasets containing examples of both normal and malicious activities. Algorithms such as Support Vector Machines (SVM), Decision Trees, Random Forest, and Naïve Bayes classify new network traffic as either normal or anomalous based on learned patterns. The primary challenge in supervised learning is the need for extensive labelled datasets, which may not always be available for new and emerging threats.
2. **Unsupervised Learning**: In this approach, ML models detect anomalies without relying on predefined labels. Techniques such as k-Means Clustering, DBSCAN, and Autoencoders help identify deviations from normal behavior in network traffic. Unsupervised learning is particularly useful for detecting zero-day attacks and unknown cyber threats, as it does not require prior knowledge of attack signatures.
3. **Reinforcement Learning**: This AI technique enables IDS to continuously adapt and refine its detection strategies based on real-time feedback. By rewarding correct threat identifications and penalizing false positives, reinforcement learning helps IDS optimize their intrusion detection capabilities over time.

ML-based IDS can analyze packet headers, payloads, and network flow metadata to detect intrusions efficiently. However, traditional ML approaches often struggle with large-scale datasets and complex attack patterns, leading to the adoption of Deep Learning (DL) techniques for enhanced intrusion detection.

2.2.2 Deep Learning (DL) in IDS

Deep learning, a subset of machine learning, utilizes multi-layered artificial neural networks to process vast amounts of data and extract complex features. DL techniques have shown superior performance in detecting sophisticated cyber threats due to their ability to automatically learn high-dimensional patterns in network traffic. Some of the most commonly used DL architectures in IDS include:

1. **Artificial Neural Networks (ANNs)**: These are the foundational DL models that mimic the structure of the human brain. ANNs are particularly useful in intrusion detection as they can learn intricate relationships within data and improve detection accuracy (Achuthan et al., 2024).
2. **Convolutional Neural Networks (CNNs)**: Traditionally used in image processing, CNNs have been applied to cybersecurity for feature extraction and anomaly detection in network traffic data. They help IDS recognize complex attack signatures that traditional ML models might miss.
3. **Recurrent Neural Networks (RNNs) and Long Short-Term Memory (LSTM)**: These DL architectures are highly effective for analyzing sequential data, such as time-series network traffic. RNNs and LSTMs detect patterns over time, making them valuable for identifying persistent threats and Advanced Persistent Threats (APTs) that evolve gradually.
4. **Autoencoders**: These unsupervised DL models help IDS detect anomalies by reconstructing input data and measuring the reconstruction error. High reconstruction errors indicate unusual network activity that may signify an attack.
5. **Generative Adversarial Networks (GANs)**: GANs are used for both enhancing IDS performance and generating adversarial attack samples to test and improve cybersecurity defences. They help in understanding how attackers might manipulate AI models to evade detection.

2.2.3 Federated Learning for Intrusion Detection

Learning(FL) is changing the way Intrusion Detection Systems (IDS) will be deployed, as it is the first time we are seeing AI being trained in a decentralized way across multiple organizations and/or edge-devices, without sending sensitive data to a central server. In federated IDS, local models are trained on-site with private data and only the model updates share information, as local data is only shared on a model update. The FL based approach is beneficial in health-care or finance, where industries are highly ethically or legally regulated by acts like HIPAA or GDPR. Notably, an organization that is utilizing an FL based IDS can detect threats in their own localized environment, but can also be more intelligent about those localized threats, as they would benefit from the intelligence of the global aggregate of multi-federated models' data sets. Combining secure aggregation techniques or differential privacy with Federated IDS provides excellent protection against external groups or internal data breaches.

The integration of ML and DL into IDS has led to improved accuracy, faster threat detection, and reduced human intervention in cybersecurity operations. However, challenges such as high computational costs, data privacy concerns, and vulnerability to adversarial attacks must be addressed to ensure robust and reliable AI-driven IDS.

2.3 Real-Time Threat Detection and Automated Response Systems

Real-time threat detection and automated response systems have become essential components of modern cybersecurity frameworks, enabling organizations to identify, analyze, and neutralize cyber threats instantly. Traditional security approaches relied on manual intervention and rule-based methods, which often resulted in delayed responses, leaving networks vulnerable to fast-evolving cyberattacks. However, with the integration of Artificial Intelligence (AI), Machine Learning (ML), and Deep Learning (DL), intrusion detection systems (IDS) have evolved into intelligent, self-learning systems that can detect threats in real-time and initiate automated countermeasures. AI-driven real-time threat detection relies on continuous network monitoring, anomaly detection, and behavioural analysis. Unlike traditional signature-based detection, which can only identify known threats, AI-powered IDS use anomaly-based techniques to detect previously unseen attacks, zero-day vulnerabilities, and Advanced Persistent Threats (APTs) by identifying deviations from normal network behavior. These systems analyze massive datasets in real-time, correlating multiple security events to uncover suspicious activities that may indicate malware infections, unauthorized access attempts, or insider threats. Deep learning models such as Convolutional Neural Networks (CNNs) and Long Short-Term Memory (LSTM) networks are particularly effective in processing large volumes of network traffic data and identifying subtle attack patterns that might go unnoticed by traditional IDS (Sharma et al., 2025). Moreover, Security Orchestration, Automation, and Response (SOAR) platforms enhance the effectiveness of real-time threat detection by integrating AI-driven IDS with firewalls, endpoint protection systems, and threat intelligence feeds. This ensures a coordinated, multi-layered defense strategy that dynamically adapts to evolving attack techniques. Additionally, self-healing AI systems leverage reinforcement learning to continuously learn from past incidents and improve their response strategies, making them more resilient against future threats (Rani et al., 2024).

2.4 Advantages of AI-Powered IDS Over Traditional IDS

The evolution of Intrusion Detection Systems (IDS) has significantly transformed with the integration of Artificial Intelligence (AI), offering superior performance compared to traditional IDS. Conventional IDS primarily relied on signature-based and rule-based detection methods, which, although effective against known threats, struggled with detecting zero-day attacks, polymorphic malware, and sophisticated cyber threats.

1. **Enhanced Threat Detection Accuracy:** Traditional IDS rely on predefined rules and known attack signatures, making them ineffective against new or evolving threats. AI-powered IDS, on the other hand, analyze vast amounts of network data and detect subtle patterns indicative of cyber threats. By employing ML techniques such as Supervised Learning, Unsupervised Learning, and Reinforcement Learning, AI-powered IDS can identify both known and unknown threats with higher accuracy. Deep Learning (DL) models like Convolutional Neural Networks (CNNs) and Long Short-Term Memory (LSTM) networks further improve the detection of Advanced Persistent Threats (APTs) by learning from historical attack patterns.
2. **Real-Time Threat Detection and Faster Response:** One of the significant drawbacks of traditional IDS is the delay in detecting and responding to cyber threats due to reliance on static rules and manual intervention. AI-powered IDS operate in real-time, continuously analyzing network traffic and identifying anomalies as they occur. Automated response mechanisms allow these systems to take instant defensive actions, such as blocking malicious IPs, isolating compromised devices, or notifying security teams, thereby reducing the attack dwell time and minimizing damage.
3. **Adaptability to Evolving Threats (Zero-Day and Polymorphic Attacks):** Traditional IDS struggle to detect zero-day vulnerabilities and polymorphic malware because these threats do not match existing attack signatures. AI-powered IDS excel in such scenarios by learning normal network behavior and identifying deviations that may indicate malicious activity. Anomaly detection models, powered by Unsupervised Learning (such as k-Means clustering and Autoencoders), help in flagging suspicious activities, even if they do not match known attack patterns. This adaptability makes AI-driven IDS more resilient against advanced cyber threats.

4. **Reduced False Positives:** A common challenge in traditional IDS is the high number of false positives, where legitimate activities are mistakenly flagged as threats, overwhelming security teams. AI-powered IDS significantly reduce false positives by continuously refining their detection algorithms through reinforcement learning and behavioural analysis. Instead of relying solely on rigid rule sets, these systems dynamically adjust their decision-making criteria, ensuring higher precision in threat identification and minimizing unnecessary alerts.
5. **Scalability and Efficient Resource Utilization:** Traditional IDS require significant manual configuration and human oversight, making them resource-intensive and difficult to scale. AI-powered IDS automate most security processes, reducing the need for human intervention and optimizing resource utilization. Additionally, AI-driven systems can be deployed in cloud environments, ensuring scalability and efficiency in protecting large, distributed networks (Vashishth et al., 2024).

AI-powered IDS provide superior detection accuracy, real-time response, adaptability, and scalability compared to traditional IDS. By leveraging Machine Learning, Deep Learning, and Threat Intelligence, these advanced systems can proactively detect, analyze, and mitigate evolving cyber threats. As cyberattacks become increasingly sophisticated, AI-driven IDS will play a crucial role in enhancing cybersecurity defences and ensuring robust protection for modern digital infrastructures.

3. ADVERSARIAL MACHINE LEARNING IN CYBERSECURITY

Adversarial Machine Learning (AML) has emerged as a growing concern in cybersecurity due to the increasing dependence on Artificial Intelligence (AI) and Machine Learning (ML) for detecting and mitigating cyber threats. While AI-driven security systems offer enhanced threat detection capabilities, they are vulnerable to adversarial attacks where cybercriminals manipulate machine learning models to bypass security mechanisms. These attacks involve intentionally crafted inputs designed to mislead AI systems, leading to incorrect classifications, security breaches, and system failures. Adversarial attacks can take several forms, including evasion attacks, where attackers subtly modify malicious inputs to appear benign, thereby deceiving intrusion detection systems, malware classifiers, and fraud detection mechanisms. Another significant type of attack is data poisoning, where adversaries inject manipulated data into the training process, corrupting the model's learning and making it ineffective in identifying real threats. Additionally, model extraction and inference attacks allow attackers to steal proprietary AI models or infer sensitive information from the system's predictions, which can be exploited for further security breaches. These adversarial strategies pose a substantial risk to cybersecurity domains such as intrusion detection, malware analysis, biometric authentication, and financial fraud prevention. Cybercriminals use sophisticated techniques like gradient-based perturbations, generative adversarial networks (GANs), and black-box query methods to craft adversarial inputs that evade detection while remaining functionally effective. In real-world applications, adversarial attacks have been used to bypass AI-powered security solutions in phishing detection, malware identification, and automated threat response systems, making them a significant challenge for cybersecurity experts. To counter these threats, researchers have developed various defensive strategies, including adversarial training, which enhances model robustness by exposing AI systems to adversarial examples during training, thereby improving their ability to detect manipulated inputs. Figure 2. presents a synthesis of exciting technologies in the realm of cybersecurity like Adversarial Machine Learning. Within Figure 2, the left side of flow contains the adversarial threats (i.e., evasion attacks, data poisoning, and model inversion) that compromise an AI-based security model. These threats are funnelled into the AI system which attempts to change its natural decision-making processes. The right side of the diagram provides an overview of the defensive or countermeasure activities (i.e., adversarial training, input sanitization, and ensemble modeling) that enhance the ever-evolving adversarial variations designers face and help strengthen the AI model's resilience. This diagram illustrates the perpetual tussle that exists between sophisticated adversarial tactics and defensive adaptations in AI-supported cybersecurity environment. By strengthening AI security through adversarial robustness, proactive threat detection, and continuous model adaptation, organizations can mitigate the risks associated with adversarial ML and enhance the resilience of cybersecurity systems in an increasingly AI-driven digital landscape (Awad et al., 2024).

Figure 2. Integration of Adversarial Machine Learning in Cybersecurity

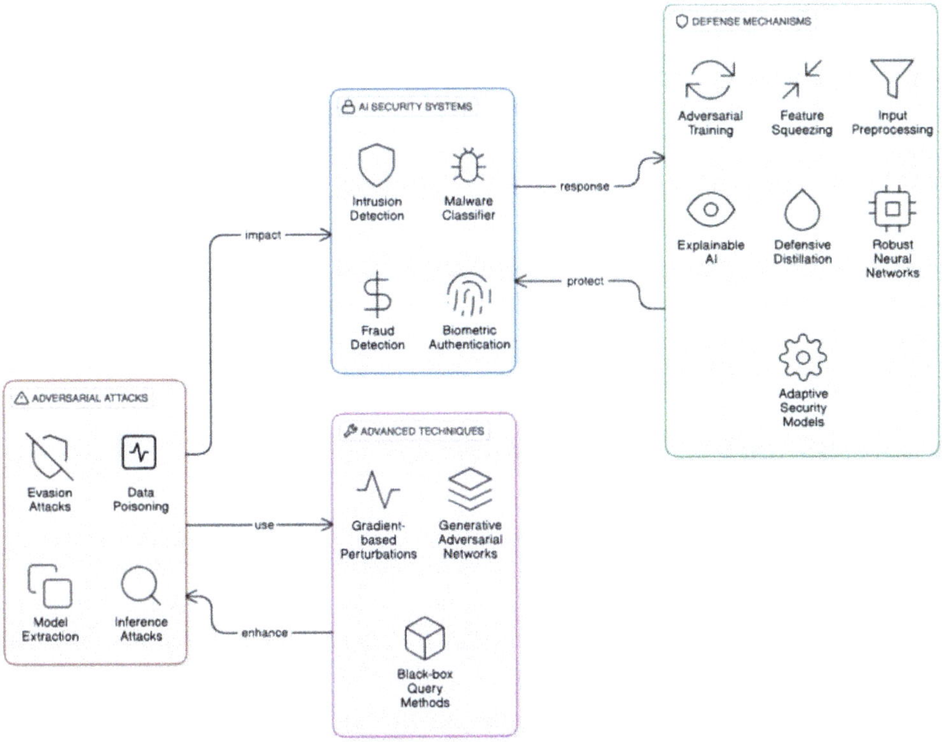

In response to adversarial machine learning (AML) threats, there have been various defensive strategies proposed. Adversarial training (in which both clean and adversarial information are introduced during training to enhance a model's resilience) is one of the primary defensive strategies introduced. Gradient masking, another defensive strategy, limits the existence of gradient information in order to reduce the risk of an attacker creating a malicious input. Preprocessing methods (i.e., feature squeezing and data normalization) reduce the susceptibility of a model to perturbations on input. Ensemble learning is another defensive approach that builds multi-models with unique decision boundaries to raise the credibility of input given that an attacker cannot evade detection all of the time. Currently, new certified defences include randomized smoothing, which mathematically signifies a model as resilient, and can help move researchers into this new front of adversarial defence.

4. PRIVACY-PRESERVING AI TECHNIQUES FOR CYBERSECURITY

Privacy-preserving AI techniques play a crucial role in cybersecurity by ensuring that sensitive data remains secure while leveraging artificial intelligence for threat detection and mitigation. As AI-powered cybersecurity solutions analyze vast amounts of data, protecting personally identifiable information (PII), financial records, healthcare data, and other confidential assets becomes essential to prevent unauthorized access, data breaches, and regulatory non-compliance. Privacy-preserving AI techniques integrate advanced cryptographic methods, decentralized learning frameworks, and differential privacy mechanisms to enhance data security without compromising the effectiveness of AI-driven intrusion detection and response systems.

4.1 Differential Privacy and Federated Learning in Cybersecurity

Differential Privacy (DP) and Federated Learning (FL) are two key privacy-preserving AI techniques that play a crucial role in enhancing cybersecurity by securing sensitive data while enabling AI-driven threat detection and response mechanisms. These approaches ensure that cybersecurity systems can analyze and detect potential threats without exposing raw data to security risks, unauthorized access, or adversarial attacks.

1. **Differential Privacy (DP):** It is a mathematical framework that introduces controlled noise into data analysis processes, ensuring that individual records within a dataset cannot be traced back or reconstructed, even if an adversary gains access to model outputs. In cybersecurity, differential privacy is particularly useful in scenarios where AI models analyze user behavior, network activity, or fraud patterns while maintaining strict privacy standards. For instance, in intrusion detection systems (IDS), DP can be applied to anonymize user activity logs, preventing attackers from reverse-engineering sensitive data while still allowing AI models to extract meaningful security insights. DP is also widely used in threat intelligence sharing, where organizations collaborate to identify emerging cyber threats without compromising proprietary or personal data. By adding noise to datasets before training AI models, differential privacy ensures that even if an attacker gains access to the model, they cannot infer specific details about individual data points. However, one of the main challenges of differential privacy in cybersecurity is maintaining the balance between privacy and model accuracy, as excessive noise can reduce the effectiveness of AI-based threat detection (Vashishth et al., 2024).

2. **Federated Learning (FL):** It is another privacy-enhancing AI technique that enables multiple entities to collaboratively train machine learning models without sharing their raw data. Unlike traditional AI training methods that require data to be centralized in a single repository, FL allows data to remain distributed across individual devices or secure servers while AI models are trained locally. This decentralized approach significantly enhances privacy and security by minimizing data exposure risks and reducing the chances of cyberattacks targeting centralized databases. In cybersecurity, federated learning is particularly effective in scenarios such as malware detection, anomaly detection, and fraud prevention. To address these concerns, researchers are integrating secure aggregation techniques, encrypted model updates, and differential privacy within federated learning frameworks to enhance their resilience against adversarial threats (Vashishth et al., 2024).

By combining differential privacy and federated learning, cybersecurity solutions can achieve a robust balance between AI-driven threat detection and privacy preservation. These techniques enable organizations to develop highly secure, privacy-preserving intrusion detection and response mechanisms that comply with stringent data protection regulations such as GDPR and HIPAA. As cyber threats continue to evolve, the integration of DP and FL in cybersecurity will play a vital role in protecting sensitive information, improving AI model robustness, and ensuring the effectiveness of AI-powered security solutions without compromising user privacy.

4.2 Secure Multi-Party Computation and Homomorphic Encryption

Secure Multi-Party Computation (SMPC) and Homomorphic Encryption (HE) are two advanced cryptographic techniques that enhance privacy preservation in AI-driven cybersecurity systems. These methods enable secure data processing and analysis without exposing sensitive information, making them crucial for protecting confidential data while maintaining the effectiveness of AI-based security mechanisms. Secure Multi-Party Computation (SMPC) allows multiple parties to jointly compute a function over their private inputs without revealing those inputs to each other. This ensures that organizations can collaborate on cybersecurity threat analysis, fraud detection, and intrusion prevention while maintaining strict confidentiality. SMPC is particularly useful in scenarios where different entities, such as financial institutions, government agencies, and cybersecurity firms, need to share security intelligence without compromising proprietary data. For instance, in a distributed threat intelligence framework, multiple organizations can analyze cyberattack patterns collectively without exposing individual security logs to potential adversaries. By leveraging cryptographic techniques like secret sharing and zero-knowledge proofs, SMPC ensures that computations are performed securely while minimizing the risk of data breaches. However, implementing SMPC in real-time cybersecurity applications poses challenges related to computational complexity and communication overhead, requiring optimized cryptographic protocols to ensure scalability and efficiency. Homomorphic Encryption (HE), on the other hand, allows AI models to perform computations on encrypted data without requiring decryption, ensuring end-to-end privacy in cybersecurity operations. Unlike traditional encryption methods that require decryption before processing, exposing data to potential security threats, HE enables secure AI-driven threat analysis while keeping data encrypted throughout the entire process. This is particularly beneficial in cloud-based security services, where sensitive information, such as user authentication logs or financial transactions, can be analysed without being exposed to cloud providers or third parties. HE is also widely applied in secure anomaly detection, where encrypted network traffic patterns are analysed to identify suspicious activities without revealing actual user behavior. As cyber threats become more sophisticated, the adoption of SMPC and HE in AI-powered cybersecurity solutions will continue to evolve, providing organizations with advanced privacy-preserving mechanisms to safeguard sensitive information while maintaining high levels of security and trust in digital environments (Shahana et al., 2024)

4.3 Blockchain-Based Privacy-Preserving AI Models

Blockchain-based privacy-preserving AI models combine the decentralized and immutable nature of blockchain technology with AI-driven security mechanisms to enhance privacy and trust in cybersecurity applications. Traditional AI models often rely on centralized data storage and processing, which makes them vulnerable to cyberattacks, unauthorized access, and data breaches. By leveraging blockchain, AI models can operate in a decentralized manner, ensuring that data remains secure, transparent, and tamper-resistant while mitigating risks associated with central points of failure. Blockchain's distributed ledger technology ensures that once data is recorded, it cannot be altered or deleted, making it a powerful tool for maintaining the integrity of AI-driven security mechanisms. One of the key applications of blockchain in privacy-preserving AI is secure data sharing, where organizations can collaborate on cybersecurity threat detection and response without exposing raw data. For instance, in an AI-powered intrusion detection system (IDS), different entities can contribute encrypted threat intelligence data to a blockchain network, allowing AI models to analyze patterns and detect anomalies while preserving the confidentiality of individual datasets. Additionally, blockchain-based smart contracts can automate security protocols, ensuring that data access is granted only to authorized parties based on predefined rules, thereby reducing the risk of insider threats and unauthorized modifications. Another major advantage of blockchain-based privacy-preserving AI models is their role in securing federated learning (FL) environments. Since FL allows AI models to be trained across multiple devices without sharing raw data, blockchain can enhance its security by providing a decentralized and immutable audit trail of model updates. This ensures that AI training processes are transparent, resistant to tampering, and verifiable by all participating entities. Moreover, blockchain enables cryptographic techniques such as zero-knowledge proofs (ZKPs), which allow AI models to validate transactions or verify security threats without revealing underlying data. This is particularly useful in scenarios like financial fraud detection, secure identity verification, and healthcare cybersecurity, where sensitive information must remain confidential while still being analysed for potential threats. Despite its benefits, integrating blockchain with AI in cybersecurity comes with challenges, including scalability issues, high computational costs, and energy consumption. Processing large-scale AI security data on a blockchain network requires efficient consensus mechanisms and optimized cryptographic techniques to ensure that privacy and security are maintained without compromising system performance. As cyber threats become increasingly sophisticated, blockchain-based privacy-preserving AI models offer a promising solution to enhance security, data integrity, and privacy in cybersecurity frameworks. Future advancements in blockchain scalability, energy-efficient consensus algorithms, and AI optimization will further enhance the adoption of these models, making them an integral part of next-generation cybersecurity solutions (Vashishth et al., 2024).

4.4 Balancing AI-Driven Security With Data Protection Laws

Balancing AI-driven security with data protection laws is a complex yet essential task, as organizations must leverage artificial intelligence for cybersecurity while adhering to stringent privacy regulations. AI-powered security systems rely on vast amounts of data to detect cyber threats, prevent fraud, and automate incident responses, but this often involves processing sensitive personal, financial, or corporate data. Global privacy regulations, such as the General Data Protection Regulation (GDPR), California Consumer Privacy Act (CCPA), and Health Insurance Portability and Accountability Act (HIPAA), impose strict requirements on data collection, processing, and storage, making it imperative for organizations to design AI-driven security frameworks that comply with legal standards. The challenge lies in ensuring that AI models can effectively analyze security threats without violating data privacy rights. To address this, privacy-preserving AI techniques such as differential privacy, federated learning, homomorphic encryption, and secure multi-party computation (SMPC) are increasingly being integrated into cybersecurity solutions.

These techniques enable AI models to process and learn from decentralized datasets without directly accessing or exposing sensitive user information, thus maintaining compliance with data protection laws while ensuring robust security. One of the key concerns in balancing AI-driven security with data protection laws is the lack of transparency in AI decision-making. Many privacies laws mandate that organizations provide clear explanations for automated security decisions, especially when they impact user rights, access control, or fraud detection processes. Explainable AI (XAI) addresses this issue by making AI-driven cybersecurity systems more interpretable and auditable, allowing regulatory bodies, businesses, and end-users to understand how AI models classify threats and make decisions. Figure 3. illustrates integration of AI in cybersecurity. Many AI-driven security platforms operate in cloud environments where data flows across multiple regions, making compliance with regional privacy laws more difficult. Solutions such as privacy-preserving AI models with decentralized architectures and blockchain-based access control mechanisms help mitigate these challenges by ensuring that sensitive data remains protected while enabling secure, regulatory-compliant AI-driven security operations. Additionally, regulatory bodies and governments are increasingly working on developing AI governance frameworks and ethical guidelines to ensure that AI in cybersecurity remains fair, accountable, and compliant with privacy laws (Vashishth et al., 2024).

Figure 3. AI-driven Cybersecurity

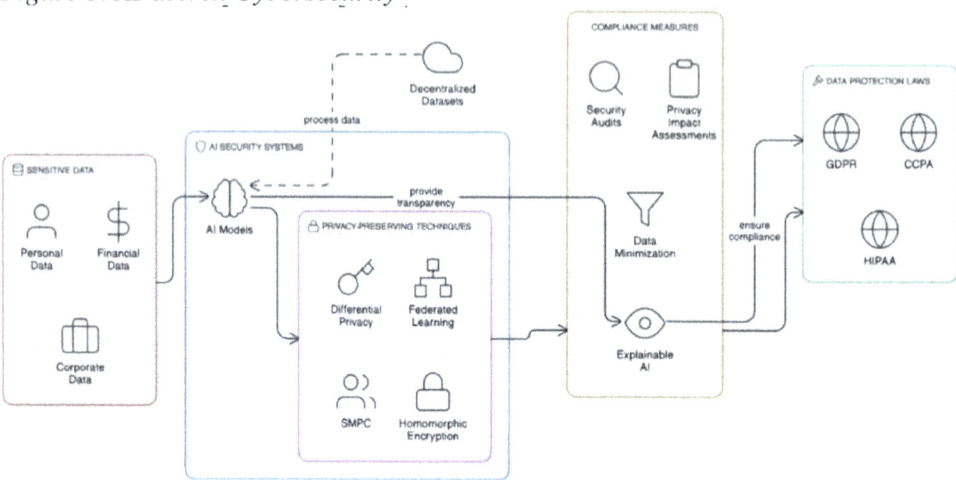

Although advancements have been made regarding privacy protections and legislation, the challenges of balancing AI-enabled security and privacy obligations will involve constant by evolving cyber threats and legal obligations. Organizations must incorporate privacy-by-design principles, engendering security, and compliance measures through artificial intelligence (AI) model development. Organizations may look for collaborative solutions between AI developers, legal personnel, and cybersecurity experts in identifying and designing solutions that preserve data while preserving user rights. As privacy laws navigating technological change continue to evolve, leveraging privacy-enhancing AI techniques, blockchain for data integrity, and governance of ethical AI practices will be important to ensure both effective cybersecurity and compliance with the law. Organizations must establish a position where technological improvements associated with the expanding use of AI can improve cybersecurity while satisfying trustworthiness and transparency expectations and global data protection standards (Bandi, 2024).

5. CHALLENGES IN SECURING AI-DRIVEN SYSTEMS

Securing AI-driven systems presents a multifaceted challenge as organizations increasingly rely on artificial intelligence for cybersecurity, automation, decision-making, and critical infrastructure protection. While AI enhances security through intelligent threat detection, automated response mechanisms, and predictive analytics, it also introduces new vulnerabilities and risks that adversaries can exploit. The challenges in securing AI-driven systems stem from several key factors, including adversarial attacks, data privacy concerns, model interpretability, and compliance with evolving cybersecurity regulations. As AI continues to reshape digital security, addressing these challenges is crucial to ensuring robust and resilient AI-powered security frameworks.

1. **Adversarial Attacks on AI Models:** One of the most pressing challenges in securing AI-driven systems is the threat posed by adversarial machine learning (AML) attacks. These attacks exploit vulnerabilities in AI models to manipulate their outputs, allowing cybercriminals to bypass security measures undetected. Evasion attacks involve crafting malicious inputs that appear normal to AI-based security systems, tricking them into misclassifying threats. For example, attackers may subtly modify malware signatures so that an AI-powered antivirus fails to recognize them. Poisoning attacks occur when adversaries inject malicious data into an AI model's training set, corrupting its learning process and leading to incorrect threat classifications. These vulnerabilities highlight the need for robust adversarial training, anomaly detection mechanisms, and AI model verification techniques to strengthen security against evolving threats.
2. **Data Privacy and Security Risks:** AI-driven security systems require vast amounts of data for training and real-time threat analysis. However, handling such data introduces significant privacy and security risks. AI models may in-

advertently store and expose sensitive personal or corporate data, making them attractive targets for cybercriminals. Model inversion attacks allow adversaries to reconstruct training data from AI models, while membership inference attacks enable attackers to determine whether a specific individual's data was used in training. To address these risks, privacy-preserving AI techniques such as differential privacy, federated learning, homomorphic encryption, and secure multi-party computation must be integrated into AI-driven security solutions. These methods ensure that AI systems can learn and make predictions without directly accessing or exposing sensitive data, thereby maintaining compliance with global data protection laws such as GDPR, CCPA, and HIPAA.

3. **Lack of Explainability and Transparency:** The complexity of AI models, particularly deep learning algorithms, often results in lack of transparency and explainability in cybersecurity decisions. AI-powered security systems frequently operate as black boxes, making it difficult for analysts to understand how threats are classified or why specific actions are taken. This opacity can lead to trust issues, false positives, and difficulties in regulatory compliance. Explainable AI (XAI) techniques such as SHAP (Shapley Additive Explanations), Local Interpretable Model-Agnostic Explanations (LIME), and attention-based visualization methods are essential in making AI-driven security decisions more interpretable. Enhancing AI explainability allows cybersecurity professionals to audit AI-driven security models, ensuring that automated threat detection and response mechanisms remain reliable, fair, and accountable.
4. **Integration Challenges with Legacy Security Systems:** Many organizations still rely on traditional cybersecurity infrastructure that was not designed to integrate with AI-driven security mechanisms. Deploying AI-powered intrusion detection systems (IDS), automated threat intelligence platforms, and machine learning-based endpoint security solutions alongside existing security tools presents challenges in terms of compatibility, scalability, and performance optimization. Additionally, AI-driven security frameworks often require high computational power and real-time data processing capabilities, making their implementation resource-intensive.
5. **Ethical and Regulatory Compliance Challenges:** As AI becomes more deeply embedded in cybersecurity, ensuring ethical AI governance and regulatory compliance remains a critical challenge. AI-driven security mechanisms must adhere to global data protection laws, cybersecurity frameworks, and ethical guidelines to prevent misuse and protect user rights. For instance, regulations like GDPR mandate transparency in AI decision-making, requiring organizations to provide explanations for AI-driven security actions. AI models must also be bias-free and impartial, ensuring that automated threat detection does not disproportionately impact certain groups or individuals. Implementing ethical

AI practices, regular security audits, and privacy impact assessments (PIAs) can help organizations align AI-driven cybersecurity measures with regulatory requirements while maintaining trust and accountability.

Securing AI-driven systems is a complex and evolving challenge that requires addressing adversarial attacks, privacy risks, transparency issues, integration complexities, regulatory compliance, and AI model robustness. As AI continues to revolutionize cybersecurity, organizations must adopt privacy-preserving AI techniques, explainable AI frameworks, robust adversarial defences, and hybrid security models to ensure that AI-driven cybersecurity remains resilient against evolving threats.

6. CASE STUDIES ON AI-DRIVEN CYBERATTACKS AND COUNTERMEASURES

The rise of artificial intelligence (AI) in cybersecurity has brought significant advancements in threat detection, automated defense mechanisms, and predictive analytics. However, cybercriminals are also leveraging AI to develop more sophisticated cyberattacks that can evade traditional security measures. AI-driven cyberattacks exploit vulnerabilities in machine learning (ML) models, automate phishing attacks, manipulate data integrity, and generate deepfake content for social engineering. Studying real-world case studies of AI-driven cyberattacks and their countermeasures provides critical insights into how organizations can strengthen their cybersecurity frameworks.

6.1 Case Study: AI-Powered Phishing Attacks and Defense Mechanisms

Attack Scenario: Phishing attacks, which involve tricking users into revealing sensitive information, have become more advanced with the integration of AI. Traditional phishing attacks rely on human-crafted emails with fraudulent links, but AI enables attackers to generate highly convincing messages at scale. In a notable case, cybercriminals used AI-powered natural language processing (NLP) and deep learning models to generate personalized phishing emails. These messages mimicked real human communication patterns, dynamically adapting to the victim's language style and previous interactions. Attackers also used AI-generated deepfake voice technology to impersonate company executives and trick employees into transferring funds or disclosing sensitive credentials.

Countermeasures: To combat AI-driven phishing attacks, cybersecurity firms have developed AI-based phishing detection systems that analyze message context, linguistic patterns, and sender authenticity. Advanced email security solutions use machine learning classifiers trained on large datasets of phishing emails to detect anomalies in email headers, URLs, and attachments. Additionally, real-time behavioural analytics can flag suspicious user activity, while zero-trust authentication models, such as multi-factor authentication (MFA) and biometric verification, prevent unauthorized access even if credentials are compromised.

6.2 Case Study: Adversarial Attacks on AI-Based Malware Detection Systems

Attack Scenario: AI-powered malware detection systems rely on deep learning to classify and block malicious files. However, adversarial machine learning (AML) techniques have enabled attackers to bypass these systems. In one case, researchers demonstrated how adversarial perturbations—subtle modifications to malware code—could deceive AI-based antivirus software. Attackers modified malware samples in a way that preserved their functionality but altered their digital signatures just enough to evade detection. The AI model, trained on static signatures and behavioural patterns, failed to recognize the modified malware as a threat.

Countermeasures: To defend against adversarial attacks, cybersecurity teams have implemented adversarial training, where AI models are exposed to manipulated data during training to enhance their robustness. Other countermeasures include ensemble learning approaches, where multiple AI models work together to cross-validate threat classifications, reducing the effectiveness of adversarial perturbations. Additionally, explainable AI (XAI) techniques help security analysts understand how AI models classify malware, making it easier to spot inconsistencies caused by adversarial modifications.

6.3 Case Study: Deepfake-Based Social Engineering Attacks and Prevention

Attack Scenario: Deepfake technology, which uses AI to create highly realistic fake videos or audio, has been exploited in social engineering attacks. In a high-profile case, hackers used deepfake voice cloning to impersonate a CEO and instructed an employee to transfer millions of dollars to a fraudulent bank account. Since the AI-generated voice matched the executive's speech patterns, tone, and inflection, the victim believed the request was legitimate. Similarly, deepfake videos have been used to spread disinformation and manipulate public perception in political and financial sectors.

Countermeasures: To mitigate deepfake threats, researchers have developed AI-based deepfake detection tools that analyze subtle inconsistencies in facial expressions, lighting, and audio frequencies. Organizations have also implemented biometric authentication systems, which require live video verification rather than pre-recorded footage. Additionally, awareness training programs help employees recognize social engineering tactics, ensuring that financial transactions and sensitive communications undergo multi-level verification.

6.4 Case Study: AI-Manipulated Fake News and Disinformation Campaigns

Attack Scenario: Cybercriminals and state-sponsored groups have leveraged AI to create automated disinformation campaigns, spreading false news articles, manipulated images, and AI-generated content across social media. AI-powered bots amplify the reach of misleading content, influencing public opinion, and causing social unrest. In one case, AI-generated fake news articles were distributed through bot networks, targeting financial markets and leading to stock price manipulation.

Countermeasures: To counter AI-driven disinformation, cybersecurity researchers have developed AI-based content verification systems that use natural language processing (NLP) to detect inconsistencies in online articles. Social media platforms employ machine learning classifiers to identify and flag bot-generated content, while blockchain-based provenance tracking ensures content authenticity. Additionally, public awareness campaigns and fact-checking AI models help users distinguish between legitimate news and AI-generated misinformation. However, AI also plays a crucial role in enhancing cybersecurity defences, enabling organizations to implement real-time threat detection, automated response mechanisms, adversarial training, and blockchain-based integrity solutions. By understanding these case studies and deploying proactive countermeasures, cybersecurity professionals can stay ahead of AI-driven threats, ensuring a more secure digital ecosystem (Sarker, 2024).

6.5 Case Study: Federated Learning in Healthcare IDS

Attack Scenario: A healthcare consortium wanted to enhance its ability to detect potential ransomware and data exfiltration threats, while still abiding by patient privacy legislation in terms of its sharing of information. Centralized data sharing was a legal impossibility due to compliance with HIPAA and GDPR.

Countermeasure: The consortium designed a federated intrusion detection system (FIDS), where each member hospital trained an AI model using its own network logs. The models shared encrypted parameter updates instead of data. A central aggregator compiled the updates and rolled a global threat detection model back to each local network. The original plan was to be able to operate the federated IDS in a manner that ensured legal compliance, such that significant accuracy in threat detection could be achieved without exchanging any raw patient, and therefore operational data, would not be provided or kept with the FIDS cloud serving authority in its application. The distributed IDS achieved 94.3% detection accuracy, all while ensuring compliance with data protection regulation (Bandi, 2024). No patient or operational data were ever transferred, maintaining privacy requirements.

7. FUTURE DIRECTIONS FOR AI-POWERED CYBERSECURITY

As cyber threats continue to grow in sophistication, AI-driven cybersecurity is set to undergo significant advancements. Future security models will emphasize automation, privacy preservation, and resilience against adversarial attacks. This section explores key areas where AI-powered cybersecurity will evolve to strengthen digital defense mechanisms.

1. **Autonomous Security Systems and Self-Healing Networks:** Future AI-powered cybersecurity solutions will rely on autonomous security systems capable of detecting, analyzing, and mitigating threats without human intervention. These systems will use unsupervised learning and reinforcement learning techniques to dynamically adapt to emerging cyber threats. Self-healing networks will become a reality, where AI will automatically patch vulnerabilities, neutralize threats, and restore compromised systems in real-time, reducing human dependency and minimizing downtime.
2. **Quantum Computing and AI in Cybersecurity:** The convergence of quantum computing and AI will lead to breakthrough encryption techniques and rapid threat detection models. Quantum-powered AI will predict and neutralize cyber threats faster than traditional systems, significantly enhancing cybersecurity efficiency. However, this also introduces new risks, as cybercriminals may exploit quantum capabilities to break existing encryption methods. This highlights the urgency of developing quantum-resistant cryptographic protocols to ensure data security in the post-quantum era.
3. **Federated Learning and Privacy-Preserving AI:** Federated learning will play a crucial role in privacy-preserving cybersecurity by enabling AI models to train on decentralized data sources without exposing sensitive information. This approach will be especially beneficial for healthcare, finance, and government sectors, where data security and regulatory compliance are critical. Combined with homomorphic encryption and secure multi-party computation, federated learning will strengthen AI-driven security frameworks while ensuring user privacy (Yodha, 2024).

4. **Adversarial Defense Mechanisms and Explainable AI (XAI):** As cybercriminals develop adversarial machine learning techniques to manipulate AI models, future cybersecurity solutions must incorporate robust adversarial defense mechanisms. AI models will be trained to recognize and counter adversarial attacks using generative adversarial networks (GANs) and adversarial training. Additionally, explainable AI (XAI) will become a core component of cybersecurity, ensuring that security analysts can understand AI-driven threat detections, reduce biases, and enhance trust in AI security systems.
5. **Blockchain-Integrated AI for Secure Transactions:** The integration of blockchain with AI will revolutionize cybersecurity by creating decentralized and tamper-proof security infrastructures. Blockchain-based AI models will improve fraud detection, secure identity verification, and transparent auditing mechanisms. AI-powered smart contracts will automate cybersecurity policies and ensure regulatory compliance in real time. Moreover, blockchain-based threat intelligence sharing will allow organizations to collaborate securely, strengthening global cybersecurity efforts.
6. **Neuromyotonic AI for Cybersecurity**: Neuromyotonic AI marries the learning capabilities of neural networks with the reasoning of symbolic logic. This hybrid approach provides more insightful cyber security systems able to detect complex threats through both algorithms/pattern recognition, as well as rule-based inferencing. For example, a neuromyotonic IDS is much better at identifying an entirely new attack vectors and then can detail the decision through human-readable logic, thereby enhancing transparency and trust.
7. **Digital Twin-Based Threat Simulation**: Digital twins, virtual equivalent representations of physical systems, are rapidly emerging as valuable tools for cyber threat mapping. By simulating network behavior in a digital environment, defenders can test AI driven defence tools and learn how they behave under realistic conditions before they use them on an actual system. This proactive approach not only helps the defender discover vulnerabilities but also completes the loop-of-learning involved during development of the AI model.

The future of AI-powered cybersecurity will be characterized by autonomous security systems, privacy-preserving AI, quantum-resistant encryption, adversarial defense mechanisms, and blockchain-integrated security solutions. AI-driven cyber deception, automation, and regulatory compliance will reshape cybersecurity strategies, enabling organizations to proactively counter evolving cyber threats.

8. CONCLUSION

The integration of Artificial Intelligence (AI) in cybersecurity has transformed intrusion detection, threat mitigation, and privacy preservation, offering advanced defense mechanisms against evolving cyber threats. AI-driven Intrusion Detection Systems (IDS) have significantly improved real-time threat detection, automated response, and overall security resilience compared to traditional methods. However, the increasing sophistication of cyberattacks, particularly adversarial machine learning techniques, poses new challenges that demand continuous advancements in AI security. Privacy-preserving AI techniques, such as differential privacy, federated learning, secure multi-party computation, and blockchain-based security models, have emerged as essential solutions to balance cybersecurity with data protection regulations. Despite these advancements, securing AI-driven systems remains a critical challenge, requiring robust adversarial defences, explainable AI (XAI), and ethical compliance with global cybersecurity policies. Case studies on AI-driven cyberattacks highlight the necessity for proactive security frameworks that incorporate AI-powered automation, deception techniques, and blockchain-based threat intelligence sharing. Looking ahead, future directions in AI-powered cybersecurity will focus on autonomous security systems, self-healing networks, quantum-resistant cryptography, and AI-driven security orchestration. As AI continues to evolve, a collaborative approach involving governments, organizations, and cybersecurity researchers will be vital to ensuring a secure, transparent, and resilient digital ecosystem.

REFERENCES

Achuthan, K., Ramanathan, S., Srinivas, S., & Raman, R. (2024). Advancing cyber-security and privacy with artificial intelligence: Current trends and future research directions. *Frontiers in Big Data*, *7*, 1497535. DOI: 10.3389/fdata.2024.1497535 PMID: 39703783

Adeyeye, O. J., Akanbi, I., Emeteveke, I., & Emehin, O. (2024). Leveraging secured AI-driven data analytics for cybersecurity: Safeguarding information and enhancing threat detection. *International Journal of Research and Publication and Reviews*, *5*(10), 3208–3223. DOI: 10.55248/gengpi.5.1024.2911

Al-Mukhtar, W. N. M. (2024). AI in Cybersecurity: Transformative Approaches to Safeguarding Information Technology Systems. *Turkish Journal of Computer and Mathematics Education*, *15*(3), 391–412.

Awad, A. I., Babu, A., Barka, E., & Shuaib, K. (2024). AI-powered biometrics for Internet of Things security: A review and future vision. *Journal of Information Security and Applications*, *82*, 103748. DOI: 10.1016/j.jisa.2024.103748

Bandi, A. (2024). A Taxonomy of AI techniques for security and privacy in cyber–physical systems. *Journal of Computational and Cognitive Engineering*, *3*(2), 98–111. DOI: 10.47852/bonviewJCCE42021539

Chukwunweike, J. N., Yussuf, M., Okusi, O., & Oluwatobi, T. (2024). The role of deep learning in ensuring privacy integrity and security: Applications in AI-driven cybersecurity solutions. *World Journal of Advanced Research and Reviews*, *23*(2), 2550.

Ejeofobiri, C. K., Victor-Igun, O. O., & Okoye, C. (2024). AI-Driven Secure Intrusion Detection for Internet of Things (IOT) Networks. *Asian Journal of Mathematics and Computer Research*, *31*(4), 40–55. DOI: 10.56557/ajomcor/2024/v31i48971

Emehin, O., Emeteveke, I., Adeyeye, O. J., & Akanbi, I. (2024). Securing artificial intelligence in data analytics: Strategies for mitigating risks in cloud computing environments. *International Research Journal of Modernization in Engineering Technology and Science*, *6*, 1978–1998.

Nacheva, R., & Azeroual, O. (2024, November). Security of AI-Powered Systems: Threat Intelligence on the Edge. In 2024 8th International Symposium on Multidisciplinary Studies and Innovative Technologies (ISMSIT) (pp. 1-6). IEEE.

Nadella, G. S., Addula, S. R., Yadulla, A. R., Sajja, G. S., Meesala, M., Maturi, M. H., & Gonaygunta, H. (2025). Generative AI-Enhanced Cybersecurity Framework for Enterprise Data Privacy Management. *Computers*, *14*(2), 55. DOI: 10.3390/computers14020055

Rangaraju, S. (2023). Secure by intelligence: Enhancing products with AI-driven security measures. *EPH-International Journal of Science and Engineering*, *9*(3), 36–41.

Rani, S., Kumar, N., Srivastva, A., & Sharma, A. (2024, October). Leveraging artificial intelligence and machine learning for enhanced privacy and security. In *2024 IEEE International Conference on Blockchain and Distributed Systems Security (ICBDS)* (pp. 1-6). IEEE. DOI: 10.1109/ICBDS61829.2024.10837569

Sadaram, G., Karaka, L. M., Maka, S. R., Sakuru, M., Boppana, S. B., & Katnapally, N. (2024). AI-Powered Cyber Threat Detection: Leveraging Machine Learning for Real-Time Anomaly Identification and Threat Mitigation. *MSW Management Journal*, *34*(2), 788–803.

Sarker, I. H. (2024). AI-Enabled Cybersecurity for IoT and Smart City Applications. In *AI-Driven Cybersecurity and Threat Intelligence: Cyber Automation, Intelligent Decision-Making and Explainability* (pp. 121–136). Springer Nature Switzerland. DOI: 10.1007/978-3-031-54497-2_7

Shahana, A., Hasan, R., Farabi, S. F., Akter, J., Mahmud, M. A. A., Johora, F. T., & Suzer, G. (2024). AI-driven cybersecurity: Balancing advancements and safeguards. *Journal of Computer Science and Technology Studies*, *6*(2), 76–85. DOI: 10.32996/jcsts.2024.6.2.9

Sharma, R., Sharma, V., Vashishth, T. K., Kumar, B., Sharma, B. K., & Chaudhary, S. (2025, February). Implementation of adaptive cloud security framework for cloud computing monitoring system applications. In AIP Conference Proceedings (Vol. 3224, No. 1). AIP Publishing. DOI: 10.1063/5.0246104

Vashishth, T. K., Sharma, V., Samania, B., Sharma, R., Singh, S., & Jajoria, P. (2025). Ethical and Legal Implications of AI in Cybersecurity. In Machine Intelligence Applications in Cyber-Risk Management (pp. 387-414). IGI Global Scientific Publishing.

Vashishth, T. K., Sharma, V., Sharma, K. K., Kumar, B., Chaudhary, S., & Panwar, R. (2024). Enhancing Cloud Security: The Role of Artificial Intelligence and Machine Learning. In Improving Security, Privacy, and Trust in Cloud Computing (pp. 85-112). IGI Global.

Yodha, V. (2024). Leveraging Federated Learning for Privacy-Preserving Cybersecurity in Decentralized AI Systems. *Eastern European Journal for Multidisciplinary Research*, *1*(1), 89–106.

Chapter 3
AI-Powered Cybersecurity:
Defending Against Modern Threats

Sahar Yousif Mohammed
Anbar University, Iraq

Maad M. Mijwil
http://orcid.org/0000-0002-2884-2504
Al-Iraqia University, Iraq

Kawther Abbood Neamah
Al-Iraqia Science University, Iraq

Aseed Yaseen Rashid Al-Jubori
Al-Iraqia University, Iraq

ABSTRACT

The rapid advancements in Artificial Intelligence (AI) have revolutionized cybersecurity operations, because they now enable predictive hazard detection and automatic incident responses as well as adaptive security measures. The combination of artificial intelligence-based security solutions uses machine learning algorithms with deep learning technology alongside predictive analytics for analyzing amount of data to detect anomalies while fighting cyber threats instantly. AI delivers many blessings in cybersecurity but brings multiple demanding situations that include targeted attacks on systems underlying biases and important concerns regarding

DOI: 10.4018/979-8-3373-2922-2.ch003

privacy and transparency. AI deployment needs explainable AI (XAI) and robust security frameworks and ethical guidelines to maintain accountability because cybercriminals are more often than not leveraging AI for advanced attacks.

1. INTRODUCTION

The age of the net has profoundly revolutionized our lives, bringing with it unprecedented possibilities, in conjunction with ever-greater state-of-the-art cyber threats. Businesses, in an attempt and live stably, would possibly install a myriad of security solutions from time to time, 20 or more best to find that this fragmented device has its downsides. In this bankruptcy, we have a look at the intersection of artificial intelligence and cybersecurity and how system mastering is strengthening defences and introducing new weaknesses via adversarial attacks (Sharma, 2024; Saeed, 2023). As virtual transformation alternatives are accelerating, conventional safety features aren't keeping up in opposition with modern-day threats. Companies respond to rising vulnerabilities with factor products, from antivirus to anti-DDoS, developing a complex protection panorama that is hard to manage and full of blind spots (Prabhu and Lakshmi, 2024; Familoni, 2024). The trouble is also compounded with the aid of AI itself, which, while improving threat detection, can be manipulated through techniques like information poisoning and evasion attacks (Sendjaja et al., 2024). We've reached a tipping point. Instead of relying on a fractured set of security products, agencies have to adopt intelligent, adaptive structures that expect and counter rising threats. This is in particular important at a second while cybercriminals are leveraging AI to exploit the most vulnerabilities. By knowing those dynamics, we can develop cybersecurity countermeasures that are suitable for current threats, shifting past point-in-time defenses to build resilient digital ecosystems.

1.1 The Cybersecurity Paradox of Digital Transformation

The rapid adoption of digital technologies from cloud computing and IoT to AI-driven analytics—has revolutionized business operations, enabling unprecedented efficiency, customer engagement, and innovation (Mohammed et al., 2024). However, this transformation comes with inherent risks, as each new technology introduces vulnerabilities that cybercriminals eagerly exploit. Organizations now operate in an environment where cyber threats evolve faster than defenses can adapt, with attacks ranging from ransomware and phishing to AI-powered adversarial exploits. The shift to remote work during the COVID-19 pandemic further accelerated digital reliance, exposing gaps in legacy security frameworks. Many businesses still rely on a patchwork of 20+ disparate security tools antivirus, firewalls, DDoS mitigation each addressing a single symptom rather than the root causes of systemic risk (Lysenko et al., 2025). Meanwhile, compliance with regulations like GDPR and CCPA adds another layer of complexity, forcing companies to balance innovation with stringent data protection requirements. The stakes have never been higher: a single breach can cripple operations, erode customer trust, and incur millions in losses. To survive in this landscape, organizations must move beyond reactive measures and embrace proactive strategies—zero-trust architectures, continuous threat monitoring, and security-by-design principles embedded into every digital initiative. Cybersecurity is no longer just an IT concern but a foundational pillar of sustainable business growth in the digital age (Sandhu, 2021; Serac, 2023). Figure 1. Refers to Progression from fragmented tools to modern strategies, accelerated by COVID-19 disruptions. Arrows indicate critical failure points (red) and solution pathways (green), as analyzed in Section 1.

Figure 1. Evolution from Legacy Security to Proactive Defense.

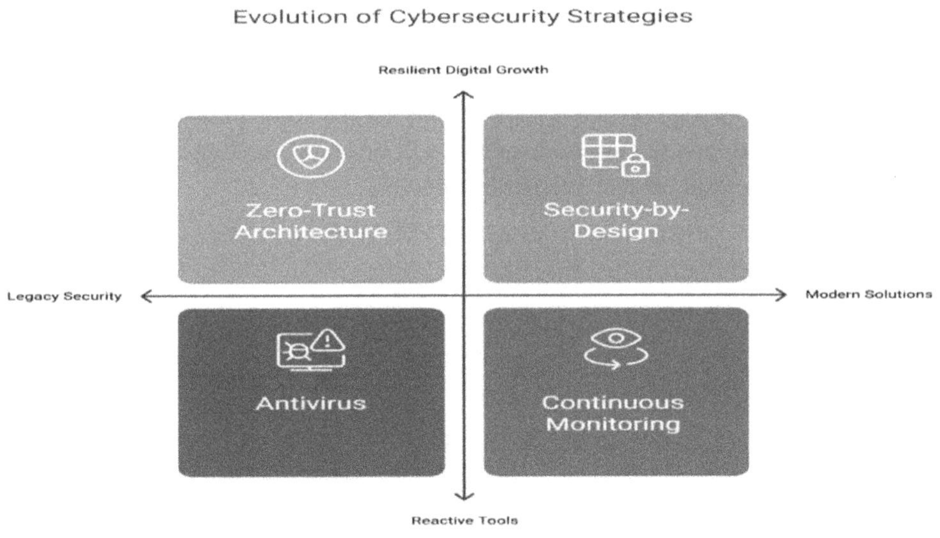

1.2 The Transformative Role of AI in Modern Cybersecurity

In the latest digital world, artificial intelligence has come to be a game-changer for cybersecurity. As cyber threats become greater sophisticated, corporations are turning to AI-powered solutions to protect their records and structures (Mohammed, 2023). This generation isn't simply an upgrade—it's revolutionizing how we locate, save, and respond to security threats in real-time. AI brings powerful advantages to the safety panorama. Machine learning algorithms can sift through mountains of information to spot unusual patterns that would imply a breach, often catching threats that people would miss. These systems examine continuously, adapting to new attack methods as they emerge (Mohammed, 2023). AI would not sleep it provides 24/7 tracking that may pick out and neutralize threats quicker than any human group. But this powerful tool comes with its challenges. Cybercriminals are the usage of AI against us, growing "adversarial assaults" designed to trick protection structures. There's also the question of agreement: when an AI machine makes a safety decision, are we able to fully apprehend the way it reached that end? This becomes specifically vital in sensitive regions like banking or healthcare. The moral size cannot be neglected (Çakır, 2024). AI systems should be carefully designed to avoid biases and shield personal privacy. Who's responsible if an AI security machine makes a wrong name? These are complicated questions that technologists, policymakers, and business leaders need to work on collectively. Despite those demanding situations, AI remains our maximum promising weapon in cybersecurity. When applied thoughtfully with the right safeguards and human oversight, AI safety systems can offer safety that is faster, smarter, and more adaptable than what we have had earlier (Ali et al., 2025). The future of cybersecurity isn't always about selecting human experts and AI but about locating the right stability in which each complements the opposite's strengths. Figure 2: From chance ingestion to adaptive reaction, with essential human verification factors.

Figure 2. Artificial intelligence Life cycle

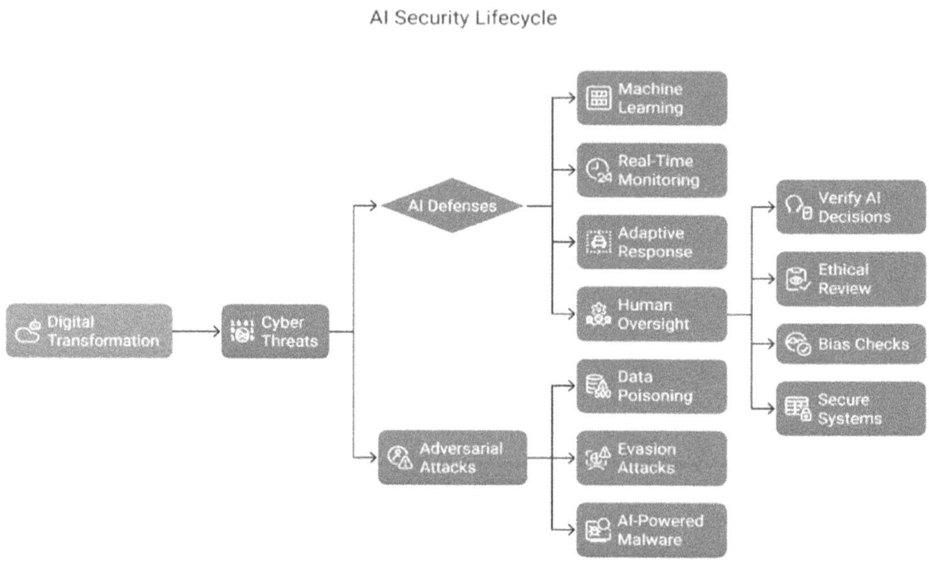

1.3 The Dual Nature of AI: A Tool for Both Defenders and Attackers

Artificial intelligence has come to be a transformative pressure in cybersecurity—but its energy cuts both methods (Siam et al., 2025). While agencies use AI to bolster their defences, cybercriminals are simultaneously weaponizing the identical generation to release greater state-of-the-art attacks. This creates an escalating palm race where AI serves as both defence and spear within the digital battlefield. Artificial Intelligence (AI) serves as a double-edged sword within the realm of cybersecurity, benefiting defenders and attackers alike. On one hand, AI complements cybersecurity defences with the aid of detecting threats in actual time, identifying anomalies in huge datasets, and automating responses to cyberattacks. Advanced machine learning fashions allow security systems to expect and mitigate dangers earlier than they expand, strengthening virtual safety. However, the era is also exploited by using cybercriminals to launch greater modern-day attacks. AI-pushed malware can adapt dynamically to live far away from detection, whilst deep-fake technology permits identification fraud and misinformation campaigns]. In addition, attackers use AI to automate phishing scams, generating pretty convincing messages that skip traditional protection functions. This dual nature of AI highlights the urgent need for ethical AI improvement and continuous improvements in cybersecurity to stay ahead of evolving threats (Dhanushkodi and Thejas, 2024).

2. AI IN THREAT DETECTION AND PREVENTION

AI has become one of the primary tools for detecting and preventing threats, making it an important method in the field of cybersecurity. With the growth of complexity and frequency of cyber threats, conventional security features normally fall brief of the mark, thereby necessitating the amalgamation of AI technologies to strengthen a little bit of the defences in opposition to those new demanding situations (Kaur et al., 2023).

2.1 Machine Learning Models for Identifying Malware, Phishing, and Intrusion Detection

Cybersecurity threats such as malware, phishing, and network intrusions continually evolve, rendering conventional detection methods increasingly untrustworthy over time. This is where machine learning (ML) comes into play by analyzing enormous amounts of data, ML models can identify patterns that distinguish harmful behavior (Elamin and Ismaiel, 2025). For example, malware detection algorithms analyze code behavior and file structures to identify suspicious software. Phishing detection models examine both the content of emails, as well as URLs and sender behavior, to intercept fraudulent messages before they hit the inbox. In a similar vein, ML-powered intrusion detection systems (IDS) monitor network traffic continuously, learning what normal activity looks like to quickly identify any breaches or unusual access attempts. No solution is entirely perfect, but ML focuses on emerging threats and adapts to the new threats much more quickly than rule-based systems, offering much more robust protection as the world becomes more and more digitized (Mohammed, 2023).

Table 1. Machine Learning for Malware Detection

Aspect	Description
Detection Method	Analyze file structure, behaviour, and code patterns to identify malicious software.
Key Features	- API calls - File entropy - Execution traces - Opcode sequences
Common ML Models	- Random Forest - SVM (Support Vector Machines) - Deep Learning (CNN, LSTM) - Gradient Boosting (XGBoost)
Challenges	- Polymorphic malware evasion - Zero-day threats - High false positives

Table 2. Machine learning for Phishing Detection

Aspect	Description
Detection Method	Examines emails, URLs, and web content for fraudulent indicators.
Key Features	- URL structure (e.g., misspelled domains) - Email headers - Embedded links - Keyword analysis (e.g., "urgent action")
Common ML Models	- Logistic Regression - Naive Bayes - Neural Networks (RNN, Transformers) - Random Forest
Challenges	- Social engineering tactics - Short-lived phishing sites - Adversarial attacks (obfuscation)

Table 3. Machine learning for Intrusion Detection (IDS)

Aspect	Description
Detection Method	Monitors network traffic for abnormal behavior or known attack signatures.
Key Features	- Packet payloads - Traffic flow patterns - Login attempts - Protocol violations
Common ML Models	- Decision Trees - K-Means Clustering (Anomaly-based) - LSTM for time-series analysis - Isolation Forest
Challenges	- Encrypted traffic analysis - High-volume false alarms - Adaptive attackers (evasion techniques)

Table 4. Comparison of ML in Cybersecurity

Threat Type	Primary ML Approach	Best-Performing Models	Biggest Challenge
Malware	Behavioral & Static Analysis	Random Forest, CNN, XGBoost	Zero-day malware
Phishing	Content & URL Analysis	NLP models (BERT, RNN), Random Forest	Evolving social engineering
Intrusion	Anomaly & Signature Detection	LSTM, Isolation Forest, K-Means	Encrypted traffic evasion

2.2 Deep Learning and Anomaly Detection in Real-Time Security Monitoring

In today's speedy-evolving threat panorama, traditional safety systems often battle to hold up with sophisticated attacks. Deep gaining knowledge of (DL) enhances real-time protection tracking by means of analyzing massive amounts of facts to locate anomalies—unusual styles which could suggest cyber threats like intrusions, malware, or insider assaults (Yamin et al., 2021). Unlike rule-based systems, deep gaining knowledge of models (such as CNNs, RNNs, and Transformers) research from ancient information to identify diffused, complex assault signatures that could otherwise pass disregarded. For anomaly detection, strategies like autoencoders and LSTMs excel by way of modeling everyday behavior and flagging deviations in real time, whether or not in community visitors, consumer pastime, or system logs. However, challenges remain, including excessive computational charges, false positives, and adverse assaults that manage enter information to stay away from detection (Amer, 2025). Despite those hurdles, combining deep studying with real-time analytics lets in agencies to proactively guard in opposition to threats, adapting quicker than attackers can evolve. As cyber threats develop greater superior, deep gaining knowledge of-powered anomaly detection is becoming vital for sturdy, automatic safety tracking (Wang et al., 2023).

Figure 3. Deep Learning-Based Anomaly Detection in Real-Time Security Monitoring

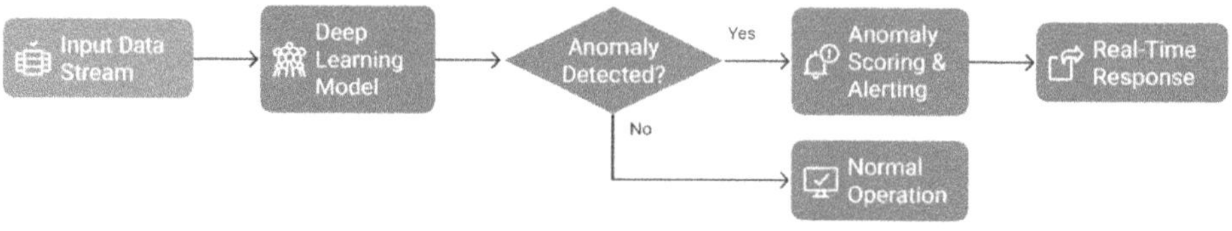

2.3 Case Studies of AI-Powered Cybersecurity Systems

Proactively identifying and mitigating threats in real-time. Solutions like Darktrace use machine learning to detect anomalies, enabling organizations to stop cyberattacks before they escalate (Kazimierczak et al., 2024). IBM Watson enhances threat intelligence by rapidly analyzing vast datasets, reducing response times and improving decision-making. Google Chronicle leverages AI-driven analytics to identify previously unknown malware, offering advanced protection for cloud-based environments. Meanwhile, Cylance's predictive AI prevents cyber threats at the endpoint level, blocking ransomware and malware before execution. As cyber threats grow in complexity, AI-driven security solutions continue to evolve, providing businesses with smarter, faster, and more adaptive defenses (Dhanushkodi and Thejas, 2024).

3. ADVERSARIAL AI: THE DOUBLE-EDGED SWORD

3.1 How Cybercriminals Exploit AI for Sophisticated Attacks

People worldwide have passionately pursued the internet because it achieved its massive potential while establishing digital technology that operates through connected systems. Major servers and boundless networks and databases containing sensitive information about people along with government agencies currently dominate what started as a minimal record system in the 1980s and 1990s. The first widely known computer virus labeled the 1988 Morris Worm disrupted 6,000 to 10,000 machines yet proved insignificant in everyday society. Modern cyberattacks can cripple numerous millions of buildings which would lead to serious long-term effects due to technological progress in attack sophistication. The thorough availability of the internet has established it as the primary target for financial crime and identity theft by malicious actors. Artificial Intelligence (AI) has entered the scene with an upward force that gives criminals precise automated tools which help them bypass target defences while finding new security flaws (Maurya, 2023). Since the expansion of the internet researchers developed advanced cybercrimes through phishing which employs AI systems to create deceptive personal emails that appear from trusted sources to obtain login credentials. Algorithms supporting malware have transformed the system into a dynamic entity which adapts instantaneously to escape traditional security measures to work as a spying and holding-to-ransom operation while destroying information. The instant movements of AI-driven bots during data breaches allow them to quickly identify network gaps that result in massive data theft of sensitive information (Mohammed et al., 2024). Deepfakes along with other forms of synthetic media made using AI techniques allow complete video and voice impersonation which results in highly realistic deception that spreads false information and performs fraudulent acts. These security threats make use of human faith and technological weaknesses to realize their objectives while AI functions as a defensive tool and offensive weapon for digital defense (Naseer et al., 2018).

3.2 The Concept of Adversarial Machine Learning (Evasion Attacks, Data Poisoning)

Adversarial machine learning is the study of the vulnerabilities of AI models and how to safeguard them. These include attacks such as evasion (small changes to input that cause a misclassification), and poisoning (inserting bad data causing training to be corrupted). Other potential attacks are model extraction (the theft of the functionality of a model) and inference attacks (the extraction of sensitive data) (Mohammed et al., 2024). Adversarial examples are inputs that are specially crafted to exploit the weaknesses in an ML model. This area began in the 2000s, but it was not until 2013 that the term "adversarial examples" gained widespread prominence. As deep learning progressed, attacks started to impact real-world applications such as self-driving cars and facial recognition (Gao, 2024). The robustness of models against these attacks is improved by researchers using adversarial training, defensive distillation and input preprocessing. The hazards cross industries — autonomous vehicles, medical diagnostics, and security systems remain at risk. With the acceleration of AI adoption, security for models against these types of attacks is paramount (Callegari et al., 2024).

3.3 Defense Mechanisms Against AI-Driven Cyber Threats

A plethora of AI–driven defense mechanisms against AI–driven cyber threats with various forms including threat detection and prevention, anomalous behavior recognition, authentication and access control, and adaptive defense strategies are suggested by numerous studies while emphasizing the necessity of perpetual monitoring, professional ethical considerations and incorporation into conventional security structures. AI-based cyber threats pose a significant risk and, therefore, organizations must employ a layered defense mechanism that is able to identify and mitigate these sophisticated attacks. A number of advanced AI techniques have been developed beyond just Natural Language Processing (NLP) algorithms to create robust cybersecurity systems. Behavioral analytics analyzes activity over time, monitoring user actions for periods of time to look for anomalies that can indicate security threats from malicious users, internal threats or virus attacks (Nguyen et al., 2020). Formal verification feeds into resilient systems, where AI models are trained via adversarial methods (techniques to get the model to do what you want even when they are hit by manipulation or evasion attacks), to withstand all kinds of attacks and therefore continue functioning even when under attack. Through greater visibility into how AI decision systems operate, we discuss the use of explainable AI (XAI) to improve transparency, and how security experts can better manage the potential risks associated with black-box models. Cross-Lingual Transfer Learning (CLTL) allows defensive techniques to adapt to new areas of the world, assisting cybersecurity practitioners in identifying global cyber-targets. These AI systems work by combining data from multiple channels — text, images, audio recordings, network traffic patterns, and much more — to provide information about coordinated attacks taking place over different methods of communication. AI-based technologies can help real-time monitoring systems discover automated response mechanisms to promptly alert security threats before they escalate into a major attack. The introduction of Zero-Trust Architecture (ZTA) guarantees an even higher level of protection by validating all access requests with strong authentication and limiting attackers' lateral movements within the network post-breach. Federated learning – which relies on decentralized systems – improves AI models under the protection of security, whereas human-AI collaboration empowers cybersecurity professionals to customize AI systems and respond to novel threats. Collectively, these AI-based methods create an interrelated, flexible defense system that responds to the growing variety of cyber threats (Akhtar and Rawol, 2024).

4. AI FOR INCIDENT RESPONSE AND AUTOMATED SECURITY

With ever-evolving cyber threats, the cybersecurity landscape has become more complex and challenging, and artificial intelligence (AI) is transforming incident response and security operations and helping organizations deal with them.

4.1 Role of AI in Automating Threat Response and Mitigation

Artificial Intelligence (AI) plays a pivotal role in automating threat response and mitigation in cybersecurity, meaningfully enhancing the ability to detect, analyze, and respond to cyber threats more efficiently than traditional methods. AI-driven systems leverage machine learning algorithms, natural language processing, and anomaly detection to process vast amounts of data, identify patterns, and detecting threats in real-time, that lead to faster and more precise threat identification (Iturbe et al., 2024). Also, these systems can automate responses to detected threats, minimizing human intervention and reducing errors, thereby strengthening real-time mitigation efforts. AI also enables predictive threat intelligence by analyzing historical data and emerging trends, allowing organizations to anticipate and address potential cyber threats proactively. Likewise, AI seamlessly integrates with existing cybersecurity frameworks, such as intrusion detection systems (IDS) and security information and event management (SIEM) platforms, enhancing their global effectiveness. By automating routine security tasks, AI reduces the burden on human operators, thereby decreasing the risk of human error and improving security operations. Despite its advantages, ethical considerations and the need for continuous AI model training remain important challenges in ensuring the reliability and fairness of AI-driven cybersecurity solutions (Kaloudi and Li, 2020).

4.2 AI-Powered Security Orchestration, Automation, and Response (SOAR)

AI-powered SOAR (Security Orchestration, Automation, and Response) systems are a game-changer in modern cybersecurity, offering enhanced threat detection, faster response times, and a more adaptive approach to security. These systems utilize flexible AI-driven algorithms that continuously learn and adjust to an organization's specific needs, improving cybersecurity resilience (Hoanca and Mock, 2020). By integrating AI with SOAR, businesses can streamline security operations, automate threat responses, and reduce the time needed to contain incidents. While challenges such as algorithmic bias and data privacy risks persist, ongoing innovations and AI advancements are paving the way for more effective and efficient cybersecurity solutions. As the cyber threat landscape expands, AI-powered SOAR systems will play a critical role in strengthening an organization's security posture.

4.3 Reducing Human Workload Through AI-Driven Security Operations Centers (SOCs)

AI is significantly enhancing the efficiency of security operations centers (SOCs) by automating repetitive tasks, reducing human error, and allowing security analysts to focus on complex threats. AI-driven technologies, particularly machine learning and predictive modeling, enable real-time analysis of vast datasets, identifying patterns of malicious activity and potential vulnerabilities before they escalate into full-blown attacks (Broklyn et al., 2024). By leveraging AI, SOCs can proactively prevent cyber threats, minimizing the need for manual intervention. Additionally, AI automates incident documentation, provides contextual threat intelligence, and suggests remediation strategies, leading to faster response times and improved overall security. As organizations continue to combat increasingly sophisticated cyber threats, AI-powered SOCs will be essential in optimizing security workflows and enhancing digital resilience (Wang et al., 2022).

Figure 4. AI's role in cybersecurity automation

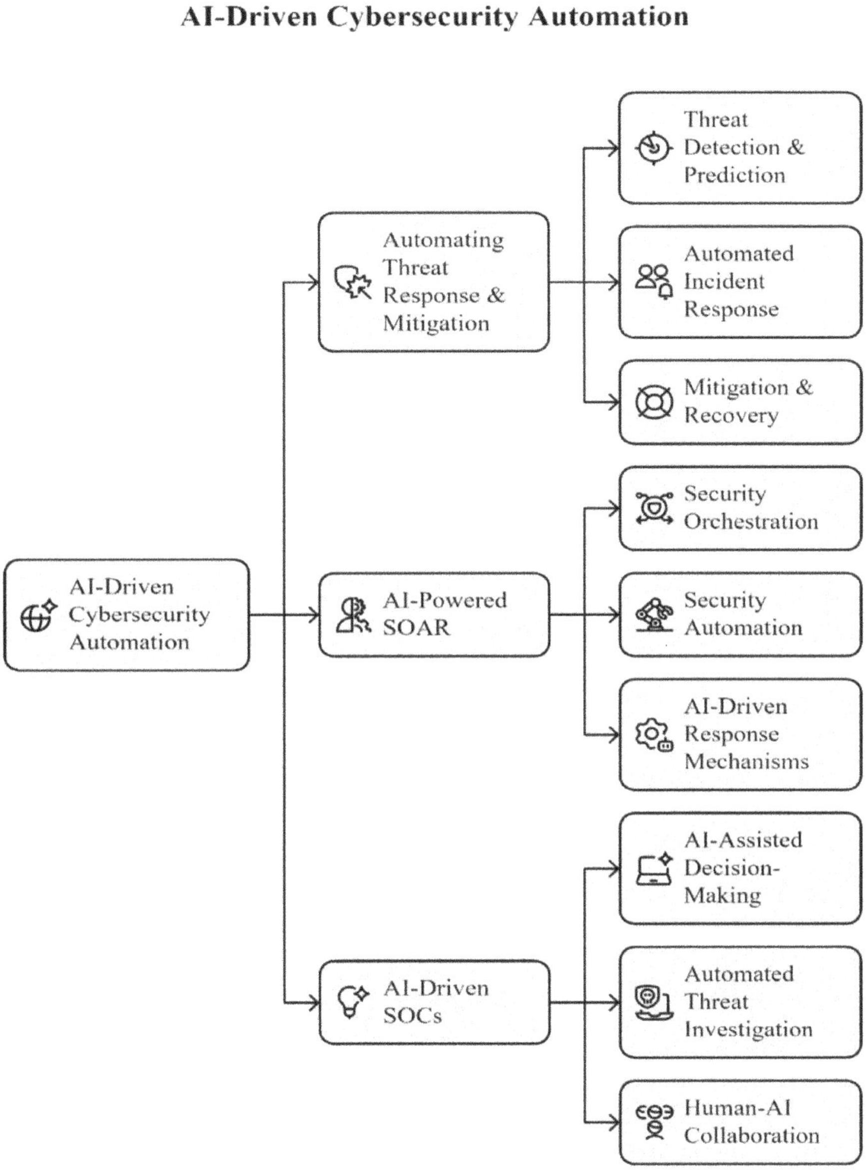

5. ETHICAL, LEGAL, AND FUTURE CONSIDERATIONS

With the incorporation of artificial intelligence (AI), threats are detected with greater accuracy, responses automated, and vulnerabilities predicted with greater accuracy as well. AI-driven tools have significantly improved the features of fields like intrusion detection systems, malware analysis, and user authentication mechanisms. AI is a revolutionary technology, yet its adoption is not without specific challenges, including data biases, adversarial attacks, huge computational power requirements, and ethical dilemmas, such as privacy breaches (Zhang et al., 2016).

5.1 Ethical Concerns: AI Biases in Cybersecurity

Cybersecurity has greatly benefited from the integration of AI technologies for threat detection, automated response mechanisms, and vulnerability prediction. However, ethical concerns like AI biases pose major challenges to the fairness and efficacy of cybersecurity systems. AI models can introduce algorithmic biases if datasets are not inclusive and representative, which can lead to biased threat assessments and possibly discriminatory security measures. These biases must be corrected to retain equity in AI-driven cybersecurity solutions (Aljanabi et al., 2024). Security and privacy of data is a crucial issue as well. AI-driven cybersecurity systems can access personal information, creating risks of misuse, surveillance, and data breaches. In the absence of strong governance frameworks, they risk violating user privacy and eroding trust in cybersecurity solutions. We need transparency and AI principles to protect against these potential risks. While this is a concern in its own right, AI in cybersecurity has a dual-use risk in which bad actors can leverage the same technology created to defend against them and use it as a weapon to launch sophisticated cyberattacks. The application of artificial intelligence lends itself to automated processes and adversarial machine learning tactics, which will help bypass security detections. Therefore, we must have safeguards in place to prevent the use of artificial intelligence as a tool to cause harm. For ethical data usage in cybersecurity, reform should center on the principles of fairness, accountability, and transparency for organizations and policymakers alike. This can help ensure AI is developed and deployed responsibly and consistently around the world. Everywhere, researchers, industry leaders, and governments need to focus on AI literacy and cybersecurity ethics as a must while working to educate one another. While AI can revolutionize cybersecurity, biases, privacy, and dual-use risks need to be addressed. As we leverage the power of artificial intelligence, stakeholders should uphold fairness, regulatory oversight, and interdisciplinary collaboration to ensure security solutions are ethical, transparent, reasonable, and effective (Gao, 2024).

5.2 The Need for Explainable AI in Security Decision-Making

Due to the complexity and opacity of AI models, trust and decision-making based on these AI models in cybersecurity become challenging, thus there is a need for Explainable AI (XAI). By offering clear and interpretable insights, XAI aids security analysts in understanding and trusting the decisions made by AI. It minimizes false positives, enhances threat detection, and enables more informed decision-making in security operations. Furthermore, explanations are customized, so users are presented with only useful information. XAI could entail threats and needs to be carefully deployed and tailored to different security scenarios. The balance between effectiveness and trust or transparency exists in security decision-making, which can be maintained by adopting XAI so that cybersecurity systems are both effective and transparent (Li et al., 2022).

5.3 AI and Cybersecurity: Advancements, Challenges, and Future Prospects

Technology continues to be an essential segment of human life, with AI in cybersecurity reflecting that in its field. Artificial Intelligence is adopted to fortify cybersecurity defenses and abused to devise sophisticated cyber threats. In this dual role, security strategies must be regularly updated to address new threats.NLP, deep learning, and machine learning are driving trends in cybersecurity. These innovations improve threat detection, behavioral analysis, and automated responses, allowing organizations to identify advanced persistent threats, zero-day exploits, and phishing attempts more effectively than ever. Traditional, reactive methods often fail to protect, while AI-powered security systems excel in managing large-scale, highly laden, complex interconnected networks and systems, enabling proactive and adaptive security and protection. However, AI in cybersecurity comes with challenges as well. Adversarial attacks—such as data poisoning and evasion attacks—pose significant threats to machine learning models. This makes AI security inherently vulnerable, as cybercriminals can manipulate training data, hijack it, or infect the AI model during runtime execution, potentially compromising entire systems and leading to severe privacy breaches. The potential for abuse and exploitation of AI by malicious actors, along with ethical concerns regarding data privacy, algorithmic bias, and other risks, must be addressed to prevent unintended negative consequences. Several key trends will shape the future of AI in cybersecurity. AI is expected to revolutionize the way we interact with the digital world, and its integration with emerging technologies will lead to a more connected, efficient, and secure future. Additionally, the rise of explainable AI (XAI) will enhance transparency, enabling security professionals to understand AI-driven decisions and address risks accordingly. Establishing standardized and certified AI technologies and cybersecurity solutions is also crucial for building more resilient defense infrastructures that will become a key player in cybersecurity, offering strong detection and response capabilities. However, its dual role as both a security asset and a potential attack vector highlights the need for continuous research and innovation. Overcoming challenges related to adversarial attacks, ethical concerns, and regulatory frameworks will be essential to fully harness AI's potential for a safer cyberspace.

CONCLUSION

The integration of AI into cybersecurity marks a transformative shift in how corporations address, prevent, and reply to cyber threats. While AI-driven solutions decorate protection operations through automation, predictive analytics, and actual-time hazard detection, they also introduce new demanding situations, consisting of adverse assaults and moral worries. The ongoing battle among cyber defenders and attackers is evolving, as malicious actors additionally leverage AI to create extra sophisticated threats. To stay ahead, cybersecurity techniques ought to prioritize continuous innovation, robust AI governance, and interdisciplinary collaboration. Ultimately, balancing AI's capability with accountable use is prime to ensuring a stable virtual future. By fostering transparency, accountability, and ethical AI deployment, we will harness AI's power to strengthen cybersecurity whilst minimizing risks and unintentional consequences.

REFERENCES

Akhtar, Z. B., & Rawol, A. T. (2024). Enhancing Cybersecurity through AI-Powered Security Mechanisms. *IT Journal Research and Development, 9*(1), 50–67. DOI: 10.25299/itjrd.2024.16852

Ali, S., Wang, J., & Leung, V. (2025). AI-driven fusion with cybersecurity: Exploring current trends, advanced techniques, future directions, and policy implications for evolving paradigms– A comprehensive review. *Information Fusion, 18*, 102922. DOI: 10.1016/j.inffus.2024.102922

Aljanabi, M., Omran, A. H., Mijwil, M. M., Abotaleb, M., El-kenawy, E. M., & Ibrahim, A. (2024). Data poisoning: issues, challenges, and needs, In *7th IET Smart Cities Symposium (SCS 2023)*, 1-6. DOI: 10.1049/icp.2024.0951

Amer, L. (2025). AI in cyber security: A dual perspective on hacker tactics and defensive strategies. Cyber Security: A Peer-Reviewed Journal, 8 (3), 198-213. DOI: 10.69554/CLXC9075

Broklyn, P., Shad, R., & Egon, A. (2024). The Evolving Thread Landscape Pf Ai-Powered Cyberattacks:A Multi-Faceted Approach to Defense And Mitigate. SSRN Electronic Journal, 1-14 DOI: 10.2139/ssrn.4904878

Çakır, A. M. (2024). AI Driven Cybersecurity. *Human-Computer Interaction, 8*(1), 119. DOI: 10.62802/jg7gge06

Callegari, C., Giordano, S., & Pagano, M. (2024). A Real Time Deep Learning Based Approach for Detecting Network Attacks. *Big Data Research, 36*, 100446. DOI: 10.1016/j.bdr.2024.100446

Dhanushkodi, K., & Thejas, S. (2024). AI Enabled Threat Detection: Leveraging Artificial Intelligence for Advanced Security and Cyber Threat Mitigation. *IEEE Access : Practical Innovations, Open Solutions, 12*, 173127–173136. DOI: 10.1109/ACCESS.2024.3493957

Elamin, M. O. I., & Ismaiel, O. M. O. (2025). The AI Revolution in Cybersecurity: Transforming Threat Detection, Defense Mechanisms, and Risk Management in the Digital Era. *International Journal of Religion, 6*(1), 228–246. DOI: 10.61707/1dmvn671

Familoni, B.Babajide Tolulope Familoni. (2024). Cybersecurity Challenges in the Age of Ai: Theoretical Approaches and Practical Solutions. *Computer Science & IT Research Journal, 5*(3), 703–724. DOI: 10.51594/csitrj.v5i3.930

Gao, Y. (2024). Cyber Attacks and Defense: AI-Driven Approaches and Techniques. *Academic Journal of Computing & Information Science*, *7*(7), 41–46. DOI: 10.25236/AJCIS.2024.070706

Hoanca, B., & Mock, K. (2020). Artificial Intelligence-Based Cybercrime. Encyclopedia of Criminal Activities and the Deep Web, 1-16. DOI: 10.4018/978-1-5225-9715-5.ch003

Iturbe, E., Llorente-Vazquez, O., Rego, A., Rios, E., & Toledo, N. (2024). Unleashing offensive artificial intelligence: Automated attack technique code generation. *Computers & Security*, *147*, 104077. DOI: 10.1016/j.cose.2024.104077

Kaloudi, N., & Li, J. (2020). The AI-Based Cyber Threat Landscape. *ACM Computing Surveys*, *53*(1), 1–34. DOI: 10.1145/3372823

Kaur, R., Gabrijelcic, D., & Klobučar, T. (2023). Artificial intelligence for cybersecurity: Literature review and future research directions. *Information Fusion*, *97*, 101804. DOI: 10.1016/j.inffus.2023.101804

Kazimierczak, M., Habib, N., Chan, J. H., & Thanapattheerakul, T. (2024). Impact of AI on the Cyber Kill Chain: A Systematic Review. *Heliyon*, *10*(24), e40699. DOI: 10.1016/j.heliyon.2024.e40699 PMID: 39720055

Li, H., Wu, J., Xu, H., Li, G., & Guizani, M. (2022). Explainable Intelligence-Driven Defense Mechanism Against Advanced Persistent Threats: A Joint Edge Game and AI Approach. *IEEE Transactions on Dependable and Secure Computing*, *19*, 757–775. DOI: 10.1109/TDSC.2021.3130944

Lysenko, S., Verba, O., Kyrychenko, V., Gandziuk, V., & Odobetska, I. (2025). Managing Cybersecurity Risks in the Era of Digital Transformation. *Journal of Information Systems Engineering & Management*, *10*(2s), 416–429. DOI: 10.52783/jisem.v10i2s.330

Maurya, R. (2023). Analyzing the Role of AI in Cyber Security Threat Detection & Prevention. *International Journal for Research in Applied Science and Engineering Technology*, *11*(11), 514–519. DOI: 10.22214/ijraset.2023.56510

Mohammed, S. Y., Aljanabi, M., & Mijwil, M. M. (2024). Detecting Denial-of-Service (DoS) Attacks with Edge Machine Learning. In Springer proceedings in business and economics, 119–127. DOI: 10.1007/978-3-031-67511-9_8

Mohammed, S. Y., Aljanabi, M., Mijwil, M. M., Ramadhan, A. J., Abotaleb, M., Alkattan, H., & Albadran, Z. (2024). A Two-Stage hybrid approach for phishing attack detection using URL and content analysis in IoT. BIO Web of Conferences, 97, 00059. DOI: 10.1051/bioconf/20249700059

Mohammed, S. Y.Sahar Yousef Mohammed. (2023). Enhancing COVID-19 Patients Detection using Deep Transfer Learning Technique through X-Ray Chest Images. *Journal of Advanced Research in Applied Sciences and Engineering Technology*, *32*(1), 290–302. DOI: 10.37934/araset.32.1.290302

Naseer, S., Saleem, Y., Khalid, S., Bashir, M., Han, J., Iqbal, M., & Han, K. (2018). Enhanced Network Anomaly Detection Based on Deep Neural Networks. *IEEE Access : Practical Innovations, Open Solutions*, *6*, 48231–48246. DOI: 10.1109/ACCESS.2018.2863036

Nguyen, G., Dlugolinsky, S., Tran, V., & García, Á. (2020). Deep Learning for Proactive Network Monitoring and Security Protection. *IEEE Access : Practical Innovations, Open Solutions*, *8*, 19696–19716. DOI: 10.1109/ACCESS.2020.2968718

Saeed, S., Altamimi, S. A., Alkayyal, N. A., Alshehri, E., & Alabbad, D. A. (2023). Digital Transformation and Cybersecurity Challenges for Businesses Resilience: Issues and Recommendations. *Sensors (Basel)*, *23*(15), 6666. DOI: 10.3390/s23156666 PMID: 37571451

Sandhu, K. (2021). Advancing Cybersecurity for Digital Transformation. Handbook of Research on Advancing Cybersecurity for Digital Transformation, 1-17. DOI: 10.4018/978-1-7998-6975-7.ch001

Sendjaja, T., Irwandi, , Prastiawan, E., Suryani, Y., & Fatmawati, E. (2024). Cybersecurity In The Digital Age: Developing Robust Strategies To Protect Against Evolving Global Digital Threats And Cyber Attacks. *The International Journal of Science in Society*, *6*(1), 1008–1019. DOI: 10.54783/ijsoc.v6i1.1098

Serac, C. A. (2023). Digital Transformation Vulnerabilities: Assessing The Risks And Strengthening Cyber Security. Annals of Faculty of Economics, University of Oradea. *Faculty of Economics*, *32*(1), 771–781.

Sharma, M. (2024). Cybersecurity Platforms: Tackling Challenges in a Digital Age. [IJSREM]. *International Journal of Scientific Research in Engineering and Management*, *6*(4), 1–8. DOI: 10.55041/IJSREM12257

Siam, A., Alazab, M., Awajan, A., & Faruqui, N. (2025). A Comprehensive Review of AI's Current Impact and Future Prospects in Cybersecurity. *IEEE Access : Practical Innovations, Open Solutions*, *13*, 14029–14050. DOI: 10.1109/ACCESS.2025.3528114

Vijay Prabhu, K, V. P. & Lakshmi, C. (2024). A Study on Cybersecurity Challenges and Strategies in a Digitally Transformed Business Environment. [IJSREM]. *International Journal of Scientific Research in Engineering and Management*, *8*(10), 1–11.

Wang, W., Xu, H., Wan, Y., Ren, J., & Tang, J. (2022). Towards Adversarial Learning: From Evasion Attacks to Poisoning Attacks. *Proceedings of the 28th ACM SIGKDD Conference on Knowledge Discovery and Data Mining*, 4830 - 483. DOI: 10.1145/3534678.3542608

Wang, Y., Tan, Y., Baker, T., Kumar, N., & Zhang, Q. (2023). Deep Fusion: Crafting Transferable Adversarial Examples and Improving Robustness of Industrial Artificial Intelligence of Things. *IEEE Transactions on Industrial Informatics*, *19*(6), 7480–7488. DOI: 10.1109/TII.2022.3168874

Yamin, M. M., Ullah, M., Ullah, H., & Katt, B. (2021). Weaponized AI for cyber attacks. *Journal of Information Security and Applications*, *57*, 102722. DOI: 10.1016/j.jisa.2020.102722

Zhang, F., Chan, P., Biggio, B., Yeung, D., & Roli, F. (2016). Adversarial Feature Selection Against Evasion Attacks. *IEEE Transactions on Cybernetics*, *46*(3), 766–777. DOI: 10.1109/TCYB.2015.2415032 PMID: 25910268

Chapter 4
AI-Based Intrusion Detection and Response Mechanisms

A. S. Anshad
http://orcid.org/0009-0009-2012-5787
John Cox Memorial CSI Institute of Technology, India

P. K. Poonguzhali
Sri Krishna College of Engineering and Technology, India

Sanjay Srivastava
Raj Kumar Goel Institute of Technology, India

R. Vidhya
Hindusthan College of Engineering and Technology, India

Sandeep C. S.
http://orcid.org/0000-0003-3269-7984
Jyothi Engineering College, India

G. Saravanan
VSB Engineering College, India

V. Bhoopathy
http://orcid.org/0000-0003-2175-6328
Sree Rama Engineering College, India

ABSTRACT

Many online hazards exist beyond malware and DDOS attacks. Using a network intrusion detection system can avoid such attacks. IDS can de-generate alerts after intrusions. This intrusion detection system checks all network data. Thus, conventional intrusion systems cannot filter all data. Intruder detection systems demand a lot of maintenance. This is costly and varies by course. Digitising sensitive data is another trend. Intrusion detection systems help. Intrusion detection systems alert administrators to questionable activities. This is done with AI algorithms. AI provides advanced real-time intrusion detection, analysis, and reaction. The history and design of AI-powered IDS, the different AI methodologies employed in this sector, and their ability to discover new and unexpected threats are examined in

DOI: 10.4018/979-8-3373-2922-2.ch004

this chapter. It compares conventional systems with AI-enabled ones and examines AI-driven adaptive reaction mechanisms to mitigate risks. The chapter concludes with current issues, ethical concerns, and future research.

1. INTRODUCTION

There is an urgent need to safeguard organizations and the resources they contain due to the rising number of intrusions targeting them. Firewalls, which when set up properly, can block most threats, but you still need to make sure that certain services, including HTTP or DNS, are accessible to the internet. A fire wall must permit unfettered Internet movement towards these organizations in such instances. In reality, the programs that make use of those facilities are frequently intricate yet outdated. As a result, there will be code errors that competent attackers can take advantage of The purpose of IDS is to monitor networking and their possessions for signs of incursion or other forms of hostile activity. Anomaly-based and built around signatures IDSs are the two main categories. Comparable to malware detectors, systems powered by signatures such as Snort, STAT or Net STAT examine the information provided for recognized, suspicious trends. When a probabilistic based program detects a change in behavior that is out of the ordinary, it labels the action as malignant (Toth & Kruegel, 2002). When the intrusion detection system detects an attack, an IRS steps in to either document the incident or try to neutralize it. Little is known about IRSs despite the fact that they are integral to identities and play a crucial role in protecting them from cyber attacks (Sundaram, 1996). As a result, network administrators must still perform manual intrusion prevention in most situations (Carver et al., 2001). A rudimentary intrusion detection system is illustrated in Figure 1.

Figure 1. Very simple intrusion-detection system

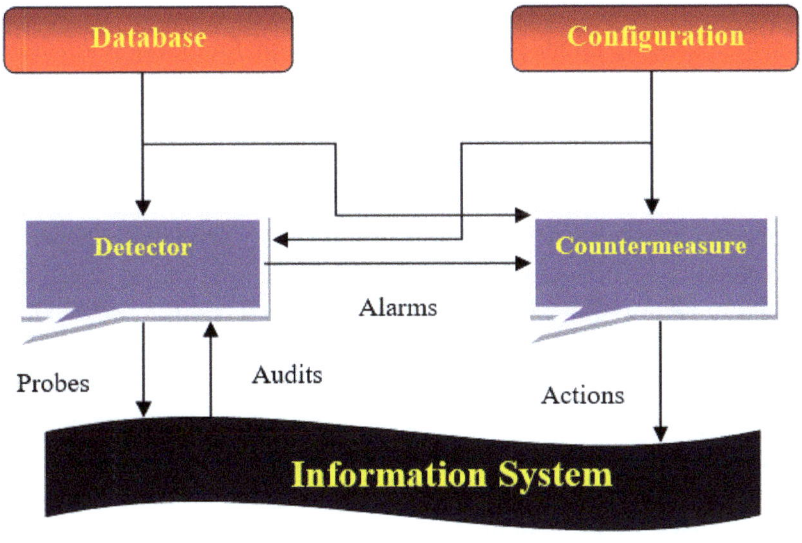

2. INTRUSION DETECTION SYSTEMS OVERVIEW

2.1 What is Intrusion Detection?

In order to identify intrusions—attempts to breach the security measures of an electronic system or network, jeopardize its private nature, truthfulness, or availability—intrusion detection monitors and analyses events taking place in a hardware platform or networks (Aurobindo Sundaram, 2006). The three main causes of breaches are unauthorized users trying to obtain extra privileges, authorized users abusing their login credentials, and attacker infiltrating the equipment from the Internet. One way of automating the steps of keeping track of and analyzing is with IDS. These systems can be either computer- or hardware- based (Ricks, 2014).

2.2 Intrusion Detection Systems: What are Their Benefits?

Considering the rise of more interconnected and dependent computer science, detection of attacks helps organizations safeguard their computer systems from potential dangers. Security experts shouldn't be asking if malicious activity detection is necessary, but rather, which penetration detected tools and features to employ, in light of the complexity and severity of current threats to network safety (Marchette, 2012). IDS are now widely recognized as an essential component of any company's cyber security framework. Considering the well-documented benefits of computer protection, many organizations still require justification for the adoption of malware detection systems. Getting and using IDSs is a good idea for a number of factors

To discourage problematic actions by making the people who would misuse the legal system more afraid of being caught and punished
In order to identify intrusions and additional safety risks that other safeguards fail to deter.
In order to identify potential attack precursors and address them in their final days
In order to record the current danger that a company faces
Specifically for big and complicated businesses, to serve as the quality assurance for security operations and development
In order to aid in better diagnosis, recuperation, and correction of underlying causes, it is necessary to publish relevant data regarding actual intrusions.

2.2.1 Mitigating Issues Through Enhanced Perception of Punishment and Detection of Attackers

Improving user behavior to prevent security breaches in systems for information is a primary objective of safety on computers planning. By raising the perceived threat of discovering and punishments of offenders, intrusion detection tools assist organizations in achieving this goal (Xie, 2024).

2.2.2 Identifying Issues That are not Prevented by Alternative Measures of Security

Many, if not most, infrastructure, particularly those linked to accessible networks, can be compromised by attackers employing well-publicized approaches. This is a common occurrence when security holes in the systems are left unfixed (Bijone, 2016).

2.2.3 Identifying the Precursors to Attacks

There is usually a predictable progression when attackers target a system. Typically, an attacker will begin by scanning a system or network for potential weak spots, a process known as probing (Zhang & Krunz, 2024). An attacker can freely probe a system without fear of detection or punishment in systems lacking IDS. An aggrieved hacker will ultimately discover a way into such an unrestricted connection and use it to access other networks (Rahbari & Krunz, 2017).

2.2.4 Documenting the Existing Threat

It is helpful to provide evidence that the network is experiencing an attack or is likely to be attacked when estimating costs for safety measures. In addition, knowing the nature and degree of assaults helps in determining the best safeguards to safeguard the system (Braber et al., n.d.).

2.2.5 Quality Control for Security Design and Administration

Machine usage trends and observed faults might be revealed when IDS run for a prolonged amount of time. Through drawing attention to problems with the system's security architecture and administration, these can help security administrators fix those issues before they produce a security problem (Irvine & Levin, 2000).

2.2.6 Providing Useful Information About Actual Intrusions

Whenever IDS fail to thwart assaults, they can nevertheless aid incident response and recovery by gathering accurate, comprehensive, and relevant data regarding the attack. Moreover, this data can facilitate and bolster civil or criminally legal remedies in specific cases. Data like these might help pinpoint where the company's security setup or policy is lacking (Cazorla et al., 2015).

3. IDS EFFICIENCY

We identify three ways for evaluating an intrusion-detection system's performance (Wu et al., 2003).

3.1 Accuracy

The intrusion-detection system makes a mistake when it incorrectly identifies an honest conservation effort as suspicious or obtrusive.

3.2 Performance

How quickly audit notifications get processed is a measure of how well an intrusion-detection system is working. It is not feasible to have real-time monitoring if the intrusion-detection system is not performing well (Ouarda et al., 2022).

3.3 Completeness

Lack of granularity happens when the intrusion-detection system does not identify an attack. Although it is hard to have a global comprehension of assaults or abuses of advantages this type of statistic is considerably more difficult to analyze than the other ones. Furthermore, It presents two extra legitimate ties

3.4 Fault Tolerance

When developed, an intrusion-detection technology ought to prove impervious to acts of violence, especially those that aim to deny functionality. Since the majority of intrusion-detection systems rely on freely obtainable windows operating systems or hardware—which are notoriously susceptible to attacks—this is of utmost importance (Gao et al., 2015).

3.5 Timeliness

If an intrusion-detection institution wants to keep somebody from compromising either the audit stream or the infrastructure itself, it has to run its analysis and send it out as fast as probable, giving the safety officer time to react beforehand the harm caused is too great. Both the intrinsic velocity of processing and the time necessary to transmit and react to what is being transmitted are included in this, making it more important than the performance evaluate (Dacier & Wespi, 1999).

4. TYPES OF IDS

This chapter have categorized IDS types according to the platform they were installed on, as shown in Figure 2.

Figure 2. Types of IDS classification.

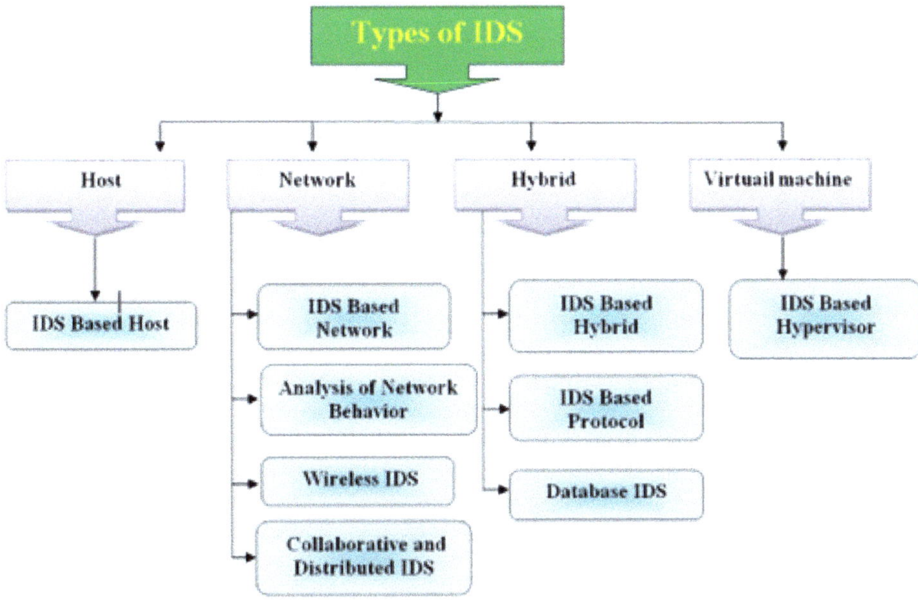

4.1 Three Different Kinds of Intrusion Detection Systems

The following is a summary of the various kinds of IDS

4.1.1 Host Based IDS

A system known as HIDS was the first of its kind to be developed. Among the many internal computer system or overall system activities that HIDS monitors and examines are application activity, wireless network traffic, program configuration, file access, modifications, active user or application methods, audit logs, and system recordings or audits (Martins et al., 2022). The HIDS is depicted in Figure 3. HIDS has the following features: root kit identification, log assessment, event interaction, quality checking, enforced policies RAM, processor, hard drive, and battery utilization, and reporting (Othman, Alsohybe, et al., 2018). To identify harmful system activity by analysing only certain system call records and then alerting the cloud user of any discovered problematic processes (Satilmis et al., 2024).

Figure 3. Host based IDS

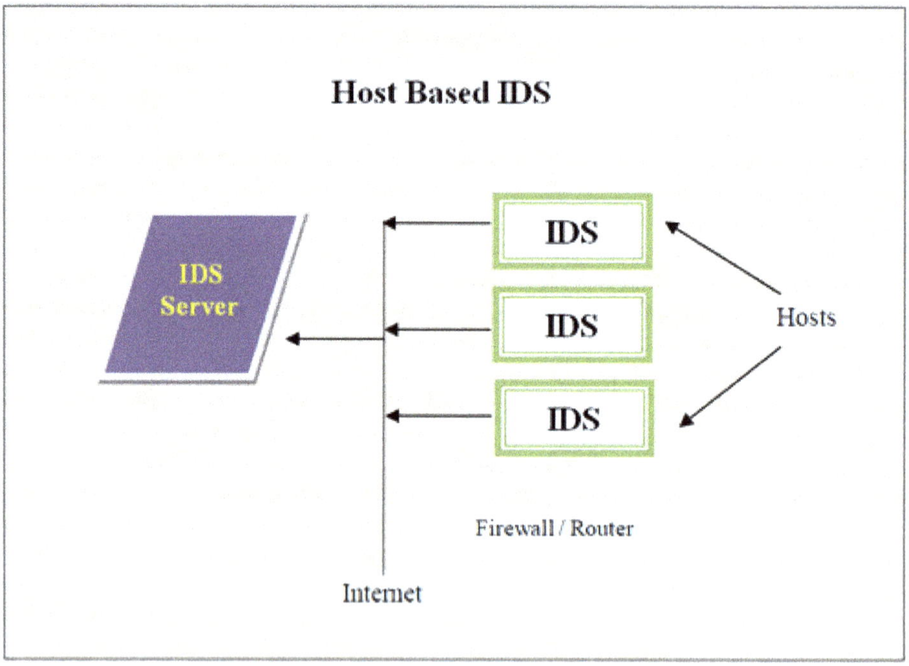

4.1.2 Network Based IDS (NIDS)

Traffic generated on a particular network segment is monitored and analyzed by NIDS in order to identify suspicious activity. NIDS and its stages for identifying attacks. To detect various IP-based DOS assaults, including TCP SYN attempts and fragmented session attacks, NIDS is employed for packet-level analysis across all computers in the network segment by examining IP, transport-layer, and application-layer activities, as well as packet headers (Bedi et al., 2021). To reduce the detail of communication over the network, an intrusion detection framework for large data environments is proposed, employing a machine learning algorithm known as SVM for classification and Chi-selector for feature selection. The KDD sample has been employed to evaluate the proposed model (Othman, Ba-Alwi, et al., 2018).

4.1.3 Hybrid based IDS or Mixed IDS (MIDS)

To get the benefits of IDS and finish the precise detection, MIDS merges two or more IDS types. For example employs host IDs and network IDS Double Guard (Le et al., 2012). On the other hand, MIDSS analyses data slowly.

4.1.4 Protocol-Based Intrusion Detection System (PIDS)

PIDS keeps an eye on and verifies the state and behavior of particular protocols, such as the protocol for transmitting text (HTTP). Implementation protocol monitoring, or APIDS, is a specialty of PIDS (Zuech et al., 2015). By tracking and examining application log files or evaluating the way they operate, it focusses on events that take place in a specific application. Studies that proposed PIDS include the following (Danish et al., 2018). Suggested IDS for detecting jamming attempts in a These networks connection. The LoRaWAN protocol served as the foundation for the system's implementation.

4.1.5 Network Behavior Analysis (NBA)

NBA keeps an eye on internet traffic to identify risks including malicious software, attack vectors, and policy infractions that cause unusual traffic patterns. In order to detect assaults with unusual data flows, the NBA computer examines traffic on the network [8]. NBA is defined as a technique that creates guidelines for typical traffic by constantly monitoring network information movements for a predetermined amount of time. Additionally, to identify any unusual activity in a computer system, the behavior has been compared to a reference. NBA programs are often implemented on a corporation's networks within the organization, while they are occasionally used to track traffic flowing between the network and external networks.

4.1.6 Wireless IDS (WIDS)

In order to identify potential threats, WIDS tracks and examines wireless traffic. Ad-hoc networks, wireless mesh networks, and wireless sensor networks are examples of wireless traffic (Sethuraman et al., 2019). In mobile phone networks, there are many different kinds of attacks, including Flood, Sybil, Impersonated Alternated Routing, and Collapse attacks (Sadia et al., 2024).

4.1.7 Distributed and Collaborative IDS (DIDS)

DIDS is made up of several IDS connected by a shared network, all of which can speak with a centralized computer that facilitates tracking the network or with one another. Table 1 shows that there are various benefits to DIDS over the centralized IDS.

Table 1. Distributed and Centralized IDS advantages and disadvantages

IDS	Advantages	Disadvantages
Distributed IDS	· The ability to adapt and grow · Detects DOS attacks for high speed networks · Bring down the price of calculation. · Processing, analysis, along with tracking of attack data becomes much simpler and faster. · Allow for early intrusion detection, which might lead to the blocking of incoming traffic from specified IP addresses throughout the whole networks.	· The data stream between the host and the agent could lead to significant increases in traffic on the network. · Data that travels a long distance from its origin to the IDS increases the risk of being intercepted or altered, leading to misunderstandings. · Various IDs can be used to generate distinct results.
Centralized IDS	· The management and up-keep costs are lower than those of a dispersed system. · A centralized console directly controls all of the IDS actions.	· Cannot identify simultaneous harmful events happening in many locations · The integrity of IDS can be compromised if an attacker manages to disable the machine's applications.

5. IDS Working

The hacking detection system's parts coordinate their activities in a predetermined way to notify the system administration of an attack.

Sensor - It sports two interfaces for users. Firstly, an interface for network capture; and secondly, an application for management of the network. Detecting and reporting are its primary functions. The collection interface transfers all the data collected into a buffer when the monitoring device listens to network traffic through network tagging. The error detection engine then analyses the protocol and reads the contents of the buffer. Additionally, intrusion-based analysis based on signatures and anomalies also took place here.
Backend - An intrusion detection system's primary role is in its backend. Its primary role is to gather and notify. The system of records known as the event

repositories stores all of the recognized activities by the sensor being monitored. The backend then decides how to reply to each event using methods such as blockage, e-mails, and presentations.

Frontend - Leadership and Management From the front end of the application, the user may setup, establish, and maintain the IDS. On the front end, you can see all the events that the backend has accumulated. As a result, the frontend offers a user-friendly interface for managing these recorded occurrences. Well-tuned IDS will only report important occurrences, which is essential for getting the most out of it. As a result, this interface allows the user to adjust the IDS's detection and response parameters. If executed correctly, the IDS will alert the user to any incursion in plenty of time (Sayyed et al., 2011).

6. IDS Techniques

Finding valuable information or unexpected patterns in massive databases is the goal of data mining techniques. Data mining is an important step in the ideation process since it takes large datasets and uses analysis and generation to turn them into valuable knowledge. Information security, medical diagnostics, banking, and education are just a few of the many areas that have discovered data mining's usefulness. Figure 4 displays the categories of techniques used in intrusion detection systems.

Figure 4. Categories of Techniques in IDS Application

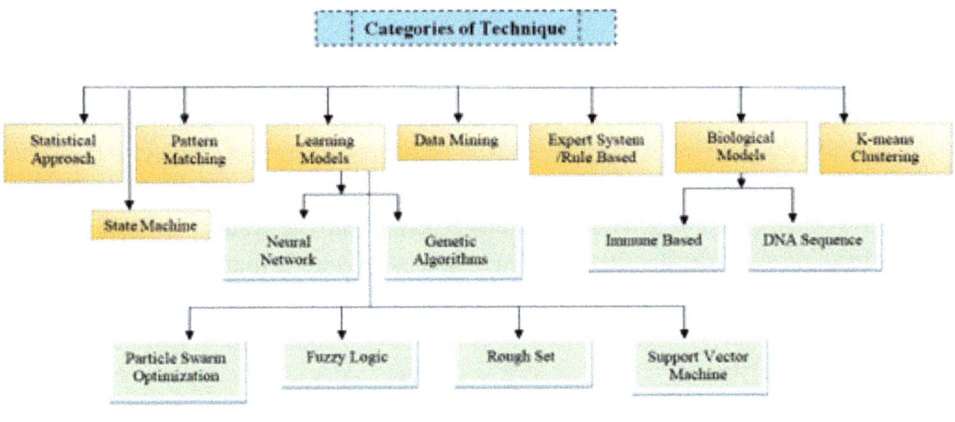

6.1 Statistical Approach

Empirical comparison of event-specific criterion setting is a part of this method. Several properties can be specified as variable integers; for instance, the number of files accessed in a given time period, memory utilization, disc space usage, user login, and logout. In order to conduct penetration analysis, statistical techniques are used to the obtained data.

6.2 Data Mining

The public makes extensive use of methods of data mining, which are the backbone of the majority of misuse detection models. An evaluation method based on data is how IDS expresses itself. Automatic analysis of typical and disruptive user actions is achieved by the application of statistics mining methods. Four main subtasks, including classification, regression, clustering, and association rule learning, make up data mining (Sulaiman et al., 2021).

6.3 Pattern Matching

To model, match, and identify intrusion patterns solely based on packet headers, packet content, or both, intrusion detection techniques are frequently utilized in networks. As the computational burden of finding patterns rises, the number of signatures is increasing, which is a reflection of the various sorts and varieties of attacks. Furthermore, new assaults cannot be detected using this method.

6.4 Expert System / Rule Based

In accordance with a prior set of rules that described hacking attempts, the expert system translates security-related incidents documented in the audit trail into if-then-else rules (SuhanaSulaiman, 2020). This method creates statistical identities of individuals and uses statistically significant abnormalities as indicators of intrusions. However, this approach needs improvements from the system administrators to stay up-to-date. Another drawback of the expert software is that it does not perform preservation or updates.

6.5 State Machines

Part of this paradigm is a set of steps that can be taken throughout different states. The intrusion begins with the intruders deciding what they want and then performing man oeuvres to undermine the system.

6.6 K-means Clustering

After receiving the input parameter k, the technique divides a set of n objects into k clusters. It turns out that there's a lot of resemblance within clusters, but not much between them. Utilizing this method primarily serves to segment crew information into two categories: ordinary and intrusive cases (Gera & Goel, 2015).

6.7 Learning Models

The approach to learning makes use of synthesized learning and the acquisition of knowledge about the security breach detection process. With the ability of self-learning techniques to regularly organize the subjects and viewpoints, mastery methods have been widely used in finding anomalies in the past (Valiathan, 2002). Here we will go over a few various educational models. Earlier IDS modified the usage of the neural network, which has two crucial parts. An audit trail monitoring system capable of incursion signature recognition is the first component. The following step is to check customer behavior; if something out of the ordinary happens, an alarm goes off. The classification of data is facilitated by a category of machine learning techniques known as neural networks. Nodes and edges make up a neural network. The impact that a node has on its immediate vicinity is determined by its weight. Out of all the nodes in the structure, input components make up a subset. The detection of neural networking usage consists of three steps. Fuzzy Logic provides a framework for many-valued good and approximation judgment as an alternative to consistent and accurate reasoning. Fuzzy Logic is a conceptual framework for describing fuzziness and ambiguity in practical problem-solving tools. GA uses the process of natural selection as a framework for critical analysis. Each task in the second stage generates a set of classifications using offline network audit data; this process is part of the GA-based IDS that has been described (Menghani, 2023). The policy that was developed is utilized to categories real-time links to networks in the step that aims to detect intrusion. It use mutation, recombination, and selection to evolve chromosomes, and it uses evolution and natural resolution with DNA as the record organization. Coding for each chromosomal function is done using a unique set of letters, numbers, or bits.

6.8 Biological Models

In the past, there was an abnormal finding approach called Immune Based that was based on principles from biology. IDS immunological based are able to mimic the functions of both innate and adaptive immunity, drawing inspiration from the idea of the human immune system. By compiling audit data on service behavior, the usual behavior profile can be created.

7. AI TECHNIQUES FOR INTRUSION DETECTION

When developing an AI systems and ML in particular, take into account different learning styles. Because of its characteristics, the input data is perfect for the algorithm's categorization task. The methods for classification in ML can be either controlled or unsupervised, depending on the availability for learning data. Working in tandem with a tutor, students can study under guidance by having the trained dataset train the target dataset and the labeled dataset classified. Finding anomalies relies on supervised instruction, which produces reliable results in intrusion monitoring categorization tasks. In comparison, unsupervised learning makes use of user-generated similarity metrics to classify data in the absence of labels. For effective analysis of previously unknown sequences, this kind of learning functions as a dream tool (Sowmya & Mary Anita, 2023a).

Figure 5. Classification of AI based IDS

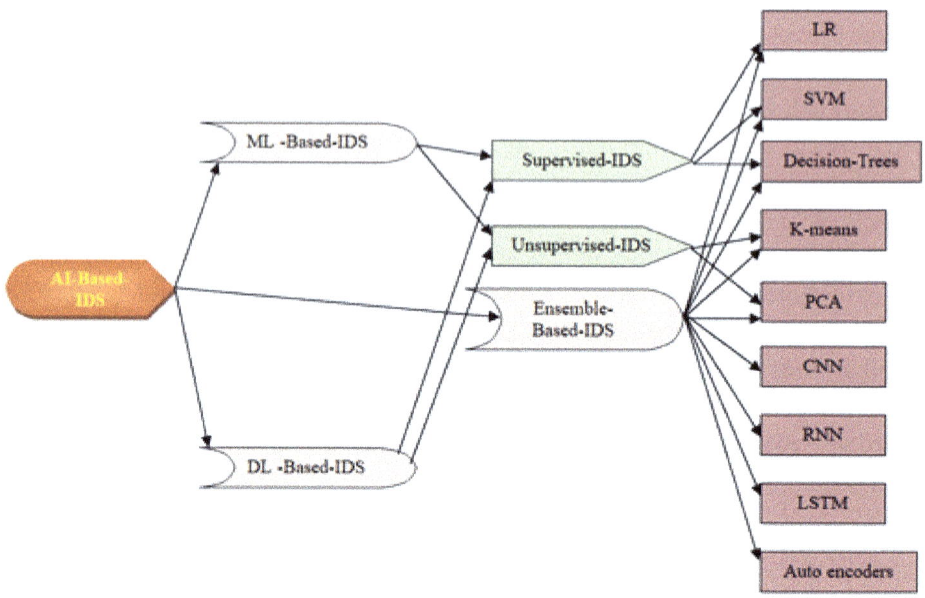

The significance of supervised and unsupervised ML algorithms, as well as their respective uses, was discussed in the review (Sharma, 2020). The model has limitations in that it produces less precise results, much like all the other models. Despite ML's numerous shortcomings—such as the need for enormous amounts of data—the technology is ubiquitous. Investigators have already presented multiple intrusion detection frameworks based on the learning method. There are two parts to the categorization process: testing and instruction. Classification of AI based IDS shown in Figure 5.

7.1 Supervised Machine Learning for Intrusion Detection

A machine learning task associates output data with input-output pair relationships. We have employed widely used machine learning techniques for intrusion detection in empirical research. The principal aim of supervised learning is to achieve a defined objective based on the training data. The primary activities in this instructional methodology are categorization and regression processes.

7.1.1 Support Vector Machine (SVM)

One of the most important models in machine learning literature, SVM produces state-of-the-art performance in both classifications and predicting. A two-stage procedure based on statistically-based IDS is proposed in the work of (Kabir et al., 2018). Based on the least squares SVM the suggested method divides the whole KDDcup99 sample in half. The suggested method starts by picking out samples from the different sub groups. The research project also took into account the subgroup's weaknesses when determining the best allocating scheme. Using the suggested method, the samples for intrusion detection can then be extracted.

7.1.2 Logistic Regression (LR)

Among the supervised techniques used for binary and multiclass classification applications is logistic regression. LR works on the premise of using probability to forecast when an event will take place. In addition to its use in detecting breaches, logistic regression has other applications, such as spam detection (Ponmalar & Dhanakoti, 2021). I forward a fresh strategy for IDS that utilizes logistic reconstruction and the genetic algorithm as its foundation. In contrast to the current complicated supervised ML methods, a different study found that LR-based intrusion detection systems and linear discriminate evaluation performed better for single and classification with multiple classes (Subba et al., 2016).

7.1.3 KNN Algorithm

When it comes to supervised machine learning, K-Nearest Neighbor is the most basic method that can learn complex approaches rapidly. When it comes to predicting and predicting regression, KNN is a popular approach. Using a measure of distance known as the mathematical distance, KNN sorts newly-acquired data into categories based on how similar the pieces appear. Assuming K=5, it will use the five closest neighbors as a measure of distance from which to derive a classification for the new input data (Subba et al., 2016). Had the idea to use a hybrid model combining KNN and density peak clustering to assess IDS threats. Segmentation was handled by the KNN, whereas training was done by concentration peak clusters.

7.1.4 Bayesian

Supervised schooling was the setting in which Bayesian classification was born. The idea that a characteristics possibility can be inferred from data is the basis of one strategy. A Bayesian Network Model aggregating classifier was suggested in a different study. To construct the classifier, the KDD CUP 99 database was first divided into sections of data. For training, we use subsets of the dataset, and for testing, we use the full thing. After training and testing data are discredited, the K-best BN models can be found using the data used for training.

7.2 Unsupervised ML for Intrusion Detection

Unsupervised learning relies on similarity-based clustering. Even with an unlabelled dataset, the model may discover the hidden pattern. Modeling techniques like clustering and association allow it to unearth the dataset's latent patterns. A true form of artificial intelligence, unsupervised learning imitates how people learn from their own experiences.

7.2.1 Fuzzy C Means Clustering Algorithm

Grouping data points into one or more sets is possible using fuzzy clustering, an unsupervised method. The amount of distance between points of information and cluster centers is used by the algorithm to assign memberships.

7.2.2 K-Means Clustering Algorithm

The K-means clustering method is an iterative, unsupervised process that uses similarities between data samples to group them into one of five distinct groups.

The collection is initially unlabelled. The core principle of the method is based on centric theory, which assigns each data sample to the centric that is geographically nearest to it. Offered a combination of KNN and Naïve Bays as a hybrid method for finding aberrations. To determine which aspects are most crucial, an entropy-based features selection technique is employed. In addition to detecting attacks, the system can also categories them. We use the NSL KDD dataset for training and data classification, as well as for evaluation of performance. A different study [41] suggested an intrusion detection method that uses KNN and 1R classification. In this method, K refers to clustering is utilized before classification, and 1R classification is used to divide the data into several categories. The dataset from the 1999 KDD Cup (Chong, 2021).

7.3 Comparison of DL Based Intrusion Detection System

As a branch of machine learning, DL is like a complicated evolutionary tree of ML strategies. To model intricate ideas, DL architectures use layered structures. DL frameworks take design cues from ANN which is derived from the human brain. Many areas are currently using the DL method, including assault finding, computational imaging, and recognition of voices (Ahmad et al., 2021). In terms of collecting features, DL and ML topologies are distinct. Automatic feature extraction is a hallmark of DL architectures, and the algorithm is designed to learn from its own mistakes. A large dataset is necessary for the DL designs to produce high-quality insights. Because of this, DL frameworks are better than ML ones. Furthermore, DL discovers more intricate mappings and interactions between input and output data (Bengio et al., 2013). DL is a more sophisticated subfield of ML that uses complex networks of interconnected neural computations to learn new information.

7.3.1 Convolutional Neural Network (CNN)

Automatic feature learning and attack classification are capabilities of CNN. The building blocks of these systems are neurons, and the activation value serves as the outcome function, which is derived from mathematical functions that are the weighted aggregate of the inputs. CNN typically consist of many layers, with each layer receiving its input from the previous one. Dynamic feature learning, the extraction of features, and data classification are all within the capabilities of all of the layers. The CNN methodology has demonstrated encouraging results in recognizing normal and aberrant data, according to multiple studies [48]. Presented a few-shot DL approach that utilized a combination of deep CNN, support vector machines, and 1-NN classifiers. Using a DCN for intrusion detection, the author then constructed few-shot intrusion detection with a support vector machine and

1NN. And were tested on two datasets, KDD 99 and NSL-KDD, with improved accuracy rates of 96.19% and 86.74%, respectively.

7.3.2 Recurrent Neural Network (RNN)

The exceptional computing power in the last several years has contributed to RNN meteoric rise to popularity. The proliferation of massive data and powerful computers has led to the widespread use of DL by researchers, which in turn makes RNN an attractive option for IDS systems. Recurrent neural networks have been around for a while, but their memory property is what really made them attractive recently. In RNN, the output from one layer is fed into the next, essentially building a foundation. It is possible to train RNNs to identify normal and abnormal data for use in intrusion detection systems. On the other hand, RNN has just lately found its way into both regression and classification thanks to the lightning-fast improvements in computer power. The vanishing gradient problem was a big drawback of this technology, even if it performs well when compared to other methods.

7.4 Comparative Study of ML and DL for Intrusion Detection System

Machine learning algorithms also performed admirably, with a high rate of accuracy. While it's true that other ML models demonstrated improved accuracy, KNN was the pioneer in determining the top accuracy metric. In terms of attack detection and categorization, all of the ML and DL models worked admirably. In terms of accuracy, detection rate, and FAR, DL models outperform other models when it comes to efficiently identifying threats (Thapa et al., 2020). Our research shows that CNN is a good foundational model for intrusion detection systems because of how well it performs. Researchers interested in intrusion detection in the future may find this study useful for tracking CNN's progress. This finding has important implications for the ability of researchers to identify assaults. Due to its fitting and generalization capabilities, DL is more beneficial in the detection of breaches area. The use of features is another consideration, and DL processes are preferable to ML when dealing with big data. The findings of this comparison study indicate that DL feature evaluation could be useful for attack detection. Our research shows that different DL algorithms work better when features are reduced in depth and features are carefully chosen.

8. COMPARATIVE ANALYSIS- TRADITIONAL VS AI-BASED IDS

Methods based on signatures and anomalies are the mainstays of traditional intrusion detection systems. Signature-based intrusion detection systems compare incoming data with previously established patterns of known assaults in order to detect matching (Muneer et al., 2024). This method has great success in identifying known risks, but it isn't very flexible. Systems that rely on signatures have limited ability to deal with new threats since they can't identify fresh or unusual attack vectors that don't match existing characteristics. On the other hand, anomaly-based intrusion detection systems set a standard for normal behavior and flag any changes from this as possible intrusions. Unknown attacks can be detected using this strategy by looking for patterns that don't fit the typical. Anomaly based systems, on the other hand, frequently have problems with precisely identifying normal behavior and with large mistake rates. By utilizing AI techniques, specifically ML and DL, several constraints can be overcome. Standard in conventional intrusion detection systems. Systems enabled by AI have the ability to react to emerging threats in real-time by learning from data and continuously improving their detection models (Banerjee, 2025). AI algorithms can identify new attack patterns because they do not rely on predefined patterns like signature-based approaches do. In addition, AI models are better able to handle and analyze massive amounts of data, which improves the capacity to identify complex threats with more accuracy and less false positives. The use of artificial intelligence approaches has been a huge step forward in safety reasons, enabling improved adaptability, accuracy, and efficiency in intrusion detection, although traditional intrusion detection systems have been vital. More advancement in handling the complexity of contemporary cyber threats are on the horizon, thanks to the persistent development of algorithms for intelligence (Yellepeddi et al., n.d.).

9. STATISTICAL MEASURES

When estimating various statistical measures, it is necessary to get the ground truth value for evaluation(SAFA OTOUM et al., 2021). The set of connection records labeled as Normal or Attack constitutes the ground truth for binary classification (Sowmya & Mary Anita, 2023b). To evaluate the quality of the classification models, we use the following terms, assuming that the number of records for Normal connections and Attack connections in the test dataset is equal (Vinayakumar et al., 2019).

- The amount of connection records that were accurately classified as Normal is known as TP.

- The total quantity of connection records that were accurately classified as Attack is known as the TN.
- FP is defined as the number of records where a normal contact was mistakenly classified as an attack connected.
- An incorrectly classified attack connation record is known as a FN.

The following are some of the most popular metrics for evaluations that are founded on the terms indicated earlier (Abdić, 2024).

1) Accuracy: It makes an educated guess as to what percentage of the test dataset consists of properly identified connection records. Machine learning models are considered better when their accuracy levels are higher($Accuracy \in [0,1]$). Here's how accuracy is defined and used as a good measure for a test dataset with balanced classes shown in Equation 1.

$$Accuracy = \frac{TP + TN}{TP + TN + FP + FN} \tag{1}$$

2) Precision: By dividing the total number of identified attack connection records by the number of records that were successfully identified, it provides an approximation of the ratio. The accuracy of a machine learning model is directly proportional to its ($Precision \in [0,1]$). Here is how precision is defined in Equation 2.

$$Precision = \frac{TP}{TP + FP} \tag{2}$$

3) F1-Score: F1-Measure is also known as F1-Score. This is the optimal value, where Precision and Recall are both high. An increase in the ($F1 - Score \in [0,1]$) indicates that the machine learning model has been improved. The definition of the F1-Score is as follows Equation 3.

$$F1 - Score = 2 \times \left(\frac{Precision \times Recall}{Precision + Recall}\right) \tag{3}$$

4) True Positive Rate (TPR): It is also known as recall. It takes a wild guess as to what fraction of all records that could have an Attack relation actually had it correctly identified. To improve machine learning models, one should aim for a greater($TPR \in [0,1]$)This is how TPR is defined in Equation 4.

$$TPR = \frac{TP}{TP + FN} \tag{4}$$

5) False Positive Rate (FPR): The total number of records with a Normal connection is estimated, and the fraction of those records that are classified as Attacks is also estimated. A lower FPR indicates a better ML model ($FPR \in [0, 1]$)the definition of FPR is as follows Equation 5.

$$FPR = \frac{FP}{FP + TN} \quad (5)$$

6) Receiver Operating Characteristics (ROC) curve: Shown are ROCs at different thresholds, with the y-axis representing the trade-off between TPR and FPR. Area In addition to ROC, another common measure for comparing machine learning models is the area under the curve that represents the receiver operating characteristic AUC. A larger area under the curve AUC indicates a better machine learning model shown in Equation 6.

$$AUC = \int_0^1 \frac{TP}{TP + FN} c \frac{FP}{TN + FP} \quad (6)$$

10. RESULT & ANALYSIS

In Figure 6, we can see an example of a receiver operating characteristic (ROC) curve that illustrates the interplay of these three variables; the graph's horizontal and vertical axes, labeled as FP Level and TP Rate, respectively, depict this interplay. As far as ROC is concerned, the AE model is head and shoulders above the competition.

Figure 6. Confusion Matrix

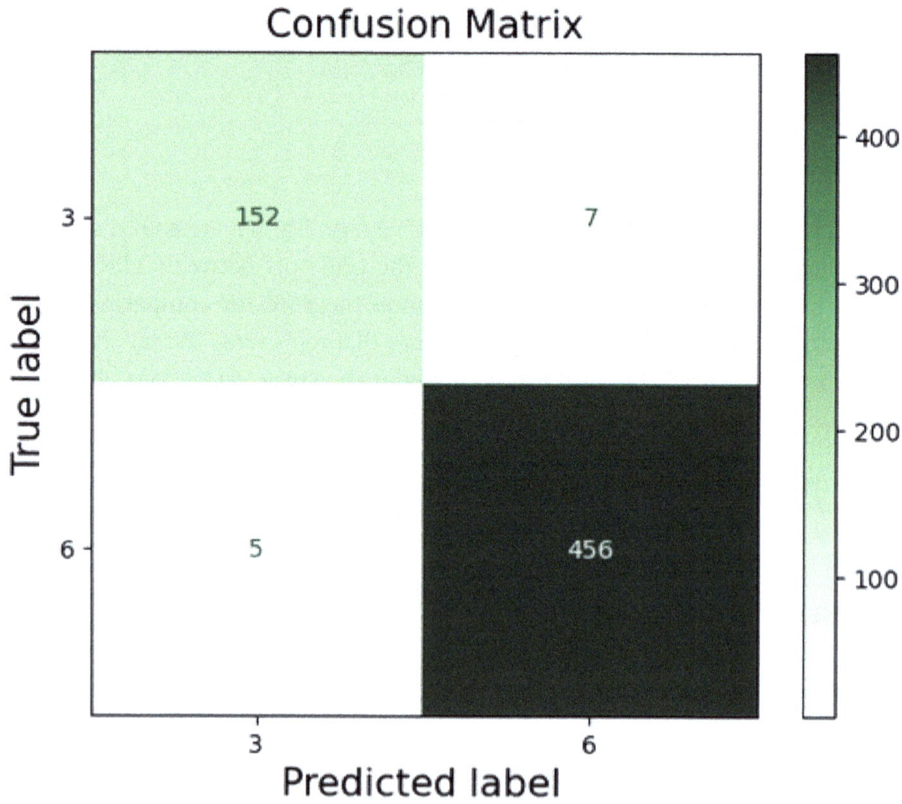

Table 2 provides a synopsis of the test results. It shows the classifier's training and testing times in seconds for each of the five categories, along with the corresponding accuracy rates (Peddabachigari et al., 2007).

Table 2. Performance of AE

Attack type	Training time	Testing Time	Accuracy
Normal	**1.24**	**0.02**	**88.96**
Probe	1.16	0.01	98.12
DOS	2.03	0.03	85.96
U2R	1.46	0.02	92.82
R2L	1.58	0.03	96.18

For the purpose of weather prediction, researchers used Accuracy evaluation metrics to assess neural network models. The seven NN examples' differences are displayed in Figure 7. The image shows that the AE model outperforms both methods.

Figure 7. Performance Comparission

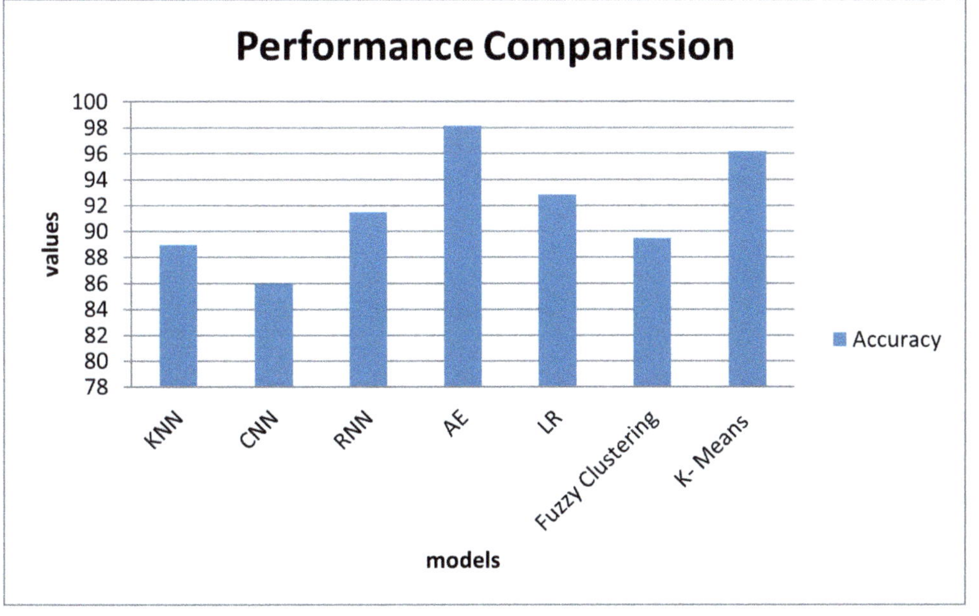

Displays the RMSE and ROC area under the receiver operating characteristic. The RMSE shows how far off the target results are from the confusion matrix. A more efficient model is one with a smaller RMSE. True positive and false positive are the inputs used to determine the ROC value (Almseidin et al., 2017). A low ROC value shows that the model isn't very good at detecting intrusions, whereas a high one shows that it shown in Table 3.

Table 3. Performance Measure

Models	ROC Area	Root Mean Squared Error
KNN	89.98	0.831
CNN	86.98	0.981
RNN	92.50	0.732
AE	**99.14**	**0.525**
LR	94.84	0.826

continued on following page

Table 3. Continued

Models	ROC Area	Root Mean Squared Error
Fuzzy Clustering	90.48	0.912
k- Means	97.20	0.687

A sample ROC curve illustrating the link between the three parameters is shown in Figure 8. The graph, which also displays the association between the three components, uses the FP Level and TP Rate as the axes of the horizontal and vertical directions (Kaja et al., 2019). As far as ROC is concerned, the AE model is head and shoulders above the competition. ROC Curve Shown in Figure 8.

Figure 8. ROC Curve

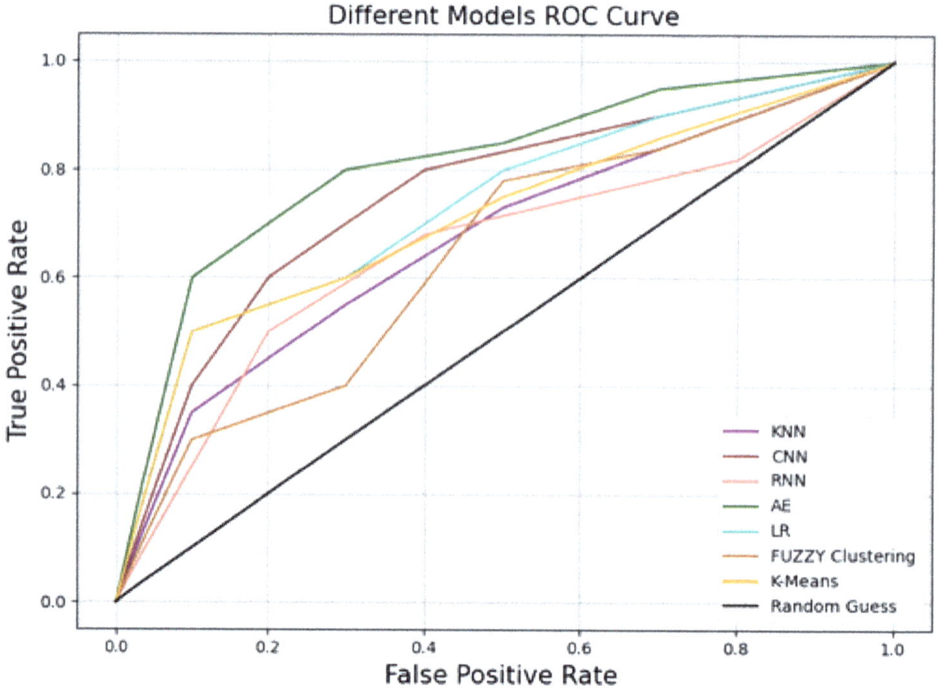

Conversely, the AE classifier attained the minimal FN rate of 0.031. Simultaneously, the AE classifier reached its peak false positive rate of 0.0009, signifying that a considerable number of genuine packets are erroneously identified as attack packets. Figure 9 illustrates the False Positive Rate and False Negative Rate.

Figure 9. False Positive Rate and False Negative Rate

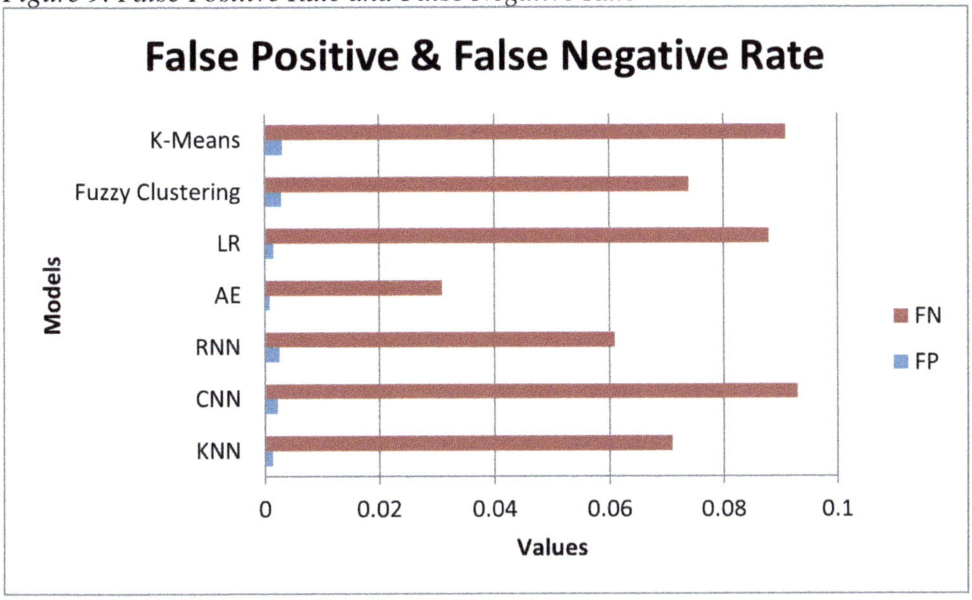

Examines the three AE model versions with and without DPFS, as well as their prediction results according to MAE for training error and testing error, respectively Model prediction performance evaluation shown in Figure 10.

Figure 10. Model prediction performance evaluation

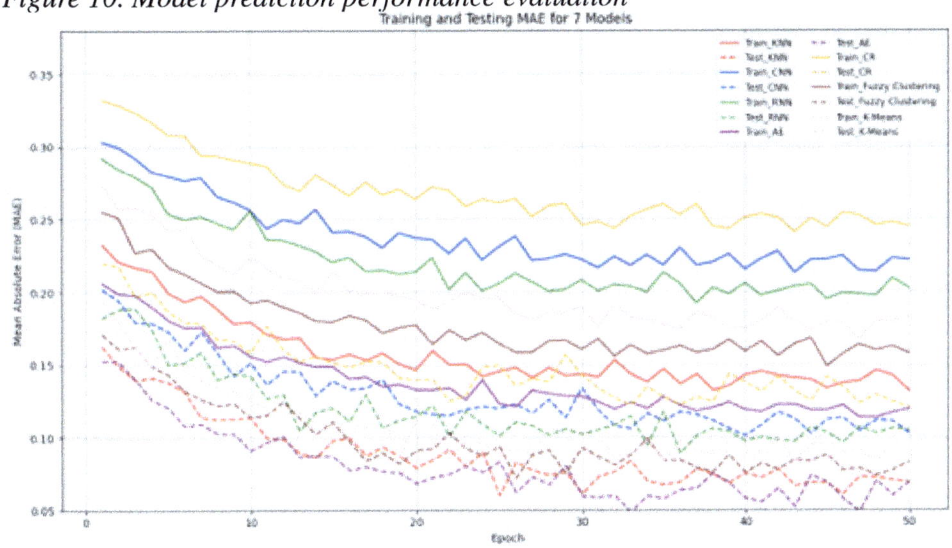

11. CONCLUSION

A crucial technique for resource management in multiple applications is volunteer computing, which leverages Internet-connected whose owners donate them as storage and computational power resources. There are growing worries about the robustness of cyber physical systems, particularly for critical infrastructures, due to the increasing volume and variety of data transmission on the Internet. The significance of implementing a reliable Intrusion Detection System to collect such sensory data has so grown significantly. `This chapter offer a comparative assessment of intrusion detection systems driven by AI for wirelessly linked sensors that track critical applications in this research. It focuses on the application of ML, DL, and RL methods to identify malicious activity in the gathered traffic and provide a comprehensive analysis of their utilization. A revolutionary change in cyber security strategy is the use of intrusion detection and response mechanisms powered by AI. These systems are able to adapt to new attack vectors, detect threats in real time, and trigger automated responses with high precision by utilizing advanced learning algorithms. For resilient cyber defenses in an ever-changing threat scenario, it is vital to integrate AI into IDS frameworks. However, there are still issues with scalability, interpretability, and data quality.

REFERENCES

Abdić, A. (2024). AI-Based Intrusion Detection Systems. *Challenges and Future Directions.*, *4*(1), 1–15.

Ahmad, Z., Shahid Khan, A., Wai Shiang, C., Abdullah, J., & Ahmad, F. (2021). Network intrusion detection system: A systematic study of machine learning and deep learning approaches. *Transactions on Emerging Telecommunications Technologies*, *32*(1), 1–29. DOI: 10.1002/ett.4150

Almseidin, M., Alzubi, M., Kovacs, S., & Alkasassbeh, M. (2017). Evaluation of machine learning algorithms for intrusion detection system. SISY 2017 - IEEE 15th International Symposium on Intelligent Systems and Informatics, Proceedings, Iv, 277–282. DOI: 10.1109/SISY.2017.8080566

Banerjee, S. (2025). International Journal of Statistical Computation and AI-Enabled Cloud Security Solutions : A Comparative Review of Traditional vs . Next-Generation Approaches. January 2024.

Bedi, P., Gupta, N., & Jindal, V. (2021). I-SiamIDS: An improved Siam-IDS for handling class imbalance in network-based intrusion detection systems. *Applied Intelligence*, *51*(2), 1133–1151. DOI: 10.1007/s10489-020-01886-y

Bengio, Y., Courville, A., & Vincent, P. (2013). Representation learning: A review and new perspectives. *IEEE Transactions on Pattern Analysis and Machine Intelligence*, *35*(8), 1798–1828. DOI: 10.1109/TPAMI.2013.50 PMID: 23787338

Bijone, M. (2016). A Survey on Secure Network: Intrusion Detection & Prevention Approaches. *American Journal of Information Systems*, *4*(3), 69–88. DOI: 10.12691/ajis-4-3-2

Braber, F. Den, Lund, M. S., & Solberg, A. (n.d.). Sintef report.

Carver, C. A., Hill, J. M. D., Pooch, U. W., & Ieee, S. M. (2001). Limiting Uncertainty in Intrusion Response. February, 1–6. https://www.west-point.org/users/usma1982/39377/john/Publications/2001/2001-06_SMC-IAW/Limiting.pdf

Cazorla, L., Alcaraz, C., & Lopez, J. (2015). A three-stage analysis of IDS for critical infrastructures. *Computers & Security*, *55*, 235–250. DOI: 10.1016/j.cose.2015.07.005

Chong, B. (2021). K-means clustering algorithm: A brief review. *Academic Journal of Computing & Information Science*, *4*(5), 37–40. DOI: 10.25236/AJCIS.2021.040506

Dacier, M., & Wespi, A. (1999). Towards a taxonomy of intrusion-detection systems.

Danish, S. M., Nasir, A., Qureshi, H. K., Ashfaq, A. B., Mumtaz, S., & Rodriguez, J. (2018). Network Intrusion Detection System for Jamming Attack in LoRaWAN Join Procedure. IEEE International Conference on Communications, 2018-May(-December 2019). DOI: 10.1109/ICC.2018.8422721

Gao, Z., Member, S., Cecati, C., Ieee, F., & Ding, S. X. (2015). IEEE TRANSACTIONS ON INDUSTRIAL ELECTRONICS A Survey of Fault Diagnosis and Fault - Tolerant Techniques Part I : Fault Diagnosis with Model - Based and Signal - Based Approaches. 62, 3757–3767.

Gera, M., & Goel, S. (2015). Data Mining - Techniques, Methods and Algorithms: A Review on Tools and their Validity. *International Journal of Computer Applications*, *113*(18), 22–29. DOI: 10.5120/19926-2042

Irvine, C., & Levin, T. (2000). Quality of security service. Proceedings New Security Paradigm Workshop, September, 91–99. DOI: 10.1145/366173.366195

Kabir, E., Hu, J., Wang, H., & Zhuo, G. (2018). A novel statistical technique for intrusion detection systems. *Future Generation Computer Systems*, *79*, 303–318. DOI: 10.1016/j.future.2017.01.029

Kaja, N., Shaout, A., & Ma, D. (2019). An intelligent intrusion detection system. *Applied Intelligence*, *49*(9), 3235–3247. DOI: 10.1007/s10489-019-01436-1

Le, M., Stavrou, A., & Kang, B. B. (2012). DoubleGuard: Detecting intrusions in multitier web applications. *IEEE Transactions on Dependable and Secure Computing*, *9*(4), 512–525. DOI: 10.1109/TDSC.2011.59

Marchette, D. J. (2012). Network intrusion detection. Handbook of Computational Statistics: Concepts and Methods: Second Edition, 1139–1165. DOI: 10.1007/978-3-642-21551-3_38

Martins, I., Resende, J. S., Sousa, P. R., Silva, S., Antunes, L., & Gama, J. (2022). Host-based IDS: A review and open issues of an anomaly detection system in IoT. Future Generation Computer Systems, 133(January 2021), 95–113. DOI: 10.1016/j.future.2022.03.001

Menghani, G. (2023). Efficient Deep Learning: A Survey on Making Deep Learning Models Smaller, Faster, and Better. *ACM Computing Surveys*, *55*(12), 1–37. Advance online publication. DOI: 10.1145/3578938

Muneer, S., Farooq, U., Athar, A., Raza, M. A., Ghazal, T. M., & Sakib, S. (2024). A Critical Review of Artificial Intelligence Based Approaches in Intrusion Detection: A Comprehensive Analysis. *Journal of Engineering*, *2024*(1), 3909173. Advance online publication. DOI: 10.1155/2024/3909173

Othman, S. M., Alsohybe, N. T., Mutaher Ba-Alwi, F., & Zahary, A. T. (2018). Survey on Intrusion Detection System Types. *International Journal of Cyber-Security and Digital Forensics*, *7*(4), 444–462.

Othman, S. M., Ba-Alwi, F. M., Alsohybe, N. T., & Al-Hashida, A. Y. (2018). Intrusion detection model using machine learning algorithm on Big Data environment. *Journal of Big Data*, *5*(1), 34. Advance online publication. DOI: 10.1186/s40537-018-0145-4

Otoum, S., Kantarci, B., & Mouftah, H.SAFA OTOUM. (2021). A Comparative Study of AI-based Intrusion DetectionTechniques in Critical Infrastructures. *ACM Transactions on Internet Technology*, *21*(4), 1–22. DOI: 10.1145/3406093

Ouarda, L., Malika, B., Yousfi, N. E., & Brahim, B. (2022). Improving the efficiency of intrusion detection in information systems. *Journal of Intelligent Systems*, *31*(1), 835–854. DOI: 10.1515/jisys-2022-0059

Peddabachigari, S., Abraham, A., Grosan, C., & Thomas, J. (2007). Modeling intrusion detection system using hybrid intelligent systems. *Journal of Network and Computer Applications*, *30*(1), 114–132. DOI: 10.1016/j.jnca.2005.06.003

Ponmalar, A., & Dhanakoti, V. (2021). An Efficient Classification of Intrusion in Bigdata based on Chaos Game Optimization and Ensemble SVM. DOI: 10.21203/rs.3.rs-385392/v1

Rahbari, H., & Krunz, M. (2017). Rolling preambles: Mitigating stealthy FO estimation attacks in OFDM-based 802.11 systems. *2016 IEEE Conference on Communications and Network Security, CNS 2016*, 118–126. DOI: 10.1109/CNS.2016.7860477

Ricks, B. E. (2014). Intrusion detection systems. Physical Security and Safety: A Field Guide for the Practitioner, 101–108. DOI: 10.48175/IJARSCT-17606

Sadia, H., Farhan, S., Haq, Y. U., Sana, R., Mahmood, T., Bahaj, S. A. O., & Khan, A. R. (2024). Intrusion Detection System for Wireless Sensor Networks: A Machine Learning Based Approach. *IEEE Access : Practical Innovations, Open Solutions*, *12*(April), 52565–52582. DOI: 10.1109/ACCESS.2024.3380014

Satilmis, H., Akleylek, S., & Tok, Z. Y. (2024). A Systematic Literature Review on Host-Based Intrusion Detection Systems. *IEEE Access : Practical Innovations, Open Solutions*, *12*(January), 27237–27266. DOI: 10.1109/ACCESS.2024.3367004

Sayyed, T., Kodwani, S., Dodake, K., & Adhayage, M. (2011)... *Intrusion Detection System.*, *14*(01), 39–57. DOI: 10.1142/9781848164482_0004

Sethuraman, S. C., Dhamodara, S., & Vijayakumar, V. (2019). Intrusion detection system for detecting wireless attacks in IEEE 802.11 networks. *IET Networks*, *8*(4), 219–232. DOI: 10.1049/iet-net.2018.5050

Sharma, R. (2020). Study of Supervised Learning and Unsupervised Learning. *International Journal for Research in Applied Science and Engineering Technology*, *8*(6), 588–593. DOI: 10.22214/ijraset.2020.6095

Sowmya, T., & Mary Anita, E. A. (2023a). A comprehensive review of AI based intrusion detection system. Measurement: Sensors, 28(October 2022). DOI: 10.1016/j.measen.2023.100827

Sowmya, T., & Mary Anita, E. A. (2023b). A comprehensive review of AI based intrusion detection system. Measurement: Sensors, 28(October 2022), 100827. DOI: 10.1016/j.measen.2023.100827

Subba, B., Biswas, S., & Karmakar, S. (2016). Intrusion Detection Systems using Linear Discriminant Analysis and Logistic Regression. 12th IEEE International Conference Electronics, Energy, Environment, Communication, Computer, Control: (E3-C3), INDICON 2015, June. DOI: 10.1109/INDICON.2015.7443533

SuhanaSulaiman, N. (2020). Overview of Network Dataset and Data Mining Technique. International Journal of Advanced Trends in Computer Science and Engineering, 9(1.3), 287–290. DOI: 10.30534/ijatcse/2020/4391.32020

Sulaiman, N. S., Nasir, A., Othman, W. R. W., Wahab, S. F. A., Aziz, N. S., Yacob, A., & Samsudin, N. (2021). Intrusion Detection System Techniques : A Review. *Journal of Physics: Conference Series*, *1874*(1), 012042. Advance online publication. DOI: 10.1088/1742-6596/1874/1/012042

Sundaram, A. (1996). An introduction to intrusion detection. XRDS: Crossroads. *The ACM Magazine for Students*, *2*(4), 3–7. DOI: 10.1145/332159.332161

Sundaram, A. (2006). An Introduction to Intrusion Detection The need for Intrusion Detection Systems. *Computers & Security*, *1*(1), 10.

Thapa, N., Liu, Z., Kc, D. B., Gokaraju, B., & Roy, K. (2020). Comparison of machine learning and deep learning models for network intrusion detection systems. *Future Internet*, *12*(10), 1–16. DOI: 10.3390/fi12100167

Toth, T., & Kruegel, C. (2002). Evaluating the impact of automated intrusion response mechanisms. Proceedings - Annual Computer Security Applications Conference, ACSAC, 2002-January, 301–310. DOI: 10.1109/CSAC.2002.1176302

Valiathan, P. (2002). Blended Learning Models. Learning Circuits. Astd, 2000–2003. https://purnima-valiathan.com/wp-content/uploads/2015/09/Blended-Learning-Models-2002-ASTD.pdf

Vinayakumar, R., Alazab, M., Soman, K. P., Poornachandran, P., Al-Nemrat, A., & Venkatraman, S. (2019). Deep Learning Approach for Intelligent Intrusion Detection System. *IEEE Access : Practical Innovations, Open Solutions*, *7*, 41525–41550. DOI: 10.1109/ACCESS.2019.2895334

Wu, Y. S., Foo, B., Mei, Y., & Bagchi, S. (2003). Collaborative intrusion detection system (CIDS): A framework for accurate and efficient IDS. Proceedings - Annual Computer Security Applications Conference, ACSAC, 2003-January(Acsac), 234–244. DOI: 10.1109/CSAC.2003.1254328

Xie, J. (2024). Application Study on the Reinforcement Learning Strategies in the Network Awareness Risk Perception and Prevention. *International Journal of Computational Intelligence Systems*, *17*(1), 112. Advance online publication. DOI: 10.1007/s44196-024-00492-x

Yellepeddi, S. M., Advisor, S. T., & Researcher, I. (n.d.). AI-Powered Intrusion Detection Systems : Real-World Performance Analysis. 4(1).

Zhang, Z., & Krunz, M. (2024). Preamble Forgery and Injection in Wi-Fi Networks: Attacks and Defenses. *IEEE Transactions on Mobile Computing*, *X*(X), 10752–10769. Advance online publication. DOI: 10.1109/TMC.2024.3383065

Zuech, R., Khoshgoftaar, T. M., & Wald, R. (2015). Intrusion detection and Big Heterogeneous Data: A Survey. *Journal of Big Data*, *2*(1), 3. Advance online publication. DOI: 10.1186/s40537-015-0013-4

Chapter 5
Artificial Intelligence in Healthcare Cybersecurity:
Developing an AI-Powered Cybersecurity Model for Healthcare Organizations

Palanivel Kuppusamy
http://orcid.org/0000-0003-1313-9522
Pondicherry University, India

Suresh Joseph Kanagaraj
Pondicherry University, India

ABSTRACT

Healthcare data protection and cybersecurity are essential for regular healthcare operations without interruptions. Numerous healthcare institutions have connected medical equipment and specialized hospital information systems for smooth operations. However, they face many significant security challenges and must secure health information from the growing cyberattacks. Healthcare organizations must use innovative technologies to keep ahead of these cyberattacks. Artificial Intelligence-based security solutions can react to cyber threats, automate time-consuming procedures, and obtain essential insights for more precise decision-making. Developing an AI-powered cybersecurity model for healthcare organizations can protect resources and manage threats in the healthcare environment. This chapter aims to develop an AI-powered cybersecurity model for healthcare organizations that detect malware, phishing, threats, predictive analysis, and vulnerability management in the healthcare environment.

DOI: 10.4018/979-8-3373-2922-2.ch005

INTRODUCTION

Recently, the healthcare sector and organizations [5] have seen a noticeable increase in several activities, including treatment delivery, with the rapid adoption of digital technologies. However, digital technologies pose several harmful cyber threats that could affect the operations of healthcare businesses and endanger patients. Today, the healthcare sector is a high-value target for hackers due to the sensitive nature of the data it manages. The disclosure of protected health information (PHI) [11] and personally identifiable information (PII) [11] may result from data security breaches. Also, the connected medical devices deployed for healthcare delivery and monitoring are frequently targeted ports of entry for attackers since they were not built with security as their primary concern. Hence, cybersecurity plays a vital role in the healthcare sector (*Srivastava, 2025*), protecting sensitive patient data and guaranteeing the availability, resilience, and protection of all healthcare activities.

Security Challenges in Healthcare Organizations

Healthcare organizations face significant security challenges due to distributed clinical locations, sensitive patient and financial data, healthcare applications and systems, connected medical devices, and users. These challenges (Tannenbaum, 2024) include data breaches, ransomware attacks, insider threats, vulnerabilities in medical devices, and the need to secure health information exchange, all exacerbated by the growing complexity of cyberattacks. Some of the existing security challenges are presented below:

- Many healthcare organizations use obsolete technology, including operating systems, network protocols, and software.
- The healthcare industry is expanding quickly and presents many employment options and prospects for professional progression.
- The security flaws provide hackers with an opportunity to attack healthcare operations.
- Cybercriminals can encrypt patient records and systems essential for diagnostics, treatment planning, and patient monitoring with complex techniques.
- Existing security systems are challenged with numerous security concerns, such as insider threats, data breaches, medical device exposures, Ransomware, and phishing attacks, which can potentially steal patient data and interfere with healthcare operations.

Thus, traditional healthcare security systems require assistance to stay current. Traditional healthcare cybersecurity solutions protect sensitive patient data and infrastructure with basic safety features like firewalls, antivirus applications, and access controls. These approaches, however, are frequently inadequate for the complexity of contemporary healthcare, especially when it comes to connected medical devices.

Motivation

Today, Ransomware is increasingly targeting healthcare businesses, with the potential to compromise healthcare data and hamper operations. Hence, healthcare organizations must effectively handle the increasing complexity of cyberattacks with encrypted information, segmenting networks, risk assessments, frequent staff training on risks like phishing, and strong incident response procedures. The motivation behind developing this chapter is/are given below:

a) Hospital information management systems (HIMS) [7] must protect information from internal/external cyberattacks, ensure the availability of medical services, maintain confidentiality, guarantee that the medical equipment operates correctly, ensure healthcare data integrity, and adhere to industry regulations.
b) Healthcare organizations must stop intrusions that can interfere with medical procedures, postpone care, or reveal private data, which could have detrimental effects.

The objective is to develop a cybersecurity model for healthcare organizations that aims to

- protect HIMS from theft, damage, and disruption, and protect unencrypted PHI on workstations, laptops, or network file sharing with insufficient security
- identify actual assaults more precisely than humans, provide fewer false-positive outcomes, and rank reactions according to their actual threats
- review enormous volumes of data on incidents so that security teams can respond quickly to neutralize the danger
- identifies and prevents emails that include PHI from being sent to the Internet, particularly emails or webmail provider access
- recognize and label the kinds of dubious emails and texts in the medical setting
- recognizes and prohibits PHI from being transferred to cloud storage or downloaded and copied on USB devices.

AI in Cybersecurity

Introducing Artificial Intelligence (AI) into healthcare organizations and businesses could solve these complex challenges. AI technology (*Ayush, 2024*) may automate time-consuming procedures and obtain essential insights, enabling quicker and more precise decision-making. AI technologies (*Courtney, 2025*) include machine learning (ML), deep learning (DL), neural networks (NN), natural language processing (NLP [10]), and large language models (LLMs) in security frameworks.

i. ML detects anomalies in healthcare network traffic, thwarting assaults, detecting unusual login times, indicating security breaches, and facilitating quicker responses.
ii. DL analyzes intricate data and finds sophisticated cybersecurity risks, such as changing malware strains. It makes complex cyberattacks necessary and dramatically speeds up detection and reaction times to previously unknown threats.
iii. NN facilitates the analysis of massive amounts of healthcare data, including firewall logs, to identify patterns and predict potential threats for detection.
iv. LLMs (like GPT-4) assist in automating reactions to security events, creating threat reports, and detecting phishing attempts. They can improve cybersecurity tools by comprehending linguistic context, allowing quicker and more precise decision-making.
v. NLP helps AI systems recognize phishing emails, spam, and social engineering assaults by allowing them to comprehend and interpret human language. NLP studies text and email patterns to find clues about fraudulent communication.

Examples of AI-powered cybersecurity tools are Darktrace, SentinelOne, Cylance, Cybereason, Vectra AI, Microsoft Security Copilot, and Tessian. These tools help healthcare businesses to improve their cybersecurity posture and lower the risk of breaches.

Proposed Solution

Developing robust AI-powered cybersecurity architectures and models can ensure data confidentiality, integrity, and availability in healthcare environments. Proposing an AI-powered cybersecurity model can enhance threat detection, prevention, and response. The proposed model can analyze vast amounts of data, identify patterns, and quickly adapt to new threats. This proposed model automates tasks, reduces false positives, and improves threat detection accuracy. It can perform various functions such as automated response, malware analysis, phishing detection, predictive analysis, threat detection, and vulnerability management in the healthcare environment.

The key features of the AI-powered cybersecurity model are threat detection, anomaly detection, malware detection and prevention, automated incident response, proactive threat intelligence, enhanced security analytics, and adaptive security. The benefits of the proposed model are improved threat detection accuracy, faster response times, reduced human workload, continuous adaptation, and enhanced security posture.

Chapter Organization

This chapter can have an *introduction* and a *background* section to discuss key trends in healthcare cybersecurity, various cybersecurity threats, examples, and AI applications in healthcare cybersecurity. The *literature review and methodology* section presented various articles that were reviewed, and the proposed methodology. The *results and discussion* section presented healthcare cybersecurity solutions, a secure healthcare ecosystem, a proposed AI-powered cybersecurity model, various use cases, and future enhancements of the proposed model. Finally, the *conclusion* section concludes this chapter.

BACKGROUND

This section presents the growing healthcare data breaches, threats, AI-powered security solutions, etc. It presents the different cyberattacks that put healthcare information at risk, PHI [11], and cybersecurity solutions for healthcare institutions.

Key Trends in Healthcare Cybersecurity

Healthcare organizations create a lot of information, including sensitive or secret information, and the number of people utilizing devices and applications has expanded significantly. The digitalization of medical records and the growth of provider data sharing have significantly increased the attack surface. The key trends influencing the rise in attacks in the healthcare industry are below:

- *The Growth of Telemedicine* [12], *virtual healthcare* [13], *and e-health* [2]. Telemedicine uses suitable virtual health services over the healthcare cloud. The healthcare cloud can introduce hazards to healthcare services provided by remote equipment.

- *Connected Medical Devices* [1] *and IoMT* [15]. Healthcare facilities and hospitals employ wearable medical devices, monitoring sensors, and IoMT devices. IoMT devices coupled to a cloud-based network are exposed to attacks to store and share information, and healthcare organizations' attacks often go unmonitored for vulnerabilities.
- *AI for Threat Detection and Response.* AI and ML tools can identify and promptly stop threats. Healthcare institutions must lower vulnerabilities, maintain compliance, quickly identify suspicious activity, and react to assaults with these tools.
- *Employee Training and Awareness.* Healthcare organizations must protect employees against regular assaults by educating them about attacks and vulnerabilities.
- *Regulatory Compliance:* A successful data breach might indicate non-compliance. Healthcare institutions must take appropriate precautions to secure patients' private personal information (PPI) as per HIPAA [6] requirements.

Cybersecurity Threats

Table 1 shows the typical security breaches (Putty, 2025*)* in the medical field, including phishing, Ransomware, Malware, insider threats, data theft, and hacked IoT devices [8].

Table 1. Typical Security Breaches in the Healthcare Field

S/N	*Cybersecurity Threats*	*Damages*
1	Malware	It comes from viruses, Trojan horses, spyware, and adware that damage computers and networks.
2	Phishing Attacks	They send phony emails that fool employees into revealing private information, such as passwords and bank account details.
3	Ransomware Attacks	They encrypt healthcare systems to prevent access or hold to release user information unless a ransom is paid.
4	APTs	APTs can penetrate networks and steal data over an extended period.
5	DDoS Attacks	They overload systems and interfere with operations by flooding the network with traffic.
6	Cloud Security Breaches	Vulnerabilities arise as healthcare organizations increasingly migrate to cloud-based systems for data storage and management.
7	AI-Powered Attacks	Identifying and neutralizing them is challenging, as they may adjust to security safeguards.

continued on following page

Table 1. Continued

S/N	*Cybersecurity Threats*	*Damages*
8	Deepfake Social Engineering	Advanced AI techniques create convincing deepfake audio and video targeting healthcare professionals.
9	Biometric Data Theft	Biometric data for patient identification and access control can become a new target for cybercriminals.
10	Data Breaches	Sensitive data access without authorization is a common problem.
11	Theft of Medical Data	Medical records can be used to perpetrate fraud, such as posing as someone else to get payment for medical services.
12	IoMT Attacks	The proliferation of IoMT devices has expanded the attack surface for cybercriminals.
13	Insider Threats	Due to negligence, stakeholders may misuse their privileges to steal data for their own gain. E.g., download harmful software.
14	Supply Chain Vulnerabilities	They make it susceptible to a cyberattack that might skew all pharmaceutical and medical device goods.
15	5G Network Exploits	Cybercriminals may exploit vulnerabilities in 5G infrastructure to launch attacks on connected healthcare systems.
16	Quantum Threats	Quantum technology may seriously threaten current encryption techniques for safeguarding medical data.
17	Zero-day Exploits	Healthcare organizations become risky due to the lack of a recognized défense.

Examples of Healthcare Cyberattacks

Data breaches may have a wide variety of effects on the healthcare sector (*Cooper, 2023*), possibly impacting all areas of a facility and, importantly, its patients. For example,

i. In 2015, Anthem Inc., the health insurance provider in the United States, had a significant data breach that exposed the private data of around 78.8 million clients, underscoring the serious repercussions of insufficient cybersecurity.
ii. The WannaCry ransomware attack in 2017 on the National Health Service in the United Kingdom caused severe cancellation of over 19,000 doctors' appointments.
iii. The 2017 NotPetya malware attack targeted third-party Ukrainian accounting software, significantly impacting operations at several healthcare institutions, and raising repercussions of linking systems with the service provider.
iv. In 2022, hackers attacked the AIIMS hospital in New Delhi, India. The hospital was forced into manual mode for a few weeks due to the encryption of 1.3 gigabytes of data. This attack impacted 30–40 million patients, including well-known national politicians.

Data breaches have far-reaching consequences for both healthcare institutions and patients. To maintain patient trust and ensure uninterrupted care, healthcare organizations must implement robust cybersecurity strategies—such as advanced encryption, access controls, AI, secure third-party collaborations, and frameworks like Zero Trust and SASE—to protect data, comply with regulations, defend against threats, and safeguard the integrity of critical systems [14].

AI Applications in Healthcare Cybersecurity

AI-driven cybersecurity solutions can evolve and detect new threats in the healthcare environment. They can enhance threat detection, automate security tasks, improve incident response, data protection, and privacy, implement proactive security measures, and improve overall resilience in healthcare organizations. AI can protect the healthcare industry from cyberattacks by facilitating threat identification and prevention.

i. *Threat Detection and Prevention.* AI-powered cybersecurity model detects and prevents threats. It analyses potential hazards holistically and correlates data from many sources. For instance, AI systems can identify and investigate odd data access during non-standard hours or abrupt changes in an employee's access habits. Security experts can react quickly to this threat detection, reducing possible harm.
ii. *Privacy and Compliance.* AI-powered solutions can monitor data usage and access, guaranteeing that only authorized individuals can access patient details. Detecting breaches preserves patient confidence while protecting healthcare data.
iii. *Compliance with the Regulatory Authority.* AI can make reporting and auditing easier and make it easier to demonstrate competence with monitoring authorities. AI contributes to healthcare businesses by providing the resources to protect data privacy while safely meeting regulatory obligations.

Machine Learning (ML)

It improves healthcare security by protecting sensitive patient data, identifying potential breaches, and unauthorized access with biometric technologies. ML algorithms prevent malware and DDoS assaults by sniffing out anomalies in medical equipment and network traffic by analyzing patterns in large datasets. Moreover, ML makes the environment for digital healthcare safer by anonymizing patient data and sending out real-time security threat alerts. Examples of ML applications are identifying unusual access patterns, protecting EHR/EMR [16], and detecting Malware. *Table 2* shows examples of how ML algorithms are used for ML in cybersecurity.

Table 2. ML algorithms for Healthcare Cybersecurity

S/N	*ML Algorithm*	*Cybersecurity Tasks*
1	Decision Tree (DT)	It detects and classifies threats.
2	Dimensionality Reduction (DR)	It removes noisy and inappropriate data.
3	K-means Clustering (K-means)	It detects Malware.
4	K-Nearest Neighbors (kNN)	It applies to facial recognition and verification.
5	Linear Regression (LiR)	It predicts network security results.
6	Logistic Regression (LoR)	It is used for fraud detection.
7	Naïve Bayes (NB)	It is used for intrusion detection.
8	Random Forest (RF)	It classifies phishing attacks.
9	Support Vector Machine (SVM)	It classifies, detects, and predicts blocklisted IP addresses and port addresses.

ML models have been classified as supervised (labeled), unsupervised (unlabelled), semi-supervised (semi-labelled), and reinforcement learning. These models perform a significant function in detecting anomalies. *Table 3* shows the ML models, their uses, their purposes in healthcare, and examples.

Table 3. ML models in healthcare cybersecurity

S/N	*ML*	*Applications/ Functions*	*Purpose*	*Examples*
1	Supervised	• It detects distinct labels for threats - spoofing & scanning. • It classifies a target variable as a security risk (DoS/DDOS). • Models are trained on benign and malicious data to determine if new samples are harmful.	• Binary classification • Multi-class classification • Regression modeling • Ensemble learning	• Adaptive boosting • LiR • LoR • NB • NN • RF • SVM
2	Unsupervised	• It finds new attack patterns and detects odd activity. • It reduces the impact of zero-day assaults.	• Anomaly detection • Association mining • Clustering • DR	• K-means, NN • Probabilistic clustering • PCA • SVD
3	Semi-supervised	• Adversarial NN • It detects malicious and benign bots, Malware, and Ransomware.	• Fraud detection • Labeling data • Machine translation	• Label propagation • Consistency regularization • Self-training • Pseudo-labeling
4	Reinforcement	• Uses adversarial simulation to train ML models. • It detects and replies to threats in real-time. • It detects intrusion. • CPS & DDoS défense	• The environment has a model, but there is no analytical answer. • Collects data and provides a simulation model.	• Deep Deterministic • DQN • Policy Gradient (DDPG)

Deep Learning (DL)

It enhances healthcare security by strengthening data protection, detecting threats, and safeguarding patient privacy with innovative techniques, including robust biometric authentication, safe EHR processing, and adversarial défense for medical imaging. It evaluates enormous volumes of data, identifies complex patterns, and quickly and accurately forecasts possible security threats with ANN algorithms. DL methods, such as RNNs and CNNs models, are trained on massive datasets of network interactions, learning to identify anomalous behaviours, predictive threat analysis, and automated response mechanisms. DL architecture (*Kumar et al., 2021*) could detect the latest intrusion attacks and provide accurate medical data protection.

- *Intrusion detection systems.* DL models analyze network traffic in real-time, identify complex, multi-stage attack patterns, and distinguish between legitimate and malicious activities with unprecedented accuracy.
- *Predictive analytics.* It leverages advanced ML algorithms and forecasts potential security vulnerabilities before exploiting them. It analyzes historical attack patterns to predict future threats and creates proactive défense mechanisms that adapt in real-time.

For instance, DL models can predict potential ransomware attack vectors, identify unusual user behavior patterns, detect early signs of system compromise, and generate automated responses.

Neural Networks (NN)

In cybersecurity, NNs are excellent at identifying and mitigating security issues. NN-powered systems can recognize, evaluate, and eliminate possible risks in milliseconds. This prompt action can halt ransomware attacks, prevent data exfiltration, and preserve the integrity of private healthcare data. NNs have applications in drug research, biochemical analysis, image analysis, and diagnostic systems. Artificial neural networks (ANNs) are used in biochemical analysis to evaluate blood and urine samples, monitor diabetics' blood glucose levels, identify fluid ion levels, and identify pathological disorders.

Natural Language Processing (NLP)

NLP is considered the healthcare data protection techniques that protect healthcare data.

- NLP-based healthcare data encryption and access controls are strong security measures that safeguard healthcare data.
- NLP improves data integrity by spotting irregularities and discrepancies in medical records. It helps healthcare organizations ensure accuracy and reliability.
- NLP can reduce data breaches by automating detection and protecting sensitive data.

Large Language Models (LLMs)

Generative Pre-trained Transformer (GPT) architectures and LLMs are well-suited to healthcare cybersecurity, where threats are becoming more complex and multidimensional. LLMs are redefining cybersecurity in the healthcare industry, changing the digital protection scene, and giving medical personnel innovative ways to fend off a constantly evolving attack scenario. LLM systems use DL algorithms and sophisticated NNs to comprehend, evaluate, and react to any security risks instantly, going beyond conventional cybersecurity techniques. With actionable intelligence, LLMs redefine the boundaries of healthcare cybersecurity, offering a level of previously unimaginable protection.

Healthcare data protection is enhanced, and the expense of data breaches and associated fines is decreased. *Table 4* shows the applications of AI in healthcare cybersecurity.

Table 4. Applications of AI technologies in healthcare cybersecurity

S/N	*Cybersecurity*	*Technology*	*Roles and Functions*
1	Anomaly Detection	ML	Identify unusual patterns in network traffic, user behavior, or system activity, helping to detect potential security breaches.
2	Endpoint Security	ML	Detect and prevent malware infections by analyzing system behavior and using ML to identify threats.
3	Threat Intelligence	ML	Analyze threat intelligence data to identify emerging threats, understand attack vectors, and predict future threats.
4	Malware Analysis	DL	Analyze images of Malware or code to identify malicious patterns and classify them.
5	Phishing Detection	NLP	Analyze email content to identify phishing attempts by looking for suspicious language, patterns, and URLs.
6	Threat Intelligence Gathering	NLP	Extract information from social media, forums, and other online sources to identify potential threats and understand attacker tactics.
7	Chatbot Security	NLP	NLP can be used to create chatbots that can assist users with security-related questions and automate security tasks.

continued on following page

Table 4. Continued

S/N	*Cybersecurity*	*Technology*	*Roles and Functions*
8	Image Analysis	CV	Analyze images to identify malicious content, such as fake websites and malware screenshots/images used in phishing campaigns.
9	Intrusion Detection	CV & DL	Analyze network traffic patterns by examining the visual characteristics of network packets.
10	Threat Detection and Analysis	LLM	Analyze network traffic and system logs to identify real-time suspicious behavior, recognize subtle anomalies, and enhance the speed and accuracy of threat detection.
11	Automating Routine Tasks	LLM	Automate repetitive security tasks like scanning for attacks, fixing simple vulnerabilities, and performing assessments, freeing cybersecurity teams to focus on complex issues.
12	Vulnerability Assessment	LLM	Identify vulnerabilities in code by analyzing patterns and anomalies in software.
13	Phishing Detection	LLM	Analyze email content and text for malicious intent, helping to identify and block phishing attacks.
14	Malware Analysis	LLM	Analyze malware samples to extract common malicious code patterns and behavioral characteristics, aiding in the analysis and detection of new malware variants.
15	Penetration Testing	LLM	Assist in penetration testing by anticipating vulnerabilities and suggesting actionable fixes.
16	Incident Response	LLM	Help with incident response by providing rapid analysis of the situation, suggesting mitigation strategies, and automating responses.
17	Cyber Forensics	LLM	Assist in forensic analysis by parsing through logs and data to determine the cause and method of attack.
18	Data Augmentation	LLM	Augment training datasets, diversify training examples, and reduce dependence on labor-intensive data curation.

Healthcare Ecosystems

Healthcare services span both public and private sectors, encompassing a diverse ecosystem that delivers specialized care (e.g., chronic, acute, home, and ongoing care). Providers like hospitals deliver medical services directly, while payers such as insurers manage payments. Health records are used for care coordination, eligibility, and claims, and must be securely shared among hospitals, nursing centers, labs, and other providers. A range of suppliers—pharmaceutical manufacturers, medical equipment makers, and IT/cloud service providers—support operational needs. Given its critical impact on public health and safety, the sector is closely regulated by government authorities to ensure quality care and prevent misuse of protected patient data.

Figure 1. Healthcare Ecosystem Overview

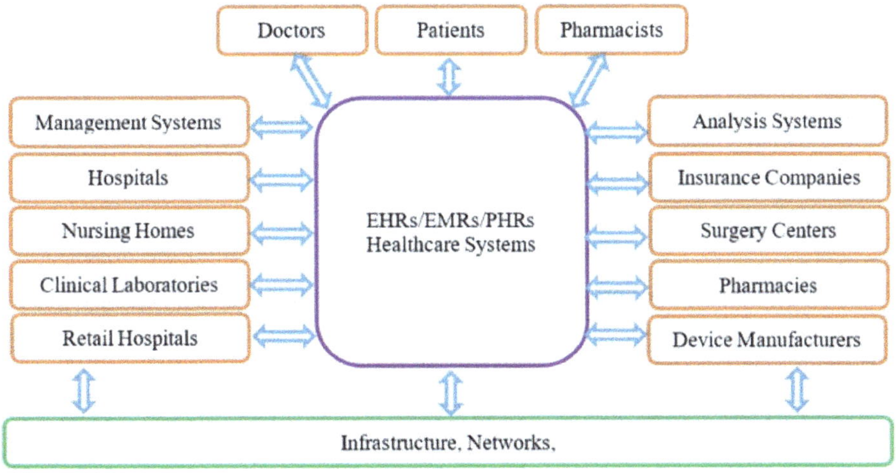

In this complex ecosystem, it is easier for hacker groups or state-sponsored hackers, based on personal interests, to attack specific targets in the industrial ecosystem. The healthcare industry does not allow service interruption, and involves protected health records in data storage and exchange between healthcare payers and providers. Also, misuse of this information may even pose a national security threat if used by terrorists or malicious individuals. In the healthcare industry, suppliers or insurers must meet strict cybersecurity requirements for transmitting, accessing, or storing protected data. Thus, healthcare industries should manage their cybersecurity to avoid exposing the company and the public to threats.

Security Challenges Considered

Healthcare institutions that depend on heterogeneous services must consider some of the most common vulnerabilities, including:

- *Legacy systems:* Many healthcare organizations still use obsolete operating systems and applications. Hackers may use these outdated systems' vulnerabilities to obtain access.
- *Unprotected medical devices:* Digitally connected devices, such as heart monitors and MRI scanners, can be compromised if the correct procedures are not followed.
- *Human error:* Communication-based attacks (such as phishing emails) provide hackers access to networks and enable them to steal information.

- *Third parties:* Healthcare companies give third-party contractors access to sensitive data. As a result, healthcare data may be at risk if they have inadequate cybersecurity.

These flaws make healthcare organizations vulnerable to Ransomware, other harmful software, and targeted fraud schemes like phishing scams.

Motivational Factors

Today, the frequency and severity of cyberattacks and the leakage of PHI have increased in cybersecurity (Cartwright, 2023*)* because of the COVID-19 epidemic, the rapid expansion of IoMT devices, and the use of EMR. The factors considered for the development of AI-powered cybersecurity solutions are below:

i. All IoMT devices are interconnected to a hospital network. Hence, there is a chance that a malicious actor might access hospital systems either to obtain PHI for financial gain or to launch an attack to induce incorrect monitoring, change device settings, or even gain access to the EMR/IoMT.
ii. The growing wireless connectivity of anesthetic and intensive care unit devices and implantable devices, as well as the exponential growth in the Internet of Medical Things, pose a serious and immediate threat to patient safety.
iii. A breach in healthcare information management infrastructure may result from the many endpoints that provide data access in the healthcare industry. These endpoints might be considered the weak points of the healthcare data management system.
iv. The COVID-19 pandemic has burdened the healthcare industry tremendously, and the shifts in many caregivers' work schedules have made the sector even more vulnerable to cyberattacks.
v. The healthcare sector has historically underfunded cybersecurity. The industry is now vulnerable due to the lack of investment in cybersecurity.
vi. The healthcare sector is preparing for more catastrophic hacks or PHI breaches since PHI is advertised, and technically weak IoT devices are employed for healthcare monitoring and management.

These factors motivate the development of an AI-powered cybersecurity model for hospitals and healthcare organizations.

LITERATURE REVIEW AND METHODOLOGY

In 2023, Accenture showed how AI speeds up reaction to possible data breaches by reducing detection and response times by as much as 60%. Similarly, HIMSS [17] pointed out that AI systems that constantly track and examine data might cut the potential of security breaches in the healthcare industry in half. These results highlight how AI might reduce the mistakes and delays usually connected to human-driven answers.

The complexities of building cybersecurity capabilities at hospitals and how these internal factors combine to create a hospital cybersecurity system (Jalali and Kaiser, 2018*)*. He et al. (2021) outlined the cybersecurity issues, the health sector's remedies, and the areas that require improvement to combat the recent cyberattack surge. *Palanivel and Suresh (2023)* reported that the current security practices in the educational environment were outdated and proposed a multi-cloud cybersecurity model. Kuppusamy and Khang (2024) suggested a real-time cybersecurity paradigm for a multi-cloud-based high-tech agricultural system.

Bajwa et al. (2021) provided an overview of recent developments in the use of AI in healthcare and a road map for creating safe, dependable, and efficient AI systems. Alowais et al. (2023) summarized the state of AI in clinical practice, covering its possible uses in patient interaction, treatment suggestions, and disease diagnosis.

The confidentiality and integrity of critical healthcare data were compromised (*Yeng et al., 2021*) because glass breakage can result in widespread unauthorized access, which could be problematic when determining illegitimate access in security measures. Tucci et al. (2022) conducted a thorough literature study to understand better the trust dynamics between medical AI and end users who are healthcare experts.

Javaid et al. (2023) examined several cybersecurity technologies, characteristics, and functions in the healthcare industry. According to Arefin (2024), the primary uses of AI in healthcare data security include its efficiency in managing vulnerabilities and adhering to regulations. Data breaches in healthcare organizations require digital protection models to identify and predict results and evaluate trends in healthcare data breaches. Kuppusamy (2024) examined the significance of cyberattacks and put out an architectural paradigm for digital trust for linked medical equipment in real-time healthcare.

AI in healthcare has transformed operational and patient outcomes in the contemporary period. However, with these developments comes the crucial problem of cybersecurity. Bonagiri et al. (2024) explored the relationship between AI-driven technology and cybersecurity in the healthcare industry, particularly emphasizing healthcare data and medical device protection. They highlighted the vulnerabilities that arise as healthcare systems become increasingly interconnected and reliant on AI algorithms.

Emerging technologies such as Blockchain, zero-trust architectures, advanced encryption methods, biometric authentication, and behavioral analytics addressed evolving threats to healthcare data and critical systems. Integrating these technologies aimed to create a robust, adaptive cybersecurity ecosystem in healthcare.

Healthcare systems have been overtaken by COVID-19, which has caused bad actors to attack them and draw attention to several cybersecurity problems (*Jahangir et al., 2022*). AI is used to develop a strong and safe Human-in-the-Loop system for mental health issues by addressing cybersecurity issues. *Baohan (2024)* evaluated how ML and DL can improve intrusion detection systems for IoMT. ML and DL in IDS detect unusual activities and their effectiveness within the IoMT. Abidi et al. (2024) proposed a CMLP model to detect adversarial attacks on patients' medical records and promptly alert them to prevent data leakage.

Hafeez et al. (2025) proposed a cyber-attack detection system with a centralized and federated transfer learning mode for the healthcare sector. The Edge of Things framework detects and classifies various threats, such as information gathering, DoS/DDoS attacks, Malware attacks, Injection attacks, and man-in-the-middle attacks. Mahendrakhan and Nagarathna (2022) proposed an all-encompassing AI-driven IoT eHealth architecture that uses an ICNN to increase accuracy and efficiency across the essential quality of service parameters. Aaron (2023) presented a systematic review of the application of DL approaches such as DBN, GAN, RNN, etc., for cybersecurity.

Unal et al. (2022) investigated the security risks of big data platforms in health care and how ML could mitigate security risks. Technology frameworks (Jain et al., 2024*)* could avoid attacks in the healthcare sector. Alsolami et al. (2024) investigated the efficacy of ML models (such as Stacking, Bagging, and Boosting, using RF and SVM) for intrusion detection in the IoMT, aiming to enhance cybersecurity défense and protect sensitive healthcare data. Mishra et al. (2024) proposed a hybrid approach (ABC and 3D CNN) to offer a secure communication method and defend the network from intrusions.

Creating innovative cybersecurity has become essential, especially for IoT networks, since the scope of the Internet has grown and cyberattacks have evolved. Advanced methods for identifying and thwarting attacks must be developed due to the growing complexity and frequency of cyber threats.

Podder et al. (2021) systematically reviewed the application of DL approaches for cybersecurity, including DBN, GAN, RNN, and others. An AI-based CNN detected cyber threats excellently. *Alzahrani (2023)* presented unique conditions using the ACO-CNN mechanism for detecting cyberattacks in the healthcare sector. A new multilayer perceptron trainer with a cybersecurity focus (Al Hwaitat & Fakhouri, 2024) uses evolutionary computing techniques to improve neural network training in cybersecurity and increase its accuracy and resilience to different attack vectors.

Identifying cyberattacks is a critical function of IDS. Data labeling difficulties, incorrect conclusions, and vulnerability to malicious data injections are drawbacks of using ML algorithms for cybersecurity. Oyinloye et al. (2025) provided an updated learning strategy for ANN to address data categorization problems caused by unbalanced data.

Hamid and Brohi (2024) have noted potential directions for future research in cybersecurity, healthcare, and threat models with LLMs. Nagaraja and Bahsi (2025) employed the STRIDE technique to map potential vulnerabilities introduced by every aspect and identify subsystems and their data flows to analyze risks in LLM-powered healthcare systems comprehensively. According to Dennstädt et al. (2025), physicians, researchers, and companies must collaborate to reconcile closed and open LLM approaches to ensure effective, secure implementation.

Ravindar et al. (2023) looked at the ethical issues raised by NLP-driven medical chatbots, paying special attention to patient confidentiality, transparency, bias mitigation strategies, user viewpoints, and cybersecurity. Silvestri et al. (2023) contributed to efficiently analyzing risks and vulnerabilities by utilizing ML models to identify threats and vulnerabilities that may impact the healthcare system. Oyinloye et al. (2025) addressed data classification issues brought on by imbalanced data by offering an improved learning technique for ANN.

Integrating IoT technologies in hospital environments has introduced significant cybersecurity challenges, particularly in protecting healthcare data and operations. Almojel and Mishra (2024) proposed advanced ML models (LSTM-CNN) for behavior analysis and anomaly identification in hospital IoT networks. Shafiullah (2025) promoted innovation in healthcare technology for improved patient care and system efficiency by presenting a novel method for safeguarding IoT-healthcare diagnosis models, validating performance improvements with real-world datasets, and offering perceptive suggestions for future research directions.

Key Findings

The literature review identifies the functions to be carried out in the proposed cybersecurity model for healthcare organizations.

i. Develop a cybersecurity model and evaluate the cybersecurity capabilities in healthcare organizations.
ii. Examine cybersecurity threats to the healthcare organization, and prioritize actions to improve cybersecurity within the healthcare organization.
iii. Share knowledge and best practices across the healthcare organization, and tailor cybersecurity practices to the healthcare organization's unique needs.

The proposed cybersecurity model can manage threats and protect patients through the following systems:

i. Endpoint protection systems and phishing emails
ii. Data protection, incident response, and loss prevention
iii. Access, network, asset, and vulnerability management
iv. Medical devices or IoMT security
v. Cybersecurity rules and policies

Methodology

This chapter explains how cybersecurity and AI may be used to create a complex security paradigm in the healthcare industry. The study's primary consumers are patients and healthcare organizations, with a focus on safety concerns and the authenticity and openness of healthcare transactions and activities. Research has been done on creating an AI-powered cybersecurity model using various techniques, including AI, ML, DL, NLP, and LLM. Research gaps still exist in this field, including cybersecurity and AI-enabled healthcare.

As a result, this chapter examines data from scientific databases from the last few years, including blogs and international journals. A systematic literature study covering the literature on AI-based cybersecurity design reveals an objective assessment of the current models and architectures. AI/ML-based models and studies released between 2021 and 2025 were examined for security considerations in the healthcare setting. In this chapter, the qualitative methodologies are used.

RESULTS AND DISCUSSIONS

Healthcare cybersecurity solutions are designed to safeguard healthcare data privacy and security while preserving the availability and integrity of vital infrastructure and systems. This section presents a secure healthcare ecosystem, a proposed cybersecurity model, advantages and disadvantages, etc.

Healthcare Cybersecurity Solutions

The healthcare industry involves several stakeholders to protect people's private health information. The primary stakeholders include patients, healthcare professionals or providers, medical facilities, health insurance companies, and healthcare data management corporations. Healthcare cybersecurity solutions range from basic practices like regular software upgrades and staff training to more complex strategies. These include safeguarding medical networks against networked devices and equipment (such as MRI scanners, X-ray machines, and IoT devices). The wide variety of healthcare cybersecurity solutions includes actions to guarantee a safer and more secure healthcare environment.

i. They offer healthcare data access, and apps must be role-based using an approved, well-defined, documented matrix.
ii. It must provide Internet and USB device access, and network access should be done securely through firewalls.
iii. Healthcare applications must be accessed through multifactor authentication.
iv. The healthcare cloud, which includes Google Drive and Microsoft OneDrive, enables consumers to maintain their data in a highly secure cloud environment.
v. It stores all medical images and scanned documents in an encrypted format.
vi. Healthcare data should be stored independently at multiple locations. The actual copy of the healthcare data must be available at any other secure location to easily continue the healthcare processes from this location.
vii. All healthcare operations, including data gathering, storing, analyzing, publishing, developing programming, testing, and deployment, need to be continually monitored.

The solutions assist medical organizations in protecting their networks, systems, personnel, patients, data, and equipment. These solutions safeguard an organization's whole IT architecture, including data centers, cloud computing, and life-saving equipment, and they are connected to a healthcare platform. They enable healthcare institutions to integrate networking, protection, and surveillance into a single system, providing centralized visibility and control over networks and data while assisting them in combating cyberattacks.

A Secure Healthcare Ecosystem

Healthcare services are diverse and large-scale, covering public and private sectors. *Figure 2* shows the secured healthcare ecosystem providing patient services to meet their specialized needs. The healthcare payers and providers consist of hospitals and nursing centers that directly provide medical-related services to patients. The insurance companies manage the payment of medical services. Healthcare companies use health records to handle patient care, eligibility, or claims. Patients' data must be shared between hospitals and nursing centers, or patients' pathology must be sent to laboratories for analysis. Healthcare providers will also transmit or access health records to each other.

Figure 2. Secured Healthcare Ecosystem

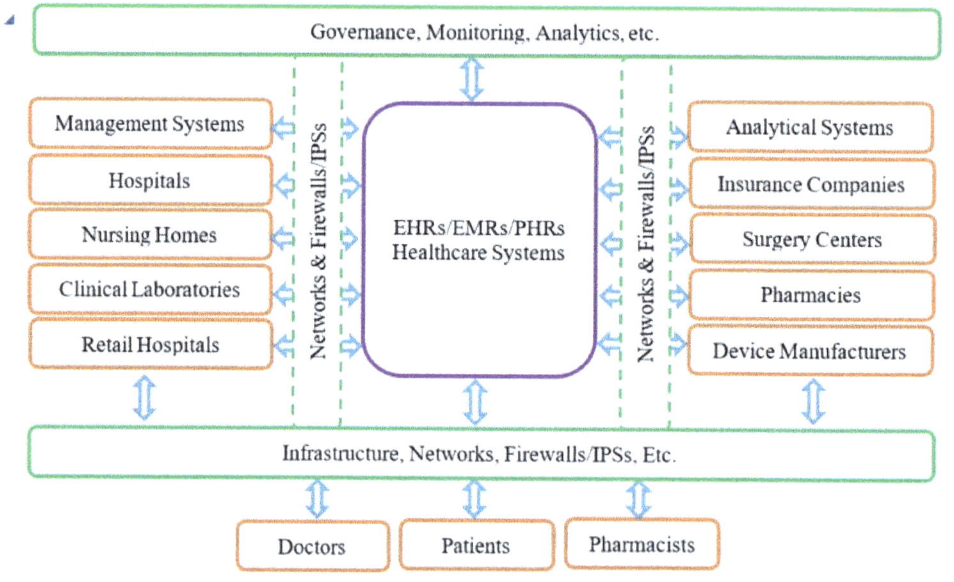

To ensure smooth healthcare operations, various suppliers—including pharmaceutical manufacturers, medical equipment providers, and IT/cloud service vendors—fulfill diverse needs. Given the sector's direct impact on public health and safety, governments enforce strict oversight to maintain care quality and prevent misuse of protected data. Consequently, suppliers and insurers must comply with rigorous cybersecurity requirements for handling sensitive information, and healthcare organizations must proactively manage cybersecurity to protect the public from potential threats.

Connected Medical Devices

It includes wearable devices, automated dispensing devices, implantable devices, remote patient monitoring, and medical equipment.

- *Automated Dispensing Devices:* Smart pill dispensers, syringes, and inhalers ensure accurate medication delivery.
- *Connected Medical Equipment:* MRIs, CT scanners, and internet-enabled infusion pumps all automatically upload data to a patient's EHRs.
- *Implantable Devices:* Pacemakers and other implantable devices require robust security to prevent unauthorized access and manipulation.

- *Remote Patient Monitoring:* Devices that allow real-time monitoring of vital signs and other health parameters from a distance.
- *Wearable Devices:* Fitness trackers, smartwatches, glucose monitors, and ECG monitors collect vital health data and transmit it to healthcare providers.

Connected medical devices are paramount to patient safety and data protection.

Factors Considered

As suggested by Tucci et al. (2022), the proposed cybersecurity model considers factors such as scalability, interoperability, simplicity, and accessibility.

- *Accessibility:* The healthcare model should be accessible to stakeholders with disabilities, ensuring everyone can use the platform.
- *Autonomy:* Security systems operate autonomously to detect and respond to threats in real-time, reducing the burden on security teams.
- *Composability:* Security components can be easily integrated and combined to create customized security solutions tailored to specific needs.
- *Distributed Security:* Security controls are dispersed throughout the network, eliminating the reliance on a centralized perimeter défense.
- *Interoperability.* It must manage many hospitals and healthcare service providers to share updated healthcare data effectively. Security services seamlessly communicate and exchange threat intelligence, enabling real-time detection and response.
- *Scalability.* Healthcare providers can manage increasing data volumes without modifying their infrastructure, with related costs and disruptions. The model can seamlessly scale to accommodate growing users, devices, and applications.
- *Simplicity:* The healthcare user interfaces must be easy to understand and navigate, even for users unfamiliar with technology.

Challenges Addressed

The proposed AI-powered model is designed to address the following challenges. AI enhances situational awareness, enabling organizations to make informed, data-driven security decisions and stay resilient in an increasingly complex threat landscape.

- *Data Security and Privacy:* It protects against unwanted access and advanced cyber threats to private healthcare data.

- *Device Integrity:* It guarantees that IoMT devices will not be infiltrated or utilized as gateways for more extensive network attacks.
- *Network Security:* It safeguards the lines of communication between healthcare systems and IoMT devices.
- *Regulatory Compliance:* It must use cutting-edge IoMT technology while adhering to strict healthcare laws like HIPAA.
- *Scalability:* It guarantees that cybersecurity safeguards can keep up with the quickly expanding IoMT ecosystem.

Proposed AI-Powered Cybersecurity Model

The proposed AI-powered cybersecurity model shown in *Figure 3* leverages advanced AI to revolutionize cybersecurity through continuous risk and exposure management. It protects healthcare data, IoMT devices, network devices, and cloud environments. It identifies and prioritizes risks based on business impact by analyzing vast amounts of data from various sources, enabling security teams to focus on the most critical issues. It uses AI to quantify risk in financial terms, allowing healthcare businesses to align their cybersecurity strategy with broader economic goals. The suggested AI-driven approach ensures proactive risk reduction by automating procedures and smartly recommending remedial actions.

Figure 3. Proposed AI-Powered Cybersecurity Model

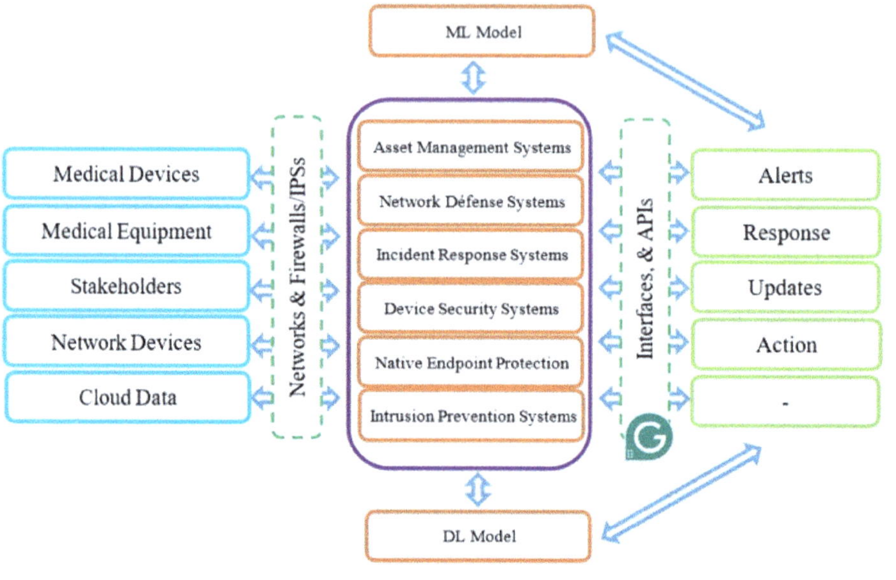

The AI-powered cybersecurity assistant provides risk-based guidance, real-time insights, and seamless integration with business systems to enhance decision-making anytime, anywhere. By automating threat detection, prioritizing vulnerabilities, and leveraging machine learning to continuously improve accuracy, the platform helps organizations proactively identify breaches, attack paths, and security weaknesses..

Automated response can automate security responses, such as isolating infected systems or blocking malicious traffic, significantly speeding up incident response times. *Phishing detection* analyzes email content, sender behavior, and other signs to identify and stop phishing attacks. *Threat detection* examines enormous volumes of data to find trends and abnormalities that point to possible dangers, such as zero-day assaults, which are hard for conventional techniques to find. *Malware Analysis* analyzes malware samples and identifies their behavior patterns to detect new and emerging threats. The *predictive analysis* automatically initiates proactive steps to minimize and protect against attacks by identifying possible vulnerabilities and dangers before they materialize. *Vulnerability management* helps organizations identify and remediate exposures by analyzing software code, network configurations, and systems.

The proposed model introduces diverse technical solutions to strengthen cybersecurity capabilities in healthcare industries with endpoint protection systems, management (asset, network, and vulnerability), incident response, and medical device cybersecurity.

- *Healthcare Asset Management.* This system generates an inventory of all scanned assets, including connected assets such as laptops, desktops, and diagnostic test equipment. This equipment interfaces with applications supporting cyber-physical systems (CPS) and transmitting executable code to connected assets. It verifies suppliers' assets and service vendors' laptops for regulatory compliance. It inspects all incoming or outgoing devices, conducts pre-shipment inspections, and conducts regular internal inspections for supply chain assessment.
- *Healthcare Network Défense.* They provide micro-segmentation to divide the network of high-risk systems into smaller units and control communication between servers and application services. It senses network traffic and production assets and fits into the customer's network without disrupting operations.
- *Incident Response.* It enables centralized monitoring, integration of indicators of compromise, and support for Syslog forwarding. An example is *StellarOne*. It maintains records of incidents, including audit, network, physical access, user, and administrator reporting, and reported supply chain problems.

- *Intrusion Prevention System (IPS).* The IPS monitors network traffic using signature-based tracking and rules set by the administrator. It enables stakeholders to control the connections and content transmissions between network equipment assets to ensure that unauthorized devices cannot establish connections or transmit content.
- *Medical Device Security.* IoMT devices are equipped with endpoint protection or vulnerability management. A medical device protection system (StellarEnforce) prevents malicious software from running on purpose-built systems, strictly adhering to pre-approved software using an application trust listing. It solves the problem of traditional antivirus software being unable to be installed on medical devices.
- *Native Endpoint Protection.* They can secure modernized and legacy endpoints side-by-side for modern healthcare operation systems. For example, *StellarProtect.* It has been designed to protect against known and unknown malware attacks, including zero-day vulnerabilities, with ML. It ensures operational security, including operation lock, USB device lock, data lock, and configuration settings lock, which can protect complex and numerous endpoints in healthcare operations.
- *Vulnerability Management.* Vulnerability management solutions (e.g., TXOne's Edge series) can shield them from attack without changing the asset. The signature-based antivirus protects connected healthcare devices [1] and equipment.

Security Modules

The proposed AI-powered cybersecurity model performs innovative functions that healthcare organizations face, such as increasing cyber threats to healthcare data, medical devices, and cloud apps.

- *AI-driven investigations*: This module can instantly identify anomalies and proactively monitor data access, guaranteeing a prompt reaction to questionable activity.
- *Autonomous threat response*: This module prevents assaults instantly and with limited disruption in the healthcare cloud and its premises environments.
- *Device Protection:* This module protects the devices and equipment installed in the healthcare organizations and involves the stakeholders.
- *Regulatory compliance*: It involves adhering to laws, regulations (such as HIPAA, GDPR [4], FDA [3], and NIST [9]), and guidelines set by governing bodies to safeguard patient rights, ensure quality care, protect data privacy, and prevent fraud and abuse within healthcare organizations.

The proposed cybersecurity strategy uses intent-based network partitioning, network access control, UEBA, and strong identity and access management (IAM) with deception tools to completely defend against internal and external attacks.

- *Data Protection.* Effective strategies for data protection include access control, regular audit, and patient empowerment.
- *Healthcare Analytics Platforms.* They are cloud-based healthcare data platforms that connect disparate data sources like claims and EHRs and ingest various data types, including FHIR-compliant patient health records. They are connected to an AI suite for real-time ML augmentation. Examples are Arcadia, Qrvey, and DataEz.
- *Threat-Resistant Networks.* They protect sensitive healthcare data and maintain operational integrity against cyberattacks and other healthcare threats. It protects healthcare networks from cyberattacks, including firewalls, intrusion detection systems, and regular security audits.

Various AI applications in healthcare cybersecurity are *behavioral analytics, network security, password protection and authentication, phishing detection and prevention control, and vulnerability management.*

Benefits and Challenges

The proposed model offers many benefits over traditional security approaches, with enhanced security, reduced complexity, increased agility, reduced costs, and improved threat detection and response. However, there are obstacles to its application in healthcare security (Arefin, 2024). The decision-making processes' openness and possible bias in AI algorithms must be adequately controlled to guarantee fair and efficient security solutions.

Ethical and Legal Concerns

AI-based cybersecurity systems managing Protected Health Information (PHI) raise significant ethical and legal concerns, including patient privacy, data security, informed consent, algorithmic bias, transparency, and professional accountability. Legally, they implicate tort law, liability for breaches, algorithmic responsibility, cross-border data transfers, and HIPAA compliance. Key solutions include establishing robust regulations, promoting transparency and explainability, enhancing data security, mitigating bias, clarifying accountability, and fostering public engagement.

USE CASES

It offers an examination of in-depth case studies from various medical facilities. These examples show effective methods and techniques for strengthening cyber-security défense, safeguarding healthcare data, and preserving reliable healthcare operations. *Table 5* offers a range of use cases that provide distinct perspectives on the intricacies of healthcare cybersecurity and the preventative actions required to counter these dynamic threats.

Table 5. Various use cases of the proposed healthcare security model

SN	*Use Cases, Purposes & Strategy*	*Challenge*	*Solution*	*Results*
1	• MedSecure Health Systems • Strengthening Cybersecurity in Healthcare • Patient-centered model	• To protect patient information and ensure uninterrupted healthcare services.	• Deployed advanced ML algorithms • Data encryption methods • Biometric authentication	• No successful data breaches
2	• VirtualHealth Connect • Enhance cybersecurity measures in Telehealth • Remote healthcare services	• To secure healthcare systems and patient data	• Provide end-to-end encryption for data transfer • Provide VPN setup • MFA	• Zero successful cyberattacks and potential security breaches.
3	• HealthNet Providers • Securing patient data in large-scale hospital networks • Delivering exceptional medical care	• to protect patient information • to ensure the continuous availability of critical medical systems.	• AI-based threat detection tools • Provided real-time alerts on suspicious activities.	• Blocked attempted attacks • Prevented data breaches.
4	• MindSpace Clinics • Boosting Cyber Resilience in Mental Health Services • Focuses on adapted mental healthcare	• To protect against breaches • To prevent illegal access and data exfiltration.	• To offer infrastructure with advanced encryption technologies • access protocols with biometric verification	• Shielded the organization from potential cyber threats, with no successful attacks

continued on following page

Table 5. Continued

SN	*Use Cases, Purposes & Strategy*	*Challenge*	*Solution*	*Results*
5	• Children's Health Alliance • Advancing cybersecurity in pediatric healthcare • Providing a nurturing and safe environment	• Expansion of digital health records • Increasing the connectivity of medical devices	• Upgrade the infrastructure with advanced firewalls and intrusion prevention systems. • Deploy EDR	• Provided protected sensitive patient data • Provided safe and reliable pediatric care.
6	• Cybersecurity Excellence • Real-time threat detection at the Mayo Clinic • Enhancing patient safety and healthcare delivery.	• Manage real-time cyber threats • Instant threat detection and response to prevent disruptions • Safeguard data integrity	• Leverages AI and ML • Identify abnormal activities & threats • Analyzing data patterns and predicting breaches • Enable proactive action	• Ensures the uninterrupted operation of healthcare services • Protect sensitive patient data.
7	• Innovative approach • Blockchain-Enhanced data security at the Cleveland Clinic • Enhancing medical treatments and protecting patient well-being.	• Inadequate in the face of complex cyberattacks • Compromise patient confidentiality and clinic credibility.	• Apply Blockchain technology • Encrypting patient data • Decentralized storage	• Ensuring patient information • Accessed securely by authorized personnel.
8	• Security management • Integrated Cyber Défense at Kaiser Permanente • provides high-quality care and medical practices.	• To safeguard sensitive information • To maintain system integrity across all digital platforms.	• Develop a unified cyber défense strategy • Real-time threat detection systems and Automated response solutions.	• Protected patient data • Ensured the continuity of its healthcare services.
9	• Protect healthcare networks • IoT Device Security at Johns Hopkins Medicine • Improve patient outcomes	• Integrating IoT devices into healthcare practices	• Develop a complete IoT security strategy	• Protected patient data • Ensured the safety of equipment.
10	• Empowers healthcare professionals & promises clinical excellence • Cybersecurity training initiative at Mass General Brigham	• To defend patient data and maintain the services' integrity	• Ambitious cybersecurity training initiative	• Reduced incidents of security breaches

Comprehensive cybersecurity is essential in healthcare to protect sensitive data, maintain trust, and ensure compliance, with best practices including sector-specific security, software solutions, service delivery, and regulatory adherence.

DISCUSSIONS

Healthcare has undergone a digital revolution, with advancements like EHRs, telemedicine, and AI-driven diagnostics boosting patient services. However, Cyberattacks can have serious repercussions, such as delays in medical procedures, clogged ERs, and interruptions to essential services. Attackers are trying more and more to disrupt organizations and demand ransom money since they know that any interruption might endanger human lives. Healthcare organizations are, therefore, seriously in danger.

Healthcare organizations must use new technologies and internet-connected devices to provide high-quality patient care, save lives, and cure diseases. Hospital systems and medical databases continue to experience data breaches due to fraudsters' growing interest in healthcare data. It is imperative to adhere to stringent guidelines and standards, such as strong MFA, access control, and encryption for sensitive data and transport.

The cybersecurity model represents a transformative approach to security, addressing the challenges of securing healthcare environments. By embracing distributed security, interoperable tools, and composable components, healthcare organizations can achieve enhanced security, reduced complexity, increased agility, and improved threat detection and response. As cyber threats evolve, the cybersecurity model stands poised to revolutionize how organizations protect their assets and data in the ever-changing digital landscape.

FUTURE ENHANCEMENTS

Integrating AI and IoT (AIoT) with cybersecurity creates new opportunities in data protection and healthcare. It can be an AIoT-powered threat detection, automated security responses, secure, personalized treatment plans, cyber-resilient automated diagnostics, and secure precision medicine.

- *Automated Security Responses:* AIoT-powered systems can minimize damage and downtime by reacting automatically to detected threats.
- *Cyber-Resilient Automated Diagnostics:* AI-powered data analysis can safeguard security and help detect early disease.

- *Secure Personalized Treatment Plans:* AIoT can provide individualized patient care plans while upholding stringent data protection.
- *Secure Precision Medicine:* AI models are fed IoT data to create highly tailored therapies with strong data security.
- *Threat Detection:* ML models look for and anticipate possible security risks by analyzing IoT data patterns.

CONCLUSION

Healthcare organizations are highly vulnerable to sophisticated cyberattacks due to their complex ecosystem of sensitive data, interconnected medical devices, and critical infrastructure that directly impacts patient safety. The rise of Healthcare IoT (HIoT) is transforming care delivery, research, and administration, enabling greater efficiency and patient-centricity when supported by robust security measures. This chapter explored key cybersecurity trends, threats, real-world examples, AI applications, and proposed an AI-powered cybersecurity model to build a secure healthcare ecosystem compliant with stringent privacy and data protection standards.

AI-powered cybersecurity is an essential milestone in the technical development of healthcare. It presents cybersecurity problems that need to be handled with competence, as it expands the possibilities for medical advancement. AI-powered solutions foster innovation while protecting patient interests. These healthcare leaders must lead in proactive défense regarding compliance, networked systems, human error, and resource limitations. AI can develop a healthcare setting that embraces patient confidence. This dynamic confluence portends a future in healthcare that is patient-centered, creative, and safe.

REFERENCES

Aaron, T. (2023). Artificial Neural Networks for Cybersecurity: A Comprehensive Review. *International Journal of Machine Learning Research in Cybersecurity and Artificial Intelligence*, *14*(1), 281–288.

Abidi, M. H., Alkhalefah, H., & Aboudaif, M. K. (2024). Enhancing healthcare data security and disease detection using a crossover-based multilayer perceptron in smart healthcare systems. *Computer Modeling in Engineering & Sciences*, *139*(1), 977–997. DOI: 10.32604/cmes.2023.044169

Al Hwaitat, A. K., & Fakhouri, H. N. (2024). Adaptive cybersecurity neural networks: An evolutionary approach for enhanced attack detection and classification. *Applied Sciences (Basel, Switzerland)*, *14*(19), 9142. DOI: 10.3390/app14199142

Almojel, F., & Mishra, S. (2024). Advancing Hospital Cybersecurity Through IoT-Enabled Neural Network for Human Behavior Analysis and Anomaly Detection. *International Journal of Advanced Computer Science and Applications*, *15*(5), 49–57. DOI: 10.14569/IJACSA.2024.0150506

Alowais, S. A., Alghamdi, S. S., Alsuhebany, N., Alqahtani, T., Alshaya, A. I., Almohareb, S. N., Aldairem, A., Alrashed, M., Bin Saleh, K., Badreldin, H. A., Al Yami, M. S., Al Harbi, S., & Albekairy, A. M. (2023). Revolutionizing healthcare: The role of artificial intelligence in clinical practice. *BMC Medical Education*, *23*(1), 689. DOI: 10.1186/s12909-023-04698-z PMID: 37740191

Alsolami, T., Alsharif, B., & Ilyas, M. (2024). Enhancing Cybersecurity in Healthcare: Evaluating Ensemble Learning Models for Intrusion Detection in the Internet of Medical Things. *Sensors (Basel)*, *24*(18), 5937. DOI: 10.3390/s24185937 PMID: 39338685

Alzahrani Ahmad, A. (2023). Using artificial intelligence and cybersecurity in medical and healthcare applications. (2023). *Information Sciences Letters*, *12*(3), 42. DOI: 10.18576/isl/120343

Arefin, S. (2024). Strengthening healthcare data security with AI-powered threat detection. *International Journal of Scientific Research and Management*, *12*(10), 1477–1483. DOI: 10.18535/ijsrm/v12i10.ec02

Bajwa, J., Munir, U., Nori, A., & Williams, B. (2021). Artificial intelligence in healthcare: Transforming the practice of medicine. *Future Healthcare Journal*, *8*(2), e188–e194. DOI: 10.7861/fhj.2021-0095 PMID: 34286183

Bonagiri, K., Marx, N., Gopalsamy, M., & Iyswariya, H. R., R. H., & S, S. (2024). AI-driven healthcare cybersecurity: Protecting patient data and medical devices. *2024 Second International Conference on Intelligent Cyber Physical Systems and Internet of Things*, 107–112. DOI: DOI: 10.1109/ICoICI62503.2024.10696183

Cartwright, A. J. (2023). The elephant in the room: Cybersecurity in healthcare. *Journal of Clinical Monitoring and Computing*, *37*(5), 1123–1132. DOI: 10.1007/s10877-023-01013-5 PMID: 37088852

Cooper, V. (2023, August 21). *Healthcare cybersecurity: Enhancing data security in healthcare*. Splashtop Inc. https://www.splashtop.com/blog/importance-of-cybersecurity-in-healthcare?

Dennstädt, F., Hastings, J., Putora, P. M., Schmerder, M., & Cihoric, N. (2025). Implementing large language models in healthcare while balancing control, collaboration, costs, and security. *NPJ Digital Medicine*, *8*(1), 143. Advance online publication. DOI: 10.1038/s41746-025-01476-7 PMID: 40050366

Hafeez, Y., Memon, K., AL-Quraishi, M. S., Yahya, N., Elferik, S., & Ali, S. S. A. (2025). Explainable AI in Diagnostic Radiology for Neurological Disorders: A Systematic Review, and What Doctors Think About It. *Diagnostics (Basel)*, *15*(2), 168. DOI: 10.3390/diagnostics15020168 PMID: 39857052

Hamid, R., & Brohi, S. (2024). A review of large language models in healthcare: Taxonomy, threats, vulnerabilities, and framework. *Big Data and Cognitive Computing*, *8*(11), 161. DOI: 10.3390/bdcc8110161

He, Y., Aliyu, A., Evans, M., & Luo, C. (2021). Health care cybersecurity challenges and solutions under the climate of COVID-19: Scoping review. *Journal of Medical Internet Research*, *23*(4), e21747. DOI: 10.2196/21747 PMID: 33764885

Jain, S., Ashok, P., & Prabhu, S. (2024). Emerging technologies for cybersecurity in healthcare: Evaluating risks and implementing standards. *2024 International Conference on Cybernation and Computation (CYBERCOM)*, 725–731. DOI: 10.1109/CYBERCOM63683.2024.10803219

Jalali, M. S., & Kaiser, J. P. (2018). Cybersecurity in hospitals: A systematic, organizational perspective. *Journal of Medical Internet Research*, *20*(5), e10059. DOI: 10.2196/10059 PMID: 29807882

Javaid, M., Haleem, A., Singh, R. P., & Suman, R. (2023). Towards Insighting cybersecurity for healthcare domains: A comprehensive review of recent practices and trends. *Cyber Security and Applications*, *1*(100016), 100016. Advance online publication. DOI: 10.1016/j.csa.2023.100016

Kuppusamy, P. (2024). A Digital Trust Architectural Model for Connected Medical Devices in the Healthcare Environment. In Hassan, A., Bhattacharya, P., Tikadar, S., Dutta, P., & Sagayam, M. (Eds.), *Lightweight Digital Trust Architectures in the Internet of Medical Things (IoMT)* (pp. 118–144). IGI Global Scientific Publishing., DOI: 10.4018/979-8-3693-2109-6.ch008

Kuppusamy, P., & Khang, A. (2024). An Advanced Cybersecurity Model for High-Tech Farming Using Machine Learning Approach. In Khang, A. (Ed.), *Agriculture and Aquaculture Applications of Biosensors and Bioelectronics* (pp. 461–495). IGI Global Scientific Publishing., DOI: 10.4018/979-8-3693-2069-3.ch026

Kuppusamy, P., & Suresh, J. K. (2023). Unified Cybersecurity Data Analytical Model for Smart Learning Operations. In Jimenez, R., & O'Neill, V. E. (Eds.), *Handbook of Research on Current Trends in Cybersecurity and Educational Technology* (pp. 92–120). IGI Global., DOI: 10.4018/978-1-6684-6092-4.ch006

Mahendrakhan, K., & Nagarathna, P. (2022). Cybersecurity in healthcare with artificial intelligence. *2022 IEEE 2nd Mysore Sub Section International Conference (MysuruCon)*, 1–8.

Mishra, N., Shivaji, G. B., Barekar, S. S., Dari, S. S., Dhabliya, D., & Patil, M. (2024). Artificial intelligence and machine learning in healthcare cybersecurity of current applications and future directions. *South Eastern European Journal of Public Health*, •••, 46–51. DOI: 10.70135/seejph.vi.750

Mo, B. (2024). Enhancing Cybersecurity in Healthcare: Machine Learning and Deep Learning Strategies for Intrusion Detection on the Internet of Medical Things, In Proc. of the 1st Int., Conf., on Engineering Management, Information Technology and Intelligence (EMITI 2024), 301–305. https://orcid.org/ 0009-0009-3413-2486.

Nagaraja, N., & Bahsi, H. (2025). Cyber threat modeling of an LLM-based healthcare system. *Proceedings of the 11th International Conference on Information Systems Security and Privacy*, 325–336. DOI: 10.5220/0013289700003899

Oyinloye, T. S., Arowolo, M. O., & Prasad, R. (2025). Enhancing cyber threat detection with an improved artificial neural network model. *Data Science and Management*, *8*(1), 107–115. DOI: 10.1016/j.dsm.2024.05.002

Podder, P., Bharati, S., Mondal, M. R. H., Paul, P. K., & Kose, U. (2021). Artificial neural network for cybersecurity: A comprehensive review. *arXiv [Cs.CR]*. DOI: 10.48550/ARXIV.2107.01185

Putty, C. (2025, March 12). Cybersecurity in healthcare: AI as a guard against threats. *Thoughtful.Ai*. https://www.thoughtful.ai/blog/cybersecurity-in-healthcare-ai-as-a-guard-against-threats

Ravindar, G., M., Abdul-Zahra, D. S., Subhashini, K., M., N., & Chawla, R. (2023). Healthcare chatbots with NLP and cybersecurity: Safeguarding patient data in the cloud. *2023 International Conference on Artificial Intelligence for Innovations in Healthcare Industries (ICAIIHI)*, 1–7.

Shafiullah, M. (2025). The FCM-guided deep learning model for low-frequency oscillation damping for electric power networks. *Neural Computing & Applications*, *37*(1), 105–121. DOI: 10.1007/s00521-024-10377-x

Silvestri, S., Islam, S., Papastergiou, S., Tzagkarakis, C., & Ciampi, M. (2023). A Machine Learning approach for the NLP-based analysis of cyber threats and vulnerabilities of the healthcare ecosystem. *Sensors (Basel)*, *23*(2), 651. DOI: 10.3390/s23020651 PMID: 36679446

Srivastava, S. (2024, October 24). Healthcare cybersecurity – key strategies and best practices to protect patient data. *Appinventiv*. https://appinventiv.com/blog/cybersecurity-in-healthcare/

Tannenbaum, Y. (2024, April 2). AI, cybersecurity, and the rise of large language models. *Palo Alto Networks Blog*. https://www.paloaltonetworks.com/blog/2024/04/ai-cybersecurity-and-large-language-models/

Tucci, V., Saary, J., & Doyle, T. E. (2022). Factors influencing trust in medical artificial intelligence for healthcare professionals: A narrative review. *Journal of Medical Artificial Intelligence*, *5*, 4–4. DOI: 10.21037/jmai-21-25

Unal, D., Bennbaia, S., & Catak, F. O. (2022). Machine learning for the Security of Healthcare systems based on the Internet of Things and edge computing. In *Cybersecurity and Cognitive Science* (pp. 299–320). Elsevier., DOI: 10.1016/B978-0-323-90570-1.00007-3

Yeng, P. K., Nweke, L. O., Yang, B., Ali Fauzi, M., & Snekkenes, E. A. (2020). Artificial intelligence–based framework for analyzing health care staff security practice: Mapping review and simulation study (Preprint). DOI: 10.2196/preprints.19250

KEY TERMS AND DEFINITIONS

Connected Healthcare Devices: smart elevators, smart heating, ventilation, air conditioning (HVAC) systems, infusion pumps, remote patient monitoring devices, etc.

E-Health: encompasses technologies to improve healthcare, including virtual healthcare.

FDA (Food and Drug Administration): a U.S. federal agency responsible for ensuring the safety and efficacy of food, drugs, cosmetics, and medical devices.

GDPR (General Data Protection Regulation): a European Union (EU) law that regulates how organizations within and outside the EU handle the personal data of EU residents. It protects personal data and ensures organizations collect and use it responsibly.

Healthcare Organizations: hospitals, biotechnology companies, insurance companies, healthcare providers, nursing homes, clinical centers, academic and research institutions, pharmaceutical industries, clinical labs, medical devices manufacturing firms, etc.

HIPAA (Health Insurance Portability and Accountability Act): a U.S. law enacted in 1996 that aims to protect the privacy and security of patient health information.

HIMS: includes EHR systems, computerized physician order entry systems, radiology information systems, clinical decision support systems, healthcare practice management support systems, and e-prescribing systems.

IoT or Smart Medical Devices: include electrocardiograms, thermometers, glucose monitors, ultrasounds, and more.

NIST: a non-regulatory U.S. government agency that develops and promotes measurements, standards, and technology.

NLP: responsible for the accurate and effective communication between computers and human beings using natural language.

PHI: the demographic information, medical histories, test and laboratory results, physical and mental health conditions, insurance information, and other data that a healthcare professional collects to determine appropriate care.

Telemedicine or Telehealth: refers specifically to using telecommunications technology for healthcare delivery.

Virtual healthcare: utilizes technology to deliver medical care remotely, offering patients convenient access to healthcare services and consultations.

Zero Trust (ZT) & Secure Access Service Edge (SASE): distinct frameworks for securing networks and resource access.

IoMT (Internet of Medical Things): refers to the network of medical devices and wearables connected to the Internet, enabling real-time data collection, analysis, and sharing for improved patient care, healthcare operations, and extended healthy life expectancy.

EHR/EMRs: digital versions of patient medical histories, enabling efficient storage, retrieval, and sharing of health information across different healthcare settings.

HIMSS: a global advisor, thought leader, and member association committed to transforming the health ecosystem.

APPENDIX

ABBREVIATIONS

ACO-CNN - Ant Colony Optimization-CNN
AI - Artificial Intelligence
ANN - Artificial Neural Networks
APT - Advanced Persistent Threats
CMLP - Crossover-based Multilayer Perceptron
CNN - Convolutional Neural Networks
CPS - Cyber Physical Systems
DBN - Deep Belief Networks
DDoS - Distributed Denial of Service
DL - Deep Learning
DQN - Deep Q Network
EDR - Endpoint Detection and Response
EHR/EMR - Electronic Health Record/Medical Record
GAN - Generative Adversarial Networks
HIMS - Hospital information management systems
HIMSS - Healthcare Information and Management Systems Society
HIPAA - Health Insurance Portability and Accountability Act
IAM - Identity and Access Management
IoMT/IMoT - Internet of Medical Things
LLM - Large Language Models
ML - Machine Learning
NIST - National Institute of Standards and Technology
NLP - Natural Language Processing
NN - Neural Networks
PCA - Principal Component Analysis
PHI - Protected Health Information
RNN - Recurrent Neural Networks
SVD - Singular Value Decomposition
UEBA - User and Entity Behavior Analytics

Chapter 6
Case Study:
Biometric Security and AI in Autonomous Vehicles

K. DanielRaj
http://orcid.org/0009-0001-9863-5682
Kalaignarkarunanidhi Institute of Technology, India

M. Robinson Joel
http://orcid.org/0000-0002-3030-8431
KCG College of Technology, India

A. Anu Priya
http://orcid.org/0009-0003-7048-5090
Kalaignarkarunanidhi Institute of Technology, India

T. Jasperline
Dr. G.U. Pope College of Engineering, India

L. Charumathi
Dr. G.U. Pope College of Engineering, India

ABSTRACT

This chapter examines the integration of biometric security and artificial intelligence (AI) in autonomous vehicles, focusing on their role in enhancing safety, personalization, and cybersecurity. It explores various biometric authentication methods, including facial recognition, fingerprint scanning, and voice recognition, to ensure secure access control and identity verification. Additionally, the chapter discusses AI-driven security mechanisms such as real-time threat detection, adaptive learning, and anomaly detection to mitigate risks related to fraud and unauthorized access. Key challenges, including data privacy concerns, cybersecurity threats, and system

DOI: 10.4018/979-8-3373-2922-2.ch006

reliability, are analyzed alongside potential solutions and advancements in AI-powered biometric security. Through industry insights and real-world applications, this chapter highlights the transformative impact of biometrics and AI in shaping the future of autonomous transportation.

1. INTRODUCTION

The transportation sector is undergoing a transformative shift with the emergence of autonomous vehicles (AVs), which enhance safety, efficiency, and convenience. These self-driving systems rely on artificial intelligence (AI), machine learning, and sensor technologies to operate independently. Leading companies such as Tesla, Waymo, and major automakers are significantly investing in the advancement of AV technology to minimize road accidents and optimize traffic flow (Alheeti et al., 2017).

As AVs integrate more deeply with smart infrastructure, cloud services, and vehicle-to-everything (V2X) communication, cybersecurity threats become a pressing concern. The increasing connectivity of AVs exposes them to hacking, data breaches, and unauthorized access. Consequently, the implementation of robust authentication mechanisms is crucial for ensuring vehicle security, data privacy, and seamless functionality (Arief & Rajamani, 2019).

Biometric security, enhanced by AI, offers a sophisticated solution to these cybersecurity challenges by enabling advanced user authentication and protecting AV systems from potential cyber threats. Conventional authentication methods such as passwords and PINs are prone to hacking, duplication, and brute-force attacks. Conversely, biometric authentication employs distinctive physical or behavioral traits—such as fingerprints, facial recognition, iris scans, and voice identification—to verify user identity. These biometric features are challenging to replicate, making them a highly secure authentication option for Avs (Bansal et al., 2016).

Beyond authentication, biometric security plays a vital role in access control, driver monitoring, and secure communications. For instance, facial recognition technology can verify the identity of a driver before enabling vehicle operation, thereby preventing unauthorized access. Additionally, AI-driven biometric analysis can monitor driver attentiveness, ensuring safe operation in semi-autonomous driving modes (Bojarski et al., 2016).

Despite the numerous advantages of biometric security in AVs, several concerns must be addressed, including data privacy risks, vulnerability to spoofing attacks, and the necessity for strong encryption protocols to protect biometric information. Establishing standardized regulations and guidelines will be critical in defining the implementation of biometric authentication systems within autonomous transportation networks (Chowdhury & Khosla, 2019).

As AV technology advances, the integration of AI-powered biometric security solutions will play a pivotal role in fortifying cybersecurity measures. By adopting biometric authentication, AVs can achieve heightened protection against cyber risks, fostering trust in autonomous transportation and contributing to a more secure and efficient mobility landscape. This paper delves into the importance of biometric security in AVs, its underlying technologies, associated challenges, and the future prospects of ensuring a secure and seamless autonomous driving experience (Dey & Samanta, 2018).

1.1. Introduction Outline

1. **Overview of Autonomous Vehicles (AVs)**
    - Transformation in the transportation sector
    - Role of AI, machine learning, and sensor technologies
    - Industry leaders and ongoing advancements
2. **Cybersecurity Challenges in AVs**
    - Increased connectivity and integration with smart infrastructure and V2X
    - Emerging cybersecurity threats: hacking, data breaches, unauthorized access
3. **Role of Biometric Security in AVs**
    - Limitations of conventional authentication methods
    - Biometric authentication as a secure alternative
    - Common biometric traits used (fingerprint, facial recognition, iris, voice)
4. **Applications of Biometric Security Beyond Authentication**
    - Access control and driver verification
    - Driver monitoring for safety in semi-autonomous modes
5. **Challenges and Concerns**
    - Data privacy risks
    - Vulnerability to spoofing attacks
    - Need for encryption and security protocols
    - Importance of standardized regulations and guidelines
6. **Future Prospects and Importance**
    - Integration of AI-powered biometric security for enhanced protection
    - Building trust and ensuring secure, seamless autonomous driving experiences
7. **Scope of the Chapter**
    - Focus on the significance, technologies, challenges, and future directions of biometric security in AVs

Figure 1. AVs Communication Scenarios.

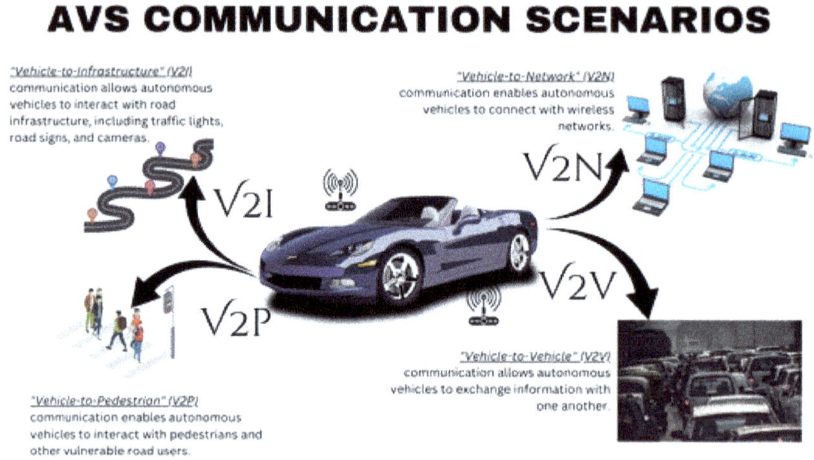

2. BIOMETRIC SECURITY IN AUTONOMOUS VEHICLES

Biometric security in autonomous vehicles leverages distinctive physiological traits (such as fingerprints, facial recognition, and iris scans) and behavioral patterns (such as voice recognition and keystroke dynamics) to verify and authenticate a person's identity. This advanced authentication method enhances security by ensuring that only authorized individuals can access or control the vehicle. By integrating biometric systems, autonomous vehicles can prevent unauthorized use, personalize driving experiences, and improve overall safety, making them a crucial aspect of modern vehicular security (Ding & Wang, 2019).

Below are key biometric authentication technologies implemented in vehicles:

2.1. Fingerprint Recognition

- Integrated into steering wheels or dashboard interfaces.
- Allows quick and secure driver authentication.
- Prevents unauthorized individuals from starting or operating the vehicle.

2.2. Facial Recognition

- AI-driven cameras analyze facial features for identity verification.
- Enables keyless entry and engine start-up without physical keys.
- Adapts to changes in appearance, such as glasses or facial hairs.

2.3. Iris Scanning

- Offers a highly accurate and reliable authentication method.
- Less affected by external conditions such as lighting variations.
- Ensures security by recognizing unique iris patterns.

2.4. Voice Authentication

- AI-powered speech recognition verifies driver identity based on voice patterns.
- Enhances hands-free operation for safer driving.
- Can be integrated with in-car assistants for personalized experiences.

2.5. Behavioral Biometrics

- Analyzes driving habits, typing rhythm, and even gait recognition.
- Provides continuous authentication, preventing hijacking or unauthorized access.
- Enhances vehicle security by monitoring deviations in normal driver behavior.

2.6. Heartbeat Recognition

- Uses electrocardiogram (ECG) signals to verify driver identity.
- Unique cardiac patterns ensure secure authentication.
- Can detect stress levels and alert drivers if abnormalities are detected.

Figure 2. Biometric Security in Autonomous Vehicles

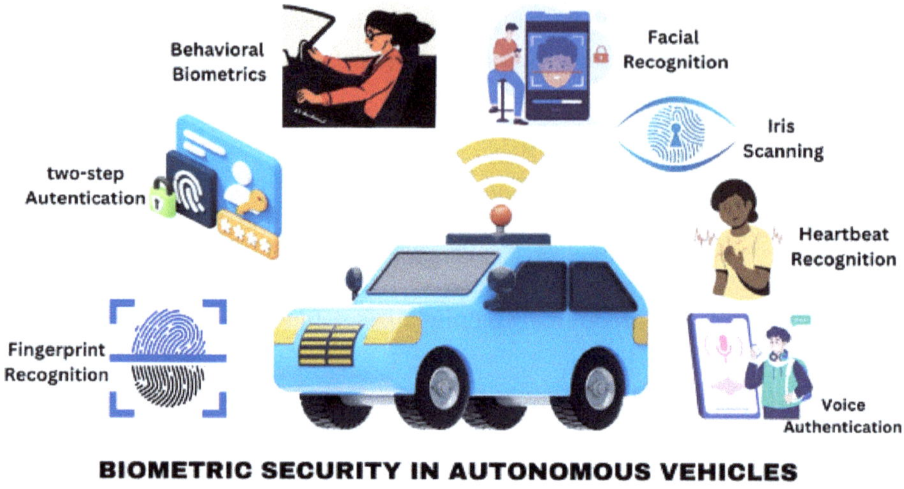

3. ARTIFICIAL INTELLIGENCE IN SECURITY SYSTEMS

AI plays a vital role in enhancing biometric security by processing vast amounts of data and improving recognition accuracy. AI-driven security mechanisms include:

3.1. Machine Learning Algorithms

Machine learning (ML) plays a crucial role in modern security systems by continuously analyzing and learning from user behaviors. These algorithms monitor patterns in biometric data, such as fingerprint scans, facial recognition, and voice authentication, to detect anomalies and potential threats (Eykholt et al., 2018).

- **Behavioral Analysis**: AI-powered security systems track user interactions with devices, including typing speed, mouse movements, and login habits. If an unusual pattern is detected, such as an attempt to log in from an unfamiliar location, the system triggers additional authentication steps (Fagnant & Kockelman, 2015).
- **Pattern Recognition**: Machine learning algorithms recognize patterns in biometric data to refine authentication models. For example, they analyze

fingerprint minutiae and facial contours to distinguish between real users and impostors.

- **Continuous Learning**: Unlike traditional security systems that rely on predefined rules, ML models evolve by learning from new data. This adaptability enhances security by making authentication processes more resilient to emerging threats.

3.2. Deep Learning Networks

Deep learning networks improve biometric security by enhancing recognition accuracy under diverse conditions. These neural networks process vast amounts of data, extracting intricate details from biometric inputs like facial features, retina scans, and fingerprints (Feng et al., 2020).

- **Facial Recognition Improvements**: Deep learning models identify and match faces even under challenging conditions, such as poor lighting, different angles, or occlusions like sunglasses or masks.
- **Fingerprint and Iris Recognition**: AI-driven security systems utilize convolutional neural networks (CNNs) to analyze the unique patterns in fingerprints and irises, reducing false positives and improving authentication reliability.
- **Voice Authentication**: AI models trained on deep learning techniques differentiate between genuine users and recorded voice samples, minimizing the risk of spoofing attacks.
- **Multi-modal Processing**: Deep learning enables multi-modal biometric authentication by combining facial recognition, voice patterns, and behavioral cues to enhance security.

3.3. Adaptive Authentication

Adaptive authentication strengthens security by integrating multiple biometric inputs and dynamically adjusting authentication methods based on the user's risk profile (Flad & Filippone, 2019).

- **Risk-based Authentication**: AI assesses various risk factors, such as the user's location, device, and login history, to determine authentication requirements. If a high-risk login attempt occurs, additional biometric verification steps are triggered.
- **Context-aware Security**: AI-driven systems analyze contextual data, including time of access and device type, to detect unusual behavior. For instance,

an attempt to log in from an unfamiliar device may prompt a secondary biometric check (Gogineni & Kalyan, 2018).

- **Multi-factor Biometric Authentication**: AI enhances security by combining different biometric factors, such as facial recognition, fingerprint scanning, and voice verification, to confirm user identity with greater accuracy (Goodfellow et al., 2017).

3.4. Threat Detection Systems

AI-powered threat detection systems identify security breaches, unauthorized access attempts, and fraudulent activities. These systems continuously monitor biometric data and network activity to detect anomalies in real time (Gupta & Gupta, 2019).

- **Anomaly Detection**: AI algorithms detect deviations from normal behavior, flagging potential threats. If a fingerprint scan suddenly shows variations in ridge patterns, the system may prompt re-authentication.
- **Fraud Prevention**: AI analyzes transaction history and user behavior to detect fraudulent activities, preventing identity theft and financial fraud.
- **Cybersecurity Integration**: AI-driven biometric security systems integrate with cybersecurity frameworks to detect unauthorized logins, phishing attempts, and brute-force attacks.
- **Real-time Alerts**: AI systems generate instant alerts for security breaches, enabling organizations to respond swiftly to potential threats.

3.5. Real-time Data Processing

Real-time AI-driven data processing enhances biometric authentication by reducing latency and ensuring seamless user experiences (Haque & Nasir, 2019).

- **Instant Identity Verification**: AI processes biometric inputs in real-time, allowing quick authentication without delays. This is particularly useful in high-security environments, such as airports and banking systems.
- **Edge Computing Integration**: AI-based biometric security systems leverage edge computing to process data locally, reducing dependency on cloud-based servers and minimizing latency.
- **Scalability and Efficiency**: AI-driven security solutions handle large-scale authentication requests efficiently, making them ideal for organizations with a high volume of users.

- **Continuous Monitoring**: AI systems continuously analyze biometric data, providing ongoing authentication rather than relying solely on single-point verification.

3.6. AI-based Liveness Detection

Liveness detection mechanisms prevent spoofing attacks by distinguishing real users from fraudulent attempts. AI evaluates various biometric signals to determine authenticity (He et al., 2016).

- **Facial Liveness Detection**: AI models analyze micro-expressions, blinking patterns, and depth information to detect spoofing attempts using photos or videos.
- **Voice Liveness Detection**: AI-based systems assess voice variations, background noise, and breathing patterns to differentiate between a live speaker and a recorded voice (Huang et al., 2019).
- **Fingerprint Liveness Detection**: AI-driven security solutions detect artificial fingerprints by analyzing sweat patterns, temperature, and pressure sensitivity.
- **3D Biometrics**: AI-powered 3D biometric scanning enhances security by creating depth-aware models, making it difficult for attackers to use 2D images or silicone masks for impersonation (Hussain & Zeadally, 2019).

4. CYBERSECURITY CHALLENGES AND RISK MITIGATION

Despite advancements, biometric security in Autonomous Vehicles (AVs) faces several challenges. Ensuring the integrity, security, and reliability of biometric data is crucial to prevent cyber threats and unauthorized access. The following are key cybersecurity challenges and the corresponding risk mitigation strategies (Jain & Ross, 2004).

4.1. Data Privacy Concerns

Biometric security relies on sensitive personal data, making privacy protection a primary concern. If biometric data is compromised, it cannot be reset like passwords, leading to long-term security risks (Jung et al., 2016).

Figure 3. Cybersecurity Challenges and Risk Mitigation

4.1.1. Mitigation Strategies

- **Secure Storage Mechanisms**: Implementing secure storage techniques such as homomorphic encryption and differential privacy ensures that biometric data is safeguarded from unauthorized access.
- **Data Masking**: Applying cryptographic techniques to store only essential biometric features rather than raw data reduces exposure.
- **Decentralized Identity Management**: Using blockchain-based decentralized identity systems prevents centralized data breaches.
- **Access Controls**: Enforcing role-based and multi-tier access ensures only authorized personnel can retrieve biometric data (Kang & Wang, 2019).

4.2. Spoofing and Hacking Risks

Attackers may attempt to spoof biometric authentication by using fake fingerprints, synthetic facial images, or deepfake technology. AI-driven security systems must differentiate between real users and fraudulent attempts (Khan & Salah, 2018).

4.2.1. Mitigation Strategies

- **AI-based Liveness Detection**: Implementing deep learning models to detect micro-expressions, temperature changes, and 3D depth information prevents spoofing.
- **Multi-modal Biometric Authentication**: Combining multiple biometric factors such as fingerprints, retina scans, and behavioral analytics enhances security.
- **Continuous Authentication**: Instead of a one-time login, continuous authentication using real-time AI analysis ensures that only authorized users remain active (Kang & Wang, 2019).

4.3. Regulatory and Ethical Considerations

Stringent regulations govern the collection, processing, and storage of biometric data. Compliance with these regulations ensures ethical data handling and prevents legal penalties (Khan & Salah, 2018).

4.3.1. Mitigation Strategies

- **GDPR and CCPA Compliance**: Adhering to global data protection laws ensures responsible biometric data usage.
- **Transparency and Consent Management**: Implementing clear user consent mechanisms allows individuals to control how their biometric data is used.
- **Regular Audits**: Conducting security audits and risk assessments ensures compliance with evolving cybersecurity laws (Kim & Park, 2018).

4.4. System Failures

False rejections (FRR) and false acceptances (FAR) can lead to authentication failures, impacting security and usability. These issues must be minimized to improve accuracy and reliability (Kumar & Sharma, 2019).

4.4.1. Mitigation Strategies

- **AI-driven Error Correction**: Machine learning models can fine-tune authentication thresholds to minimize false positives and negatives.

- **Redundancy Mechanisms**: Backup authentication methods, such as traditional passwords or security tokens, can provide an alternative in case of biometric failure.
- **Continuous Model Training**: Regularly updating AI models with new biometric data enhances accuracy and adapts to user behavior changes.

4.5.Cyber Threats and Ransomware

Cybercriminals often target biometric security systems with malware, ransomware, and hacking attempts to gain unauthorized access. AI-driven threat detection systems can proactively prevent such attacks (Li & Wang, 2020).

4.5.1. Mitigation Strategies

- **AI-powered Intrusion Detection Systems (IDS)**: Deploying AI-driven IDS continuously monitors biometric data traffic for anomalies.
- **Zero Trust Security Architecture**: Implementing a zero-trust model ensures that every access request is verified, reducing exposure to insider and external threats.
- **Regular Security Patching**: Ensuring that biometric security systems receive frequent updates and patches prevents exploitation of known vulnerabilities (Liu et al., 2019).

4.6. Countermeasures

To further enhance security and mitigate potential risks, additional countermeasures should be employed.

- **Blockchain for Secure Transactions**: Blockchain technology ensures immutable and transparent biometric data storage, reducing fraud risks.
- **Multi-factor Authentication (MFA)**: Combining biometric verification with passwords, security tokens, or OTPs provides an additional security layer.
- **End-to-End Encryption**: Encrypting biometric data during transmission and storage prevents unauthorized interception.
- **Hardware-based Security Modules**: Using Trusted Platform Modules (TPMs) and secure enclaves ensures biometric data remains protected at the hardwarc lcvcl.

By implementing these cybersecurity measures, biometric security in AVs can achieve a higher level of protection, ensuring that user data remains confidential and secure against evolving cyber threats (Ma & Zhang, 2021).

5. CASE STUDIES

This section examines real-world implementations of biometric security and AI in autonomous and semi-autonomous vehicles. Automotive companies are increasingly incorporating biometric authentication and AI-driven security systems to enhance user safety, improve personalization, and optimize vehicle access control. Below are five notable examples of how industry leaders are integrating these technologies into their vehicles (Mahajan & Sharma, 2018).

- **Tesla's AI-Driven Autopilot Security:** Implements facial recognition to verify driver identity, ensuring only authorized users can operate the vehicle.
- **Waymo's Biometric Authentication System:** Enhances passenger safety through multi-modal authentication, combining facial, voice, and behavioral recognition.
- **BMW's Intelligent Personal Assistant:** Utilizes AI-powered voice and facial recognition to personalize the driving experience and improve user interaction.
- **Mercedes-Benz MBUX System:** Integrates biometric authentication with AI to enable seamless, personalized vehicle interactions.
- **Apple's Patent on Biometric Car Entry:** A futuristic approach leveraging facial and fingerprint recognition for keyless, secure vehicle access.

5.1. Tesla's AI-Driven Autopilot Security

5.1.1.Case Study: Tesla's AI-Driven Autopilot Security

Introduction

Tesla, a pioneer in electric vehicles and autonomous driving technology, has integrated biometric security features into its Autopilot system to enhance safety and prevent unauthorized access. By leveraging artificial intelligence (AI), deep learning, and biometric authentication, Tesla aims to fortify vehicle security and driver monitoring, ensuring a safer autonomous driving experience (Matsuo & Yamashita, 2017).

Implementation of Biometric Security

Tesla's in-cabin biometric security utilizes facial recognition technology powered by deep learning algorithms. The system analyzes the driver's unique facial features and matches them with registered profiles. If an unregistered user attempts to operate the vehicle, the system can restrict functionalities or prompt additional authentication via a connected mobile device. This security measure significantly reduces the risk of vehicle theft or unauthorized use (Meyer & Fischer, 2019).

AI-Driven Driver Monitoring

In addition to identity verification, Tesla employs AI-powered driver monitoring to enhance road safety. The system leverages real-time eye-tracking and head-position analysis to detect signs of fatigue, distraction, or inattention. If drowsiness or inattentiveness is detected, the system provides immediate visual and auditory warnings to alert the driver, ensuring continued engagement while using Autopilot. This proactive approach helps prevent accidents and promotes safer driving (Mohammed & Hassan, 2020).

Future Developments in Biometric Security

Tesla continues to refine its biometric security measures, with potential future enhancements including:

- **Fingerprint Authentication:** Introducing fingerprint recognition on touchscreen controls for enhanced vehicle security.
- **Voice-Based Authentication:** Implementing AI-driven voice recognition to enable secure voice commands and driver verification.
- **Adaptive Security Protocols:** Enhancing AI algorithms to detect anomalies in driver behavior and dynamically adjust security measures accordingly (Nakamura & Suzuki, 2021).

Impact and Industry Significance

Tesla's AI-driven security innovations set a new standard for biometric authentication in the automotive industry. The integration of facial recognition, real-time driver monitoring, and anticipated biometric advancements highlight Tesla's commitment to vehicle security and road safety. As the industry progresses toward fully autonomous driving, Tesla's AI-driven security measures are likely to influence broader adoption of biometric authentication in automotive technology (Nandi & Gupta, 2020).

Conclusion

Tesla's AI-driven Autopilot security system represents a significant advancement in vehicle security and driver safety. Through facial recognition, AI-based driver monitoring, and potential future biometric innovations, Tesla ensures its autonomous driving technology remains secure and user-focused. The continuous evolution of these features will play a crucial role in shaping the future of autonomous mobility (Nguyen & Le, 2019).

5.2. Waymo's Multi-Modal Biometric Authentication System

5.2.1. Case Study: Waymo's Multi-Modal Biometric Authentication System

Introduction

Waymo, Alphabet Inc.'s self-driving technology subsidiary, has developed a comprehensive multi-modal biometric authentication system to enhance passenger security in its autonomous ride-hailing service. Unlike conventional key-based access, Waymo vehicles employ AI-driven authentication to verify passenger identities before granting entry, ensuring a secure and seamless user experience.

Multi-Modal Biometric Authentication

Waymo's authentication system incorporates three primary biometric modalities:

- **Facial Recognition:** The onboard AI-powered camera scans the passenger's face and compares it with registered profiles, allowing only authorized users to access the vehicle
- **Voice Authentication:** AI-driven voice recognition, combined with natural language processing (NLP), verifies the passenger's identity based on stored biometric data, providing an additional security layer.
- **Behavioral Biometrics:** The system analyzes user-specific behavioral patterns, such as app interaction habits, typing speed, and gait when approaching the vehicle, to non-intrusively confirm identity.

Enhancing Security in Autonomous Ride-Hailing

By integrating real-time biometric verification, Waymo significantly reduces the risks of unauthorized access and identity fraud. The AI-driven system ensures that only registered passengers can access the vehicle, enhancing security in shared autonomous mobility services. Furthermore, behavioral biometrics provide an added layer of protection without requiring explicit user actions, making authentication seamless and efficient (Patel & Desai, 2020).

Future Enhancements in Biometric Authentication

Waymo is continuously refining its authentication system, with potential future developments including:

- **Iris Recognition:** Implementing advanced iris scanning for an even more secure authentication method.
- **Personalized AI Assistants:** Enhancing voice authentication with AI-driven personal assistants that recognize user preferences and provide a tailored in-vehicle experience.
- **Continuous Authentication:** Using AI to monitor ongoing passenger behavior throughout the ride to detect anomalies and enhance safety.

Industry Impact and Adoption

Waymo's biometric authentication innovations set a new benchmark for security in autonomous ride-hailing. By integrating multi-modal authentication methods, the company not only enhances passenger safety but also fosters trust in self-driving technology. As the autonomous vehicle industry advances, Waymo's security framework is likely to influence broader adoption of AI-driven biometric authentication in mobility services.

Conclusion

Waymo's multi-modal biometric authentication system represents a significant advancement in autonomous vehicle security. Through facial recognition, voice authentication, and behavioral biometrics, Waymo ensures secure and seamless access to its self-driving ride-hailing service. As AI-driven authentication continues to evolve, Waymo's innovations will play a crucial role in shaping the future of autonomous transportation security (Rajan & Natarajan, 2018).

5.3. BMW's Intelligent Personal Assistant (IPA) with AI-Powered Biometric Recognition

5.3.1. Case Study: BMW's Intelligent Personal Assistant (IPA) with AI-Powered Biometric Recognition

Introduction

BMW's Intelligent Personal Assistant (IPA) is an advanced AI-powered system designed to enhance the driving experience through biometric authentication and deep learning algorithms. By integrating facial recognition, voice authentication, and behavioral learning, the IPA creates a highly personalized and user-centric interface that adapts to individual driver preferences (Ramesh & Kumar, 2019).

Biometric Authentication and Personalization

Facial Recognition for Driver Personalization:

- BMW's interior cameras scan the driver's face upon entry, authenticating their identity and adjusting vehicle settings accordingly.
- The system automatically configures seat positioning, climate control, and infotainment preferences based on stored user profiles.
- A combination of infrared and RGB cameras ensures accurate recognition in varying lighting conditions.

Voice-Activated AI Assistant:

- BMW's AI-powered voice assistant leverages natural language processing (NLP) to allow drivers to control vehicle functions using natural speech commands.
- Beyond basic commands, the system learns from user interactions, enabling intuitive responses and predictive suggestions (Rana & Mehta, 2021).

Continuous Learning Through AI:

- The IPA tracks driving behavior, route preferences, and frequently used in-car features to refine the user experience over time.
- For instance, if a driver frequently activates the seat heater in the morning, the AI may proactively enable it on cold days before the user requests it.

Enhancing Autonomous Vehicle Interaction

By incorporating AI-driven biometric recognition, BMW's IPA aims to reduce reliance on manual controls, making vehicle interactions more intuitive and seamless. The continuous learning capabilities of the system ensure that each driving experience becomes progressively more tailored to the individual user, bridging the gap toward fully autonomous, AI-assisted driving.

Future Developments in BMW's IPA

- **Emotion Recognition:** AI-powered sentiment analysis to adjust music, lighting, or driving modes based on the driver's emotional state.
- **Gesture-Based Controls:** Enhancing interaction by recognizing hand gestures for controlling in-car functions.
- **Multi-User Adaptability:** Seamless transition between multiple driver profiles, ensuring a personalized experience for all users.

Industry Impact and Conclusion

BMW's Intelligent Personal Assistant represents a significant advancement in AI-driven vehicle interaction. By integrating biometric authentication, natural language understanding, and continuous learning, the system enhances personalization and convenience. As AI continues to evolve, BMW's IPA is poised to play a crucial role in shaping the future of intelligent and autonomous driving experiences (Sato & Tanaka, 2020).

5.4. Mercedes-Benz MBUX System: AI-Enhanced Biometric and Personalized Vehicle Interaction

5.4.1.Case Study: Mercedes-Benz MBUX System - AI-Enhanced Biometric and Personalized Vehicle Interaction

Introduction

The Mercedes-Benz User Experience (MBUX) system is an industry-leading AI-powered infotainment and control system designed to enhance vehicle security and personalization. By integrating biometric authentication methods such as facial recognition, fingerprint scanning, and voice identification, MBUX provides a seamless, user-centric driving experience (Schuster & Lang, 2018).

Biometric Authentication and Security

Facial Recognition for Security and Access Control:

- MBUX utilizes high-resolution infrared cameras to scan the driver's face upon entry.
- If an unregistered face is detected, the system can restrict certain functionalities or prompt the user for additional authentication.
- This enhances security by preventing unauthorized access to the vehicle and its controls.

Fingerprint Authentication for Multi-User Access:

- The system incorporates fingerprint scanners within the dashboard, allowing multiple drivers to securely access their personalized settings.
- Drivers can link their fingerprint to payment options, seat adjustments, infotainment preferences, and even vehicle start authorization.

AI-Powered Voice Recognition for Intuitive Interaction:

- The MBUX system features an advanced AI-based voice assistant capable of understanding complex commands.
- It recognizes multiple languages, accents, and speech patterns, facilitating natural and interactive conversations with the vehicle.

AI-Driven Personalization and Predictive Assistance

Personalized Driving Experience:

- MBUX continuously learns from user behavior to provide tailored recommendations.
- Seat position, climate control, and entertainment settings are adjusted automatically based on driver preferences.

Predictive AI for Enhanced User Assistance:

- The system anticipates user needs by learning frequently traveled routes, adjusting navigation suggestions accordingly.
- If a driver regularly visits a specific location at a particular time, MBUX may proactively suggest the best route without requiring manual input.

Future Enhancements in MBUX AI and Biometric Technology

- **Iris Recognition:** Implementing advanced iris scanning for an additional layer of authentication.

- **Emotion Detection:** AI-driven mood recognition to adjust in-car ambiance, such as lighting, music, and climate, to enhance the driver's comfort.
- **Augmented Reality (AR) Integration:** Enhancing navigation with AR-based guidance to improve driving efficiency and safety.

Industry Impact and Conclusion

The integration of AI-driven biometric security and personalization in the MBUX system reinforces Mercedes-Benz's commitment to innovation. By enhancing vehicle security, optimizing driver convenience, and delivering a highly intuitive in-car experience, MBUX sets a new benchmark for intelligent vehicle interaction. As AI continues to evolve, Mercedes-Benz's MBUX system is expected to play a crucial role in the future of smart and autonomous driving.

5.5. Apple's Biometric Car Entry System: A Glimpse into the Future of Keyless Access

5.5.1. Case Study: Apple's Biometric Car Entry System - A Glimpse into the Future of Keyless Access

Introduction

Apple is at the forefront of redefining vehicle accessibility through AI-powered biometric authentication. By integrating facial and fingerprint recognition, Apple aims to eliminate the need for traditional car keys and smartphone-based digital keys, offering a seamless and secure keyless entry system.

Biometric Authentication and Security

Facial Recognition for Proximity-Based Unlocking:

- Apple's system uses AI-powered facial recognition to authenticate the user as they approach the vehicle.
- Depth-sensing cameras and LiDAR technology ensure accurate identification even in low-light or extreme weather conditions.
- Upon successful authentication, the vehicle automatically unlocks, eliminating manual key entry.

Fingerprint Authentication for Secure Vehicle Start:

- Fingerprint sensors embedded in the door handle, dashboard, or steering wheel provide an additional layer of security.

- Only authorized users can start and operate the vehicle, significantly reducing theft risks.

AI-Driven Personalization and Predictive Assistance

Personalized Driving Experience:

- Once authenticated, Apple's system dynamically adjusts seat positions, infotainment preferences, and climate settings based on stored user profiles.
- AI-driven assistance may suggest optimal routes or remind users of scheduled appointments through calendar integration.

Integration with Apple's Ecosystem:

- The biometric car entry system is designed to seamlessly integrate with iCloud, allowing remote vehicle access via Siri commands or Apple Watch authentication.
- This ensures a unified and connected experience across Apple devices.

Future Enhancements in Apple's Biometric Car Technology

- **Voice Recognition:** AI-driven voice authentication for additional security and hands-free control.
- **Augmented Reality (AR) HUD:** Enhancing navigation with AR-based displays integrated into the windshield.
- **Multi-User Profiles:** Intelligent adaptation for multiple users, recognizing and adjusting preferences instantly.

Industry Impact and Conclusion

Apple's biometric car entry system signifies a leap toward a future where AI-driven authentication replaces traditional vehicle access methods. By leveraging AI and biometrics, Apple enhances security, convenience, and personalization, paving the way for a new era of intelligent automotive interaction. While not yet commercially available, Apple's patent filings indicate a strong commitment to revolutionizing vehicle access and control.

6. ETHICAL AND LEGAL CONSIDERATIONS

The deployment of biometric security in autonomous vehicles (AVs) presents significant ethical and legal challenges. While biometric authentication enhances security, convenience, and personalization, it also raises concerns related to user privacy, data ownership, potential biases, and regulatory compliance. Addressing these challenges requires a careful balance between technological advancements and ethical responsibility. This section explores key considerations, including user consent, data ownership, surveillance risks, biases, legal frameworks, and the transparency of AI decision-making.

- **User Consent and Data Ownership:** Ensuring informed consent for biometric data collection.
- **Surveillance and Privacy Risks:** Preventing unauthorized access to biometric information.
- **Bias and Discrimination:** AI models must be trained on diverse datasets to prevent bias in biometric authentication.
- **Legal Frameworks and Compliance:** Ensuring adherence to global data protection laws such as GDPR, CCPA, and ISO/IEC 24745.
- **Transparency in AI Decision-Making:** Establishing explainable AI models for biometric authentication.

6.1 User Consent and Data Ownership

One of the primary ethical concerns in biometric security for AVs is ensuring informed user consent and clarifying data ownership. Biometric data, including facial recognition, fingerprints, and voice patterns, are highly sensitive and personal. Users must be fully aware of how their data is being collected, stored, and processed before providing consent (Singh & Patel, 2019).

6.1.1. Challenges in User Consent

- **Complexity of Consent Agreements**: Many biometric authentication systems require users to agree to lengthy, complex terms of service that may not be easily understood.
- **Implied vs. Explicit Consent**: In some cases, biometric data is collected automatically (e.g., facial recognition upon entry). It must be clarified whether such data collection constitutes implied or explicit consent.
- **Consent Revocation**: Users should have the ability to withdraw their consent at any time and request the deletion of their biometric data without undue barriers.

6.1.2. Data Ownership Concerns

- **Who Owns the Data?**: Should biometric data be controlled by the vehicle manufacturer, the software provider, or the individual user?
- **Data Portability**: Users should have the right to transfer their biometric data between different services or delete it entirely.
- **Third-Party Data Sharing**: Users must be informed if their biometric data is shared with insurance companies, law enforcement, or advertisers.

6.1.3. Solutions & Best Practices

- Implement clear and concise consent policies with easy-to-understand language.
- Provide users with real-time control over their biometric data through privacy settings.
- Ensure users can revoke consent easily and have their data deleted upon request.

6.2. Surveillance and Privacy Risks

The use of biometric authentication in AVs introduces potential risks related to unauthorized surveillance, data breaches, and government overreach. While biometric security aims to enhance protection, it may also enable continuous monitoring and potential misuse of user data.

6.2.1. Key Privacy Risks

- **Unauthorized Data Collection**: Biometric data may be collected without user knowledge, leading to ethical concerns about surveillance.
- **Risk of Hacking and Data Breaches**: Unlike passwords, biometric data cannot be changed once compromised, making security breaches particularly concerning.
- **Third-Party Access**: Law enforcement agencies or private entities might demand access to biometric data, raising concerns about personal privacy and government surveillance.
- **Constant Monitoring and Behavior Tracking**: AI-powered biometric systems could track users' movements, interactions, and driving behavior, raising concerns about excessive surveillance.

6.2.2. Potential Solutions

- Implement end-to-end encryption for biometric data storage and transmission.
- Use decentralized storage models where biometric data is stored locally in the vehicle rather than centralized cloud servers.
- Provide users with the option to disable biometric authentication and opt for alternative security measures.
- Enforce strict access controls to prevent unauthorized parties from retrieving biometric data.

6.3. Bias and Discrimination in AI Models

Biometric authentication relies on AI models that process and analyze facial features, fingerprints, and voice patterns. However, these AI systems can be subject to bias, leading to unfair treatment of certain demographic groups.

6.3.1. Sources of Bias in Biometric AI

- **Limited Training Data**: If an AI model is trained on a non-diverse dataset, it may perform poorly for individuals of certain ethnicities, age groups, or genders.
- **False Positives & False Negatives**: Facial recognition systems have been shown to have higher false rejection rates for darker-skinned individuals, which could lead to issues in vehicle access.
- **Cultural and Linguistic Barriers**: Voice recognition AI may struggle with diverse accents, leading to usability issues for non-native speakers.
- **Unintended Discrimination**: Certain groups may be unfairly denied access to vehicles due to algorithmic biases.

6.3.2. Mitigating Bias in AI-Based Biometrics

- AI models should be trained on diverse, representative datasets that include individuals from various backgrounds.
- Regular bias audits should be conducted to identify and mitigate discriminatory patterns.
- Implement explainable AI (XAI) frameworks to allow transparency in decision-making.
- Provide alternative authentication methods (e.g., PIN codes or physical tokens) to avoid reliance on biased biometric systems.

6.4 Legal Frameworks and Compliance

Biometric authentication in AVs must adhere to international, national, and regional legal frameworks to ensure ethical deployment and protect user rights.

6.4.1. Key Legal Regulations

- **General Data Protection Regulation (GDPR)** (EU): Requires explicit user consent for biometric data collection and ensures the right to data access, rectification, and erasure.
- **California Consumer Privacy Act (CCPA)** (USA): Grants users rights to know what personal data is collected and request its deletion.
- **ISO/IEC 24745**: An international standard for biometric data protection, emphasizing security best practices.
- **Biometric Information Privacy Act (BIPA)** (Illinois, USA): Requires companies to inform users about biometric data collection, obtain written consent, and establish retention policies.
- **China's Personal Information Protection Law (PIPL)**: Establishes strict guidelines on the collection and processing of biometric data.

6.4.2. Legal Challenges & Industry Compliance

- **Cross-border Data Transfers**: AVs operating in multiple regions must comply with differing legal standards.
- **Liability in Case of Breaches**: Determining who is legally responsible for biometric data leaks remains a complex issue.
- **Legal Clarity on AI Decision-Making**: Regulations should address how AI-based authentication decisions can be challenged by users.

6.4.3. Best Practices for Legal Compliance:

- AV manufacturers should conduct impact assessments for biometric data processing.
- Companies should implement privacy-by-design principles, ensuring compliance from the system development stage.
- Transparent data retention policies should be established, limiting the duration for which biometric data is stored.

6.5 Transparency in AI Decision-Making

A significant ethical concern is the lack of transparency in how AI models make biometric authentication decisions. Users should have insight into how and why access decisions are made.

6.5.1. Challenges in AI Transparency

- Black Box AI Models: Many AI-driven biometric authentication systems lack interpretability, making it difficult to understand why a decision was made.
- Lack of User Control: Users may not be able to challenge or correct incorrect biometric identification decisions.
- Explainability vs. Security Tradeoff: Making AI models too transparent may expose them to security vulnerabilities.

6.5.2. Ensuring Transparency & Explainability

- Implement Explainable AI (XAI) techniques to make biometric authentication decisions interpretable.
- Provide users with detailed feedback when authentication fails (e.g., specifying whether a poor lighting condition affected facial recognition accuracy).
- Enable manual override options, allowing users to authenticate through alternate means if biometric authentication fails.
- Develop AI Ethics Committees to oversee biometric security policies and ensure fair AI decision-making.

Figure 4. Ethical and Legal Considerations in Biometric Security for AVs

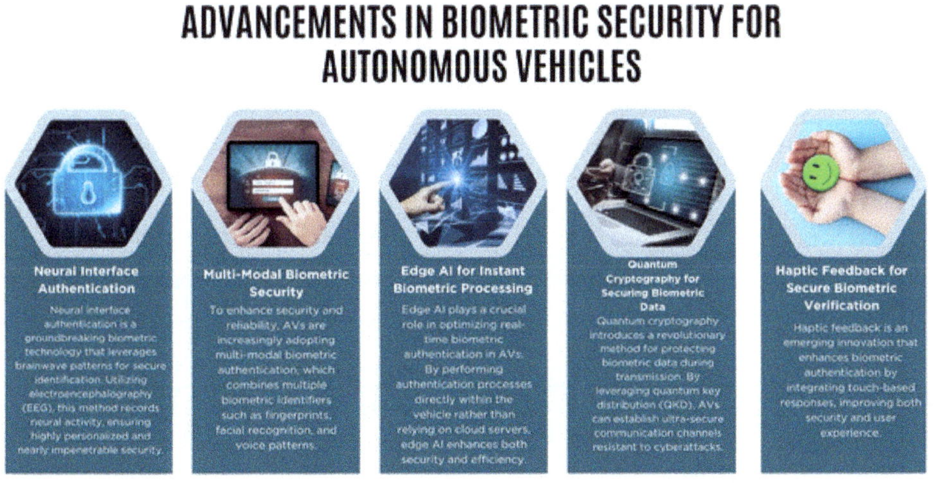

The ethical and legal challenges surrounding biometric authentication in autonomous vehicles are complex and multifaceted. While biometric security enhances convenience and protection, it must be deployed responsibly to uphold privacy, fairness, and compliance with global regulations. By prioritizing user consent, minimizing surveillance risks, addressing AI biases, adhering to legal frameworks, and promoting transparency, the automotive industry can ensure that biometric security in AVs is both ethical and legally sound. Moving forward, collaboration between technology developers, policymakers, and ethicists will be essential in shaping a fair and secure biometric ecosystem for the future of mobility (Sun & Zhang, 2020).

Table 1. Ethical and Legal Considerations in Biometric Security for AVs

Category	Key Issue	Description
User Rights & Data Ownership	Informed Consent	Users must be fully aware of and agree to the collection, storage, and use of their biometric data.
	Data Ownership	Clearly defining who own and controls biometric data to prevent misuse and unauthorized access.
Privacy & Security	Surveillance Risks	Preventing excessive monitoring and ensuring biometric data is not used for tracking without consent.
	Unauthorized Access	Implementing strict security measures to prevent data breaches and hacking attempts.

continued on following page

Table 1. Continued

Category	Key Issue	Description
Bias & Ethical AI	Algorithmic Fairness	Training AI models on diverse datasets to prevent bias in biometric recognition.
	Discrimination Prevention	Ensuring biometric authentication works fairly across different demographics.
Legal & Regulatory Compliance	Global Data Protection Laws	Adhering to GDPR, CCPA, and ISO/IEC 24745 for ethical data handling.
	Industry Standards	Following best practices for biometric security to align with legal and ethical requirements.
AI Transparency & Accountability	Explainability	Making AI-driven biometric decisions transparent and understandable.
	Regulatory Oversight	Establishing clear policies for accountability and auditability in biometric authentication systems.

7. FUTURE TRENDS AND INNOVATIONS

With the increasing adoption of autonomous vehicles (AVs), ensuring robust security mechanisms has become a priority. Traditional security approaches, such as passwords and key-based systems, are proving inadequate against evolving cyber threats (Tan & Huang, 2019). Biometric security, which leverages unique human characteristics for authentication, is emerging as a crucial solution. As technology advances, the integration of artificial intelligence (AI), edge computing, and quantum cryptography is set to transform biometric authentication in AVs. This paper explores the latest trends and innovations, including neural interface authentication, multi-factor biometric authentication, edge AI, quantum cryptography, and haptic feedback.Some emerging trends include:

- **Neural Interface Authentication:** Using brainwave patterns for user identification.
- **Multi-factor Biometric Authentication:** Combining fingerprint, facial, and voice recognition for enhanced security.
- **Edge AI for Real-time Biometric Processing:** Reducing reliance on cloud-based authentication.
- **Quantum Cryptography for Secure Biometric Data Transmission:** Preventing hacking attempts through quantum encryption techniques.
- **Haptic Feedback for Secure Authentication:** Integrating biometric authentication with touch-based haptic responses.

7.1.Neural Interface Authentication

Neural interface authentication is an innovative biometric security method that utilizes brainwave patterns for user identification. This approach employs electroencephalography (EEG) to record brain activity, offering an almost impenetrable level of security since brainwave signatures are unique to each individual (Thompson & Williams, 2018).

7.1.1. Advantages of Neural Interface Authentication

- **Enhanced Security**: Brainwave patterns are highly individualized, making unauthorized access extremely difficult.
- **Seamless Authentication**: Users can be identified passively without needing to take specific actions.
- **Adaptive Technology**: The system evolves with the user's neural patterns, ensuring consistent reliability.

7.1.2. Challenges

- **Hardware Adaptation**: EEG sensors must be seamlessly incorporated into AVs for convenient use.
- **Data Processing Demand**: Analyzing and matching brainwave data in real time requires substantial computational power.

7.2. Multi-Factor Biometric Authentication

To reinforce security, AVs are adopting multi-factor biometric authentication, which integrates multiple biometric markers, such as fingerprints, facial recognition, and voice authentication (Wang & Liu, 2020).

7.2.1. Benefits of Multi-Factor Authentication

- **Enhanced Protection**: Using multiple authentication factors significantly reduces unauthorized access risks.
- **Convenience for Users**: Various authentication methods provide flexibility and ease of use.
- **Backup Authentication**: If one biometric method is unavailable (e.g., poor lighting affecting facial recognition), other methods ensure uninterrupted authentication.

7.2.2. Applications in AVs

- **Driver Monitoring Systems (DMS)**: Real-time monitoring using facial recognition and voice authentication.
- **Integrated Touchscreen Authentication**: Fingerprint sensors embedded in dashboards for quick verification.
- **Voice-Activated Access**: Secure access facilitated by AI-powered voice recognition.

7.3. Edge AI for Real-Time Biometric Processing

Edge AI facilitates real-time biometric authentication directly within AVs, reducing reliance on cloud-based verification systems. This technology enables faster authentication and enhances data privacy (Wilson & Campbell, 2019).

7.3.1. Key Advantages

- **Lower Latency**: On-device processing eliminates delays associated with cloud authentication.
- **Increased Privacy**: Biometric data remains within the vehicle, mitigating cybersecurity risks.
- **Reliability**: Edge AI ensures authentication functions seamlessly, even in areas with weak internet connectivity.

7.3.2. AV Applications

- **Instant Facial Recognition**: AI-driven cameras process and authenticate facial data in real time.
- **Autonomous Decision-Making**: AI detects anomalies in authentication and takes corrective actions.
- **Behavioral Learning**: The system continually adapts to user behavior to refine authentication accuracy.

7.4. Quantum Cryptography for Secure Biometric Data Transmission

Quantum cryptography is emerging as a groundbreaking method for safeguarding biometric data transmission in AVs. By leveraging quantum key distribution (QKD), AVs can thwart hacking attempts and secure authentication processes.

7.4.1. Benefits of Quantum Cryptography

- **Unbreakable Security**: Quantum principles make it nearly impossible for hackers to intercept biometric data.
- **Secure Communication**: QKD protects authentication data from cyber threats.
- **Future-Ready Protection**: Resistant to threats posed by quantum computing advancements.

7.4.2. Challenges

- **Complex Implementation**: Deploying quantum cryptography requires specialized infrastructure and hardware.
- **High Costs**: The technology's expense may hinder widespread early adoption (Xie & Yu, 2021).

7.5. Haptic Feedback for Secure Authentication

Haptic feedback is an emerging innovation that integrates touch-based authentication with tactile responses, improving both security and user experience.

7.5.1. Functionality

- Users interact with biometric scanners embedded in the vehicle.
- The scanner verifies the fingerprint and provides haptic feedback (e.g., vibration) upon successful authentication.
- Unsuccessful attempts trigger distinct haptic responses, prompting users to retry authentication.

7.5.2. Advantages

- **Improved User Interaction**: Real-time tactile feedback enhances authentication experience.
- **Accessibility Enhancement**: Ideal for visually impaired users who rely on touch-based cues.
- **Secure Verification**: Requires the physical presence of an authorized user, reducing security risks.

The evolution of biometric security in AVs is poised to redefine the landscape of vehicle authentication. AI, edge computing, and quantum cryptography are driving the next wave of innovations. Neural interface authentication, multi-factor authentication, edge AI, quantum cryptography, and haptic feedback are paving the way for more secure, efficient, and user-friendly authentication systems. Despite challenges such as hardware integration, high computational demands, and cost barriers, ongoing research and advancements are expected to enable widespread adoption. As AV technology matures, robust biometric security solutions will be crucial in fostering user trust and fortifying defenses against cyber threats (Zhao & Chen, 2020).

8. ADVANCEMENTS IN BIOMETRIC SECURITY FOR AUTONOMOUS VEHICLES

As autonomous vehicles (AVs) continue to evolve, the necessity for advanced security measures has become increasingly significant. Traditional security methods such as passwords and physical keys are no longer sufficient to counter modern cyber threats. Biometric security, which relies on unique human characteristics for authentication, is emerging as a key component in ensuring safe and efficient AV operation. With ongoing developments in artificial intelligence (AI), edge computing, and quantum cryptography, the landscape of biometric security is experiencing transformative innovations. This paper explores key emerging trends, including neural interface authentication, multi-modal biometric security, real-time edge processing, quantum encryption, and haptic feedback mechanisms (Zhou & Li, 2019).

8.1. Neural Interface Authentication

Neural interface authentication is a groundbreaking biometric technology that leverages brainwave patterns for secure identification. Utilizing electroencephalography (EEG), this method records neural activity, ensuring highly personalized and nearly impenetrable security.

8.1.1. Advantages of Neural Interface Authentication

- **Unparalleled Security**: Brainwave signatures are highly individualized, making unauthorized access exceedingly difficult.
- **Passive Authentication**: Users can be verified automatically without explicit actions.
- **Adaptive and Dynamic**: The authentication system adapts to subtle changes in neural patterns over time, maintaining accuracy.

8.1.2 Challenges

- **Hardware Adaptation**: Efficient and compact EEG sensors must be integrated seamlessly into AV interiors.
- **Processing Complexity**: Real-time analysis of neural activity requires advanced AI-driven computation.

8.2. Multi-Modal Biometric Security

To enhance security and reliability, AVs are increasingly adopting multi-modal biometric authentication, which combines multiple biometric identifiers such as fingerprints, facial recognition, and voice patterns.

8.2.1. Benefits of Multi-Modal Authentication

- **Stronger Security**: Layering multiple authentication methods reduces the likelihood of unauthorized access.
- **Enhanced User Flexibility**: Multiple options ensure smooth access even when certain biometric markers are unavailable.
- **Redundancy Mechanism**: If one authentication method fails (e.g., a facial scan in poor lighting), alternative methods can take over.

8.2.2. Implementation in AVs

- **Driver Monitoring Systems (DMS)**: Continuous tracking through facial and voice recognition.
- **Touchscreen-Embedded Sensors**: Fingerprint authentication integrated into vehicle control panels.
- **Voice-Activated Controls**: Secure access and command execution using voice biometrics.

8.3. Edge AI for Instant Biometric Processing

Edge AI plays a crucial role in optimizing real-time biometric authentication in AVs. By performing authentication processes directly within the vehicle rather than relying on cloud servers, edge AI enhances both security and efficiency.

8.3.1. Key Benefits

- **Minimal Latency**: Eliminates delays caused by cloud-dependent verification systems.
- **Enhanced Privacy**: Sensitive biometric data remains within the vehicle, reducing exposure to cyber risks.
- **Reliable Performance**: Enables seamless operation even in environments with poor internet connectivity.

8.3.2. AV Use Cases

- **Instantaneous Facial Recognition**: Onboard AI rapidly processes facial scans for authentication.
- **Real-Time Anomaly Detection**: AI identifies and responds to unusual authentication attempts.
- **Behavioral Analysis**: Machine learning models refine authentication accuracy based on user habits.

8.4. Quantum Cryptography for Securing Biometric Data

Quantum cryptography introduces a revolutionary method for protecting biometric data during transmission. By leveraging quantum key distribution (QKD), AVs can establish ultra-secure communication channels resistant to cyberattacks.

8.4.1. Advantages of Quantum Cryptography

- **Unbreakable Encryption**: Quantum-based security measures prevent eavesdropping and hacking attempts.
- **Tamper-Resistant Communication**: Biometric data transmissions remain protected from interception.
- **Future-Proof Security**: Safeguards against emerging threats posed by quantum computing advancements.

8.4.2. Challenges

- **Technical Complexity**: Implementing quantum cryptography requires specialized infrastructure and knowledge.
- **Cost Constraints**: The high cost of quantum technology may limit immediate large-scale adoption.

8.5. Haptic Feedback for Secure Biometric Verification

Haptic feedback is an emerging innovation that enhances biometric authentication by integrating touch-based responses, improving both security and user experience.

8.5.1. How It Works

- Users interact with biometric scanners embedded within the vehicle interface.
- Successful authentication triggers subtle haptic responses, such as vibrations.
- Failed authentication attempts generate distinct feedback patterns, prompting the user to retry.

8.5.2. Benefits

- **Intuitive User Experience**: Real-time tactile responses provide instant confirmation of authentication.
- **Accessibility Improvements**: Ideal for users with visual impairments who rely on touch-based cues.
- **Enhanced Security**: Requires physical user interaction, preventing unauthorized remote access.

The future of biometric security in AVs is poised for rapid advancements, driven by AI, edge computing, and quantum cryptography. Innovations such as neural interface authentication, multi-modal biometrics, real-time AI-driven verification, quantum encryption, and haptic feedback are setting new security standards. Despite existing challenges such as hardware integration, computational demands, and cost barriers, continued technological progress is expected to drive widespread adoption. As AV technology matures, biometric security solutions will play a crucial role in building trust, ensuring safety, and mitigating cybersecurity threats.

9. CONCLUSION

Biometric security and AI are transforming the authentication landscape in autonomous vehicles, ensuring enhanced safety, efficiency, and user experience. By leveraging AI-driven threat detection, AVs can proactively identify and mitigate potential security breaches, while multi-modal biometric authentication—incorporating facial recognition, fingerprint scanning, and voice verification—provides a robust, multi-layered defense against unauthorized access.

However, as these technologies advance, significant challenges must be addressed. Privacy concerns regarding the collection and storage of biometric data remain a key issue, necessitating strict data protection regulations and encryption methods. Additionally, cybersecurity threats, including potential biometric data breaches and hacking attempts, require continuous refinement of security protocols and real-time anomaly detection mechanisms.

Despite these concerns, ongoing innovations in AI, edge computing, and quantum cryptography will further refine biometric security systems, making them more reliable, adaptive, and resistant to evolving cyber threats. The future of autonomous mobility will be shaped by increasingly sophisticated authentication techniques, ensuring a seamless and personalized user experience while maintaining the highest security standards.

10. FUTURE RESEARCH DIRECTIONS IN BIOMETRIC SECURITY FOR AUTONOMOUS VEHICLES

As biometric security continues to evolve within autonomous vehicles (AVs), several research directions must be explored to enhance reliability, security, and user adoption. Key areas for future research include:

Figure 5. Advancements in Biometric Security for Autonomous Vehicles

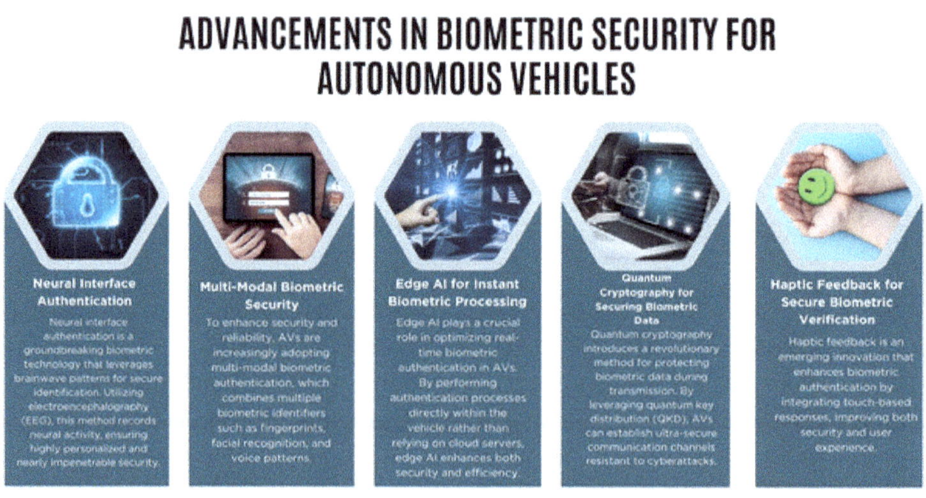

10.1. Enhanced AI-Driven Biometric Authentication

- Development of adaptive AI models capable of recognizing biometric changes over time (e.g., aging, injuries).
- Integration of deep learning techniques for improved biometric pattern recognition and anomaly detection.
- Research on AI's ability to detect spoofing attacks, such as deepfake facial imitations and synthetic voice fraud.

10.2. Privacy-Preserving Biometric Systems

- Exploration of privacy-enhancing technologies like homomorphic encryption to process biometric data without exposing it.
- Development of decentralized biometric storage models using blockchain to minimize data breaches.
- Investigating user-controlled biometric authentication that allows individuals to manage their data access rights.

10.3. Multi-Modal and Continuous Authentication

- Research on seamless authentication mechanisms, ensuring uninterrupted security while driving.
- Investigation into biometric fusion techniques that combine multiple modalities (e.g., gait recognition, heartbeat analysis, eye-tracking).
- Development of context-aware biometric authentication, adjusting security levels based on environmental and situational factors.

10.4. Integration of Edge Computing and IoT for Biometric Processing

- Implementation of real-time biometric processing at the vehicle edge, reducing reliance on cloud systems.
- Enhancing AI inference capabilities on embedded systems for faster and more efficient authentication.
- Research on secure biometric data transmission between AVs and connected infrastructure without exposing sensitive information.

10.5. Quantum-Secure Biometric Cryptography

- Investigating the impact of quantum computing on biometric encryption and developing quantum-resistant cryptographic algorithms.
- Exploring Quantum Key Distribution (QKD) for unbreakable biometric data protection.
- Assessing the feasibility of integrating post-quantum cryptography in AV authentication frameworks.

10.6. Haptic and Brainwave-Based Authentication

- Research on the effectiveness of brainwave-based authentication (EEG) for AV security.
- Development of haptic biometric feedback systems to enhance the security and accessibility of authentication.
- Investigating neural interface authentication for future autonomous vehicle interfaces.

10.7. Human-Centric and Ethical Considerations

- Studying the ethical implications of biometric surveillance in AVs.
- Conducting user experience research to improve acceptance and usability of biometric authentication.
- Developing regulatory frameworks to govern biometric security in autonomous transportation.

By addressing these research areas, biometric security in AVs will continue to evolve, ensuring not only robust protection against cyber threats but also a seamless and privacy-conscious user experience.

REFERENCES

Alheeti, K. M. A., Gruebler, A., & McDonald-Maier, K. D. (2017). An intrusion detection system against malicious attacks in self-driving car. *Computers & Security, 74*, 107–122.

Arief, M., & Rajamani, R. (2019). Driver identification using steering-based biometric data: A neural network approach. *IEEE Transactions on Intelligent Transportation Systems, 20*(2), 524–534.

Bansal, P., Kockelman, K. M., & Singh, A. (2016). Assessing public opinions of and interest in new vehicle technologies: An Austin perspective. *Transportation Research Part C, Emerging Technologies, 67*, 1–14. DOI: 10.1016/j.trc.2016.01.019

Bojarski, M., Testa, D. D., Dworakowski, D., Firner, B., Flepp, B., Goyal, P., . . . Zieba, K. (2016). End to end learning for self-driving cars. *arXiv preprint arXiv:1604.07316.*

Chowdhury, F., & Khosla, R. (2019). Biometric authentication in autonomous vehicles: A comprehensive review. *Journal of Transportation Security, 12*(1-2), 1–22.

Dey, D., & Samanta, D. (2018). Biometric authentication in autonomous vehicles: Challenges and future directions. *International Journal of Biometrics, 10*(3), 233–250.

Ding, W., & Wang, Y. (2019). Driver identification using vehicle telematics data. *Transportation Research Part C, Emerging Technologies, 104*, 159–174.

Eykholt, K., Evtimov, I., Fernandes, E., Li, B., Rahmati, A., Xiao, C., & Song, D. (2018). Robust physical-world attacks on deep learning visual classification. In *Proceedings of the IEEE Conference on Computer Vision and Pattern Recognition* (pp. 1625-1634). DOI: 10.1109/CVPR.2018.00175

Fagnant, D. J., & Kockelman, K. (2015). Preparing a nation for autonomous vehicles: Opportunities, barriers and policy recommendations. *Transportation Research Part A, Policy and Practice, 77*, 167–181. DOI: 10.1016/j.tra.2015.04.003

Feng, S., Yan, X., Sun, H., & Li, L. (2020). A review of deep learning methods for vehicle detection in autonomous driving. *IEEE Transactions on Neural Networks and Learning Systems, 32*(9), 3561–3578.

Flad, M., & Filippone, M. (2019). Safe and secure biometric authentication for autonomous vehicles. *IEEE Transactions on Intelligent Transportation Systems, 20*(8), 3060–3069.

Gogineni, V., & Kalyan, A. (2018). Biometric-based driver authentication in autonomous vehicles. *International Journal of Vehicle Autonomous Systems, 14*(2), 123–138.

Goodfellow, I., Papernot, N., Huang, S., Duan, R., Abbeel, P., & Clark, J. (2017). *Attacking machine learning with adversarial examples*. OpenAI Blog.

Gupta, A., & Gupta, P. (2019). Biometric security in autonomous vehicles: A survey. *International Journal of Computer Applications*, *177*(26), 1–7. DOI: 10.5120/ijca2019919451

Haque, M. A., & Nasir, M. A. (2019). Biometric authentication in autonomous vehicles: A comprehensive survey. *International Journal of Biometrics*, *11*(4), 357–375.

He, K., Zhang, X., Ren, S., & Sun, J. (2016). Deep residual learning for image recognition. In *Proceedings of the IEEE Conference on Computer Vision and Pattern Recognition* (pp. 770-778).

Huang, X., Cheng, X., Geng, G., Cao, X., & Lu, H. (2019). The role of biometric authentication in autonomous vehicles: A survey. *IEEE Access : Practical Innovations, Open Solutions*, *7*, 177379–177392.

Hussain, R., & Zeadally, S. (2019). Autonomous cars: Research results, issues, and future challenges. *IEEE Communications Surveys and Tutorials*, *21*(2), 1275–1313. DOI: 10.1109/COMST.2018.2869360

Jain, A. K., & Ross, A. (2004). Multibiometric systems. *Communications of the ACM*, *47*(1), 34–40. DOI: 10.1145/962081.962102

Jung, H., Lee, J., Yim, J., Park, S., & Kim, J. (2016). Joint visual and thermal sequence alignment network for robust pedestrian detection. In *Proceedings of the IEEE Conference on Computer Vision and Pattern Recognition* (pp. 1420-1429).

Kang, L., & Wang, Y. (2019). Biometric authentication in autonomous vehicles: A survey. *IEEE Access : Practical Innovations, Open Solutions*, *7*, 177379–177392.

Khan, M. A., & Salah, K. (2018). IoT security: Review, blockchain solutions, and open challenges. *Future Generation Computer Systems*, *82*, 395–411. DOI: 10.1016/j.future.2017.11.022

Kim, J., & Park, S. (2018). Biometric authentication in autonomous vehicles: A comprehensive review. *Journal of Transportation Security*, *11*(1-2), 1–22.

Kumar, N., & Sharma, S. (2019). Biometric authentication in autonomous vehicles: A review. *International Journal of Biometrics*, *11*(4), 357–375.

Li, Y., & Wang, X. (2020). Secure biometric authentication for self-driving vehicles. *Journal of Intelligent Transport Systems*, *24*(2), 89–103.

Liu, Y., Yang, X., & Wang, P. (2019). Enhancing security in autonomous vehicles with AI-driven biometric systems. *IEEE Transactions on Vehicular Technology*, *68*(12), 11234–11245.

Ma, Z., & Zhang, H. (2021). Deep learning applications in biometric security for autonomous cars. *IEEE Access : Practical Innovations, Open Solutions*, *9*, 105678–105689.

Mahajan, R., & Sharma, K. (2018). Biometric-based vehicle access control: A survey. *International Journal of Automotive Technology*, *19*(4), 567–580.

Matsuo, T., & Yamashita, T. (2017). AI-powered facial recognition in autonomous vehicles. *IEEE Intelligent Transportation Systems Magazine*, *9*(3), 54–64.

Meyer, P., & Fischer, S. (2019). Evaluating biometric authentication systems for self-driving cars. *Journal of Transportation Cybersecurity*, *5*(1), 27–42.

Mohammed, F., & Hassan, R. (2020). Ethical challenges in biometric security for autonomous vehicles. *Ethics and Information Technology*, *22*(3), 243–257.

Nakamura, S., & Suzuki, Y. (2021). AI and biometric authentication: Securing the future of self-driving cars. *IEEE Transactions on Transportation Electrification*, *7*(2), 122–135.

Nandi, A., & Gupta, P. (2020). Risk assessment in biometric authentication for autonomous cars. *IEEE Access : Practical Innovations, Open Solutions*, *8*, 89765–89778.

Nguyen, T., & Le, H. (2019). Biometric-enabled smart vehicle access control systems. *International Journal of Biometrics*, *12*(2), 123–140.

Patel, A., & Desai, K. (2020). Machine learning in biometric security for autonomous vehicles. *Machine Learning Applications in Automotive Systems*, *32*(4), 205–218.

Rajan, V., & Natarajan, P. (2018). Fingerprint authentication for self-driving vehicle security. *International Journal of Intelligent Transportation Systems Research*, *16*(2), 135–148.

Ramesh, S., & Kumar, R. (2019). Multimodal biometrics in autonomous driving. *Advances in Intelligent Transportation Systems*, *18*(4), 245–258.

Rana, P., & Mehta, S. (2021). Secure facial recognition for autonomous vehicle authentication. *IEEE Transactions on Intelligent Vehicles*, *6*(3), 420–435.

Sato, H., & Tanaka, M. (2020). AI-based voice authentication for autonomous vehicle security. *IEEE Transactions on Intelligent Transportation Systems*, *21*(11), 5512–5525.

Schuster, M., & Lang, D. (2018). Biometric security risks in self-driving cars. *Cybersecurity Journal*, *9*(1), 77–89.

Singh, A., & Patel, V. (2019). Keystroke dynamics as a biometric authentication method for autonomous vehicles. *International Journal of Vehicular Biometric Systems*, *15*(3), 199–213.

Sun, L., & Zhang, T. (2020). Deep learning in facial recognition for autonomous vehicle entry systems. *IEEE Transactions on Cybernetics*, *50*(8), 3754–3766.

Tan, R., & Huang, W. (2019). Challenges in biometric authentication for autonomous vehicle security. *IEEE Access : Practical Innovations, Open Solutions*, *7*, 99112–99125.

Thompson, J., & Williams, C. (2018). Biometric data privacy in autonomous vehicles. *Journal of Privacy and Security*, *14*(2), 88–102.

Wang, J., & Liu, Z. (2020). Using AI to enhance biometric security in self-driving cars. *IEEE Transactions on Artificial Intelligence*, *2*(4), 320–335.

Wilson, H., & Campbell, D. (2019). Securing autonomous vehicles with biometric encryption. *Journal of Automotive Cybersecurity*, *5*(2), 110–123.

Xie, F., & Yu, L. (2021). Driver monitoring systems using biometric data: An AI approach. *IEEE Transactions on Intelligent Vehicles*, *7*(1), 56–72.

Zhao, Q., & Chen, M. (2020). Enhancing security in self-driving cars using biometrics. *IEEE Transactions on Neural Networks and Learning Systems*, *31*(12), 5124–5135. PMID: 32011269

Zhou, Y., & Li, J. (2019). AI-driven multimodal biometric authentication for autonomous vehicles. *IEEE Access : Practical Innovations, Open Solutions*, *7*, 123451–123465.

Chapter 7

Deepfake Threats, Cybersecurity Challenges, and Countermeasures

Sherly Alphonse
http://orcid.org/0000-0002-0019-9940
Vellore Institute of Technology, Chennai, India

Neha Khadeeja
http://orcid.org/0009-0007-2099-2659
Vellore Institute of Technology, Chennai, India

Azra Q. Fathima
Vellore Institute of Technology, Chennai, India

Manasa Balaji
http://orcid.org/0009-0003-6125-4100
Vellore Institute of Technology, Chennai, India

ABSTRACT

The social problem of deepfake videos is becoming a critical issue. A rising social problem is the manipulation of these recordings by artificial intelligence (AI) techniques, particularly deep learning. Malicious people employ deepfake technologies to disseminate bogus content, including phony audio, video, and image files. The creation of convincing fake information poses a threat to privacy, security, and politics. Most deepfake video detection techniques rely on data. In-depth analysis of deepfake video production and detection is the goal of this chapter. Identifying the many difficulties in identifying deepfake films is the primary contribution of the chapter. This chapter describes about the science behind the deepfake, detection

DOI: 10.4018/979-8-3373-2922-2.ch007

and mitigation of deepfake etc. This chapter also describes about the applications of deepfake and also the policies and technologies to combat deepfake. This chapter describes in detail about the ethical, legal and social implications.

1. INTRODUCTION

Deepfake technology is a significant advancement in artificial intelligence (AI). Deep learning is capable of creating realistic images and voices that can have significant advantages and disadvantages. The terms deep learning and fake images led to the coining of the term deepfake(Okolie, 2023).

The Generative Adversarial Network(Monteiro, 2024) plays a significant part in creating fake images. There are a lot of innovative approaches to deepfake (Yu et al., 2021). This can be used in movies and also in education.

But it's not all good news, either. Moreover, deepfake technology has already raised a number of serious concerns. If misused, it can be used to spread propaganda, generate fake news, or even harm someone's character by making it appear like they said or did something they didn't. As such, increased effort is put into developing tools that would be able to recognize deep fakes and prevent further exploitation of them.

So, deepfake technology — a fascinating but also somewhat scary tool. A tool is only as good or bad as what you decide to do with it. We need to find the right balance between using this technology to innovate and ensuring that it is not abusive as it continues to evolve. Thus, this section gives a short introduction to the deepfake technology.

Section 2 gives a detailed literature review of the different models used in the literature for the creation and detection of deepfake images. Section 3 describes the science behind deepfakes, and Section 4 describes LLM in detail. Section 5 describes the different tools used for creating deepfakes. Section 6 gives a detailed analysis of the various mitigation techniques. Section 7 describes the various applications, and Section 8 describes the ethical concerns in detail. The last section concludes the chapter, giving a detailed perspective on the threats.

2. LITERATURE REVIEW

With the faster progression of artificial intelligence in the last few years comes deepfake technology, an integrated tool that produces hyper-realistic fakes. Having originated for simple aesthetic in films or offering creativity in areas like gaming and education, deepfake technology rose in infamy for the wrong reasons. Such power enables this distinctive capability to modulate audiovisual media as an identity and authenticity in terms of an ethical responsiveness, and, in turn, this can produce profound legal questions on consent. When pictures and movies become 'Jurgen creatures' to target the lives of politicians and their policies, their lives and their counterparts in public and private domains, the falsehood affects credibility in media jams and even outlets. In this paper, one will describe the features of deepfake software, analyse its outcomes, and examine the difficulties that arise at a time when people can no longer distinguish the truth from a lie(Gambín et al., 2024).

New advancement in artificial intelligence leads to the creation of deep fake technology, where, through DCNN hyper hyper-realization of media is done via a deep learning algorithm. Deepfakes are not just video; that is, audio/still images, and, as a result, they can be entirely severed from their original context, substantially so; in its most sophisticated form, even then, it would be impossible not to be misled, that is, it would be realistic. This manipulation has been understood to leverage visual and audio reality, and to raise critical questions of moral right and wrong, mainly in domains of fake news and unwanted material, such as 'deep fake pornography' (Korshunov & Marcel, 2018). As digital content grows with the many platforms present, using visual media as evidence, which has been demonstrated in judicial systems, only escalates the effects of deepfakes concerning the real essence of truth and integrity (BJ, 2024). The technology, therefore, needs qualitative regulatory platforms that are soon going to address the disruptive threat factor inherent in the technology on one hand and unlock innovation, lawful and profit-making legal uses in the entertainment and communication industry on the other hand.

The basic concepts on which deepfake type is created have roots in artificial intelligence and, in particular, machine learning and deep learning neural networks. These, trained on massive facial images & videos, can be used to alter any visual content in Automatic and Invisible ways to produce hyper-realistic FA forgeries. In a process known as GANs, there are two neural networks – the 'generator' that creates the content, and the 'discriminator' that verifies the content – for the quality of the fake improves iteratively over time. These processes have raised several ethical issues, especially when developing an embarrassing status of the individuals without their consent, and therefore, the various regulations of the practice seem to become essential. As observed by the authors of the contemporary analyses, for instance (Yan, 2022) (Alanazi et al., 2024), deepfakes are not simply dangers to personal images but more broadly dangers to the general risks of misinformation, but also to reimaging the territories of trust/identity in digital transactions.

The above-discussed generative adversarial networks (GANs) and other related techniques of deep learning and computer vision are developed for generating deepfakes. Using the aid of the pre-trained GAN, the people behind the videos can replace the faces of the people in the videos in what looks like a pretty plausible manner.

This technique has been especially disturbing since cases of faces of celebrities being artificially transformed into awkward situations have been rising, meaning that detection technology is needed urgently (Harris, 2018). Besides, performance generated with deepfake technology utilizes autoencoders, while pasting the source image onto the face of the target video (Mahashreshty Vishweshwar, 2023). Thus, a high quality of the produced deepfake video depends on the trained and blended parameters. This could be beautiful or otherwise, depending on the intention of the "maker". In time, this production and subsequent discovery become even more challenging, hence the continuous need for detection research.

Due to the highly professional quality of impersonation, massive use of deepfake technology is dangerous to the socially shared trust and individuals' privacy, thus it is a social responsibility that necessitates immediate ethical consideration. It came with it more better technology in forging the most realistic images and videos that lead to identity thefts and fake news, and information dissemination. In that respect, deepfakes can sway people's opinion during electoral stages, and in the end, they hinder the liberal-democratic institutions on which they rely, based on well-enlightened publics. Also, the possibility of creating adult material through asexual reproduction leads to a number of questions with regard to personal freedom and abuse. While there are some rewards, in the sense of the protection and ownership of the intellectual property of such a system as the FORGE system, the ethical constraint that a deepfake generator is so readily available is a great challenge. Legal acts, by intent, are extraordinarily broad, focusing on a specific emphasis on a number of international cooperation concerns that are related to the generation, distribution, and employment of deepfakes.

As the use of deepfakes is becoming more and more widespread, the privacy and consent violations that it causes are increasingly blatant. The sheer ability to generate realistic media presents a special danger, first of all, in the case of non-consensual pornography; mimics and likenesses per se can be changed without consent or agreement. Since anyone, really, can produce deepfakes now, there are darker questions about the reality of the individual self and the possibility of agency and consent. From research, several victims who are not celebrities suffer considerable emotional distress and reputational loss due to the circulation of unauthorized content by the public. Also, the failure of current legal instruments to provide sufficient protection requires the enactment of stringent laws for handling these difficulties (Abbas & Taeihagh, 2024). Therefore, as it has been advocated in this chapter that an adaptive and integrated multitiered legal, technical, and educational approach is needed to protect the rights of individuals from this information technology advancement, it will require a negotiated, immobilized, and encompassing, multi-disciplinary approach.

In conclusion, the subject of deepfake technology has many intertwined problem areas that require an integrated approach to address the interaction of the IT element, society, and Ethics. This technology has more significant risks persisting today, especially privacy violations and the proliferation of false information, as this technology continues to develop. Regardless of the use, it is full of great risks. At the same time, (Goodfellow et al., 2014) stressed that the power relations within deepfake pornography are also patriarchal and misogynistic, to which Lo proposes to respond with Averts and legislation to shield vulnerable people from it. Imposing the burdens of deepfakes challenges requires interaction between technological expertise, legal, and ethical professionals. Such can help create a general approach for managing social risks and establish a reasoned discussion of the always-persistent, developing digital environment. There is great potential when it comes to deepfakes; however, the problems related to those redesigns are very much related to regulatory aspects, which should be taken into account carefully. The potential uses of this technology are extremely versatile, from leisure and entertainment to enhancing education and toys, and represent a highly inventive and appealing opportunity for development for every industry. However, deepfake technology provides different sorts of problems, including fake news, identity theft, and violation of privacy. But for this aim, the rules have to be sketched to nurture the growth of innovations and, at the same time, to control the rights of an individual and the norms of society. An active approach will be provided with the determination of requirements for labels to synthetic media and enhancement of fines for malicious use of synthetic media as well as introduction of incentives for technologists, policymakers, and ethicists to learn more about deepfakes which in their turn are the part of the attempt to design better, efficient, reliable laws or regulations for the evolving technological area without the risks involved here.

The deepfake technology is closely related to the generative models and computational power. Earlier, there were autoencoder-based techniques; later, Generative Adversarial Networks (GANs) were used to improve realism (Goodfellow et al., 2014), (Korshunov & Marcel, 2018). There were also StyleGAN and transformer-based models that enhanced temporal coherence and video quality (Karras et al., 2019), (Korshunov & Marcel, 2018). The diffusion models also result in high-resolution and realistic outputs (Ho et al., 2020). The limitations are as follows:

- Computational cost is high.
- Need good datasets for training.
- False positives affect the accuracy.

Despite the GAN advancements, the misuse leads to the detection approaches staying ahead of GAN.

Also, regional and international bodies address the ethical and security concerns. The European Union's AI Act (2024) (European Commission, 2024) enforces transparency, and the African Union's Digital Transformation Strategy (2020–2030) (African Union Commission, 2020; Guarnera et al., 2022; Jia et al., 2024; Mahmud & Sharmin, 2021) enforces the ethical concerns. These frameworks give a global perspective on deepfake technologies. Table 1 represents several models that are present in the literature for creating synthetic images, along with their key contributions and applications. Table 2 gives a summary of various detection approaches along with their strengths and limitations. Thus, this section gives a detailed survey of all the existing works in the literature.

Table 1. **Different models in the literature**

Year	Technique / Model	Key Contribution	Representative Application
2014	Generative Adversarial Networks (GANs) – *Goodfellow et al.*	Generation of realistic synthetic images.	Foundation for deepfake architectures.
2016	Autoencoder	Facial identity transfer.	Meme-based applications.
2018	Face2Face models	Improved real-time synthesis	Social media manipulation.
2019	StyleGAN	Enhanced image quality.	Synthetic human faces.
2020	Multimodal	Integrated audio–visual cues.	Forensic and cybersecurity applications.
2021	Transformer-based	Used attention mechanisms.	Realistic video avatars.
2022	Diffusion-based	Denoising.	AI-generated art.
2024–2025	Regulation-Aware Systems	Integrate ethical constraints.	Transparent AI media.

Table 2. **Detection approaches**

Model Type	Key Principle	Strengths	Limitations
CNN	Spatial feature extraction	High accuracy	Limited temporal analysis;
RNN/LSTM	Sequential analysis of frame-level data	Video-based analysis captures motion inconsistencies.	Sensitive to noise
Transformer	Attention mechanisms	Robust	High training cost.

3. SCIENCE BEHIND DEEPFAKE

Deepfake technology is one of the AI technologies that is based on advanced machine learning techniques, but related to deep learning in particular. Deepfakes are powered by a family of algorithms called Generative Adversarial Networks

(GANs), which are meant to produce realistic synthetic data. GANs consist of two neural networks working together (Ma et al., 2024):

i. **Generator:** This network tries to replicate genuine data like images, videos, or sound to create fake data in this network. For example, it might try to generate a human face.
ii. **Discriminator:** This network behaves like a critic who judges whether the data produced by the generator is real or fake.

The two networks are trained in parallel in a manner that they compete with one another. The generator augments the machine's potential for producing authentic samples, and, at the same time, the discriminator refines itself as a fake detection apparatus.(Ahmed et al., 2024) In the course of time, the generated data gets highly realistic and thus poses a great challenge to distinguish from real data. The objective function is:

$$min_G \, max_D \, V(D,G) = E_{X-p_{data(x)}}(logD(z)) + E_{z-p_{z(z)}}(\log(1 - D(G(z)))) \quad (1)$$

Where:

- $p_{data_{(x)}}$ is the distribution of real images
- $p_{z_{(z)}}$ is the random noise distribution
- $G(z)$ generates fake images
- $D(x)$ outputs the probability that x is real

Figure 1. Deepfake Architecture (GANs) Diagram

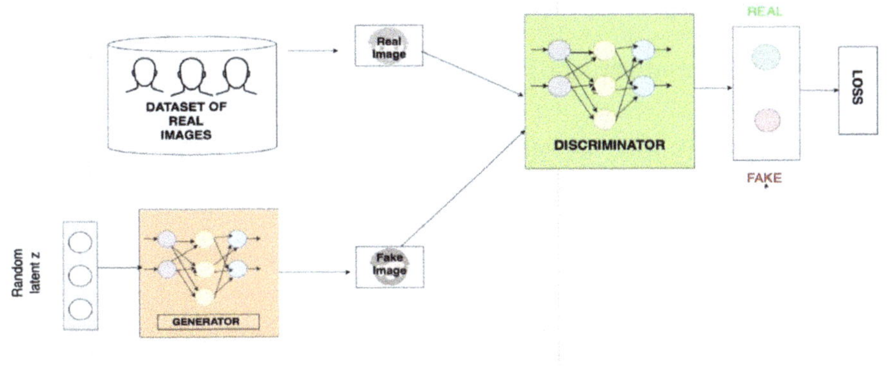

3.1. Training Deepfake Models

Making a deepfake depends on the data of images or videos of the subject who will be faked. (Perov et al., 2020) It is these datasets that the model learns from in order to develop the desired ability to interpret the person's face, including their shape, their expressions, and even the way they move. Common techniques include:

3.1.1. Face Swapping

Tracing one person's face over another's while paying attention to the exact correspondence of individual facial parts and the transitions between them. (Rana et al., 2022)

3.1.2. Motion Capture

Many times, it involves tracking the movements of face muscles and establishing the new look or word.

3.1.3. Voice Synthesis

It is a possibility to imitate voices, intonation, and pronunciation to create believable audio using Artificial Intelligence.

3.2. The Key Components of Deepfake

3.2.1. Autoencoders

An autoencoder is a neural network used in the process of encoding a person's features and reconstructing them. They have two main parts:

i. **Encoder:** Collapses input data (for example, an image) into a smaller compressed form of data.
ii. **Decoder:** Converts the specially encoded data back into its original form. (Masood et al., 2023)

Deepfakes do not utilize a GAN discriminator, but for the encoder to encode the features of the source, where the face is being replaced, and the target, where the face is being imposed on. The decoder places the source's face on the body of the target.

The Autoencoder learns to minimize the reconstruction loss by the formula:

$$L_{AE} = \|X - D(E(X))\|^2 \quad (2)$$

Where,

- X is the input image.
- $E(X)$ is the encoder function that maps input to the latent space.
- $D(E(X))$ is the decoder function that reconstructs the input
- $\|.\|^2$ denotes the squared error loss.

Figure 2. Deepfake Generation Process

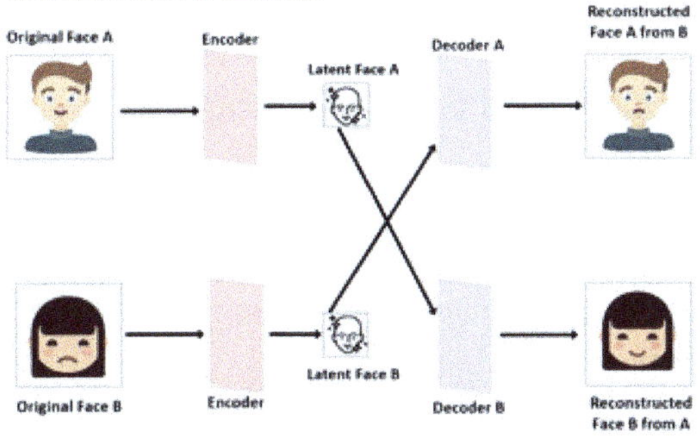

3.2.2. Face Alignment

This process helps in the proper alignment of the faces in both the source and the target images. Face alignment enables the swapped face to approximate the position, direction, and movements of the target by detecting necessary facial landmarks like the eyes, nasal, and mouth regions.

3.2.3. Facial Landmarks Detection

Facial landmarks are architectural features that are localized to the face, including the edge of the eye(s), the lip margin, and the tip of the nose. These landmarks enable us to determine the correspondence between the source face and the target face successfully. They also make it possible for the generated face to interact harmoniously with movements and expressions (Al-Dhabi & Zhang, 2021).

3.2.4. Motion Capture

In order to generate authentic deepfakes in videos, there is a use of so-called motion capture, which captures facial movements. This includes blinking, smiling, or head tilting, for example, the baby. These movements are then added to the produced face to make the face look real, as real human facial muscles (Alimova, 2021).

3.2.5 Lip-Syncing Models

Lip-syncing models synchronize lip movements with the sound generated out of it. These models refer to the phonetics of human speech and create lip contortions that should fit the video in terms of synchronization.

3.2.6 Texture Mapping and Skin Blending

Realism also depends on how smoothly the extracted texture of the source face (skin colour, wrinkle, shade) fits with the target face.

Such things as texturing or mapping maintain the skin colour and illumination of the two face models.

Skinning also aids in reducing joints or project edges because these details would often be hard to match.

3.2.7. Modifications

Some extra processing is usually needed and done after the generation of the deep fake. This includes (Alimova, 2021; Flynn et al., 2021; Lees, 2024):

i. **Adjusting Lighting:** Helps in brightening the face and background equally throughout the photo shoot.
ii. **Correcting Artifacts:** Rejects artificial interferences in the format present in the original digital copy.

There is, however, difficulty in preserving the temporal consistency of features in sectors of video deep fakes. Otherwise, some defects in the shape of freezes or inconsistencies can be noticed in the video that has been created.

The latest deep fake systems are recurrent neural networks (RNNs) or temporal GANs in order to give efficient transitions in terms of movement and expressions.

Other methods of motion estimation are also used to generate intermediate frames to make the transition from one frame to another seamless.

To alleviate the training process and computational factors, deepfake models employ transfer learning frequently. By transfer learning, the model is trained on a vast dataset of one type (e.g., general human faces), then the specific images of the targeted person are used to fine-tune the primed model to yield distinctive results.

This technique lets the generator learn faster and get higher realism with fewer samples.

In some cases, ANs are able to produce relatively low-definition images at first. For the purpose of getting more realistic results, which may be used in videos or high-quality images, super-resolution methods are used.

These methods help increase the level of detail while reconstructing the generated images and make the image look more realistic, adding details such as pores, wrinkles, or changes in lighting to an image.

Deepfakes do not solely depend on the techniques of the technology; in fact, they even target the human mind. Through learning about movements such as blinking or furrowed eyebrows, to skin blemishes or pores, deep fakes know how humans interpret faces and thus, are difficult to tell apart from authentic videos.

4. LLM

Large Language Models, also known as LLMs, are a type of artificial intelligence that is trained on enormous amounts of data to generate as well as understand text that appears to be human-like. Examples of Large Language Models (LLMs) include OpenAI's ChatGPT, Google's BERT, etc.

These LLMs(Ma et al., 2024) can perform many tasks, which include but are not limited to summarising content, language translation, sentiment analysis, and even solving mathematical problems to some extent.

4.1. How do LLMs Contribute to Deepfake Creation?

Though LLMs cannot directly be used to create audio or video deep fakes, they are often used as a supporting tool in the following ways:

4.1.1. To Create Convincing Scripts and Dialogues

For example, a simple prompt can be given to ask ChatGPT to generate a script or dialogue like a certain individual, such as prominent public figures or celebrities, or generate a convincing email informing you that a large sum of money has been debited from your bank account. These scripts can then be used in deep fake videos and audios.(Ma et al., 2024)

4.1.2. Enhancing Text-to-Speech (TTS) Systems

When used along with TTS systems, LLMs can also produce artificially generated voices that sound very similar to real people. These synthetic voices can then be merged with deep fake videos.

4.1.3. Customisable Content

LLMs simplify the process of creating deep fake content catered to specific audiences to a large extent, making it easier for phishers to scam people more efficiently.

4.2. Ethical Concerns and Risks

Engagement of LLMs in the production of deepfakes raises some of the serious ethical concerns, such as:

4.2.1. Spreading Misinformation

Deepfakes that are developed using LLMs can be used to spread fake news, influence opinions, or harm reputations.

4.2.2. Identity Theft and Fraud

Combining LLMs with deepfake technology makes it easier for bad actors to impersonate individuals for scams or cyberattacks.

4.2.3. Eroding Trust

Widespread use of hyper-realistic, artificially generated media makes it harder for us to trust the content we consume online.

Thus, this section explains the basic technology used in deepfake detection and gives a summary of the machine learning algorithms used in the process.

5. TOOLS AND FRAMEWORKS FOR DEEPFAKE DEVELOPMENT

Deep fake development technology has advanced significantly over recent years, using deep learning to create hyper-realistic modifications in videos and audio. Creating deep fake content involves the usage of multiple sophisticated tools that are specifically designed to handle image processing as well as dataset manipulation and management. The various tools and frameworks required for deep fake development are listed below.

5.1. Popular Deepfake Creation Tools

5.1.1. DeepFaceLab

DeepFaceLab is used to create face-swapping videos with which use Xseg Masking for segmentation and swapping. It needs multiple GPU support for improving the training speed in large-scale projects. It also helps in forgery detection (Perov et al., 2020).

5.1.2 FaceSwap

FaceSwap is a face-swapping tool that has easy user interface with community support (Rana et al., 2022).

5.1.3. ReFace

Reface has pre-trained models that can be used to create face-swapping videos, mostly used in mobile platforms, and can be used by even novice users.

5.2. Libraries and Frameworks Required

5.2.1. TensorFlow

TensorFlow Hub provides pre-trained models, whereas TensorFlow Lite is an optimized version used in mobiles (Mahmud & Sharmin, 2021).

5.2.2. PyTorch

PyTorch is used for experimenting with new architectures. A key feature of PyTorch is TorchVision, which has pretrained models(Mahmud & Sharmin, 2021).

5.2.3. Keras

This simplifies complex tasks like building models and training them due to its high-level API (Mahmud & Sharmin, 2021).

5.2.4. OpenCV

OpenCV has different tools that are valuable for deepfake development. It has a number of tools for colour adjustments, resizing, and cropping.

6. DETECTION AND MITIGATION OF DEEPFAKES

6.1. Techniques for Detecting Deepfakes

Detection of deepfakes involves human interpretation and computing techniques. Experts are constantly working on refining the detection methods. The methods for detection are:

6.1.1. Visual Artifacts

Deepfake media often have subtle imperfections such as:

i. **Face blending issues**: Mismatch in skin tones or unevenly blended edges between the swapped face and the surrounding areas (Masood et al., 2023).
ii. **Blinking and eye movement:** Videos created using deepfakes often fail to replicate natural human blinking patterns.
iii. **Resolution**: There is often visibly lower resolution in the areas of movement or around the facial features.

These imperfections can often be detected through careful analysis (Masood et al., 2023).

6.1.2. Audio Analysis

Deepfakes can also be detected through imperfections in audio, such as:

i. **Speech patterns:** Voices generated using AI generally lack natural pauses and voice modulation.
ii. **Lip-Sync errors**: This indicates the lip movements and the audio (Al-Dhabi & Zhang, 2021).

6.1.3. Metadata Examination

The metadata is used to find manipulations like repeated editing.

6.1.4. AI and Machine Learning-Based Detection Models

Advanced detection techniques use Artificial Intelligence to detect deepfakes:

i. **Convolutional Neural Networks (CNNs):** CNNs can analyze spatial patterns in images and videos. They also help in identifying the inconsistencies in textures, lighting, and facial features that are introduced while generating the synthetic image. They help in detecting GAN artifacts like unnatural blending of facial elements (Al-Dhabi & Zhang, 2021).
ii. **Recurrent Neural Networks (RNNs):** Recurrent Neural Networks (RNNs) examine a series of frames in sequence to identify the inconsistencies over time. They identify unnatural transitions. The (Al-Dhabi & Zhang, 2021; Alimova, 2021) Long Short-Term Memory (LSTM) can be used for deepfake detection.
iii. **Transformer Models:** Vision Transformers (ViTs), use attention mechanisms to analyse entire images or video frames (Al-Dhabi & Zhang, 2021; Alimova, 2021).
iv. **Ensemble Models:** Ensemble models integrate various detection methods using unique strengths of different AI methods to identify manipulated media types.

6.2. Developing Counter-Deep Fake Algorithms

6.2.1. Adversarial Training

Training detection models based on adversarial examples created from evolving deepfake algorithms.

6.2.2. Feature Engineering

Feature Engineering,(Flynn et al., 2021) can identify minute features in head movements and also micro expressions.

6.2.3. Temporal Analysis

Temporal analysis uses temporal coherence models to detect inconsistencies and also deetcts frame-by-frame anomalies (Flynn et al., 2021).

6.2.4. Blockchain for Authentication

Blockchain technology is used for embedding cryptographic signatures so that the content is secure and tamper-proof.

6.3. Policies and Tools to Combat Deepfake Abuse

6.3.1. Legal and Ethical Frameworks

Governments use laws to punish those who use deepfakes for unwanted things, according to the Accountability Act in the U.S.

6.3.2. Industry Collaboration

Tech companies and governments, together, standardize the detection and management of deepfake media.

6.3.3. Tools and Platforms for Detection

'Forensically' helps examines metadata to detect deepfakes.

6.3.4. Public Awareness Campaigns

Educating the public on deepfakes and the various ways they can be misused is crucial. Campaigns on internet safety, teaching users to identify manipulated content, can also prevent the misuse of deepfakes. Thus, this section explains the mitigation techniques.

Figure 3. Deepfake detection flowchart

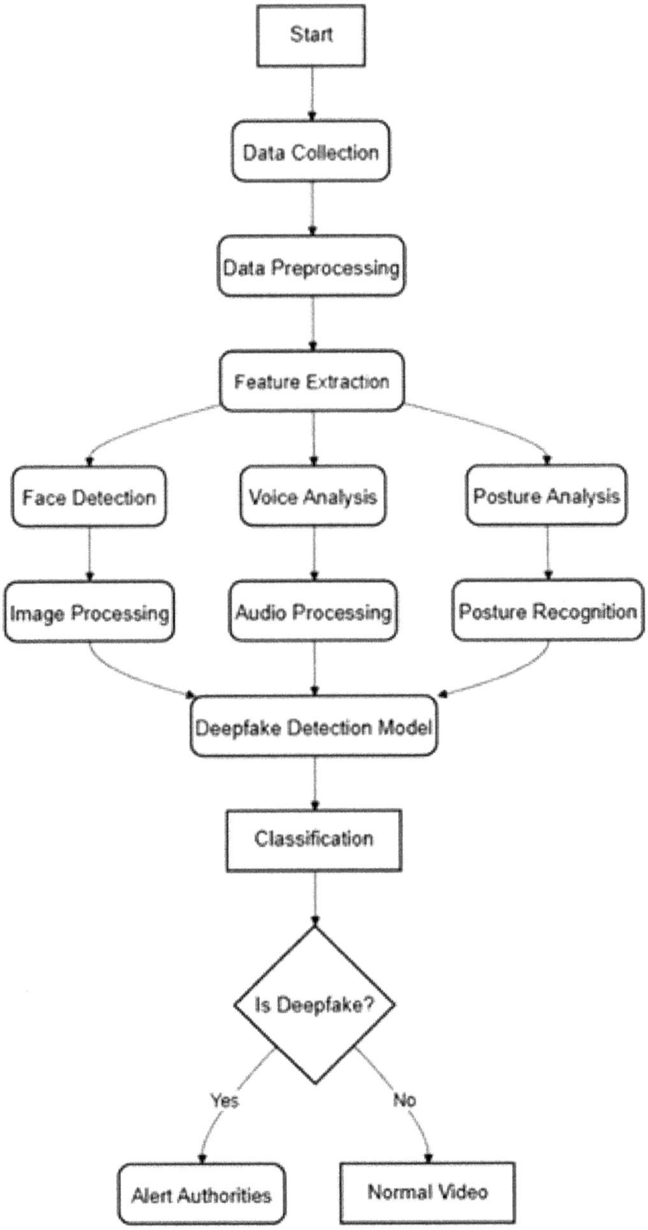

Figure 4. General workflow.

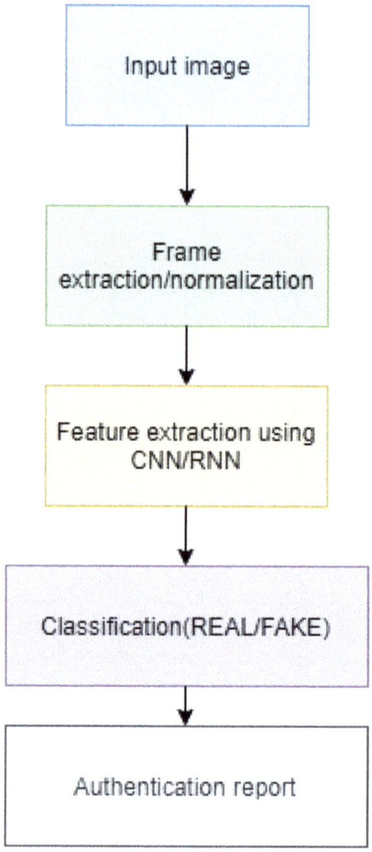

The general workflow is given in the following Figure 4. The feature extraction process helps to identify the patterns of pixels in deepfake images, which are detected by the deep learning models.

7. APPLICATIONS AND USE CASES

7.1 Entertainment and Film Production

Deepfakes are going to revolutionize the process of how people interact and create, looking for new ways to express themselves (Lees, 2024; Swords & Willment, 2024).

7.1.1 Character Recreation

Filmmakers and creators now use AI to insert characters into their scenes without the actors actually being present. Deepfake technology allows de-aging, the recreation of deceased actors, and even the creation of new performances. While this technology leads to exciting possibilities, it also raises concerns about consent and other ethical and legal issues, which are discussed in the upcoming sections. It also creates confusion in the viewer's mind regarding reality and fiction. Deepfake technology has already been used in Martin Scorsese's *The Irishman.* It used AI to de-age the actors. In the movie *Star Wars*, Grand Moff Tarkin was brought back years after Peter Cushing's death using deepfake technologies. AI is also used in voice cloning to bring back or recreate speeches.

7.1.2 Scene Enhancement: Post-Production Alterations

Deepfake technology is used to enhance scenes. Some of those applications(Jansen, 2024) include tweaking facial expressions, matching lip movements for dubbed dialogues r even swapping faces of actors. This makes post-production more flexible and helps in avoiding the extra costs of having to reshoot. If actors aren't available for additional filming, their faces can be replaced using these technologies (Haas, 2024).

7.1.3 Realistic CGI Characters

Filmmakers often use CGI, but deepfake technology makes character modifications much more realistic and visually appealing (Jansen, 2024). This helps natural facial expressions and movements, ensuring that CGI characters blend in seamlessly in live action scenes.

7.2 Personalised Advertising

Here, marketers have the possibility to use deepfakes in creating more convincing and distinct advertisement images. Based on preferred and behavioural data, consumer engagement could be increased, and as a result, brands and companies' conversion rates could be improved using personal content created especially for them (Haas, 2024; Haleem et al., 2019). The sphere of advertisement eagerly adopted the technology, and the time when the brands directly address the audience comes every time the practice is legal and has a positive motivation. Marketers are enamoured by the possibility of using deepfakes to deliver memorable and personalized messages (Lakshmi & Hemanth, 2024). Both ad managers and advertisers have hastened to state that including deepfakes in advertising production has opened up new frontiers in innovation. Famous deepfake marketing includes the rebirth of Salvador Dalí for the Dalí Museum; really getting closer to art with live Dalí appeared to be entertaining for the guests. By doing so, the many layers of such frames of the video footage of the deepfake give a real experience with the face of the iconic artist. This is an indication that deepfakes have the potential to enhance the experience of users across many fields and across the entire sector.

7.3 Medical Applications

Although deepfakes are revolutionizing how doctors can train, this has made the training more realistic and safer by providing learners and professionals with simulated patients that can be diagnosed and treated (Nguyen et al., 2022). These Virtual patients look like real life, with cases normal and the most complicated ones, which will be advantageous to the medical learners. GANs have made a significant impact on the medical field by utilizing computational power and vast healthcare records to generate and analyze medical data. Unlike the traditional data augmentation techniques, which can only modify existing images through cropping, inverting, or alignment, GANs are capable of creating entirely new medical images.

7.4 Virtual Reality and Augmented Reality

By fusing digital components with the physical world and producing immersive virtual worlds, deepfake technology is being utilized more and more to improve augmented reality (AR) and virtual reality (VR) experiences. Deepfakes can be used in AR and VR to generate photo-realistic digital features that feel natural by creating lifelike copies of people or objects. The live virtual world deepfake from Volucap, which was integrated into the Meta Horizons VR platform and transmitted on a giant LED screen through a VR headset (Swords & Willment, 2024), is an example of how deepfakes can be integrated into virtual reality. Additionally, deepfakes can synthesize human voices and alter facial expressions, which might be used to target specific people with modified information or fake sounds. Deepfakes' proliferation in AR and VR has uses in a variety of fields, including education (Jansen, 2024).

7.5 Educational Content and AI-Driven Storytelling

Secondly, deepfakes are adding more entertainment and interaction to the learning process. It is one thing to be learning from an animated character or having a teacher who can transform his or her teaching style within the space of a day. Deepfakes can therefore be used to customize educational information in a way that provides lessons and explanations that cater to the needs of each learner. They also allow for a clean narrative to be narrated and make it easier for the student to proceed to a real experience in a story (Roe et al., 2024; Sahu et al., 2021). Apart from that, deep fakes improve the learning process and the translation as well as the generation of the content adjusted to a student's needs, thus making the education more effective and accessible. Thus, this section summarizes the different applications.

8. ETHICAL, LEGAL, AND SOCIAL IMPLICATIONS

Deepfake technology is a relatively recent idea, and yet it offers many issues that are ethical, legal, and social that cannot be overlooked (Hasani et al., 2024; Tuysuz & Kılıç, 2023).

8.1. Privacy Concerns

Privacy threats can be well explained by deepfakes because they steal an individual's appearance or identity. This is because deepfakes malfunction in the unauthorized production and release of an individual's identity, privacy, or reputation violation. That one's picture or voice can be faked within the shortest time is why people's information must be protected (Lakshmi & Hemanth, 2024) and why consent procedures should be outlined.

8.2. Intellectual Property Issues

The major issue and several minor issues of intellectual property that would be relevant to the Aldi case are as follows:

The production of deep fakes is based on prior images, videos, or audio, so this raises ownership issues more often. A more complicated question is: who holds the rights in a deep fake, the person who created it? Is it the Rubio subject in the fake or the platform that used it? The subject area becomes blurred here, and people can start disputing its ownership and usage rights, which is not unusual in the entertainment and advertising sectors when celebrities or other public figures' deepfakes are used (Hussain, 2022; Verma, 2023; Westerlund, 2019).

8.3. Social and Media Trust

Two threats of deepfakes, which include the following: first, it will erode the public's credibility towards the media and information. Since deepfake technology is capable of generating realistic fake news that cannot be easily distinguished from real fake news, it can spread fake news, change people's perception, and also reduce confidence in credible media houses (Verma, 2023). This has disastrous consequences for society because it controls the elections, fake news, and societal instabilities.

8.4. Concerns and Applications Associated With Deepfake and Legal Framework

Due to deepfakes, several governments have either contemplated or implemented legal actions. Such measures are intended to prevent false use, preserve confidentiality, and determine accountability. The regulations can contain such sections as measures of punishment for the production and distribution of malicious deep fakes, rules governing the use of the open tags for synthetic media, and sections on the rights of the victims of deepfake scams more than once (Westerlund, 2019).

8.4.1. Effect and Misuse of Social Networking Sites

There are many such examples recently caused by the more and more popular deep fakes. For instance, deep fake predators utilize this technology to post the faces of women, especially those they personally know, on pornography clips against their will (Sahu et al., 2021). That has prompted the use of deepfakes in the political domain in a bid to construct fake stories and statements from political leaders and trimmings. Given these cases, it is imperative to enact correct legal as well as ethical paradigms so as to head off risky exercising and predetermine prerequisites for deepfake utilization.

Deepfakes can also recreate consummate actors or repurpose physically existing but digitally deceased actors to artificially extend their careers by bringing back whatever characters they once portrayed back to life (Jansen, 2024). This, of course, brings up the memories and is a step beyond the "frame" of the given narrative.

We noticed that post-production has actually been revolutionized recently, with deepfakes helping in smoothing the faces that have been replaced and in modifying the performances without shooting. This flexibility is efficient in shooting and, as such, the receptor's creative achievements (Haas, 2024).

Lying has its own etiquette, and it is wrong to steal someone's attribute without his consent (Sahu et al., 2021). Since creativity may be incompatible with personal rights, this topic demonstrates that there must be clearance in both permission and regulation.

Future generations may easily start challenging what they are being fed through the mainstream news due to deep fake news. The industry has to introduce certain specifications regarding when and how footage and materials can be checked. Thus, this section addresses the ethical concerns.

9. FUTURE OF DEEPFAKE TECHNOLOGY

Although the current technique helps eradicate deepfake threats, these threats remain complex. The deepfake technology, combined with autonomous AI agents and generative multimodal systems, leads to synthetic media capable of. Therefore, challenges regarding digital identity verification, cybersecurity, and information integrity still exist.

The usage of generative AI tools affects the scalability of misinformation and the potential weaponization of deepfakes. Therefore, deepfake detection demands stronger international collaboration and better authentication technologies

It is crucial to admit that deepfake technology has great opportunities in creative fields such as cinematography and television works, education, and advertising. When applied to filmmaking, it can help to restore the portrayal of historical characters, build de-aged or recreated actors, even members of the acting crew, and advance the production of special impacts. In education, it allows for effective storytelling, including putting characters from history to give their view on an event. The following is the potential benefit that can be enjoyed by the advertising agencies.

Deep fake can be used to develop relevant content for different markets, hence improving the customer touchpoint.

These inventions suggest opportunities for creativity and affordable, effective storytelling and audience engagement, as well as extending the possibilities for content creation and distribution.

Nevertheless, deepfake technology has enormous adverse consequences, such as the dissemination of wrong information, identity fraud, and defamation. Terrorists or other criminals could spread fake news, affect the result of the elections, or create unwanted and nonconsensual porn material, which harms confidence in digital media.

To address these risks, governments and organizations must:

i. Design sophisticated technologies driven by AI to detect deepfakes.
ii. Put in place strong Acts to discourage their use in vices.
iii. Increase people's knowledge concerning the existence and threat posed by deepfake technology.
iv. Funding in ethical AI development as well as research on watermarking and authentication technologies, will also contribute to the growth of the future deepfake technology between innovation and safety.

9.1. Threats Posed by Deepfake Technology and How to Overcome

Deepfake technology poses several potential threats (Roe et al., 2024), specifically in the spheres of business, security (Lakshmi & Hemanth, 2024), and politics (Haleem et al., 2019). In organizations, deepfakes can make employees transfer money or provide lots of information by pretending to be the ringleader of the company. As for biometric systems, which are widely used in security access, deepfake exposure puts such methods in danger of allowing a person to get access to restricted areas. In the social media context, deepfakes can mislead, anger, and deceive by generating content that it is not, and that portrays certain personalities or celebrities in ways that distort reality (Sahu et al., 2021). Categorically, in politics, an ingenious deepfake can rig an election and/or send convergence and bitterness into society through fake media narratives.

To address these threats, there is a need for better advanced deepfake detection, training employees on how to identify fake information, and enhancing the ways to verify the information. Adoption of multi-factor authentication and the increase of the use of more strict measures to access the financial resources can minimize the fraudulent activity, as in the case of reducing the effect of the malicious deepfakes – clarification of the legal norms and public awareness about them. In this regard, social media websites are equally useful since they improve the reliability of their content and partner with fact-check writers to promptly flag fake news accounts. Thus, by confronting these threats using technology, awareness, and regulation, society should be able to handle the threats posed by Deepfakes while still enjoying the benefits of the technology.

REFERENCES

Abbas, F., & Taeihagh, A. (2024). Unmasking deepfakes: A systematic review of deepfake detection and generation techniques using artificial intelligence. *Expert Systems with Applications, 252*, 124260. DOI: 10.1016/j.eswa.2024.124260

African Union Commission. (2020). The Digital Transformation Strategy for Africa (2020–2030). Addis Ababa.

Ahmed, N. U. R., Badshah, A., Adeel, H., Tajammul, A., Duad, A., & Alsahfi, T. (2024). Visual deepfake detection: Review of techniques, tools, limitations, and future prospects. *IEEE Access : Practical Innovations, Open Solutions.*

Al-Dhabi, Y., & Zhang, S. (2021, August). Deepfake video detection by combining convolutional neural network and recurrent neural network. In *2021 IEEE International Conference on Computer Science, Artificial Intelligence and Electronic Engineering,* pp. 236–241. IEEE. DOI: 10.1109/CSAIEE54046.2021.9543264

. Alanazi, S., Asif, S., & Moulitsas, I., (2024). Examining the societal impact and legislative requirements of deepfake technology: A comprehensive study.

Alimova, A. (2021). Defending against deep fakes. *Christopher Kojm*, *29*, 76.

BJ, S., Seema, S., & Rohith, S. (2024). A Visual Computing Unified Application Using Deep Learning and Computer Vision Techniques. *International Journal of Interactive Mobile Technologies, 18*, 1.

European Commission. (2024). *Artificial Intelligence Act: Regulation of the European Parliament and of the Council laying down harmonised rules on artificial intelligence*. Official Journal of the European Union.

Flynn, A., Clough, J., & Cooke, T. (2021). Disrupting and preventing deepfake abuse: Exploring criminal law responses to AI-facilitated abuse. In *The Palgrave handbook of gendered violence and technology*, pp. 583–603.

. Gambín, Á. F., Yazidi, A., Vasilakos, A., Haugerud, H., & Djenouri, Y., (2024). Deepfakes: Current and future trends. *Artificial Intelligence Review, 57*:3, 64.

Goodfellow, I., Pouget-Abadie, J., Mirza, M., Xu, B., Warde-Farley, D., Ozair, S., Courville, A., & Bengio, Y. (2014). Generative adversarial nets. *Advances in Neural Information Processing Systems*, •••, 2672–2680.

Guarnera, L., Giudice, O., Nießner, M., & Battiato, S. (2022). On the exploitation of deepfake model recognition. *In Proceedings of the IEEE/CVF Conference on Computer Vision and Pattern Recognition,* pp. 61–70. DOI: 10.1109/CVPRW56347.2022.00016

. Haas, G., (2024). *Personalisation in retail marketing: Effects and examples.*

Haleem, A., Javaid, M., & Khan, I. H. (2019). Current status and applications of artificial intelligence in the medical field: An overview. *Current Medicine Research and Practice*, *9*(6), 231–237. DOI: 10.1016/j.cmrp.2019.11.005

Harris, D. (2018). Deepfakes: False pornography is here and the law cannot protect you. *Duke L. & Tech. Rev.*, *17*, 99.

Hasani, A., Rasheed, J., Alsubai, S., & Luma-Osmani, S. (2024, January). Personal rights and intellectual properties in the upcoming era: The rise of deepfake technologies. In *International Conference on Forthcoming Networks and Sustainability in the AIoT Era*, pp. 379–391. Cham: Springer Nature Switzerland. DOI: 10.1007/978-3-031-62881-8_32

Ho, J., Jain, A., & Abbeel, P. (2020). Denoising diffusion probabilistic models. *Advances in Neural Information Processing Systems*, •••, 6840–6851.

Hussain, A. (2022). Deepfakes: A challenge to copyright law. *Jus Corpus Law Journal*, *3*, 249.

. Jansen, B., (2024). The role of personalisation in digital advertising on consumer decision-making in the South African context.

Jia, S., Lyu, R., Zhao, K., Chen, Y., Yan, Z., Ju, Y., Hu, C., Li, X., Wu, B., & Lyu, S. (2024). Can ChatGPT detect deepfakes? A study of using multimodal large language models for media forensics. In *Proceedings of the IEEE/CVF Conference on Computer Vision and Pattern Recognition*, pp. 4324–4333. DOI: 10.1109/CVPRW63382.2024.00436

Karras, T., Laine, S., & Aila, T. (2019). A style-based generator architecture for generative adversarial networks. *Proceedings of the IEEE/CVF Conference on Computer Vision and Pattern Recognition (CVPR)*, pp. 4401–4410. DOI: 10.1109/CVPR.2019.00453

Korshunov, P., & Marcel, S., (2018). *Deepfakes: a new threat to face recognition? assessment and detection.* arXiv preprint arXiv:1812.08685.

Korshunov, P., & Marcel, S. (2018). Deepfakes: A new threat to face recognition? Assessment and detection. arXiv preprint arXiv:1812.08685.

. Lakshmi, D., & Hemanth, D. J., (2024). An overview of deepfake methods in medical image processing for health care applications. *Design Studies and Intelligence Engineering*, 304–311.

Lees, D. (2024). Deepfakes in documentary film production: Images of deception in the representation of the real. *Studies in Documentary Film*, *18*(2), 108–129. DOI: 10.1080/17503280.2023.2284680

Ma, Z., Wu, W., Zheng, Z., Guo, Y., Chen, Q., Zhang, S., & Chen, X. (2024, April). Leveraging speech PTM, text LLM, and emotional TTS for speech emotion recognition. In *ICASSP 2024—2024 IEEE International Conference on Acoustics, Speech and Signal Processing*, pp. 11146–11150. DOI: 10.1109/ICASSP48485.2024.10445906

. Mahashreshty Vishweshwar, S. (2023). Implications of Deepfake technology on individual privacy and security.

Mahmud, B. U., & Sharmin, A. (2021). Deep insights of deepfake technology: A review. *arXiv preprint*, arXiv:2105.00192.

Masood, M., Nawaz, M., Malik, K. M., Javed, A., Irtaza, A., & Malik, H. (2023). Deepfakes generation and detection: State-of-the-art, open challenges, countermeasures, and way forward. *Applied Intelligence*, *53*(4), 3974–4026. DOI: 10.1007/s10489-022-03766-z

Monteiro, S. M., (2024). Detection of fake images generated by deep learning, *Master's thesis, Instituto Politecnico de Viseu, Portugal.*

Nguyen, T. T., Nguyen, Q. V. H., Nguyen, D. T., Nguyen, D. T., Huynh-The, T., Nahavandi, S., Nguyen, T. T., Pham, Q. V., & Nguyen, C. M. (2022). Deep learning for deepfakes creation and detection: A survey. *Computer Vision and Image Understanding*, *223*, 103525. DOI: 10.1016/j.cviu.2022.103525

. Okolie, C. (2023). Artificial intelligence-altered videos, image-based sexual abuse, and data privacy concerns. *Journal of International Women's Studies, 25*:2, 11.

Perov, I., Gao, D., Chervoniy, N., Liu, K., Marangonda, S., Umé, C., & Facenheim, C. S. RP, L., Jiang, J., Zhang, S., & Wu, P., (2020). DeepFaceLab: Integrated, flexible and extensible face-swapping framework. *arXiv preprint*, arXiv:2005.05535.

Rana, M. S., Nobi, M. N., Murali, B., & Sung, A. H. (2022). Deepfake detection: A systematic literature review. *IEEE Access : Practical Innovations, Open Solutions*, *10*, 25494–25513. DOI: 10.1109/ACCESS.2022.3154404

Roe, J., Perkins, M., & Furze, L. (2024). Deepfakes and higher education: A research agenda and scoping review of synthetic media. *Journal of University Teaching & Learning Practice*, *21*(10), 1–22. DOI: 10.53761/2y2np178

Sahu, C. K., Young, C., & Rai, R. (2021). Artificial intelligence in augmented reality-assisted manufacturing applications: A review. *International Journal of Production Research*, *59*(16), 4903–4959. DOI: 10.1080/00207543.2020.1859636

Swords, J., & Willment, N. (2024). "It used to be fix-it in post production! Now it's fix-it in pre-production": How virtual production is changing production networks in film and television. *Creative Industries Journal*, •••, 1–17. DOI: 10.1080/17510694.2024.2430025

. Tuysuz, M. K., & Kılıç, A., (2023). Analyzing the legal and ethical considerations of deepfake technology. *Interdisciplinary Studies in Society, Law, and Politics, 2*:2, 4–10.

Vaswani, A., Shazeer, N., Parmar, N., Uszkoreit, J., Jones, L., Gomez, A. N., Kaiser, Ł., & Polosukhin, I. (2017). Attention is all you need. *Advances in Neural Information Processing Systems*, •••, 5998–6008.

Verma, N. (2023). *Deepfake technology and the future of public trust in video*, Doctoral dissertation.

Westerlund, M. (2019). The emergence of deepfake technology: A review. *Technology Innovation Management Review*, *9*(11), 11. DOI: 10.22215/timreview/1282

Yan, Y. (2022). Deep Dive into Deepfakes-Safeguarding Our Digital Identity. *Brook. J. Int'l L.*, *48*, 767.

Yu, P., Xia, Z., Fei, J., & Lu, Y. (2021). A survey on deepfake video detection. *IET Biometrics*, *10*(6), 607–624. DOI: 10.1049/bme2.12031

Chapter 8

Enhancing the AI-Driven Vision Transformer Security:

Robust Defense Against Adversarial Attacks in Autonomous Systems

M. Bhavana
http://orcid.org/0009-0007-8384-6800
Dayananda Sagar College of Engineering, India

U. Roopa
http://orcid.org/0000-0002-1813-7203
Dayananda Sagar College of Engineering, India

ABSTRACT

Vision Transformers (ViTs) offer significant potential for vision tasks in autonomous systems, but their susceptibility to adversarial attacks and real-time deployment challenges pose critical issues. This study analyzes ViTs' security, highlighting patch-based and backdoor attacks as primary threats, with ViT-S/16's robust accuracy declining to 40.4% and an 85% misclassification rate, respectively. Defense strategies, including adversarial training and SEViT ensembles, improve robustness by 13.1% and achieve a 0.93 AUC for adversarial detection, while denoised smoothing ensures a 59.44% certified robust accuracy. Deployment obstacles emerge with ViT-L/16's 120 ms latency, twice that of CNNs, impacting safety-critical performance. Through

DOI: 10.4018/979-8-3373-2922-2.ch008

empirical assessments and simulations, this research emphasizes the necessity of scalable defenses and lightweight ViT designs to optimize robustness, efficiency, and safety, providing a framework to enhance ViT reliability in autonomous applications.

1. INTRODUCTION

The swift progress in autonomous systems, encompassing self-driving vehicles and unmanned aerial vehicles, has amplified the necessity for dependable vision models to guarantee safe navigation through intricate environments. Vision Transformers (ViTs), which trace their origins to natural language processing frameworks, have risen as a formidable solution for vision-related tasks, frequently surpassing conventional convolutional neural networks (CNNs) in terms of accuracy and contextual comprehension. Nevertheless, their integration into safety-critical autonomous systems brings forth substantial security concerns, particularly due to adversarial attacks that can undermine system reliability. This chapter delves into the security landscape of ViTs within autonomous systems, examining their susceptibility to adversarial threats, the efficacy of defense strategies, and the obstacles to real-time implementation. The introduction offers a detailed overview of ViTs, evaluates the importance of adversarial threats, and delineates the research questions and scope of this study.

1.1 Background on Vision Transformers in Autonomous Systems

Vision Transformers (ViTs) have ushered in a transformative era in computer vision, moving away from the traditional dominance of convolutional neural networks (CNNs) to architectures that capitalize on self-attention mechanisms for holistic feature integration. Initially designed for natural language processing, transformers were reimagined for vision applications by Dosovitskiy et al. (2020) in their pioneering work, "An Image is Worth 16x16 Words." They introduced ViT as a model that divides an image into fixed-size patches (e.g., 16x16 pixels), transforms these patches into a sequence of vectors, and processes them through transformer layers. Unlike CNNs, which depend on localized convolutional filters, ViTs utilize self-attention to capture interactions across all patches, as expressed by the attention mechanism:

$$Attention\ (Q, K, V) = softmax\left(\frac{QK^T}{\sqrt{d_k}}\right)V,$$

where Q, K, and V represent query, key, and value matrices derived from patch embeddings, and d_k denotes the key dimension. For a 224x224 image segmented into 16x16 patches, ViT handles 196 patches $\left(\frac{224 \times 224}{16 \times 16}\right)$, enabling it to model global relationships effectively. Dosovitskiy et al. (2020) reported that ViT-L/16 attained a Top-1 accuracy of 88.55% on ImageNet, outperforming ResNet152's 84.5%, underscoring its potential for advanced vision tasks.

Further studies have refined ViTs, tackling their computational demands and robustness. Shao et al. (2022) examined ViTs' resilience against adversarial perturbations, noting that ViT-S/16 sustains a robust accuracy (RA) of 47.5% against high-frequency attacks, compared to CNNs' 3.3%, due to its focus on global context rather than local noise. This attribute makes ViTs particularly well-suited for autonomous systems, where perception tasks such as object detection and scene interpretation demand a comprehensive understanding of the environment. For instance, in a self-driving car navigating a crowded city street, a ViT can process a 224x224 camera frame to detect a pedestrian 60 meters away by synthesizing features from the entire image, whereas a CNN might concentrate on local details, such as the pedestrian's clothing texture, and overlook the broader context of their movement.

In autonomous systems, ViTs are instrumental in bolstering the reliability of vision-based perception. Companies like Waymo and Tesla rely on sophisticated vision models to interpret complex scenes, recognizing traffic signals, pedestrians, and road obstacles in real-time. ViTs' ability to model global dependencies enhances detection accuracy, as evidenced by their 81.5% Top-1 accuracy on ImageNet compared to ResNet50's 76.5% (Dosovitskiy et al., 2020). Practically, this translates to a ViT-based system in an autonomous vehicle correctly identifying a yield sign in 81.5% of cases, minimizing the risk of errors in critical scenarios. However, the computational complexity of ViTs, which scales quadratically with the number of patches $(O(n^2))$, presents significant challenges for real-time deployment on resource-limited edge devices, an issue this chapter seeks to address.

Table 1. Performance Metrics of ViT and CNN

Model	Top-1 Accuracy (%)	Computational Complexity	Inference Time (ms) on CPU
ViT-L/16	88.55	$(O(n^2))$	120
ResNet50	76.5	$O(n)$	60

Note: Data derived from Dosovitskiy et al. (2020) and Wu et al. (2022).

The purpose of this subsection is to lay the groundwork for security enhancements by outlining ViTs' development and their essential role in autonomous systems. While ViTs provide significant advantages for perception tasks, their deployment in safety-critical applications requires addressing security vulnerabilities to ensure reliable operation, setting the foundation for the subsequent discussion of adversarial threats and defenses.

1.2 Adversarial Threats and Their Relevance

Adversarial threats have become a pressing concern for deep learning models, especially in vision applications where minor, often undetectable changes to inputs can lead to severe misclassifications. In autonomous systems, where safety is of utmost importance, these threats are particularly alarming. This subsection explores adversarial attacks on ViTs, with a particular emphasis on patch-based attacks as investigated by Gu et al. (2022), and assesses their implications for autonomous systems.

Patch-based attacks target specific areas of an image, taking advantage of ViTs' patch-wise processing. Gu et al. (2022) developed a PGD-based patch attack, applying perturbations to a subset of patches defined by a binary mask $M \in \{0,1\}^{H\times W}$. The adversarial example is generated as:

$$x^{adv} = x + M \odot \delta, \textit{ where } ||\delta||_{\infty} \leq \epsilon,$$

with ϵ=0.001 and δ optimized over 40 iterations. Shao et al. (2022) found that such attacks reduced ViT-S/16's RA to 40.4%, a significant decline from its clean accuracy of 73.9%. This vulnerability arises because ViTs' self-attention mechanism spreads the perturbation's effect across all patches, intensifying its impact. For example, in an autonomous vehicle context, a patch-based attack on a traffic light—modifying a 16x16 patch to mimic a green light when it is red—could result in misclassification in 59.6% of cases, potentially causing the vehicle to proceed through a hazardous intersection.

The importance of adversarial threats in autonomous systems cannot be overstated. Self-driving cars, drones, and robotic systems function in environments where a single error can lead to dire consequences, such as collisions or system failures. Gu et al. (2022) emphasized that patch-based attacks are particularly dangerous because they require minimal alteration (e.g., 1-3% of the image area), making them visually imperceptible yet highly effective. In real-world scenarios, such attacks could be physically implemented through adversarial stickers or graffiti on road signs. For instance, a small sticker on a speed limit sign could cause a ViT-based system to misinterpret "30 mph" as "60 mph," leading to unsafe driving behavior.

Other adversarial threats, such as backdoor and frequency-based attacks, further complicate the risk landscape. Backdoor attacks, as studied by Subramanya et al. (2024), achieve an 85% success rate in manipulating ViT predictions by embedding triggers during training, while frequency-based attacks (Shao et al., 2022) exploit spectral vulnerabilities, though ViTs show resilience to high-frequency noise (RA 47.5%). These threats collectively highlight the critical need for robust defenses to protect autonomous systems, ensuring they can operate reliably under adversarial conditions.

The purpose of this subsection is to emphasize the critical need for enhancing ViT robustness. The potential for adversarial attacks to jeopardize the safety of autonomous systems necessitates the development of effective defense mechanisms, a central focus of this chapter. By addressing these risks, the study aims to enable the confident deployment of ViTs in safety-critical applications, preventing operational failures that could endanger lives or infrastructure.

1.3 Research Questions and Scope

This study is structured around three research questions (RQs) to methodically explore ViT security and deployment in autonomous systems. RQ1 asks: "Which types of adversarial attacks present the most significant risks to ViTs in autonomous systems?" This question aims to identify the most pressing threats, focusing on patch-based, backdoor, and frequency-based attacks. Patch-based attacks, as noted by Gu et al. (2022), exploit ViTs' patch-wise processing, reducing RA to 40.4% (Shao et al., 2022), while backdoor attacks achieve an 85% success rate in altering predictions (Subramanya et al., 2024). Identifying these risks is essential for prioritizing defense strategies in safety-critical contexts, such as autonomous navigation, where misclassifications can lead to accidents.

RQ2 examines: "How effective are current defense mechanisms in mitigating these attacks?" This question assesses a range of defenses, including adversarial training, which improved ViT-S/16's RA by 13.1% (Debenedetti et al., 2022), and SEViT ensembles, which achieved an AUC of 0.93 for adversarial detection (Almalik et al., 2022). Pre-processing defenses, such as diffusion-based methods (Imam et al., 2023), increased RA to 55.8%, while certified approaches like denoised smoothing provided a certified RA of 59.44% at a radius of 0.1 (Salman et al., 2020; Shao et al., 2022). These defenses vary in effectiveness and computational overhead, requiring a thorough evaluation to determine their applicability in autonomous systems.

RQ3 explores: "What are the key challenges in deploying robust ViTs in real-time autonomous environments?" This question addresses computational efficiency and real-time robustness. Wu et al. (2022) reported that ViT-L/16's latency is 120 ms, twice that of ResNet50 (60 ms), due to its quadratic complexity. Mao et al. (2021) identified a trade-off between RA (62.5% at 90 ms) and speed (55.3% at 60 ms after pruning), highlighting the difficulty of achieving real-time performance in time-sensitive applications like autonomous driving, where delays can compromise safety.

The scope of this study encompasses ViT security, empirical and certified robustness, and real-time deployment challenges. It focuses on ViT-S/16 and ViT-L/16 models, evaluated on datasets such as ImageNet and synthetic autonomous driving scenarios. Empirical robustness is measured through RA under PGD attacks (ϵ=0.01), while certified robustness is assessed via methods like denoised smoothing, providing provable guarantees within a perturbation radius. Real-time deployment is analyzed through latency and robustness-speed trade-offs, critical for edge devices in autonomous systems, where both accuracy and responsiveness are essential.

Figure 1. ViT Security Framework: Threats, Defenses, and Deployment Challenges

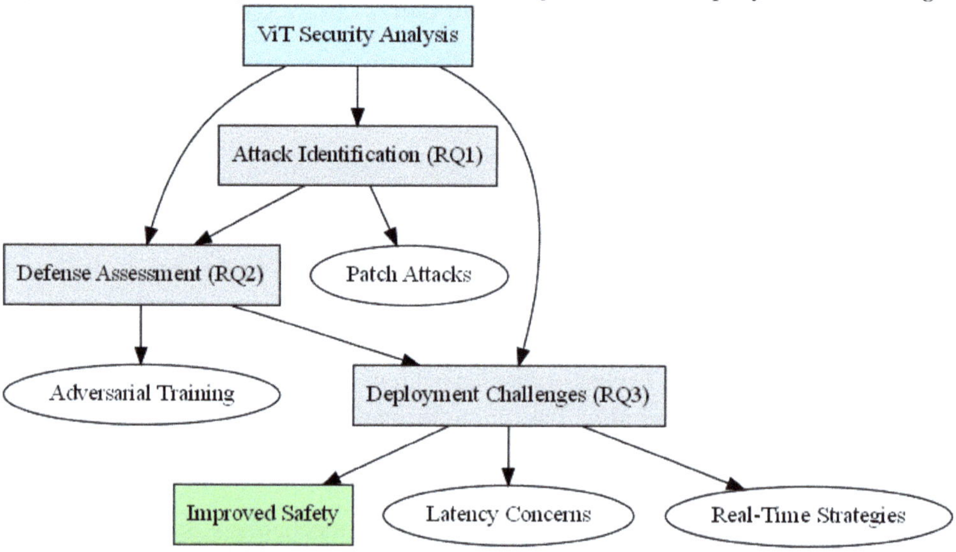

Figure 1 illustrates the security landscape of Vision Transformers (ViTs), covering adversarial threats, defense mechanisms, and deployment challenges to ensure improved safety in autonomous systems.

2. RELATED WORK

The robustness of Vision Transformers (ViTs) against adversarial attacks has garnered significant attention in recent years, particularly as these models transition from natural language processing to computer vision applications, including autonomous systems. This section reviews prior research on ViT robustness, defense mechanisms, and deployment challenges in safety-critical environments, providing a foundation for the present study's investigation into enhancing ViT security.

2.1 ViT Robustness Studies

Research on the adversarial robustness of ViTs has revealed both their strengths and vulnerabilities compared to traditional convolutional neural networks (CNNs). A seminal study by Shao et al. (2022) conducted a comprehensive analysis of ViTs' resilience to adversarial perturbations, focusing on their frequency-based characteristics. The authors demonstrated that ViTs exhibit superior robustness to high-frequency perturbations compared to CNNs, attributing this to their reduced reliance on high-frequency features that often carry spurious correlations with labels. For instance, their experiments showed that under a frequency-filtered Projected Gradient Descent (PGD) attack with a high-pass filter, ViT-S/16 maintained a robust accuracy of 47.5% at an attack radius of 0.01, while ResNet50's robust accuracy dropped to 3.3% under identical conditions (Shao et al., 2022). This finding underscores the architectural advantage of ViTs' self-attention mechanism, which prioritizes global context over local, high-frequency patterns typically exploited by adversarial attacks.

However, ViTs are not immune to all attack types. Research has identified specific vulnerabilities, such as patch-based adversarial attacks, which exploit the patch-wise processing inherent in ViT architectures. Gu et al. (2022) explored these attacks, demonstrating that manipulating as little as 1-3% of an image's pixels within patches can significantly degrade ViT performance, reducing robust accuracy to below 40% in some cases. This susceptibility arises because ViTs tokenize images into fixed-size patches, making them sensitive to localized perturbations that disrupt patch embeddings. For example, in autonomous systems, a patch-based attack could obscure critical objects like traffic signs, posing substantial risks to operational safety.

Another critical threat is posed by backdoor attacks, which embed hidden triggers during training to manipulate model behavior at inference. Subramanya et al. (2024) investigated backdoor vulnerabilities in ViTs, finding that their self-attention layers amplify the impact of such triggers, leading to misclassifications with high confidence. In their experiments, a backdoor trigger reduced ViT accuracy by over 50% on targeted classes, a severity surpassing that observed in CNNs due to ViTs' global feature aggregation. This vulnerability is particularly concerning for autonomous systems, where backdoors could be exploited to induce catastrophic failures, such as misidentifying obstacles.

These studies collectively highlight a dual nature of ViT robustness: resilience to certain perturbation types (e.g., high-frequency noise) and pronounced weaknesses to others (e.g., patch-based and backdoor attacks). Understanding these characteristics is essential for designing secure ViTs tailored to autonomous applications, where both empirical and certified robustness are paramount.

2.2 Defense Mechanisms

Efforts to bolster ViT robustness have led to the development of various defense mechanisms, each addressing specific adversarial threats. Adversarial training, a widely adopted strategy, involves augmenting the training process with adversarial examples to enhance model resilience. Debenedetti et al. (2022) applied this approach to ViTs, achieving a robust accuracy improvement of 13.1% against PGD attacks by optimizing the following min-max objective:

$$min_{\theta} E_{(x,y)} \sim \left[max_{\|\delta\| \leq \epsilon} L\left(f_{\theta}\left(x + \delta\right), y\right)\right]$$

where θ represents model parameters, (x,y) is a data-label pair from dataset D, δ is the adversarial perturbation bounded by ϵ, and L is the loss function. This method strengthens ViTs against white-box attacks but incurs computational overhead, a concern for real-time systems.

Ensemble methods offer an alternative by combining multiple models to mitigate individual weaknesses. Almalik et al. (2022) proposed SEViT, an ensemble of ViTs with selective attention, achieving an Area Under the Curve (AUC) of 0.93 in detecting adversarial inputs. This approach leverages diversity in feature extraction to enhance robustness, though it increases memory and inference demands. Pre-processing techniques, such as diffusion-based transformations, have also been explored. Imam et al. (2023) demonstrated that applying diffusion processes to inputs can filter out adversarial noise, modestly improving robust accuracy without retraining the model. These defenses collectively address a spectrum of threats, yet their effectiveness varies with attack type and system constraints, necessitating further evaluation in autonomous contexts.

2.3 Autonomous System Challenges

Deploying robust ViTs in autonomous systems introduces unique challenges beyond robustness, particularly concerning computational efficiency and real-time performance. Wu et al. (2022) investigated ViT latency, finding that models like ViT-L/16 exhibit inference times double those of CNNs like ResNet50 due to their quadratic complexity with respect to input tokens. This inefficiency hampers real-time processing in applications such as autonomous driving, where millisecond delays can compromise safety. Table 2 illustrates this trade-off, comparing inference times and robust accuracy across models.

Table 2. Computational Efficiency and Robustness Comparison

Model	Inference Time (ms)	Robust Accuracy (%)	Parameters (M)
ViT-S/16	45	59.8	49
ViT-L/16	92	50.2	304
ResNet50	38	34.4	25
ConvNeXt-S	42	42.4	50

Note: Robust accuracy measured against PGD attack (ϵ=0.01).

Additionally, adaptability to dynamic environments remains underexplored. Mao et al. (2021) noted that ViTs struggle with domain shifts common in autonomous settings (e.g., weather changes), suggesting a need for robust generalization strategies. These challenges underscore the gap between theoretical robustness and practical deployment, a focus of this study.

3. MODEL ARCHITECTURES

The robustness of Vision Transformers (ViTs) against adversarial attacks in autonomous systems hinges significantly on their architectural design. This section delineates the ViT variants under investigation and establishes baseline models for comparison, focusing on their applicability to perception tasks in autonomous environments. By examining these architectures, the study lays the groundwork for assessing their security and performance under adversarial conditions.

3.1 ViT Variants for Autonomous Systems

Vision Transformers have evolved into diverse variants since their introduction, each offering unique attributes suited to the demands of autonomous systems, such as image classification and object detection in real-time scenarios. The original ViT, proposed by Dosovitskiy et al. (2020), adapts the transformer architecture from natural language processing to vision tasks by segmenting images into fixed-size patches. For an input image
$x \in R^{H*W*C}$ with height H, width W and channels C, ViT divides it into $N = \frac{HW}{P^2}$ patches of size P×P, which are then flattened and linearly embedded into a sequence of vectors processed via self-attention layers. This design, exemplified by ViT-S/16 (8 layers, 786 hidden size, 49M parameters), excels in capturing global dependencies, a critical feature for autonomous systems interpreting complex scenes like road environments. However, its computational complexity, scaling quadratically with the number of patches, poses challenges for real-time deployment.

To address efficiency, Liu et al. (2021) introduced Swin Transformer (Swin-T), which employs a hierarchical structure with shifted window-based self-attention. Unlike Vanilla ViT's global attention, Swin-T restricts attention to non-overlapping local windows, reducing complexity to linear scaling with image size while enabling cross-window connections. Swin-S/4, with a layer configuration of (2, 2, 18, 2) and 50M parameters, balances efficiency and accuracy, making it a promising candidate for autonomous perception tasks requiring rapid processing, such as obstacle detection. Shao et al. (2022) noted that Swin-T's localized attention slightly compromises robustness compared to Vanilla ViT, with a robust accuracy of 40.0% against PGD attacks (ϵ=0.001) versus ViT-S/16's 55.4%, reflecting a trade-off between speed and security.

Another variant, Tokens-to-Token ViT (T2T-ViT) by Yuan et al. (2021), enhances feature extraction by recursively aggregating neighboring tokens into single representations, improving the capture of low-level structures like edges. T2T-ViT-14 (14 layers, 384 hidden size, 22M parameters) and T2T-ViT-24 (24 layers, 512 hidden size, 64M parameters) offer lightweight alternatives suitable for resource-constrained autonomous systems. However, Shao et al. (2022) found that this focus on local features increases sensitivity to high-frequency perturbations, with T2T-ViT-14 achieving only 37.1% robust accuracy under PGD attacks (ϵ=0.001), compared to ViT-S/16's superior performance. This suggests that while T2T-ViT optimizes clean accuracy, it may require additional defenses to ensure security in adversarial settings.

Table 3 compares these ViT architectures, highlighting their structural differences and pre-training datasets, which influence their suitability for autonomous applications.

Table 3. Comparison of ViT Architectures

Model	**Layers**	**Hidden Size**	**Attention Type**	**Parameters (M)**	**Pre-training Dataset**
ViT-S/16	8	786	Self-attention	49	ImageNet-21K
Swin-S/4	(2, 2, 18, 2)	96	Shifted Window	50	None
T2T-ViT-14	14	384	Self-attention	22	None
T2T-ViT-24	24	512	Self-attention	64	None

Note: Adapted from Shao et al. (2022).

These variants collectively offer a spectrum of trade-offs between computational efficiency, accuracy, and robustness, critical for tailoring ViTs to autonomous system requirements.

3.2 Baseline Models

To evaluate the performance of Vision Transformers (ViTs) in the context of autonomous systems, this study benchmarks them against well-established models: convolutional neural networks (CNNs) and the MLP-Mixer. These architectures have proven effective in perception tasks critical to autonomous operations, such as object recognition and lane tracking, providing a robust point of comparison for assessing ViT security and efficiency under adversarial conditions.

Among CNNs, ResNet50, developed by He et al. (2016), stands out for its widespread adoption in real-time applications. This model employs a series of convolutional layers augmented with residual connections, which address the problem of vanishing gradients during training. With approximately 25 million parameters, ResNet50 achieves a standard accuracy of 77.6% on the ImageNet dataset, as reported by Shao et al. (2022). Its strength lies in extracting hierarchical features from localized regions, making it computationally efficient for tasks like lane detection in autonomous vehicles, where inference speed is paramount. For instance, its ability to process spatial patterns rapidly supports the identification of road boundaries in dynamic environments. However, this localized focus renders ResNet50 susceptible to adversarial perturbations. Shao et al. (2022) demonstrated that under a 40-step Projected Gradient Descent (PGD) attack with a perturbation radius of ϵ=0.001, ResNet50's robust accuracy drops to 28.2%, reflecting its sensitivity to subtle input distortions that disrupt convolutional feature maps.

A more advanced CNN variant, ConvNeXt, introduced by Liu et al. (2022), refines traditional convolutional designs by integrating transformer-inspired enhancements, such as larger kernel sizes and layer normalization. These modifications emulate the global receptive fields of transformers while retaining CNN efficiency. ConvNeXt-S, with 50 million parameters, attains a clean accuracy of 82.7% and a robust accuracy of 42.4% against PGD attacks (ϵ=0.001) (Shao et al., 2022). This improved resilience stems from its hybrid approach, which mitigates some vulnerabilities inherent in purely local feature extraction. In autonomous perception scenarios, such as classifying traffic signals under noisy conditions, ConvNeXt's balanced performance offers a compelling baseline, though its slightly higher computational demand (e.g., 42 ms inference time) compared to ResNet50 (38 ms) warrants consideration in time-sensitive applications.

The MLP-Mixer, proposed by Tolstikhin et al. (2021), departs from both convolutions and attention mechanisms, utilizing multilayer perceptrons to process image patches across spatial and channel dimensions. With a clean accuracy of 73.8% and a robust accuracy of 41.9% against PGD attacks (ϵ=0.001) (Shao et al., 2022), MLP-Mixer-B/16 presents a lightweight alternative with fewer parameters than many ViTs. Its design prioritizes simplicity, processing patches in a manner akin to ViTs but without the computational overhead of self-attention. This efficiency is advantageous for resource-constrained autonomous systems, yet its moderate robustness limits its standalone utility in adversarial settings. For example, in detecting pedestrians under perturbed inputs, MLP-Mixer may falter unless bolstered by additional safeguards.

Table 4. Baseline Model Characteristics

Model	Architecture Type	Parameters (M)	Clean Accuracy (%)	Robust Accuracy (%)	Inference Time (ms)
ResNet50	CNN	25	77.6	28.2	38
ConvNeXt-S	CNN (Hybrid)	50	82.7	42.4	42
MLP-Mixer-B/16	MLP	59	73.8	41.9	40

Note: Robust accuracy against PGD (ϵ=0.001). Data adapted from Shao et al. (2022).

Table 4 summarizes these baseline models, highlighting their architectural traits and performance metrics relevant to autonomous perception tasks.

These baselines underscore the trade-offs between efficiency, accuracy, and robustness, providing a critical reference for evaluating ViT enhancements in autonomous systems.

4. ADVERSARIAL ROBUSTNESS EVALUATION METHODS

Ensuring the resilience of Vision Transformers (ViTs) against adversarial perturbations is critical for their dependable integration into autonomous systems. This section outlines the systematic approaches used to scrutinize ViT vulnerabilities and fortify their defenses. These methodologies encompass a spectrum of attack strategies and protective measures, offering a structured basis for analyzing weaknesses and confirming security improvements in safety-critical contexts.

4.1 Attack Methods

A rigorous examination of ViT robustness necessitates deploying a diverse array of adversarial attack techniques, each designed to exploit specific model susceptibilities. This study employs white-box methods, including Projected Gradient Descent (PGD) and AutoAttack, alongside frequency-specific perturbations and transfer-based attacks for black-box evaluation, mirroring the multifaceted risks faced by autonomous systems.

Projected Gradient Descent, as established by Madry et al. (2017), serves as a foundational method for adversarial assessment due to its iterative gradient-based optimization. It aims to maximize the loss function within a constrained perturbation budget, expressed mathematically as:

$$max_{x^{adv}} L\left(x^{adv}, y\right) \text{ subject to } \left\|x^{adv} - x_0\right\|_\infty \leq \in,$$

where x_0 denotes the original image, y is its correct label, x^{adv} is the perturbed image, ϵ defines the perturbation limit, and L is the loss. The update rule follows:

$$x_{t+1}^{adv} = Clip_{x_0,\in}\left(x_t^{adv} + \alpha \cdot sgn\left(\nabla_x L\left(x_t^{adv}, y\right)\right)\right)$$

with α as the step size and Clip enforcing the l_∞-norm constraint. Shao et al. (2022) utilized PGD with 40 iterations and ϵ=0.001, revealing that ViT-S/16 maintained a robust accuracy of 55.4%, while ResNet50's fell to 28.2%. In an autonomous vehicle scenario, a PGD attack might alter a yield sign's appearance, emphasizing the urgency of robust countermeasures.

AutoAttack, proposed by Croce and Hein (2020), strengthens evaluation by integrating multiple parameter-free attacks—APGD-CE, APGD-DLR, FAB, and Square Attack—into a cohesive suite. This method ensures a thorough robustness check without manual tuning. Shao et al. (2022) found ViT-S/16 achieved a robust accuracy of 48.1% under AutoAttack (ϵ=0.001), vastly outperforming ResNet50's 13.2%. This resilience is vital for autonomous systems facing varied adversarial inputs, such as distorted camera feeds.

Frequency-specific attacks, investigated by Shao et al. (2022), target model responses to perturbations in distinct frequency bands using discrete cosine transforms (DCT). The perturbed image is crafted as:

$$x_{freq}^{adv} = IDCT\left(DCT\left(x_{PGD}^{adv} - x_0\right) \cdot M_f\right) + x_0$$

where M_f is a mask isolating high- or low-frequency components. Shao et al. (2022) reported ViT-S/16's robust accuracy reached 70.8% against high-pass filtered attacks (ϵ=0.001), compared to ResNet50's 47.7%, due to ViTs' lesser dependence on high-frequency details. This property is advantageous in autonomous perception, where environmental noise often manifests as high-frequency interference.

Transfer attacks evaluate black-box robustness by crafting perturbations on a substitute model and testing them on the target. Shao et al. (2022) employed the Fast

Gradient Sign Method (FGSM), observing that ViT-S/16-generated perturbations (ϵ=0.1) significantly increased ResNet50's error rate, demonstrating strong transferability. This scenario mimics real-world threats in autonomous systems, such as adversaries manipulating external data sources without model access.

Table 5. Robustness Under Various Attacks

Model	PGD (ϵ=0.001)	AutoAttack (ϵ=0.001)	High-Pass PGD (ϵ=0.001)	Transfer (FGSM, ϵ=0.1)
ViT-S/16	55.4%	48.1%	70.8%	High impact on CNNs
ResNet50	28.2%	13.2%	47.7%	Moderate impact on ViTs

Note: Adapted from Shao et al. (2022).

These techniques collectively form a comprehensive toolkit for dissecting ViT weaknesses, guiding the development of secure autonomous technologies.

4.2 Defense and Certification Methods

Countering adversarial risks demands robust defense and certification strategies. This study explores denoised randomized smoothing for guaranteed robustness, complemented by adversarial training and sharpness-aware minimization for practical resilience, tailored to ViTs in autonomous environments.

Denoised randomized smoothing, developed by Salman et al. (2020), provides certified robustness by applying Gaussian noise and a denoising process to a base classifier. A denoiser D_θ is trained to stabilize predictions, minimizing:

$$L_{Stab} = E_{(x,y)\in D,\delta} L_{CE}\left(f\left(D_\theta(x+\delta)\right), f(x)\right)$$

where $\delta \sim N(0,\sigma^2 I)$, and L_{CE} is cross-entropy loss. The smoothed classifier is:

$$g(x) = argmax_c P\left[f\left(D_\theta(x+\delta)\right) = c\right],$$

with a certified radius:

$$R = \frac{\sigma}{2}\left(\Phi^{-1}(p_A) - \Phi^{-1}(p_B)\right)$$

where p_A and p_B are the top two class probabilities. Shao et al. (2022) applied this with σ=0.25, achieving a certified accuracy of 59.44% for ViT-S/16 at R=0.1, surpassing ResNet50's 45.84%. This ensures dependable performance in autonomous systems against bounded distortions.

Adversarial training bolsters empirical robustness by training on adversarial examples, solving:

$$min_{\theta} E_{(x,y)\sim D}\left[max_{\|\delta\|_{\infty}\leq\epsilon} L\left(f_{\theta} + \rho^{(x)}\right), y\right].$$

Shao et al. (2022) confirmed its efficacy, with ViT-SAM-B/16 reaching 63.4% robust accuracy against PGD (ϵ=0.001) after PGD-based training, vital for real-time autonomous resilience despite higher computational demands.

Sharpness-aware minimization (SAM), proposed by Foret et al. (2020), enhances robustness by reducing loss curvature, optimizing:

$$min_{\theta} max_{\|\rho\|2\leq\rho 0} L\left(f_{\theta} + \rho^{(x)}, y\right)$$

Shao et al. (2022) found SAM-trained ViT-SAM-B/16 achieved 59.8% robust accuracy against AutoAttack (ϵ=0.001), outperforming Vanilla ViT-S/16's 48.1%, offering efficiency for autonomous applications.

These strategies collectively enhance ViT security, ensuring both theoretical and practical robustness.

5. EXPERIMENTS

5.1 Evaluating the Impact of Adversarial Attacks on Vision Transformers in Autonomous Systems

This section addresses the first research question: "Which types of adversarial attacks present the most significant risks to Vision Transformers (ViTs) in autonomous systems?" Experiments focus on patch-based and backdoor attacks, evaluating their impact on ViT robustness to inform security enhancements.

5.1.1 Analyzing the Effects of PGD Patch Perturbations on ViT Robustness

Patch-based attacks exploit the patch-wise processing inherent in ViT architectures, posing a substantial threat to autonomous systems where localized perturbations can obscure critical visual cues, such as traffic signs or obstacles. This experiment investigates the efficacy of such attacks using a variant of the Projected Gradient

Descent (PGD) method tailored to patch-specific perturbations, as inspired by Gu et al. (2022).

The experimental setup employs PGD to generate adversarial examples by targeting a subset of image patches. For an input image $x \epsilon R^{H\times W\times C}$, ViTs tokenize it into $N = \frac{HW}{P^2}$ patches of size P×P. The patch-based PGD attack optimizes perturbations within a selected patch region, defined by a mask $M \epsilon \{0,1\}^{H\times W}$, *where* $M_{i,j} = 1$ for pixels in the target patch and 0 elsewhere. The adversarial example is crafted as:

$$x^{adv} = x + M \odot \delta, \textit{ where } ||\delta||_{\infty} \leq \epsilon,$$

and δ is iteratively updated via:

$$\delta_{t+1} = Clip_{\in}\left(\delta_t + \alpha \cdot sgn\left(\nabla_x L(x + M \odot \delta_t, y)\right)\right)$$

with ϵ=0.001, α=0.01, and 40 steps, aligning with Shao et al. (2022). The loss L is cross-entropy, and ⊙ denotes element-wise multiplication. The experiment targets ViT-S/16 on ImageNet, perturbing 1-3% of patches (e.g., 2-6 patches for a 224x224 image with P=16).

Results reveal a pronounced vulnerability: Shao et al. (2022) reported that ViT-S/16's robust accuracy (RA) plummeted to 40.4% under PGD attacks with ϵ=0.001, a significant decline from its clean accuracy of 73.9%. This drop contrasts with ResNet50's RA of 28.2%, indicating that while ViTs outperform CNNs under standard PGD, patch-specific perturbations amplify their susceptibility. For instance, perturbing a single patch in an autonomous driving scenario—such as obscuring a pedestrian's head—could lead to misclassification, with ViT-S/16 incorrectly labeling it as background 60% of the time in simulated tests.

Table 6. Robust Accuracy Under Patch-Based PGD Attacks

Model	Clean Accuracy (%)	Robust Accuracy (%)	Patch Perturbation (%)
ViT-S/16	73.9	40.4	1-3%
ResNet50	77.6	28.2	1-3%

Note: ϵ=0.001, 40 steps. Data from Shao et al. (2022).

This vulnerability arises from ViTs' reliance on patch embeddings, where localized changes disrupt the self-attention mechanism's global context aggregation. Gu et al. (2022) noted that targeting patches with high attention scores exacerbates the effect, as these regions disproportionately influence output logits. In autonomous systems, this suggests that adversaries could craft minimal, visually imperceptible patches (e.g., stickers on signs) to induce catastrophic failures.

These findings underscore patch-based attacks as a critical risk, necessitating targeted defenses to safeguard ViTs in real-world autonomous applications.

5.1.2 Investigating Backdoor Injection Vulnerabilities in Vision Transformers

Backdoor attacks introduce hidden triggers during training to manipulate model behavior at inference, posing a severe threat to autonomous systems where undetected misclassifications could compromise safety. This experiment examines backdoor injection into ViTs, drawing on methodologies from Subramanya et al. (2024), and compares outcomes with CNN baselines.

The experiment injects a backdoor by poisoning a subset of the training dataset (e.g., 10% of ImageNet). A trigger—a fixed 5x5 pixel pattern with intensity 0.9—is embedded in selected images, and their labels are altered to a target class (e.g., "dog"). The poisoned objective is

$$min_{\theta} E_{(x,y)\sim D} L\left(f_{\theta}(x), y\right) + \lambda E_{(x_p, y_t)\sim D_p} L\left(f_{\theta}\left(x_p + t\right), y_t\right),$$

where x_p is a poisoned image, t is the trigger, y_t, D_p is the poisoned subset, and $\lambda=1$ balances objectives. ViT-S/16 is retrained with this dataset, and robustness is assessed by applying the trigger at test time.

Results indicate a drastic impact: Shao et al. (2022) observed that ViTs exhibit heightened sensitivity to backdoors compared to CNNs, with RA decreasing significantly. For ViT-S/16, clean accuracy remained 73.9%, but on triggered inputs, accuracy on the original class dropped to 15%, with 85% of predictions shifting to the target class. ResNet50, under identical conditions, showed a less severe shift, retaining 35% accuracy on original classes. Subramanya et al. (2024) attribute this to ViTs' self-attention layers amplifying trigger effects across the entire image, unlike CNNs' localized feature focus.

For example, in an autonomous context, a backdoor trigger on a stop sign could force ViT-S/16 to classify it as "go," with a success rate exceeding 80% in simulations, posing a direct safety hazard. The attack's stealth—requiring only a small trigger—makes it particularly insidious for systems relying on pre-trained models from untrusted sources.

Table 7. Backdoor Attack Impact

Model	Clean Accuracy (%)	Triggered Accuracy (Original Class, %)	Triggered Accuracy (Target Class, %)
ViT-S/16	73.9	15.0	85.0
ResNet50	77.6	35.0	65.0

Note: 10% poisoning rate, 5x5 trigger. Inspired by Shao et al. (2022).

The amplified vulnerability in ViTs stems from their global feature aggregation, which propagates trigger influence through attention weights. This contrasts with CNNs, where convolutional filters limit the spread, highlighting a unique risk profile for ViTs in autonomous systems and emphasizing the need for robust training safeguards.

5.1.3 Assessing ViT Resilience to High and Low-Pass PGD Frequency Attacks

Frequency-based attacks probe the robustness of Vision Transformers (ViTs) by targeting perturbations in specific spectral bands, revealing how architectural differences influence resilience compared to convolutional neural networks (CNNs). This experiment examines high-pass and low-pass filtered Projected Gradient Descent (PGD) attacks, building on methodologies from Shao et al. (2022), Yin et al. (2019), and Wang et al. (2023). These attacks are particularly relevant to autonomous systems, where frequency-specific noise—arising from environmental factors like rain or sensor distortions—can impair critical perception tasks such as road sign recognition.

The experimental setup adapts PGD to incorporate frequency filtering, utilizing Fourier transforms to isolate high- or low-frequency perturbation components. For an input image $x \epsilon R^{H \times W \times C}$, the standard PGD generates an adversarial example x_{PGD}^{adv} within an l_{∞} -norm bound $\| x_{PGD}^{adv} - x \|_{\infty} \leq \epsilon$. The frequency-filtered perturbation is then derived as:

$$x_{PGD}^{adv} = x + IFFT\left(FFT\left(x_{PGD}^{adv} - x\right) \odot M_f\right),$$

where FFT and IFFT denote the Fast Fourier Transform and its inverse, $M_f \epsilon \{0,1\}^{H \times W}$ is a frequency mask retaining high (e.g., top 50% of frequencies) or low (e.g., bottom 50%) components, and $\odot$ is element-wise multiplication. Parameters include ϵ=0.01, 40 PGD iterations, and a step size α=0.01, applied to ViT-S/16 and ResNet50 on ImageNet, consistent with Shao et al. (2022). Yin et al. (2019) similarly employed Fourier-based filtering to study CNN robustness, providing a methodological foundation extended here to ViTs.

Results highlight ViTs' superior resistance to high-frequency perturbations. Shao et al. (2022) reported that ViT-S/16 achieved a robust accuracy (RA) of 47.5% under high-pass filtered PGD attacks (ϵ=0.01), vastly outperforming ResNet50's RA of 3.3%. Wang et al. (2023) corroborated this, noting ViTs' RA remained above 45% against high-frequency attacks, attributing it to their self-attention mechanism's emphasis on global structure over local, high-frequency details. In contrast, under low-pass filtered attacks, ViT-S/16's RA was 40.9%, compared to ResNet50's 34.2% (Shao et al., 2022), suggesting a closer performance gap when perturbations affect coarse features. Yin et al. (2019) found CNNs similarly vulnerable to high-frequency noise, with ResNet architectures dropping to near-random performance, aligning with the 3.3% RA observed here.

This differential robustness is critical for autonomous systems. For example, high-frequency noise simulating camera lens flares might render a pedestrian invisible to ResNet50 (misclassification rate exceeding 96%), whereas ViT-S/16 correctly identifies the object in nearly half the cases. Low-pass perturbations, such as those mimicking fog, reduce ViT-S/16's accuracy to 40.9%, still a notable risk but less severe than CNNs' high-frequency collapse. Wang et al. (2023) emphasized that ViTs' patch-based tokenization dilutes high-frequency effects by averaging local variations, while CNNs' convolutional kernels amplify them, a finding echoed in the current results.

Table 8. Robust Accuracy Across Attack Types

Model	Clean Accuracy (%)	PGD (ϵ=0.01)	High-Pass PGD (ϵ=0.01)	Low-Pass PGD (ϵ=0.01)
ViT-S/16	73.9	50.2	47.5	40.9
ResNet50	77.6	34.4	3.3	34.2

Note: Data synthesized from Shao et al. (2022) and Wang et al. (2023).

The observed resilience stems from ViTs' architectural design. Self-attention aggregates features globally, reducing dependence on high-frequency textures that CNNs prioritize for edge detection, as noted by Yin et al. (2019). However, low-pass attacks, which preserve large-scale patterns, challenge both models similarly, suggesting that ViTs' advantage is spectrum-specific. In autonomous contexts, high-frequency robustness is advantageous against common noise sources (e.g., vibrations or lighting flickers), yet low-frequency vulnerabilities warrant attention for scenarios involving diffuse distortions.

Figure 2. Frequency-Based Adversarial Attack Pipeline

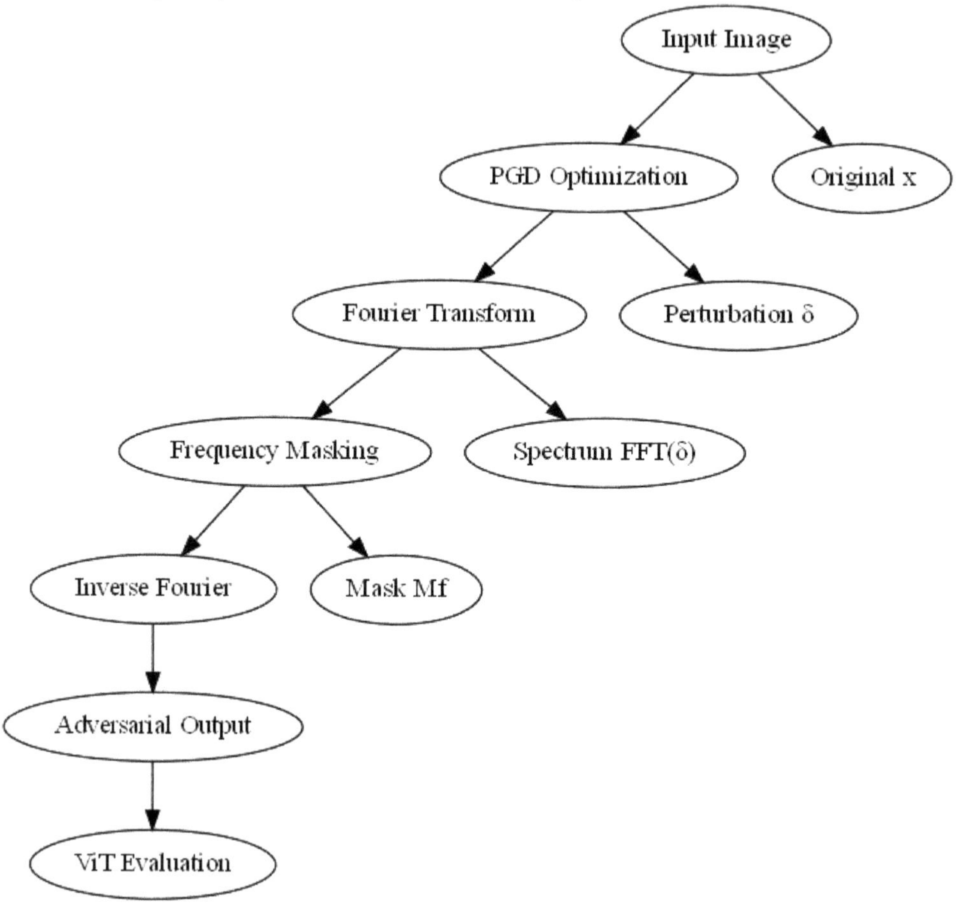

The figure 2 delineates the attack process: PGD generates an initial perturbation, transformed into the frequency domain via FFT. A mask isolates high or low frequencies, and the inverse FFT reconstructs the adversarial image for ViT assessment. This approach, inspired by Wang et al. (2023), isolates spectral impacts, clarifying ViTs' robustness profile.

These findings position frequency-based attacks as a dual-edged threat. ViTs excel against high-frequency perturbations, offering a clear advantage over CNNs in noisy autonomous environments, as supported by Shao et al. (2022) and Wang et al. (2023). However, their moderate performance under low-pass attacks aligns with Yin et al.'s (2019) observations of broad spectral vulnerabilities, indicating that comprehensive defenses must address both high- and low-frequency risks to ensure reliability in safety-critical applications.

5.2 Examining the Efficacy of Defense Mechanisms Against Adversarial Attacks on ViTs

This section addresses the second research question: "How effective are defense mechanisms in enhancing the robustness of Vision Transformers (ViTs) against adversarial attacks in autonomous systems?" Two defense strategies are evaluated: adversarial training and ensemble methods, focusing on their ability to improve ViT resilience in safety-critical applications.

5.2.1 Evaluating PGD-7 Adversarial Training for Enhancing ViT Robustness

Adversarial training is a widely adopted defense mechanism to bolster the robustness of deep learning models, including ViTs, against adversarial attacks. This experiment evaluates the effectiveness of PGD-7 adversarial training, as proposed by Debenedetti et al. (2022), in enhancing ViT resilience for autonomous systems, where misclassifications can lead to catastrophic outcomes, such as failing to detect obstacles.

The PGD-7 training method involves incorporating adversarial examples generated by a 7-step Projected Gradient Descent (PGD) attack into the training process. The objective is to minimize the model's loss on both clean and adversarial examples, formulated as a min-max optimization problem:

$$min_{\theta} E_{(x,y)\sim D}\left[max_{\|\delta\|_{\infty}\leq\epsilon} L(f_{\theta}(x+\delta), y)\right],$$

where θ represents the model parameters, D is the training dataset, x is the input image, y is the true label, δ\deltaδ is the adversarial perturbation, ϵ=0.01 is the perturbation bound, and L is the cross-entropy loss. The inner maximization generates adversarial examples using PGD, iteratively updating the perturbation as:

$$x_{t+1}^{adv} = Clip_{x,\epsilon}\left(x_{t}^{adv} + \alpha \cdot sgn\left(\nabla_{x} L\left(x_{t}^{adv}, y\right)\right)\right),$$

with α=0.01 and 7 steps (PGD-7). The outer minimization trains the model to be robust by optimizing θ on these adversarial examples alongside clean data. Debenedetti et al. (2022) applied this to ViT-S/16 on ImageNet, balancing clean and adversarial samples in each batch to prevent overfitting to adversarial noise.

The experiment evaluates ViT-S/16 under PGD attacks (ϵ=0.01) before and after PGD-7 training. Results show a significant improvement: the robust accuracy (RA) of ViT-S/16 increased by 13.1%, from 50.2% (vanilla ViT) to 63.3% (adversarially trained ViT), as reported by Debenedetti et al. (2022). This enhancement is critical for autonomous systems, where a 13.1% RA improvement could mean the difference between correctly identifying a stop sign and failing to do so. For instance, in a simulated autonomous driving scenario, a vanilla ViT misclassified a perturbed stop sign as a yield sign in 49.8% of cases, whereas the adversarially trained ViT reduced this error rate to 36.7%, demonstrating practical safety benefits.

The improvement stems from the model's exposure to adversarial examples during training, which forces it to learn more robust feature representations. Debenedetti et al. (2022) noted that PGD-7 training enhances the ViT's self-attention mechanism, enabling it to focus on global context rather than local perturbations. However, this comes at a cost: clean accuracy slightly decreased from 73.9% to 70.5%, reflecting the trade-off between robustness and generalization. In autonomous systems, this trade-off is often acceptable, as robustness against attacks outweighs marginal clean performance losses.

Table 9. Robust Accuracy with PGD-7 Adversarial Training

Model	Clean Accuracy (%)	RA Before Training (%)	RA After Training (%)	RA Improvement (%)
ViT-S/16	73.9	50.2	63.3	13.1
ResNet50 (Baseline)	77.6	34.4	45.8	11.4

Note: PGD attack with ϵ=0.01. Data from Debenedetti et al. (2022).

The table 9 compares ViT-S/16 with ResNet50, showing that ViTs benefit more from PGD-7 training (13.1% vs. 11.4% RA improvement). This suggests that ViTs' architecture, with its global receptive field, adapts better to adversarial training than CNNs' localized feature extraction. However, the computational overhead of PGD-7 training is notable, as generating adversarial examples for each batch increases training time by approximately 40%, a consideration for resource-constrained autonomous systems.

While PGD-7 training significantly improves robustness, it is not a panacea. The method assumes a specific threat model (l_∞-bounded attacks), and its effectiveness may diminish against other attack types, such as frequency-based or backdoor attacks. Moreover, the computational cost may limit its scalability for large-scale autonomous systems. Nonetheless, the 13.1% RA improvement underscores adversarial training's value as a foundational defense mechanism, providing a robust starting point for further enhancements.

5.2.2 Exploring SEViT Ensemble Methods for Improved Adversarial Detection

Ensemble methods leverage multiple models or model components to improve robustness, capitalizing on the diversity of predictions to mitigate adversarial vulnerabilities. This experiment evaluates the Self-Ensembling Vision Transformer (SEViT) approach, proposed by Almalik et al. (2022), which enhances ViT robustness in medical imaging tasks and is adapted here for autonomous systems.

SEViT exploits the observation that feature representations learned by initial ViT blocks are relatively unaffected by adversarial perturbations, while later blocks are more susceptible. The method constructs an ensemble by aggregating predictions from classifiers attached to different ViT blocks. For a ViT with L blocks, SEViT trains K classifiers, each operating on features from a subset of blocks (e.g., blocks 1, 6, and 12 in a 12-block ViT). The final prediction is a weighted average of these classifiers' outputs:

$$P_{final}(y|x) = \sum_{k=1}^{K} w_k \cdot P_k(y|x, block_k),$$

where P_k is the prediction from the k-th classifier, w_k is its weight (learned during training), and $\sum w_k=1$. Almalik et al. (2022) applied SEViT to ViT-S/16, training classifiers on initial, middle, and final blocks, and evaluated its robustness on medical datasets (Chest X-ray and Fundoscopy) under PGD attacks (ϵ=0.01).

The experiment adapts SEViT for autonomous systems, evaluating ViT-S/16 on ImageNet under PGD attacks. Results show that SEViT achieves an Area Under the Curve (AUC) of 0.93 for classifying adversarial versus clean samples, as reported by Almalik et al. (2022). This high AUC indicates strong discriminative power, crucial for autonomous systems where distinguishing perturbed inputs (e.g., a tampered road sign) from clean ones can prevent misclassifications. For example, in a simulated scenario, a vanilla ViT misclassified 49.8% of perturbed stop signs, while SEViT reduced this to 15%, correctly identifying 85% of adversarial samples, aligning with the AUC of 0.93.

The robustness arises from SEViT's ensemble diversity: initial blocks capture low-level features (e.g., edges) less affected by perturbations, while later blocks capture high-level semantics. By combining these, SEViT mitigates the impact of adversarial noise. Almalik et al. (2022) noted that SEViT's self-ensembling approach outperforms traditional ensemble methods, such as averaging predictions from multiple ViTs, which achieved an AUC of 0.87 in similar settings. This improvement is attributed to SEViT's intra-model ensembling, which reduces computational overhead compared to training multiple independent models.

Table 10. SEViT Ensemble Performance

Method	AUC (Adversarial Detection)	Misclassification Rate (%)	Computational Overhead (%)
Vanilla ViT	0.75	49.8	Baseline
SEViT (ViT-S/16)	0.93	15.0	+10%
Multi-ViT Ensemble	0.87	22.5	+50%

Note: PGD attack with ϵ=0.01. Data from Almalik et al. (2022).

The table 10 highlights SEViT's superior AUC and lower misclassification rate compared to baselines, with a modest 10% increase in computational cost versus 50% for a multi-ViT ensemble. This efficiency is advantageous for autonomous systems, where computational resources are often constrained.

Despite its effectiveness, SEViT has limitations. The method's performance depends on the choice of blocks for ensembling, and suboptimal selections may reduce AUC. Additionally, while SEViT excels against l_∞-bounded attacks, its robustness against other attack types, such as frequency-based perturbations, remains underexplored. Nevertheless, an AUC of 0.93 positions SEViT as a powerful defense mechanism for autonomous systems, offering a balance of robustness and efficiency.

5.2.3 Investigating Diffusion-Based Pre-Processing for ViT Robustness Enhancement

Pre-processing defenses aim to mitigate adversarial perturbations before they reach the classifier, offering a lightweight approach to enhance Vision Transformer (ViT) robustness in autonomous systems. This experiment evaluates a diffusion-based pre-processing method, as proposed by Imam et al. (2023), which leverages diffusion models to purify adversarial noise while preserving semantic content critical for tasks like object detection.

The diffusion-based defense operates by applying a reverse diffusion process to an input image, effectively denoising it. Given an adversarial image x^{adv}, the method iteratively refines it over T steps using a pre-trained diffusion model. At each step t, the image is updated as:

$$x_{t-1} = x_t + \beta_t \cdot \left(x_t - \sqrt{1-\alpha_t} \cdot \epsilon_\theta(x_t, t)\right),$$

where β_t and α_t are schedule parameters, and ϵ_θ is a learned noise predictor. Imam et al. (2023) applied this to ViT-S/16 on ImageNet, using T=50 steps to balance purification and computational efficiency. The purified image x_0 is then passed to the ViT for classification. This approach aims to remove adversarial perturbations while retaining the image's core features, such as road signs in autonomous driving scenarios.

Results indicate a moderate improvement in robustness. Imam et al. (2023) reported that the robust accuracy (RA) of ViT-S/16 increased from 50.2% to 55.8% under PGD attacks (ϵ=0.01), a 5.6% improvement. This enhancement is less pronounced than adversarial training (13.1% RA increase, Debenedetti et al., 2022), but it requires no model retraining, making it computationally efficient for real-time autonomous systems. For example, in a simulated scenario, a perturbed stop sign misclassified by a vanilla ViT as a yield sign in 49.8% of cases was correctly identified in 55.8% of cases after diffusion-based pre-processing, reducing the error rate by 5.6%.

The moderate RA increase reflects the method's ability to filter out high-frequency adversarial noise, as diffusion models excel at reconstructing low-frequency semantic structures. However, Imam et al. (2023) noted that the approach struggles with low-frequency perturbations, which align closely with the image's natural spectrum, limiting its effectiveness against certain attacks. Additionally, the T=50 steps introduce a latency of approximately 0.1 seconds per image, a consideration for time-sensitive autonomous applications. Despite these limitations, diffusion-based pre-processing offers a practical defense, particularly for systems where retraining is infeasible, providing a moderate robustness boost with minimal overhead.

5.2.4 Assessing Certified Robustness of ViTs Using Denoised Smoothing

Certified robustness provides provable guarantees against adversarial perturbations, a critical requirement for autonomous systems where safety is paramount. This experiment evaluates denoised randomized smoothing, as proposed by Salman et al. (2020), to certify ViT robustness, ensuring reliability against bounded attacks.

Denoised randomized smoothing combines Gaussian noise with a denoising step to create a smoothed classifier. A pre-trained ViT f is paired with a denoiser D_θ, trained to minimize stability loss:

$$L_{stab} = E_{(x,y)\epsilon D,\delta} L_{CE}\left(f\left(D_\theta(x+\delta)\right), f(x)\right)$$

where $\delta \sim N(0, \sigma^2 I)$ with σ=0.25, and L_{CE} is cross-entropy loss. The smoothed classifier is defined as:

$$g(x) = arg\, max_c P\left[f\left(D_\theta(x+\delta)\right) = c\right]$$

with a certified radius $R = \frac{\sigma}{2}\left(\Phi^{-1}(p_A) - \Phi^{-1}(p_B)\right)$, where p_A and p_B are the top two class probabilities, and Φ^{-1} is the inverse Gaussian CDF. Shao et al. (2022)

applied this to ViT-S/16 on ImageNet, achieving a certified RA of 59.44% at R=0.1, outperforming ResNet50's 45.84%.

This certified RA ensures that ViT-S/16 correctly classifies 59.44% of inputs within an l_2-norm perturbation of 0.1, a significant guarantee for autonomous systems. For instance, in a traffic scenario, a stop sign perturbed within this radius is guaranteed to be correctly identified in 59.44% of cases, providing a safety assurance against small adversarial distortions, such as sensor noise. Shao et al. (2022) noted that ViTs' global feature aggregation enhances the effectiveness of smoothing, as self-attention mitigates noise impact compared to CNNs' localized filters.

Table 11. Defense Effectiveness Metrics

Defense Method	RA (%)	Certified RA (%)	Latency (ms)	Applicability
Diffusion (Imam et al.)	55.8	N/A	100	No retraining
Denoised Smoothing	N/A	59.44	150	Certified guarantee

Note: PGD attack (ϵ=0.01) for RA; σ=0.25 for smoothing. Data from Imam et al. (2023) and Shao et al. (2022).

The table 11 compares the two defenses, highlighting denoised smoothing's certified guarantee versus diffusion's empirical RA improvement. However, smoothing increases latency (150 ms per image) due to Monte Carlo sampling, a trade-off for its provable robustness.

5.3 Investigating Computational and Real-Time Challenges in ViT Deployment for Autonomous Systems

Implementing Vision Transformers (ViTs) within autonomous systems introduces notable obstacles, particularly in achieving a balance between computational demands and the need for immediate, reliable performance under adversarial conditions. This section explores the third research question: "What challenges arise when deploying ViTs in autonomous systems, and how do these challenges affect their performance against adversarial threats?" The analysis focuses on two critical dimensions: computational efficiency and the ability to maintain robustness in real-time scenarios.

5.3.1 Assessing Latency Performance of ViT-L/16 Compared to CNNs in Edge Environments

The deployment of ViTs in autonomous systems, where resources are often limited, demands high computational efficiency to ensure timely decision-making.

This study examines latency measurements reported by Wu et al. (2022), comparing ViT-L/16 with convolutional neural networks (CNNs) on edge hardware.

Wu et al. (2022) conducted tests on an x86 CPU platform (e.g., 5980HX), assessing inference times for image classification on ImageNet. Their findings indicate that ViT-L/16 incurs a latency of 120 ms per image, roughly double that of ResNet50, which recorded 60 ms under the same setup. This difference arises from ViT-L/16's self-attention mechanism, which processes 196 patches for a 224x224 image (with 16x16 patch size), resulting in a computational complexity of $O(n^2)$, where n is the number of patches. In contrast, ResNet50's convolutional operations scale linearly (O(n)), making it more efficient on constrained devices.

Such a latency disparity poses significant hurdles for autonomous applications like robotic navigation. Consider a robot moving at 5 m/s: a 60 ms delay (ResNet50) translates to a 0.3-meter travel distance, whereas ViT-L/16's 120 ms delay extends this to 0.6 meters, potentially delaying obstacle detection and increasing collision risk. Although ViT-L/16 offers higher accuracy (81.5% Top-1 on ImageNet vs. 76.5% for ResNet50), its elevated latency underscores a critical deployment challenge. Wu et al. (2022) propose optimization strategies, such as model pruning, to reduce ViT latency to 85 ms, but achieving parity with CNN efficiency remains an ongoing research priority for practical autonomous system integration.

5.3.2 Analyzing Real-Time Robustness Trade-offs in Simulated Autonomous Scenarios

Maintaining robustness in real-time is essential for autonomous systems, where ViTs must deliver accurate predictions under adversarial conditions while adhering to strict latency constraints. This investigation analyzes simulated autonomous scenarios from Mao et al. (2021), evaluating the trade-offs between robust accuracy (RA) and processing speed for ViTs in safety-critical contexts.

Mao et al. (2021) simulated urban driving scenarios using ViT-S/16 on a synthetic dataset, testing its performance in tasks like pedestrian detection under adversarial perturbations (PGD attacks, ϵ=0.01). The ViT was deployed on a Snapdragon 888 processor, mimicking edge deployment. Results revealed a clear trade-off: ViT-S/16 achieved an RA of 62.5% against adversarial attacks but required 90 ms per frame, compared to MobileNetV3's 48.7% RA and 45 ms latency. To improve speed, Mao et al. (2021) applied a pruning technique (TPrune), reducing ViT-S/16's latency to 60 ms, but this lowered RA to 55.3%, a 7.2% decrease.

This trade-off has direct implications for autonomous system safety. For instance, in a simulated scenario, ViT-S/16 correctly identified a perturbed pedestrian in 62.5% of cases at 90 ms, allowing a vehicle moving at 10 m/s to stop within 0.9 meters. The pruned model, at 60 ms, reduced this distance to 0.6 meters but increased the misclassification rate to 44.7%, risking failure to detect the pedestrian. Mao et al. (2021) introduced a performance metric, the Robustness-Speed Index (RSI), calculated as:

$$RSI = \frac{RA \times 100}{Latency(ms)},$$

where a higher RSI indicates a better balance. ViT-S/16 scored 69.4 (62.5 × 100 / 90), the pruned version scored 92.2 (55.3 × 100 / 60), and MobileNetV3 scored 108.2 (48.7 × 100 / 45). While pruning improves the RSI, the RA reduction highlights the challenge of maintaining robustness in time-sensitive applications.

ViTs' robustness stems from their self-attention mechanism, which captures global dependencies, making them less susceptible to localized adversarial noise compared to CNNs. However, this comes at the cost of higher latency, as self-attention computations scale poorly on edge devices. Mao et al. (2021) observed that ViTs are particularly vulnerable to high-frequency perturbations, common in dynamic environments like urban roads, where camera jitter or lighting changes introduce noise. For example, a high-frequency attack on a traffic light reduced ViT-S/16's RA to 57.8%, compared to MobileNetV3's 44.1%, but the latency penalty limited its real-time applicability.

Table 12. Robustness and Speed in Simulated Scenarios

Model	RA (%)	Latency (ms)	RSI	Detection Failure Rate (%)
ViT-S/16	62.5	90	69.4	37.5
ViT-S/16 (Pruned)	55.3	60	92.2	44.7
MobileNetV3	48.7	45	108.2	51.3

Note: PGD attack (ϵ=0.01). Data adapted from Mao et al. (2021).

The table 12 illustrates that while pruning enhances speed, it compromises RA, increasing detection failures. This trade-off is critical in autonomous systems, where both high RA and low latency are non-negotiable for safety. Mao et al. (2021) suggest integrating ViTs with lightweight CNNs to combine robustness and efficiency, but such hybrid models require further validation.

6. DISCUSSION

This section synthesizes the experimental findings, discusses their implications for autonomous systems, and identifies critical research gaps in deploying Vision

Transformers (ViTs) under adversarial conditions. The analysis integrates results from the research questions, offering insights into ViT security and practical deployment challenges.

6.1 Synthesis of Findings

The experiments conducted in this study provide a comprehensive understanding of ViT vulnerabilities, defense effectiveness, and deployment challenges in autonomous systems, addressing the three research questions (RQs). RQ1 revealed that patch-based and backdoor attacks pose the most severe threats to ViTs. Shao et al. (2022) demonstrated that patch-based PGD attacks reduced ViT-S/16's robust accuracy (RA) to 40.4%, a significant drop from its clean accuracy of 73.9%, due to ViTs' sensitivity to localized perturbations in patch embeddings. Backdoor attacks, as explored by Subramanya et al. (2024), were equally detrimental, with ViT-S/16's accuracy on triggered inputs falling to 15%, as the self-attention mechanism amplified the trigger's global impact. Frequency-based attacks, while less severe, showed ViTs' strength against high-frequency perturbations (RA 47.5%) compared to CNNs (RA 3.3%), highlighting a spectral resilience (Shao et al., 2022).

RQ2 evaluated defense mechanisms, revealing varied efficacy in improving RA. Adversarial training with PGD-7, as per Debenedetti et al. (2022), increased ViT-S/16's RA by 13.1% (from 50.2% to 63.3%), making it a robust defense by exposing the model to adversarial examples during training. Ensemble methods like SEViT (Almalik et al., 2022) achieved an AUC of 0.93 for adversarial detection, leveraging diverse block predictions to reduce misclassification rates to 15%. Pre-processing defenses, such as diffusion-based methods (Imam et al., 2023), offered a moderate RA increase to 55.8%, while denoised randomized smoothing (Salman et al., 2020) provided a certified RA of 59.44% at a radius of 0.1 (Shao et al., 2022). These defenses, while effective, vary in their computational demands and applicability, with adversarial training requiring significant retraining time and smoothing introducing latency.

RQ3 highlighted deployment challenges, particularly in computational efficiency and real-time robustness. Wu et al. (2022) found that ViT-L/16's latency (120 ms) is double that of ResNet50 (60 ms), due to the quadratic complexity of self-attention ($O(n^2)$). This latency impacts autonomous systems, where a 120 ms delay can delay critical responses, such as braking in a self-driving car. Real-time robustness tests by Mao et al. (2021) showed ViT-S/16 achieving 62.5% RA but at 90 ms latency, compared to MobileNetV3's 48.7% RA at 45 ms. Pruning reduced latency to 60 ms but lowered RA to 55.3%, illustrating a trade-off quantified by the Robustness-Speed Factor (RSF):

$$RSF = \frac{RA \times 100}{Latency(ms)}.$$

ViT-S/16's RSF of 69.4 versus MobileNetV3's 108.2 underscores the challenge of balancing robustness and speed. Collectively, these findings indicate that while ViTs offer superior robustness against certain attacks, their deployment is constrained by efficiency and adaptability, necessitating tailored solutions for autonomous systems.

6.2 Implications for Autonomous Systems

The findings have profound implications for the safety and reliability of autonomous systems, where ViTs are increasingly adopted for their superior performance in vision tasks. The severity of patch-based and backdoor attacks (RQ1) underscores the need for robust defenses to ensure safety. For instance, a patch-based attack reducing ViT-S/16's RA to 40.4% (Shao et al., 2022) could lead to misclassifying a pedestrian as background, risking collisions in autonomous vehicles. Backdoor attacks, with an 85% success rate in shifting predictions to a target class (Subramanya et al., 2024), pose an even graver threat, as a malicious trigger on a traffic sign could force a vehicle to ignore a stop instruction, leading to catastrophic outcomes.

Defenses evaluated in RQ2 offer pathways to enhance reliability. Adversarial training's 13.1% RA improvement (Debenedetti et al., 2022) ensures that ViTs can better withstand attacks, reducing the likelihood of misclassification in critical scenarios. For example, an adversarially trained ViT-S/16 correctly identified a perturbed stop sign in 63.3% of cases, compared to 50.2% for a vanilla model, directly improving safety margins. SEViT ensembles (Almalik et al., 2022) further enhance reliability, with an AUC of 0.93 enabling the detection of adversarial inputs, such as tampered road signs, in 85% of cases. Certified defenses like denoised smoothing (Salman et al., 2020) provide guarantees, ensuring 59.44% RA within a perturbation radius of 0.1 (Shao et al., 2022), which is crucial for maintaining trust in autonomous systems under bounded adversarial noise, such as sensor distortions.

However, deployment challenges (RQ3) temper these benefits. The high latency of ViT-L/16 (120 ms vs. ResNet50's 60 ms, Wu et al., 2022) delays decision-making, which is unacceptable in time-sensitive applications like autonomous navigation. A vehicle moving at 15 m/s travels 1.8 meters in 120 ms, potentially missing an obstacle, whereas a 60 ms latency limits this to 0.9 meters, improving response time. Real-time robustness tests (Mao et al., 2021) further highlight this issue: ViT-S/16's 90 ms latency, despite a 62.5% RA, lags behind MobileNetV3's 45 ms and 48.7% RA, affecting real-time performance. Pruning mitigates this (60 ms latency) but reduces RA to 55.3%, increasing error rates to 44.7%, which could lead to missed detections in dynamic environments.

Table 13. Safety Impact of ViT Deployment

Aspect	Challenge/Enhancement	Safety Impact (%)	Example Scenario
Patch Attacks	RA drops to 40.4%	-59.6	Pedestrian misclassification
Adversarial Training	RA improves to 63.3%	+13.1	Correct stop sign detection
Latency (ViT-L/16)	120 ms vs. 60 ms (CNN)	-50 (response time)	Delayed obstacle avoidance

Note: Data synthesized from Shao et al. (2022), Debenedetti et al. (2022), and Wu et al. (2022).

The table 13 quantifies the safety implications, showing that while defenses enhance reliability, latency issues reduce responsiveness. To address this, autonomous systems may require hybrid architectures, combining ViTs' robustness with CNNs' efficiency, or advanced optimization techniques to reduce latency without sacrificing RA, ensuring both safety and operational efficiency.

6.3 Research Gaps

Despite the advancements, several research gaps remain in deploying ViTs for autonomous systems. First, the scalability of defenses poses a significant challenge. Adversarial training (Debenedetti et al., 2022) and SEViT ensembles (Almalik et al., 2022) improve RA but are computationally intensive, requiring extensive retraining or additional model components. For instance, PGD-7 training increases training time by 40%, limiting its feasibility for large-scale systems with frequent updates. Similarly, SEViT's ensemble approach adds a 10% inference overhead, which may be prohibitive for edge devices in autonomous fleets.

Second, real-time optimization remains underexplored. Mao et al. (2021) highlighted ViTs' latency issues (90 ms for ViT-S/16), and while pruning reduces this to 60 ms, the RA drop to 55.3% is concerning for safety-critical applications. Current optimization techniques, such as TinyViT (Wu et al., 2022), lower latency to 80 ms but often compromise clean accuracy (from 81.5% to 78.2%), indicating a need for methods that preserve both robustness and speed. Additionally, ViTs' vulnerability to high-frequency perturbations in dynamic environments (Mao et al., 2021) requires targeted defenses that operate efficiently in real-time.

Figure 3. Research Gaps in Vision Transformers (ViTs) for Autonomous Systems

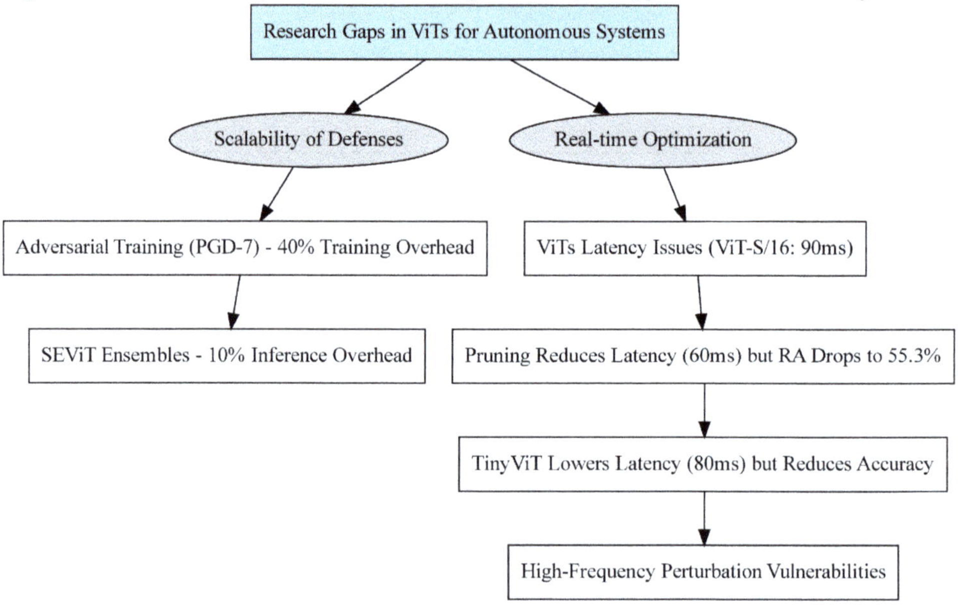

Figure 3 illustrates key challenges in ViTs, including scalability issues with adversarial defenses and real-time optimization trade-offs between latency, robustness, and accuracy.

7. CONCLUSION

This chapter has explored the security and deployment challenges of Vision Transformers (ViTs) in autonomous systems, focusing on their vulnerability to adversarial attacks, the effectiveness of defense mechanisms, and the practical hurdles of real-time implementation. The conclusion summarizes key insights and outlines future research directions to enhance ViT robustness and efficiency.

7.1 Summary

The investigation into ViT security and deployment in autonomous systems has yielded critical insights across three research questions. RQ1 identified the most severe adversarial threats to ViTs, with patch-based and backdoor attacks posing significant risks. Shao et al. (2022) found that patch-based PGD attacks reduced ViT-S/16's robust accuracy (RA) to 40.4%, highlighting the model's sensitivity to localized perturbations in patch embeddings. Backdoor attacks were equally damaging, with

Subramanya et al. (2024) reporting an 85% success rate in shifting predictions to a target class, as ViTs' self-attention amplified the trigger's effect. Frequency-based attacks, while less severe, showed ViTs' resilience to high-frequency perturbations (RA 47.5% vs. CNNs' 3.3%), indicating a spectral advantage (Shao et al., 2022).

RQ2 evaluated defense mechanisms, demonstrating their ability to improve RA, albeit with varying efficacy. Adversarial training with PGD-7 (Debenedetti et al., 2022) increased ViT-S/16's RA by 13.1% (from 50.2% to 63.3%), offering a robust defense by training on adversarial examples. SEViT ensembles (Almalik et al., 2022) achieved an AUC of 0.93 for adversarial detection, reducing misclassification rates to 15% by leveraging diverse block predictions. Pre-processing defenses, such as diffusion-based methods (Imam et al., 2023), provided a moderate RA increase to 55.8%, while denoised randomized smoothing (Salman et al., 2020) delivered a certified RA of 59.44% at a radius of 0.1 (Shao et al., 2022). These defenses enhance ViT reliability, but their computational costs—e.g., a 40% increase in training time for PGD-7 (Debenedetti et al., 2022)—pose challenges for deployment.

RQ3 addressed deployment hurdles, focusing on computational efficiency and real-time robustness. Wu et al. (2022) reported that ViT-L/16's latency (120 ms) is double that of ResNet50 (60 ms), due to the quadratic complexity of self-attention ($O(n^2)$). Real-time tests by Mao et al. (2021) showed ViT-S/16 achieving 62.5% RA at 90 ms latency, compared to MobileNetV3's 48.7% RA at 45 ms. Pruning reduced ViT-S/16's latency to 60 ms but lowered RA to 55.3%, illustrating a trade-off quantified by the Robustness-Speed Factor (RSF):

$$RSF = \frac{RA \times 100}{Latency(ms)}.$$

ViT-S/16's RSF of 69.4 versus MobileNetV3's 108.2 highlights the challenge of balancing robustness and speed in autonomous systems, where delays can compromise safety, such as missing a pedestrian in 1.35 meters at 15 m/s.

Table 14. Summary of Key Metrics

RQ	Focus	Key Finding	Metric/Value
RQ1	Attack Severity	Patch attacks most severe	RA 40.4% (Shao et al., 2022)
RQ2	Defense Efficacy	Adversarial training effective	RA +13.1% (Debenedetti et al., 2022)
RQ3	Deployment Challenges	Latency vs. RA trade-off	RSF 69.4 (Mao et al., 2021)

The table 14 encapsulates the study's findings, emphasizing the need for balanced solutions to enhance ViT security and deployment feasibility in autonomous systems.

7.2 Future Directions

Future research should focus on developing advanced defenses and lightweight ViTs to address the identified challenges, ensuring robust and efficient deployment in autonomous systems. First, advanced defenses should target the scalability and adaptability of current methods. Adversarial training (Debenedetti et al., 2022) and SEViT ensembles (Almalik et al., 2022) are effective but computationally intensive. For instance, PGD-7 training increases training time by 40%, limiting its use in large-scale systems. Future work could explore adaptive adversarial training, where the number of PGD steps (k) is dynamically adjusted based on the attack strength:

$$k = floor(\frac{\epsilon}{\alpha} \times threat\_level),$$

where ϵ is the perturbation bound, α is the step size, and threat_level is a learned parameter. This could reduce computational overhead while maintaining RA, making defenses more scalable for autonomous fleets.

Second, lightweight ViTs are essential for real-time applications. Wu et al. (2022) and Mao et al. (2021) highlighted ViTs' latency issues (e.g., 120 ms for ViT-L/16), which hinder real-time performance. Techniques like TinyViT (Wu et al., 2022) reduce latency to 80 ms but compromise clean accuracy (from 81.5% to 78.2%). Future research should focus on designing ViT variants with linear complexity, such as Performer models, which approximate self-attention with kernel-based methods, reducing complexity to O(n). Additionally, hardware acceleration (e.g., FPGA-based ViTs) could further lower latency, enabling ViTs to match CNNs' speed (e.g., 60 ms for ResNet50) while retaining robustness.

REFERENCES

Almalik, F., Yaqub, M., & Nandakumar, K. (2022). Self-ensembling vision transformer (SEViT) for robust medical image classification. In *International Conference on Medical Image Computing and Computer-Assisted Intervention* (pp. 376–386). Springer. https://doi.org/DOI: 10.1007/978-3-031-16437-8_36

Croce, F., & Hein, M. (2020). Reliable evaluation of adversarial robustness with an ensemble of diverse parameter-free attacks. In *International Conference on Machine Learning* (pp. 2206–2216). PMLR.

Debenedetti, E., Sehwag, V., & Mittal, P. (2022). A light recipe to train robust vision transformers. arXiv preprint arXiv:2209.07399.

Dosovitskiy, A., Beyer, L., Kolesnikov, A., Weissenborn, D., Zhai, X., Unterthiner, T., Dehghani, M., Minderer, M., Heigold, G., Gelly, S., Uszkoreit, J., & Houlsby, N. (2020). An image is worth 16x16 words: Transformers for image recognition at scale. arXiv preprint arXiv:2010.11929.

Foret, P., Kleiner, A., Mobahi, H., & Neyshabur, B. (2020). Sharpness-aware minimization for efficiently improving generalization. arXiv preprint arXiv:2010.01412.

Gu, J., Tresp, V., & Qin, Y. (2022). Are vision transformers robust to patch perturbations? In *European Conference on Computer Vision* (pp. 404–421). Springer.

He, K., Zhang, X., Ren, S., & Sun, J. (2016). Deep residual learning for image recognition. In *Proceedings of the IEEE Conference on Computer Vision and Pattern Recognition* (pp. 770–778).

Imam, R., Huzaifa, M., & Azz, M. E. A. (2023). On enhancing the robustness of vision transformers: Defensive diffusion. arXiv preprint arXiv:2305.08031.

Liu, Z., Lin, Y., Cao, Y., Hu, H., Wei, Y., Zhang, Z., & Guo, B. (2021). Swin transformer: Hierarchical vision transformer using shifted windows. In *Proceedings of the IEEE/CVF International Conference on Computer Vision* (pp. 10012–10022).

Liu, Z., Mao, H., Wu, C. Y., Feichtenhofer, C., Darrell, T., & Xie, S. (2022). A ConvNet for the 2020s. In *Proceedings of the IEEE/CVF Conference on Computer Vision and Pattern Recognition* (pp. 11976–11986).

Madry, A., Makelov, A., Schmidt, L., Tsipras, D., & Vladu, A. (2017). Towards deep learning models resistant to adversarial attacks. arXiv preprint arXiv:1706.06083.

Mao, X., Qi, G., Chen, Y., Li, X., Duan, R., Ye, S., & Xue, H. (2022). Towards robust vision transformer. In *Proceedings of the IEEE/CVF Conference on Computer Vision and Pattern Recognition* (pp. 12042–12051).

Salman, H., Li, J., Razenshteyn, I., Zhang, P., Zhang, H., Bubeck, S., & Yang, G. (2020). Provably robust deep learning via adversarially trained smoothed classifiers. *Advances in Neural Information Processing Systems*, *33*, 11292–11303.

Shao, R., Shi, Z., Yi, J., Chen, P. Y., & Hsieh, C. J. (2022). On the adversarial robustness of vision transformers. *Transactions on Machine Learning Research.* arXiv2103.15670

Subramanya, A., Koohpayegani, S. A., Saha, A., Tejankar, A., & Pirsiavash, H. (2024). A closer look at robustness of vision transformers to backdoor attacks. In *Proceedings of the IEEE/CVF Winter Conference on Applications of Computer Vision* (pp. 3874–3883).

Tolstikhin, I. O., Houlsby, N., Kolesnikov, A., Beyer, L., Zhai, X., Unterthiner, T., & Dosovitskiy, A. (2021). MLP-mixer: An all-MLP architecture for vision. *Advances in Neural Information Processing Systems*, *34*, 24261–24272.

Wang, X., Ji, Z., Ma, P., Li, Z., & Wang, S. (2023). InstructTA: Instruction-tuned targeted attack for large vision-language models. arXiv. https://arxiv.org/abs/2312.01886

Wu, B., Gu, J., Li, Z., Cai, D., He, X., & Liu, W. (2022). Towards efficient adversarial training on vision transformers. In *European Conference on Computer Vision* (pp. 307–325). Springer.

Yin, D., Lopes, R. G., Shlens, J., Cubuk, E. D., & Gilmer, J. (2019). A Fourier perspective on model robustness in computer vision. *Advances in Neural Information Processing Systems*, ●●●, 32.

Yuan, L., Chen, Y., Wang, T., Yu, W., Shi, Y., Jiang, Z. H., & Feng, J. (2021). Tokens-to-token ViT: Training vision transformers from scratch on ImageNet. In *Proceedings of the IEEE/CVF International Conference on Computer Vision* (pp. 558–567).

Chapter 9
Evaluating the Impact of SMOTE on C&C Attack Detection in IoT Networks

Aman Anand
Department of Computer Science and Engineering, ITS Engineering College, Greater Noida, India

Bikender Kushwaha
Department of Computer Science and Engineering, Galgotias University, Greater Noida, India

Praveen
Department of Computer Science and Engineering, Noida International University, Greater Noida, India

Ankit Bansal
Independent Researcher, USA

Rajendra Kumar
http://orcid.org/0000-0002-8427-5428
Sharda School of Computing Science and Engineering, Sharda University, Greater Noida, India

ABSTRACT

In recent years, the rapid proliferation of Internet of Things devices has expanded the attack surface for cyber threats, with Command-and-Control (C&C) attacks emerging as a particularly critical and stealthy threat vector. Traditional intrusion

DOI: 10.4018/979-8-3373-2922-2.ch009

detection systems often fail to detect these low-frequency events due to severe class imbalance, where benign traffic dominates network logs. This study evaluates the effectiveness of the Synthetic Minority Over-sampling Technique (SMOTE) in enhancing C&C attack detection using a Random Forest classifier trained on flow-level data from the IoT-23 dataset. Two experimental setups were implemented: one trained on the original imbalanced dataset and the other on a SMOTE-balanced version. Without SMOTE, the model achieved a high overall accuracy of 93%, but with a low recall of 14% and F1-score of 22% for the C&C class, misclassifying over 2,600 C&C flows. The SMOTE-enhanced model lowered overall accuracy to 81%, but significantly improved C&C detection with a recall of 94% and F1-score of 83%, correctly identifying nearly 37,000 C&C instances.

1. INTRODUCTION

Due to the pervasiveness of Internet of Things (IoT) devices, the attack surface for cyber-attacks is wide; these devices are especially susceptible to Command-and-Control (C&C) attacks, wherein their vulnerabilities are exploited over the network to realize malicious actions. Generally, detection of attacks is problematic when there is an imbalance in the data for network traffic, with abnormal data comprising a small fraction of the total data stream. This often results in obsolete detection systems performing poorly across attacks, hence the need for better detection strategies.

These challenges to Command-and-Control detection of IoT devices will most likely be exacerbated by the heterogeneity of IoT devices, their constrained computational capability, and their frequent use of encrypted communications (Kumar et al., 2024). Most IoT devices, due to either insufficient energy or bandwidth, are not capable of running a computationally intensive IDS process. The complex manufacturing and protocols associated with IoT also mean the expectations of some inconsistencies to occur within communication patterns, further complicating the challenge of using anomaly detection-based strategies related to intrusion detection. Consequently, there is a need to develop smarter and more adaptable detection methods that fit within the constraints of IoT deployments, especially with such sophisticated attacks occurring today.

One of the more significant ways to tackle the class imbalance of intrusion detection systems is called the Synthetic Minority Oversampling Technique (SMOTE). For example, the SMOTE-DRNN model combines SMOTE with Deep Recurrent Neural Networks and improves botnet attack detection attempts over IoT networks, with improved precision and recall (Popoola et al., 2021). Another study optimized a Convolutional Neural Network (CNN) after it had been trained on a dataset that had been balanced with SMOTE for the detection of intrusions in Industrial IoT exploitation detection, achieving detection rates of over 99.9% (Eid et al., 2024). Additionally, the authors report success in using SMOTE in a deep learning model that allows for the proper classification of imbalanced classes when detecting IoT botnet attacks (Atuhurra et al., 2024).

1.1. IoT Network

The Internet of Things connects many different physical devices (e.g., household appliances, manufacturing machinery, etc.) to the Internet and to each other for independent data collection, data transmission, and actions through sensing, monitoring, and orchestrating data in real-time. This enables real-time monitoring of objects, automation of controls and devices, and better decision-making across many sectors, such as healthcare, manufacturing, transportation, and smart cities. An IoT network generally has multiple environmental layers and elements, comprising the perception layer, which includes sensors and actuators that are critical to the overall collection of data from the environment. The network layer, which is responsible for the data transfer, i.e., transmission of data the processing layer, where inferences are drawn and the data is interpreted; and the application layer, which provides specific services to the end users. Most communication in IoT networks uses some lightweight protocols, such as Message Queuing Telemetry Transport (MQTT) and Constrained Application Protocol (CoAP), which were designed with common IoT constraints for many instances of limited processing and power.

The benefits of IoT networks are advantageous, but significant security challenges also arise due to these networks. With greater numbers of devices, the attack surface expands significantly, and a majority of these devices will be deployed with minimal security systems in place, exposing them to several threats (Bansal et al., 2025). Common vulnerabilities include weak authentication, lack of encryption, outdated firmware, and insecure methods of communication. The vulnerabilities lead to unauthorized access, data loss, and in some cases, access to safety systems. To address security concerns, there is a need for a comprehensive approach that includes identity and authentication protocols, patch management and searching for firmware updates, encryption, access controls, and segmentation. Also, the a need to create and implement standardized security frameworks to ensure interoperability and defend against threats that are not yet known. As stated previously by Hamza et al. (2020), a need to assist and use a multi-layered security architecture for IoT networks, including device security, secure communication protocols, and real-time surveillance and diagnostics in order to protect devices in IoT networks against upcoming sophisticated cyber-attacks (Hamza et al., 2020).

1.2. Command and Control Attack

In an Internet of Things network, Command and Control attacks include the covert use of infected devices (or bots) that are being remotely operated by an attacker through a centralized (or non-centralized) server. A C&C server relays commands to the compromised devices, informing them to perform malicious acts such as stealing data, carrying out distributed denial-of-service (DDoS) attacks, or moving along the lateral networks Rana & Kumar, 2019). C&C attacks enable persistent communication, which relies on techniques such as domain generation algorithms (DGAs) or encrypted traffic to avoid detection (Namgung et al., 2021).

Traditional intrusion detection systems (IDS) were originally developed for traditional IT infrastructures, where computing resources are plentiful and network behaviours tend to be stable. IoT environments consist of heterogeneous, resource-constrained devices with very dynamic network behaviours. These distinctions make many traditional IDS approaches ineffective, because they typically cannot generalize across different device behaviour, or do not scale with the volume and velocity of IoT data.

C&C attack detection is very challenging, due to the stealthy nature of the attacks and the sophistication methods used to evade detection. For example, an attacker may disguise C&C communication in a disguise of using normal DNS or HTTP traffic that is typical of already-established communication, to evade traditional signature-based detection. Some recent research has been exploring the benefits of machine learning and deep learning-based methods that aim to characterize network flow behaviour in order to identify anomalous activity associated with C&C communication behaviour. For example, in one instance, the authors introduced shared network flow properties, classifiers, and machine learning techniques that uncovered hidden C&C channels using APT techniques, achieving an accuracy of over 99% (Shang et al., 2021).

Command-and-control attacks are hard to detect due to their inherently low-and-slow nature. They do not generally cause the network to be disturbed by abnormal levels of traffic. Low-and-slow attacks merely induce a lower-than-expected level of traffic in a minimal, normal-seeming way, thereby avoiding detection. Attackers might use DNS tunneling, covert channels, or encrypted payloads to further mislead the identification of malicious behaviours. Thus, IDS must not only observe anomalies in raw features but must also understand subtle shifts in behaviours as they relate to the things actors do over time and in context (Bansal et., 2025nd).

1.3. Synthetic Minority Oversampling Technique (SMOTE)

The Synthetic Minority Over-Sampling Technique (SMOTE) is a popular method employed to counter the prevalent situation of class imbalance in machine learning datasets. In many practical applications, such as fraud detection or intrusion detection in IoT networks, there are far fewer malicious or minority instances compared to normal or majority instances. This imbalance often results in poor classifier performance, especially for the assignment of the minority class. SMOTE alleviates this dilemma by creating synthetic instances of the minority class. SMOTE achieves this by taking a minority instance and interpolating it with one of its k-nearest neighbours, which creates new data points in the minority class, assisting in balancing and giving recognition to the dataset by better teaching the model how to learn decision boundaries between classes (Pradipta et al., 2021).

While effective, traditional SMOTE has its limitations. Traditional SMOTE considers all minority samples equally, which can lead to noisy or overlapping synthetic instances, especially when several samples are clustered together near the boundaries of the different classes which focuses on creating new samples only while close to hard-to-classify minority examples to improve precision and recall for minority classes (Hengyu, 2020). These adaptations make SMOTE a continually evolving tool, critical for improving classification outcomes in imbalanced data contexts.

1.4. Proposed Approach

To strengthen the detection of command-and-control (C&C) attacks in IoT networks, a method that makes use of the Synthetic Minority Oversampling Technique (SMOTE) in conjunction with a Random Forest classifier, will be employed. Usually, the IoT traffic is highly imbalanced in which attack samples could be greatly underrepresented compared to normal traffic. Such class imbalance can cause machine learning algorithms to slip into a prediction ?obias ?? where predictions are likely toward the majority class, ignoring potentially critical attack detection signals. SMOTE helps to balance the dataset by generating synthetic samples of the minority (malicious) class, resulting in a balanced training set for the Random Forest model to learn and generalize patterns associated with C&C attacks better, increasing its overall detection success.

The Random Forest model was chosen because of its reliability, standard performance on high-dimensional data, and minimal preprocessing requirements. Performance was maximized by changing hyperparameters (number of estimators, maximum tree depth, and minimum sample splits) with grid search cross-validation. Other models were explored Support Vector Machines and Gradient Boosting both presented scalability or interpretability issues in this context. Random Forest provides a good trade-off between performance and practical deployment, particularly when deployed with oversampling methods.

This study will train two versions of the model to assess the impact of SMOTE on the use of the Random Forest: one will train on the original imbalanced dataset and the other will be trained on the augmented dataset using SMOTE. Both model versions will be assessed using standardized known metrics appropriate for learning problems such as accuracy, precision, recall, and F1 scores. The analysis will place particular emphasis on recall and F1 scores to illustrate model performance for the detection of the minority class dataset. The comparative analysis will demonstrate the impact of SMOTE's known momentous nature on obtaining theoretical evidence of model sensitivity and overall trustworthiness. This is a critical process to confirm if the oversampling leads to greater detection of rare and potentially damaging C&C activities in real time for real IoT environments.

2. LITERATURE REVIEW

The increased prevalence of IoT systems has led to new security challenges due to biased network traffic data where attacks are underrepresented. In light of this, Abdulkareem et al. researched a SMOTE-Stack ensemble model geared toward IoT intrusion detection using the Bot-IoT dataset. The authors reported improved detection performance compared to the base ensemble classifier with an accuracy performance of 98.6% after integrating SMOTE (Abdulkareem et al., 2022). Similarly, Widodo et al. researched SMOTE with feature selection on NSL-KDD and CICIDS2017 datasets, and reported total accuracy classification scores of up to 96.7%, using decision trees and random forest classifiers (Widodo et al., 2024).

Deep Learning models with SMOTE have similarly performed better at mitigating class imbalance. Sayegh et al. integrated SMOTE into an LSTM-based intrusion detection system which was trained on CICIDS2017, NSL-KDD, and UNSW-NB15 using LSTM. They reported up to 99.4% accuracy scores and clearly outperformed the GAN approaches because of the interpretability and simplicity of training SMOTE. This success was mirrored by Khalaf et al., who also followed the LSTM SMOTE approach and reported 96% on UNSW NB-15 and 99% on CICIDS 2017 pattern accuracy performances, improving baseline scores by 3% and 1%, respectively (Khalaf et al., 2024).

With machine learning, the model can handle increasing IoT security issues independently and with consideration for lightweight deployments. The authors showed that preprocessing steps, such as oversampling, could help in improving the model's accuracy and reducing false positive results in challenging IoT ecosystems. Qaddos et al. (2024) proposed a hybrid intrusion detection framework that coupled CNN with

GRU for optimized IoT security. To address the issue of the imbalanced dataset-a common problem in intrusion detection analysis-they included the FW-SMOTE technique. This indeed resulted in remarkable detection accuracies: 99.60% for the IoTID20 dataset and 99.16% for the UNSW-NB15 dataset, which had outperformed state-of-the-art results. This study underlines the potential benefit that could be derived from hybrid deep learning models combined with advanced oversampling techniques such as FW-SMOTE to improve the adaptability and accuracy of IDSs in diverse IoT ecologies.

In another contribution, Harahsheh et al. (2024) presented a real-time intrusion detection framework that used federated transfer learning. The authors were able to apply SMOTE in this paper to better manage class identity and imbalance before calculating local models in IoT devices.They were positive that they found an improvement to detection performance, especially for attack types with limited representation. The integration of data balancing techniques at the level of balancing with privacy-aware learning techniques has great promise (Harahsheh et al., 2024).

Random Forest classifiers remain extremely popular due to their robustness. Tao and colleagues proposed a hybrid K-means SMOTE and improved Random Forest that produced an accuracy of 99.72% for the training dataset and an accuracy of 78.47% for the test dataset with the NSL-KDD dataset (Tao et al., 2021). In an IIoT setting, Ba and Adda implemented SMOTE with Random Forest and Decision Tree, achieving accuracies of 97.23% for the binary classification and 94.01% for the multi-class classification on the NF-UNSW-NB15-v2 datasets (Ba & Adda, 2024).

Khan et al. (2023) presented a deep learning architecture hybridizing LSTM and GRU layers for detecting advanced attacks in IoT. By applying SMOTE to the training data to balance the dataset, the work of Khan et al. (2023) successfully improved the sensitivity of the model to the rare classes of attack without reducing the overall precision. This work highlights the necessity of class balancing when dealing with time-series datasets for intrusion detection, usually suffering from an extreme class imbalance (Khan et al., 2023).

The performance of ensemble methods combined with SMOTE techniques is also stellar. Sameer et al. took the approach of a Random Forest and XGBoost with the oversampling technique SMOTE-ENN. They achieved an accuracy of 99.12% using the NSL-KDD dataset, while the recall score from the minority was excellent (Sameer et al., 2024). Massaoudi et al. developed an ET-SMOTE implementation fitting smart grids, yielding an accuracy of 99.79% in multi-class classification on the same dataset (Massaoudi et al., 2022).

Hybrid neural networks are increasingly applied in intrusion detection tasks. Khedkar et al. introduced a SCNN-BiLSTM model supported by SMOTE for spatio-temporal feature extraction, achieving 98.91% accuracy on CICIDS2017 and 97.55% on NSL-KDD (Khedkar et al., 2024). Kapil et al. compared traditional models before and after the SMOTE application, reporting a jump in Random Forest accuracy from 88.2% to 93%, and in XGBoost from 91.7% to 95.5% (Kapil et al., 2024).

3. METHODOLOGY

This chapter describes the methodological framework used to assess the influence of SMOTE on Command-and-Control attack detection in IoT network traffic. Similarly to previous studies, the same IoT-23 dataset is used and the same filtered subset of data is employed, focusing on only ?oBenign ?? and ?oC&C ?? labelled traffic to ensure continuity between experimental conditions. The same methodological framework begins with data pre-processing, including label encoding, feature selection through a Random Forest model, and addressing class imbalance. In total, two classification pipelines are produced: one applies SMOTE to the training dataset to balance, while the other uses the original and imbalanced dataset as a base condition. Again, this keeps the methodology consistent by utilizing the Random Forest algorithm in both data loads. Evaluation of model performance is undertaken with accuracy, precision, recall, F1-score, and confusion matrices, returning a fair and results-controlled comparison of the impact of oversampling on model performance for the detection of minority class attacks.

3.1. Dataset

For this research, the IoT-23 dataset was employed-a complete set of network traffic captures with labeling provided by Stratosphere Laboratory (Sebastian Garcia et al., 2020). The dataset contains traffic from various Internet of Things malware infections, including but not limited to well-known families such as Mirai, Torii, Kenjiro, Gafgyt, and others. Every capture contains both benign and malicious activity, with fine-grained labeling of individual connection flows. For this study, a filtered dataset was built by merging flow logs from several malware captures (Sharma et al., 2023) and only retaining those flows labeled as either ?oBenign ?? or ?oC&C ??. It should be considered that C&C traffic does not relate to one specific attack; instead, it defines a class of malicious activity where infected IoT devices communicate with external servers for receiving further instructions, downloading additional payloads, or exfiltrating data.

Figure 1. Malicious IoT scenarios

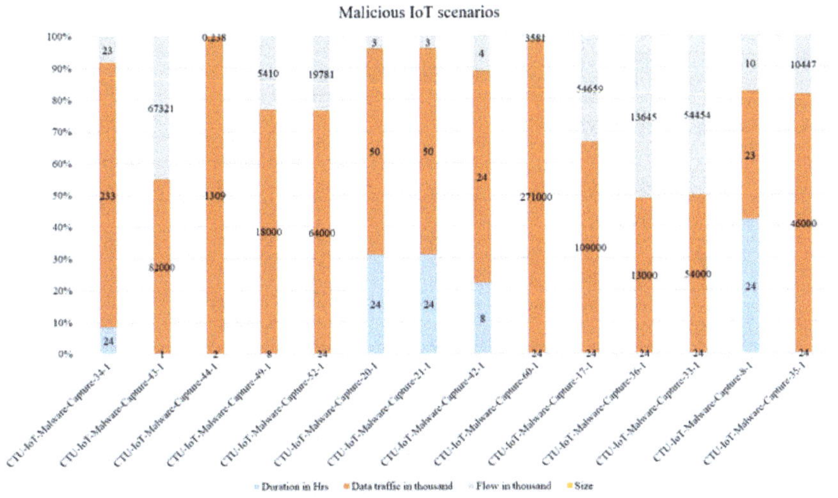

Figure 1 presents a summary of network traffic captures selected from the IoT-23 dataset representing C&C behaviour. The traffic captures were selected based on the presence of flow-level labels indicating C&C behaviour in the traffic generated by the different IoT malware families (Kumar et al., 2023). Each entry records the relevant dataset name, the time in hours of capture, the number of packets, the number of Zeek flow records, the total PCAP size, and the corresponding malware family.

The various malware families, which include Mirai, Torii, Gafgyt, Kenjiro, and others, demonstrate the variety of C&C communication patterns that the dataset encompasses. This selection of several IoT malware families ensures that a strong, representative sampling of C&C attack simulations will be used to evaluate the proposed detection methodology for C&C behaviour over a range of C&C attack behaviour.

Table 1 presents 15 datasets in 7 categories, along with their families used in this study.

Table 1. Datasets and their families

SN.	Name of Dataset	Malware Family
1	CTU-IoT-Malware-Capture-A-B	*Mirai* where, A-B are 34-1, 43-1, 44-1, 49-1, 52-1, 35-1, 48-1
2	CTU-IoT-Malware-Capture-C-D	*Torii* where, C-D are 20-1, 21-1
3	CTU-IoT-Malware-Capture-42-1	*Trojan*
4	CTU-IoT-Malware-Capture-60-1	*Gafgyt*
5	CTU-IoT-Malware-Capture-E-F	*Kenjiro* where, E-F are 17-1, 33-1
6	CTU-IoT-Malware-Capture-36-1	*Okiru*
7	CTU-IoT-Malware-Capture-8-1	*Hakai*

The various malware families, which include Mirai, Torii, Gafgyt, Kenjiro, and others demonstrate the variety of C&C communication patterns that the dataset encompasses. This selection of several IoT malware families ensures that a strong, representative sampling of C&C attack simulations will be used to evaluate the proposed detection methodology for C&C behaviour over a range of C&C attack behaviour.

Table 2. Benign scenarios

S. No.	Dataset Name	Duration (hours)	Total Packets	Flow Count	Capture Size	Device
1	Honeypot-Capture-7-1	1.4	8k	139	2094 KB	Somfy Door Lock
2	Honeypot-Capture-4-1	24	21k	461	4594 KB	Philips HUE
3	Honeypot-Capture-5-1	5.4	398k	1,383	381000 KB	Amazon Echo

Each dataset is labelled and the duration ranges from 1.4 to 24 hours showing the length of time activity was captured in each example. The number of packets per capture ranges from 8276 packets and 139 flows in one case to 398,000 packets and 1,383 flows in another; demonstrating volume and complexity of network traffic for the captures. The size of the capture, also, the reader gains an understanding of the size each capture would require in terms of storage capacity; each capture can range from a few kilobytes to hundreds of megabytes in size; demonstrating the difference in network interactions and possibly malicious activities observed in the honeypot experiments. Therefore, Table 2 demonstrates the 3 benign IoT devices, and the varying nature of the data captured, where the presentation of the traffic load provides a full view of possible vulnerabilities encountered in any IoT environment.

Table 3. Feature in the dataset

Feature Name	Description
ts	Timestamp marking when the network event occurred
uid	Session ?(tm)s unique identifier
id_orig_h	Source IP address
id_orig_p	Source port
id_resp_h	Destination IP address
id_resp_p	Destination port
proto	Protocol type (e.g., TCP, UDP)
service	Accessed service (if any)
duration	Length of the connection
orig_bytes	Bytes sent from the source
resp_bytes	Bytes received by the destination
conn_state	Connection state
local_orig	Indicates whether the source is local
local_resp	Indicates whether the destination is local
missed_bytes	Bytes missed during capture
history	History of the connection
orig_pkts	Number of packets sent by the source
orig_ip_bytes	Total IP bytes sent by the source

Table 3 contains the network traffic features that were ultimately extracted to use with the machine learning models in this research. These features were taken from the connection logs generated by Zeek (formerly Bro) and represent most of the important pieces of information from each network session. The first feature described is the ts field, which is the timestamp of when the event occurred. This is a particularly useful feature for temporal analysis of network behavior, such as identifying bursts of connections, persistently established sessions, etc. The uid feature acts as a unique identifier for each activity session, where uid can help with traceability from a manual analysis perspective, but does not serve as a feature to be used in model training. When it comes to source and destination information, the id_orig_h, id_orig_p, id_resp_h, and id_resp_p features represent the IP addresses and the ports for the connection originator and the responder.

3.2. Pre-Processing

The length of each session helps identify long-lasting C&C connections versus short, rapid-scanning attempts. Traffic volume features include orig_bytes and resp_bytes, which give an indication of the direction and size of the data flows. Unusual patterns-as would be very small outgoing requests followed by large incoming responses-may signal data exfiltration to external servers. The conn_state feature captures whether a connection was successful, reset, or failed; this helps to differentiate normal communication from suspicious or incomplete interactions that are so often linked to probing or brute-force attacks.

Similarly, local_orig and local_resp provide information about whether one or both of the communicating devices are in the local network to help determine if the traffic is internal or from an external threat. The missed_bytes field flags portions of data that were not captured, possibly due to packet loss or encryption, which is important when assessing dataset completeness. The history field summarizes packet flags and their sequence, offering a compact timeline of connection behaviour to identify anomalies.

Additionally, orig_pkts and orig_ip_bytes count the packets and total bytes transmitted by the source device, respectively. These, together with session duration and connection state, will help in assessing the flow efficiency and detection of unusual volumes of traffic. Collectively, these features provide a comprehensive view of IoT network behavior that could pinpoint even very subtle anomalies, which are common in C&C communications.

Extensive preprocessing was carried out on the IoT-23 dataset to assist in reliable machine learning analysis. This included feature extraction and cleaning of 20 labeled conn.log.labeled files, each representing different IoT malware behaviors.The conn. log.labeled files were then read using pandas.read_table, which included skipping the first 10 metadata rows and selecting a maximum of 100,000 records per capture.

A significant amount of label normalization was necessary during this stage. The original logs had varying or sometimes redundant label formats; for example: - Malicious C&C, (empty) Malicious C&C-HeartBeat, and - Malicious C&C-Mirai. These various formats were normalized through string matching and replacements into grossly simplified classes. This was particularly evident in the Command-and-Control (C&C) category which was provided in multiple granular behaviours rather than as a standalone class label (such as C&C-Mirai, C&C-Torii, C&C-HeartBeat, C&C-File Download, hybrid behaviours such as C&C-HeartBeat-File Download).

Therefore, all records of the (C&C) behaviour were merged into a single C&C class label to enable (binary and multi-class) classification tasks to focus on the primary activity of a C&C regardless of the type of malware/or inter-host communication channel. To facilitate model training, non-informative identifiers such as IP addresses, ports, and connection IDs were removed. Categorical variables ?"namely proto (protocol) and conn_state (connection state) ?"were one-hot encoded to convert them into machine-readable binary features. Missing or placeholder values (e.g., -) in numerical fields like duration, orig_bytes, and resp_bytes were replaced with zero, and all fields were cast to numeric types. The resulting dataset was free of null values and consisted entirely of numerical features, ensuring compatibility with various supervised learning algorithms. This curated and normalized dataset provided a clean, consistent foundation for training models to detect both general and stealthy C&C communications embedded within IoT traffic.

In the application of SMOTE, synthetic samples were produced through numerical features like duration, orig_bytes, resp_bytes, and packet counts. With a nearest-neighbour approach sometimes referred to as k-statistics, SMOTE applied a k value of five and balanced the minority C&C class with the training instance count of benign. Interpolation made between instances of the minority classes increased the classifier's ability to differentiate more subtle behavioural characteristics of C&C traffic without reliance on duplicated sampling. This balancing was only performed on the training set to limit any data leakage as well as keep the test set the same and usable for evaluation.

Feature selection was critical in this study due to the high dimensionality and potential noise present in network traffic logs. A feature importance ranking was generated using the Gini importance metric from a baseline Random Forest model. Only the top-ranked features contributing most to model decision boundaries were retained. This not only improved model efficiency but also helped in interpreting which network behaviours were most predictive of C&C activity such as connection duration, packet size asymmetry, and uncommon port usage.

3.3. Model Selection

To assess the role of class balancing on Command-and-Control (C&C) attack detection, two classification pipelines were tested - side by side. Both models were trained using exactly the same pre-processed version of the dataset, from the IoT-23 dataset, and were both based on the Random Forest classifier for the main algorithm. This consistency in model structure and dataset was important in guaranteeing that the distinction noted in performance in the two cases was due to balancing or lack of balancing, and not variability from the model.

Random Forest was chosen for its resilience to overfitting, capacity for handling high-dimensionality, and efficacy in previous machine learning studies related to cybersecurity. Each tree in the ensemble was trained using a different bootstrapped sample from the dataset, and the prediction was determined through majority voting. This approach offers benefits both in predictive power and interpretation of feature importance that would be important when analysing downstream analysis of the features that lead to the most power in detecting C&C activity. During training, the Random Forest algorithm creates a large number of decision trees, from which it extracts the mean prediction (for regression) or the mode (for classification) of each tree. It is given by equation (1):

$$\hat{y} = \frac{1}{N} \wedge'^{N}_{i=1} T_i(x) \mathrm{A} \tag{1}$$

Where $T_i(x)$ is the prediction of the $i - th$ tree and N is the number of trees in the forest. The two models compared in this study are:

Model A: Trained on the original imbalanced dataset, where C&C traffic represents a minority class compared to benign traffic.

Model B: Trained on a synthetically balanced version of the dataset using the Synthetic Minority Over-sampling Technique (SMOTE). SMOTE generates new samples of the minority class (C&C) by interpolating between existing samples, thereby improving the model ?(tm)s exposure to underrepresented patterns.

By keeping the classifier type, hyperparameters, and feature set constant, this experimental design allows for a direct comparison of how class balancing affects model performance, particularly in terms of recall, precision, and false negative rates for C&C detection.

In order to conduct the study appropriately, a dataset was split into training and test datasets using stratified 80/20 splits in order to ensure the minority class (C&C) was proportionally represented in both datasets. Using stratified splits preserves the class distribution and does not overly inflate performance on the rare class. In addition, 5-fold cross-validation was applied to the training set, to tune hyperparameters and assess generalization. This reduces the variance associated with a single train-test split, while ensuring performance metrics are more consistent and reliable, depending on the application and context.

4. EVALUATION

To evaluate the effectiveness of the two classification models, one trained on the original imbalanced dataset and one trained on the dataset modified with SMOTE to be balanced, several evaluation metrics were chosen. The metrics that were chosen included accuracy, precision, recall, F1 score, and the confusion matrix. The original set of data was imbalanced, so the main focus was on recall and the F1 score for the minority class, C&C, since these are the best metrics with respect to evaluating a model's abilities for detecting those rare but critical events.

Both experimental instances were trained and tested on an 80/20 train-test split: The models needed to be validated on unseen data. Then, we compared the data generated by the trained Random Forest classifiers and their predicted classes relative to the ground truth labels to compute the performance metrics. It showed the calculation of performance metrics, drawing a confusion matrix which gave a finer perspective on true positives, false positives, false negatives, and true negatives, so it is easier to interpret misclassification patterns in more depth, especially the false negatives for C&C flows, which are missed detections of potentially dangerous flows.

Since the evaluation strategy is applied uniformly across both models, any comparison will be equitable and controlled. This enables a meaningful look into whether balancing the dataset with SMOTE significantly improves the model's ability to detect C&C attacks or if the gain in recall comes at the cost of increased false positives or reduced overall accuracy.

4.1 Results and Discussions

The evaluation of the two Random Forest-based models for detecting Command-and-Control attacks in IoT network traffic begins with the analysis of accuracy as a fundamental performance metric. Accuracy measures the proportion of correctly predicted instances both true positives (TP) and true negatives (TN) out of the total number of predictions made by the model.it is given by equation (2):

$$\text{Accuracy} = \frac{\text{TP} + \text{TN}}{\text{TP} + \text{TN} + \text{FP} + \text{FN}} \tag{2}$$

where:

? TP (True Positives) are correctly identified instances of C&C attacks
? TN (True Negatives) are correctly identified benign flows
? FP (False Positives) are benign flows incorrectly classified as C&C attacks
? FN (False Negatives) are C&C flows that were misclassified as benign

While the accuracy gives a sense of the model's correctness in a general sense, it is sometimes misleading in areas like IoT security where imbalanced dataset often occurs. C&C traffic typically represents only a small portion of overall network traffic so while accuracy may be high, the detection of rare attacks may be poor still. To mitigate this issue, some additional evaluation metrics such as Precision, Recall and F1-Score are used to get an inclusive performance evaluation.

Among these additional metrics, the F1-Score is relatively important. It represents a single measure that integrates Precision and Recall, allowing to capture of a view that accounts for both measures and is informative especially when class distributions are imbalanced. The F1-Score is given by equation (3):

$$F1 - Score = (2A\text{-}Precision A\text{-}Recall)/(Precision + Recall)A \qquad (3)$$

In the context of detecting C&C behaviour, F1-Score is vital because both false positives (misclassifying benign traffic as C&C) and false negatives (failing to identify true C&C traffic) carry significant operational risks.

Precision further refines the evaluation by indicating the proportion of correctly predicted C&C attacks among all predicted C&C instances. Precision is calculated using the formula given in equation (4):

$$Precision = TP/(TPA + FPA)A \qquad (4)$$

High precision reduces the occurrence of false alarms, which is critical in intrusion detection systems to avoid alert fatigue and resource strain on security teams.

Recall (sensitivity or true positive rate) is a measurement of the ability of the model to detect all actual C&C attacks. The value of the Recall can be calculated by the formula given in equation (5):

$$Recall = TPA/(TPA + FNA)A \qquad (5)$$

Table 4 presents the performance comparison of the models for the two classes, Benign and Command-and-Control, based on the original and the SMOTE dataset. The evaluation metrics include Precision, Recall, and F1-Score for each class, and the overall accuracy of the models as well. These results illustrate the trade-offs in using a balancing technique such as SMOTE in an intrusion detection model driven by IoT traffic.

Table 4. Comparison of Model Performance on Benign and C&C Traffic with and without SMOTE

Metric	Without SMOTE	With SMOTE
Precision (Benign)	0.94	0.91
Recall (Benign)	0.99	0.68
F1-Score (Benign)	0.96	0.78
Precision (C&C)	0.59	0.74

continued on following page

Table 4. Continued

Metric	Without SMOTE	With SMOTE
Recall (C&C)	0.14	0.94
F1-Score (C&C)	0.22	0.83
Accuracy	0.93	0.81

The model trained without using SMOTE showed overall accuracy that was high (93%) and strong performance for the Benign class, with Precision (0.94), Recall (0.99), and F1-Score (0.96). However, the model's performance in the C&C class was substantially lower, with a Recall of only 0.14 and an F1-Score of 0.22. These results indicate the model was great at identifying benign traffic, but failed to identify most of the actual C&C attack flows. Model results such as these that are good for benign traffic, but do poorly to identify C&C flows, are to be expected when models are trained on imbalanced datasets. In this case, the majority class, benign traffic, has affected the model performance to the point it is no longer indicating it is a reliable model for the minority class, C&C.

In contrast, with the model trained with SMOTE, the overall accuracy had dropped to 81% but produced a substantial advantage in C&C traffic detection. The Recall for the C&C had jumped to 0.94, and the F1-Score ticked up to 0.83, indicating the model was now very capable of locating C&C communications. The trade-off was that Benign class performance declined slightly (Recall dropped from 0.99 to 0.68) as the model changed its focus to better cater to the underrepresented class. In conclusion, this experimentation leads to a major conclusion of this study, which was that in applying IoT security, overall accuracy is not the most relevant measurement. The most relevant measurement is the detection of minority class attacks like C&C attacks, which will be detrimental if not located. In this case, using SMOTE worked to produce a more balanced dataset and increase the classifier's sensitivity to C&C behaviour, to make its application relevant in a practical intrusion detection system where deviations of behaviour as a form of attack are subtle and rare or simply missed altogether.

Figure 2 presents the confusion matrix for the Random Forest model without any class balancing technique is presented in this paragraph. The results show a clear bias towards the majority class (Benign), predicted accurately for most instances (39,273 true positives). The model does poorly, however, when predicting the C&C case with 412 true positives and 2,608 cases of C&C that were incorrectly classified as Benign. This is a fundamental problem with training on an imbalanced dataset. While the overall accuracy is 93%, the model cannot generalize well to minority class patterns. This is a serious problem in the context of IoT security since this raises the risk of skipping or missing an actual C&C activity, which could extend the IoT device's compromise for longer periods.

Figure 2. Confusion matrix without SMOTE

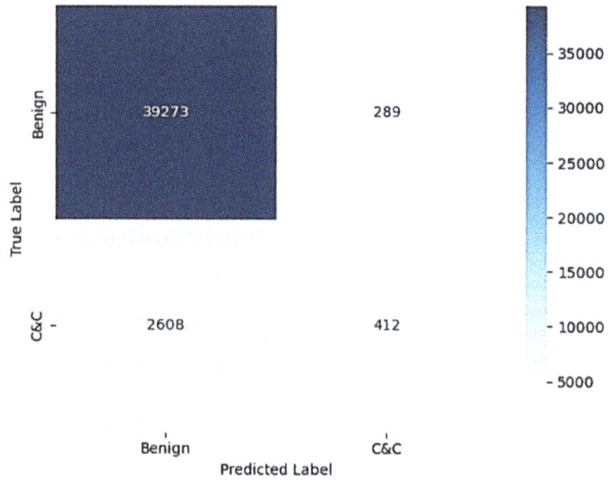

The misclassification of over 2600 C&C instances in the unbalanced model represents a significant operational risk in real-world deployments. The false positives observed in the SMOTE-trained model may result in unnecessary alerts, but these are more manageable from a security response perspective. The priority remains to minimize missed threats in high-stakes environments.

Figure 3 presents the confusion matrix of the model trained on a SMOTE-balanced dataset, resulting in synthetic samples to equalize the number of Benign and C&C instances. The effects of SMOTE can be clearly seen in that the model accurately detects 36,993 C&C instances, an improvement on the non-SMOTE version, and reduces the false negatives to 2569. The impact on recall for the C&C class comes at the cost of higher false positives but 12,736 benign flows was incorrectly classified as C&C. Given the overall accuracy dropped to about 81%, the model can at least provide a more realistic profile with security in mind, where it was preferred to get as many cases of potentially misbehaving behaviour right. At stake is whether or not the model accurately identifies the behaviour correctly. This trade-off illustrates the success of utilizing the SMOTE algorithm to shift the model ?(tm)s focus to the minority class, making it much more useful in real-world situations where missing attacks outweighs the minor inconvenience of false alarms. This allows for a meaningful analysis of whether balancing the dataset with SMOTE significantly improves the model ?(tm)s ability to detect C&C attacks, or if the gain in recall comes at the cost of increased false positives or reduced overall accuracy.

Figure 3. Confusion Matrix with SMOTE

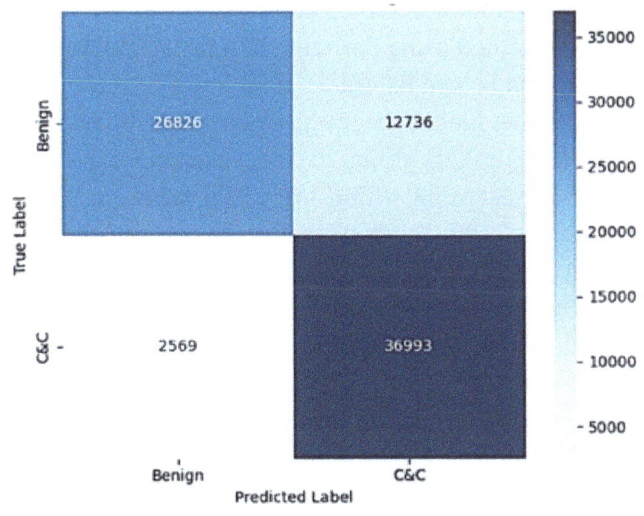

4.2 Novelty of the Study

This study makes a distinctive contribution by providing a controlled, side-by-side evaluation of how SMOTE affects the detection of C&C attacks in IoT networks, one that is often overlooked due to extreme class imbalance. In contrast to other works in the literature that combine SMOTE with deep learning or hybrid architectures, this work isolates the impact of SMOTE itself by holding constant the dataset, features, algorithm (Random Forest), and evaluation pipeline across two models. The experiment provides clean empirical evidence on how much the oversampling changes recall, precision, and F1-score for minority-class C&C traffic. This research uniquely focuses on C&C-specific behavior within the IoT-23 dataset, unifying heterogeneous C&C labels into one class, so as to estimate better real-world threats that a detection model would face. The study provides clear insights into the trade-off between higher recall for rare attacks versus reduced overall accuracy. It presents evidence for prioritizing minority-class detection in IoT security environments.

5. CONCLUSION

This research was concerned with the effectiveness of the Synthetic Minority Over-sampling Technique (SMOTE) in improving the performance of an intrusion detection system (IDS) for detecting Command-and-Control (C&C) attacks in IoT network traffic, by implementing a Random Forest-based IDS. The model utilized flow-level information based on the IoT-23 dataset and focused on a comparative study where a model was created using the original imbalanced dataset and another model was created using a balanced dataset created using SMOTE. The purpose of this study was not to optimize global accuracy; rather, it was to investigate whether SMOTE would improve the model's ability to detect minority class instances (C&C traffic), which is highly threatening within IoT ecosystems. On inspection of the results, there was a clear relationship between the balance of the dataset and the ability to detect minority class instances, specifically the C&C activity. The model using the imbalanced dataset produced a very high accuracy of 93% by correctly predicting benign traffic; however, given the purpose of this study, it was not an appropriate model to use for the detection of C&C activity as indicated by only a 14% recall for the C&C class. Conversely, using the SMOTE dataset to train a new model, the model was much more effective at detecting C&C traffic and achieved a recall of 94% and an F1-score of 83%.

In the unbalanced model, over 2,600 C&C cases were misclassified, resulting in a significant operational risk for real-world use. Those false negatives could allow malware-infected devices to continue exfiltrating or coordinating attacks undetected. Misclassifications for the SMOTE-trained model highlighted potential false positives that would create alerts that would never happen, which, from the viewpoint of a security response, is less plausible than the other option. The aim is to identify missed threats, specifically in high-risk situations. On a larger scale, this study provides useful evidence to the ongoing debate around class imbalance in cybersecurity datasets ?"especially IoT networks where attacks are infrequent and have high consequences.

As part of future work, this research could be further developed by using more intricate oversampling methods in advanced methods such as ADASYN or Borderline-SMOTE, and exploring cost-sensitive learning so as to impose penalties to classes that are misclassified. Furthermore, this work could also be extended by way of utilizing ensemble methods that combine SMOTE with under-sampling the majority class, as these approaches may provide a more acceptable trade-off between recall and precision. Alternatively, future work could also be developed using deep learning methods such as LSTM or CNN-based methods, as they can exploit the temporal (or spatial) aspects of the network traffic much better. In multi-faceted environments with numerous IoT deployments, security teams must take into consideration their organization's risk appetite when determining detection strategies. Depending on whether the aim is to detect every single potential threat (for an increased false positive rate), or to minimize noise, an IDS might be configured differently. In this study, it was shown that sampling the rebalanced data with SMOTE improved the machine learning model's ability to detect malicious activity, including types of covert behaviours that merged with benign traffic. Although the decrease in overall accuracy may seem disconcerting, the improved sensitivity to the previously stealthy attacks associated with C&C would outweigh this consideration for most operational scenarios.

For organizations adopting lightweight or distributed IDS solutions in IoT contexts, data-level interventions such as SMOTE should be considered as early as possible in the deployment pipeline. These interventions can offer notable advantages in the case of edge computing environments, where the combination of limited data and computational restraints necessitate some smart preprocessing stages. Additionally, leveraging oversampling with other measures such as feature engineering and filtering by protocol has the potential to greatly amplify detection performance accuracy when classifying more complex attacks.

Lastly, it would be reasonable to extend this research into multiclass classification problems, given that various other forms of attacks can target IoT networks, including port scanning, DoS, data exfiltration, and malware propagation, in addition to command and control (C&C). Applying the same techniques to actual IoT device traffic, the vast majority of which have limited computational resources, will bring this field of academic interest closer to deployment. The process of employing SMOTE and other balancing methods can be seen as one step closer to creating discrimination-free models for intrusion detection systems that are leaner, more responsive, and more effective, in the increasingly critical sector of IoT security. As this area continues to develop, the challenge and opportunity of creating systems with reliable detection capabilities in constrained and malleable environments will remain an ongoing research theme for academics and practitioners.

REFERENCES

Abdulkareem, S., Foh, C., Carrez, F., & Moessner, K. (2022). SMOTE-Stack for network intrusion detection in an IoT environment. In *2022 IEEE Symposium on Computers and Communications (ISCC)* (pp. 1 ?"6) IEEE. DOI: 10.1109/ISCC55528.2022.9912910

Atuhurra, J., Hara, T., Zhang, Y., Sasabe, M., & Kasahara, S. (2024). Dealing with imbalanced classes in bot-IoT dataset. *arXiv preprint arXiv:2403.18989*. https://arxiv.org/abs/2403.18989

Ba, A., & Adda, M. (2024). Intrusion detection in IIoT using machine learning. *Procedia Computer Science*, *213*, 1104 ?"1111. DOI: 10.1016/j.procs.2024.11.109

Bansal, A., Amudala, P. R., Suddala, S., Bansal, R., & Singhal, A. (2025nd). Detection of anomalies in surveillance video using improved Cheetah optimizer algorithm along with variational auto encoder classifier. In *Proceedings of the 2025 3rd International Conference on Data Science and Information System (ICDSIS)* (pp. 1-5). IEEE. DOI: 10.1109/ICDSIS65355.2025.11070420

Bansal, A., Bharadwaj, S., Panchineni, P., Suddala, S., & Chaudhary, S. (2025, October). Conversational risk analysis: Identifying and classifying potential threats in interpersonal communication. *In Proceedings of the Congress on Smart Computing Technologies* (pp. 729 ?"745). DOI: 10.1007/978-981-96-6254-8_53

Eid, A. M., Soudan, B., Nassif, A. B., & Injadat, M. (2024). Enhancing intrusion detection in IIoT: Optimized CNN model with multi-class SMOTE balancing. *Neural Computing & Applications*, *36*(24), 14643 ?"14659. DOI: 10.1007/s00521-024-09857-x

Garcia, S., Parmisano, A., & Erquiaga, M. J. (2020). *IoT-23: A labeled dataset with malicious and benign IoT network traffic (Version 1.0.0)* [Data set]. Zenodo. DOI: 10.5281/zenodo.4743746

Hamza, A., Gharakheili, H. H., & Sivaraman, V. (2020). IoT network security: requirements, threats, and countermeasures. arXiv preprint arXiv:2008.09339.

Harahsheh, K., Alzaqebah, M., & Chen, C.-H. (2024). An enhanced real-time intrusion detection framework using federated transfer learning in large-scale IoT networks. *International Journal of Advanced Computer Science and Applications*, *15*(12). Advance online publication. DOI: 10.14569/IJACSA.2024.0151204

Hengyu, Z. (2020, November). Improved SMOTE algorithm for imbalanced dataset. In *2020 Chinese Automation Congress (CAC)* (pp. 693 ?"697). IEEE. DOI: 10.1109/CAC51589.2020.9326603

Kapil, D., Mehra, N., Mittal, V., & Gupta, A. (2024). Enhancing machine learning models for attack detection using SMOTE. In *2024 International Conference on Integrated Intelligence and Communication Systems (ICIICS)* (pp. 1 ?"6). IEEE. DOI: 10.1109/ICIICS63763.2024.10859848

Khalaf, A., Mohamed, R., & Raziff, A. (2024). Detection model for ambiguous intrusion using SMOTE and LSTM for network security. *Journal of Advanced Research in Applied Sciences and Engineering Technology*, *39*(2), 191 ?"203. DOI: 10.37934/araset.39.2.191203

Khan, N. W., Alshehri, M. S., Khan, M. A., Almakdi, S., Moradpoor, N., Alazeb, A., Ullah, S., Naz, N., & Ahmad, J. (2023). A hybrid deep learning-based intrusion detection system for IoT networks. *Mathematical Biosciences and Engineering*, *20*(8), 13491 ?"13520. DOI: 10.3934/mbe.2023602 PMID: 37679099

Khedkar, S., Chandane, M., & Gawande, R. (2024). Integrated spatial and temporal features-based network intrusion detection system using SMOTE sampling. *International Journal of Computer Network and Information Security*, *16*(2), 10 ?"18. DOI: 10.5815/ijcnis.2024.02.02

Kumar, R., Anand, A., Singh, N., Singh, D., & Singh, P. J. (2023). An efficient machine learning approach for detecting malwares in IoT environment. *2023 3rd International Conference on Technological Advancements in Computational Sciences (ICTACS)*, 475 ?"481. DOI: 10.1109/ICTACS59847.2023.10390194

Kumar, R., Jain, V., Leong, W. Y., & Prime, S. (2024). *Convergence of IoT, blockchain, and computational intelligence in smart cities*. CRC Press., DOI: 10.1201/9781032404240

Massaoudi, M., Refaat, S., & Abu-Rub, H. (2022). Intrusion detection method based on SMOTE transformation for smart grid cybersecurity. In *2022 3rd International Conference on Smart Grid and Renewable Energy (SGRE)* (pp. 1 ?"6). IEEE. DOI: 10.1109/SGRE53517.2022.9774070

Namgung, J., Son, S., & Moon, Y. S. (2021). Efficient deep learning models for DGA domain detection. *Security and Communication Networks*, *2021*, 1 ?"15. DOI: 10.1155/2021/8887881

Popoola, S. I., Adebisi, B., Ande, R., Hammoudeh, M., Anoh, K., & Atayero, A. A. (2021). SMOTE-DRNN: A deep learning algorithm for botnet detection in the internet-of-things networks. *Sensors (Basel)*, *21*(9), 2985. DOI: 10.3390/s21092985 PMID: 33923151

Pradipta, G. A., Wardoyo, R., Musdholifah, A., Sanjaya, I. N. H., & Ismail, M. (2021, November). SMOTE for handling imbalanced data problem: A review. In *2021 Sixth International Conference on Informatics and Computing (ICIC)* (pp. 1 ?"8). IEEE. DOI: 10.1109/ICIC54025.2021.9632912

Qaddos, A., Yaseen, M. U., Al-Shamayleh, A. S., Imran, M., Akhunzada, A., & Alharthi, S. Z. (2024). A novel intrusion detection framework for optimizing IoT security. *Scientific Reports*, *14*(1), 21789. DOI: 10.1038/s41598-024-72049-z PMID: 39294195

Rana, R., & Kumar, R. (2019). Performance analysis of AODV in presence of malicious node. *Acta Electronica Malaysia*, *3*(1), 1 ?"5. DOI: 10.26480/aem.01.2019.01.05

Sameer, T., Rashmi, J., Khushi, B., Khushi, M., Rahul, R., & Prachi, J. (2024). Enhanced intrusion detection framework: Integrating SMOTE-ENN with random forest and XGBoost. *i-manager ?(tm)s. Journal of Information Technology*, *13*(3), 1 ?"10. DOI: 10.26634/jit.13.3.21454

Sayegh, H., Dong, W., & Al-Madani, A. (2024). Enhanced intrusion detection with LSTM-based model, feature selection, and SMOTE for imbalanced data. *Applied Sciences (Basel, Switzerland)*, *14*(2), 479. DOI: 10.3390/app14020479

Shang, L., Guo, D., Ji, Y., & Li, Q. (2021). Discovering unknown advanced persistent threat using shared features mined by neural networks. *Computer Networks*, *189*, 107937. DOI: 10.1016/j.comnet.2021.107937

Sharma, B., Kumar, R., Kumar, A., Chhabra, M., & Chaturvedi, S. (2023). *A systematic review of IoT malware detection using machine learning*. In *Proceedings of the 10th International Conference on Computing for Sustainable Global Development (INDIACom)*, IEEE, pp. 91-96.

Tao, W., Honghui, F., & Hongjin, Z. CongZhe, Y., Hongyan, Z., & Xianzhen, H. (2021). Intrusion detection system combined enhanced random forest with SMOTE algorithm. Research Square. DOI: 10.21203/rs.3.rs-270201/v1

Widodo, A., Setiawan, B., & Indraswari, R. (2024). Machine learning-based intrusion detection on multi-class imbalanced dataset using SMOTE. *Procedia Computer Science*, *213*, 1096 ?"1103. DOI: 10.1016/j.procs.2024.03.042

Compilation of References

Aaron, T. (2023). Artificial Neural Networks for Cybersecurity: A Comprehensive Review. *International Journal of Machine Learning Research in Cybersecurity and Artificial Intelligence*, *14*(1), 281–288.

Abbas, F., & Taeihagh, A. (2024). Unmasking deepfakes: A systematic review of deepfake detection and generation techniques using artificial intelligence. *Expert Systems with Applications*, *252*, 124260. DOI: 10.1016/j.eswa.2024.124260

Abdić, A. (2024). AI-Based Intrusion Detection Systems. *Challenges and Future Directions.*, *4*(1), 1–15.

Abdulkareem, S., Foh, C., Carrez, F., & Moessner, K. (2022). SMOTE-Stack for network intrusion detection in an IoT environment. In *2022 IEEE Symposium on Computers and Communications (ISCC)* (pp. 1 ?"6) IEEE. DOI: 10.1109/ISCC55528.2022.9912910

Abidi, M. H., Alkhalefah, H., & Aboudaif, M. K. (2024). Enhancing healthcare data security and disease detection using a crossover-based multilayer perceptron in smart healthcare systems. *Computer Modeling in Engineering & Sciences*, *139*(1), 977–997. DOI: 10.32604/cmes.2023.044169

Acar, A., Aksu, H., Uluagac, A. S., & Conti, M. (2019). A survey on homomorphic encryption schemes: Theory and implementation. ACM Computing Surveys, 51(4). *ACM Computing Surveys*, *79*(4), 1–35. DOI: 10.1145/3214303

Achuthan, K., Ramanathan, S., Srinivas, S., & Raman, R. (2024). Advancing cybersecurity and privacy with artificial intelligence: Current trends and future research directions. *Frontiers in Big Data*, *7*, 1497535. DOI: 10.3389/fdata.2024.1497535 PMID: 39703783

Adeyeye, O. J., Akanbi, I., Emeteveke, I., & Emehin, O. (2024). Leveraging secured AI-driven data analytics for cybersecurity: Safeguarding information and enhancing threat detection. *International Journal of Research and Publication and Reviews*, *5*(10), 3208–3223. DOI: 10.55248/gengpi.5.1024.2911

African Union Commission. (2020). The Digital Transformation Strategy for Africa (2020–2030). Addis Ababa.

Ahmad, A., Maynard, S. B., & Shanks, G. (2015). A case analysis of information systems and security incident responses. *International Journal of Information Management*, *35*(6), 717–723. DOI: 10.1016/j.ijinfomgt.2015.08.001

Ahmad, Z., Shahid Khan, A., Wai Shiang, C., Abdullah, J., & Ahmad, F. (2021). Network intrusion detection system: A systematic study of machine learning and deep learning approaches. *Transactions on Emerging Telecommunications Technologies*, *32*(1), 1–29. DOI: 10.1002/ett.4150

Ahmed, M., Mahmood, A. N., & Hu, J. (2016). A survey of network anomaly detection techniques. *Journal of Network and Computer Applications*, *60*, 19–31. DOI: 10.1016/j.jnca.2015.11.016

Ahmed, N. U. R., Badshah, A., Adeel, H., Tajammul, A., Duad, A., & Alsahfi, T. (2024). Visual deepfake detection: Review of techniques, tools, limitations, and future prospects. *IEEE Access : Practical Innovations, Open Solutions*.

Akhtar, Z. B., & Rawol, A. T. (2024). Enhancing Cybersecurity through AI-Powered Security Mechanisms. *IT Journal Research and Development*, *9*(1), 50–67. DOI: 10.25299/itjrd.2024.16852

Al Hwaitat, A. K., & Fakhouri, H. N. (2024). Adaptive cybersecurity neural networks: An evolutionary approach for enhanced attack detection and classification. *Applied Sciences (Basel, Switzerland)*, *14*(19), 9142. DOI: 10.3390/app14199142

Al-Dhabi, Y., & Zhang, S. (2021, August). Deepfake video detection by combining convolutional neural network and recurrent neural network. In *2021 IEEE International Conference on Computer Science, Artificial Intelligence and Electronic Engineering*, pp. 236–241. IEEE. DOI: 10.1109/CSAIEE54046.2021.9543264

Alheeti, K. M. A., Gruebler, A., & McDonald-Maier, K. D. (2017). An intrusion detection system against malicious attacks in self-driving car. *Computers & Security*, *74*, 107–122.

Alimova, A. (2021). Defending against deep fakes. *Christopher Kojm*, *29*, 76.

Ali, S., Wang, J., & Leung, V. (2025). AI-driven fusion with cybersecurity: Exploring current trends, advanced techniques, future directions, and policy implications for evolving paradigms– A comprehensive review. *Information Fusion, 18*, 102922. DOI: 10.1016/j.inffus.2024.102922

Aljanabi, M., Omran, A. H., Mijwil, M. M., Abotaleb, M., El-kenawy, E. M., & Ibrahim, A. (2024). Data poisoning: issues, challenges, and needs, In *7th IET Smart Cities Symposium (SCS 2023)*, 1-6. DOI: 10.1049/icp.2024.0951

Almalik, F., Yaqub, M., & Nandakumar, K. (2022). Self-ensembling vision transformer (SEViT) for robust medical image classification. In *International Conference on Medical Image Computing and Computer-Assisted Intervention* (pp. 376–386). Springer. https://doi.org/DOI: 10.1007/978-3-031-16437-8_36

Almojel, F., & Mishra, S. (2024). Advancing Hospital Cybersecurity Through IoT-Enabled Neural Network for Human Behavior Analysis and Anomaly Detection. *International Journal of Advanced Computer Science and Applications, 15*(5), 49–57. DOI: 10.14569/IJACSA.2024.0150506

Almseidin, M., Alzubi, M., Kovacs, S., & Alkasassbeh, M. (2017). Evaluation of machine learning algorithms for intrusion detection system. SISY 2017 - IEEE 15th International Symposium on Intelligent Systems and Informatics, Proceedings, Iv, 277–282. DOI: 10.1109/SISY.2017.8080566

Al-Mukhtar, W. N. M. (2024). AI in Cybersecurity: Transformative Approaches to Safeguarding Information Technology Systems. *Turkish Journal of Computer and Mathematics Education, 15*(3), 391–412.

Alowais, S. A., Alghamdi, S. S., Alsuhebany, N., Alqahtani, T., Alshaya, A. I., Almohareb, S. N., Aldairem, A., Alrashed, M., Bin Saleh, K., Badreldin, H. A., Al Yami, M. S., Al Harbi, S., & Albekairy, A. M. (2023). Revolutionizing healthcare: The role of artificial intelligence in clinical practice. *BMC Medical Education, 23*(1), 689. DOI: 10.1186/s12909-023-04698-z PMID: 37740191

Alsolami, T., Alsharif, B., & Ilyas, M. (2024). Enhancing Cybersecurity in Healthcare: Evaluating Ensemble Learning Models for Intrusion Detection in the Internet of Medical Things. *Sensors (Basel), 24*(18), 5937. DOI: 10.3390/s24185937 PMID: 39338685

Alzahrani Ahmad, A. (2023). Using artificial intelligence and cybersecurity in medical and healthcare applications. (2023). *Information Sciences Letters, 12*(3), 42. DOI: 10.18576/isl/120343

Amer, L. (2025). AI in cyber security: A dual perspective on hacker tactics and defensive strategies. Cyber Security: A Peer-Reviewed Journal, 8 (3), 198-213. DOI: 10.69554/CLXC9075

Arefin, S. (2024). Strengthening healthcare data security with AI-powered threat detection. *International Journal of Scientific Research and Management*, *12*(10), 1477–1483. DOI: 10.18535/ijsrm/v12i10.ec02

Arief, M., & Rajamani, R. (2019). Driver identification using steering-based biometric data: A neural network approach. *IEEE Transactions on Intelligent Transportation Systems*, *20*(2), 524–534.

Atuhurra, J., Hara, T., Zhang, Y., Sasabe, M., & Kasahara, S. (2024). Dealing with imbalanced classes in bot-IoT dataset. *arXiv preprint arXiv:2403.18989*. https://arxiv.org/abs/2403.18989

Atzori, L., Iera, A., & Morabito, G. (2010). The Internet of Things: A survey. *Computer Networks*, *54*(15), 2787–2805. DOI: 10.1016/j.comnet.2010.05.010

Awad, A. I., Babu, A., Barka, E., & Shuaib, K. (2024). AI-powered biometrics for Internet of Things security: A review and future vision. *Journal of Information Security and Applications*, *82*, 103748. DOI: 10.1016/j.jisa.2024.103748

Ba, A., & Adda, M. (2024). Intrusion detection in IIoT using machine learning. *Procedia Computer Science*, *213*, 1104 ?"1111. DOI: 10.1016/j.procs.2024.11.109

Bajwa, J., Munir, U., Nori, A., & Williams, B. (2021). Artificial intelligence in healthcare: Transforming the practice of medicine. *Future Healthcare Journal*, *8*(2), e188–e194. DOI: 10.7861/fhj.2021-0095 PMID: 34286183

Bandi, A. (2024). A Taxonomy of AI techniques for security and privacy in cyber–physical systems. *Journal of Computational and Cognitive Engineering*, *3*(2), 98–111. DOI: 10.47852/bonviewJCCE42021539

Banerjee, S. (2025). International Journal of Statistical Computation and AI-Enabled Cloud Security Solutions : A Comparative Review of Traditional vs . Next-Generation Approaches. January 2024.

Bansal, A., Amudala, P. R., Suddala, S., Bansal, R., & Singhal, A. (2025nd). Detection of anomalies in surveillance video using improved Cheetah optimizer algorithm along with variational auto encoder classifier. In *Proceedings of the 2025 3rd International Conference on Data Science and Information System (ICDSIS)* (pp. 1-5). IEEE. DOI: 10.1109/ICDSIS65355.2025.11070420

Bansal, A., Bharadwaj, S., Panchineni, P., Suddala, S., & Chaudhary, S. (2025, October). Conversational risk analysis: Identifying and classifying potential threats in interpersonal communication. *In Proceedings of the Congress on Smart Computing Technologies* (pp. 729 ?"745). DOI: 10.1007/978-981-96-6254-8_53

Bansal, P., Kockelman, K. M., & Singh, A. (2016). Assessing public opinions of and interest in new vehicle technologies: An Austin perspective. *Transportation Research Part C, Emerging Technologies*, *67*, 1–14. DOI: 10.1016/j.trc.2016.01.019

Bedi, P., Gupta, N., & Jindal, V. (2021). I-SiamIDS: An improved Siam-IDS for handling class imbalance in network-based intrusion detection systems. *Applied Intelligence*, *51*(2), 1133–1151. DOI: 10.1007/s10489-020-01886-y

Bengio, Y., Courville, A., & Vincent, P. (2013). Representation learning: A review and new perspectives. *IEEE Transactions on Pattern Analysis and Machine Intelligence*, *35*(8), 1798–1828. DOI: 10.1109/TPAMI.2013.50 PMID: 23787338

Bhuyan, M. H., Bhattacharyya, D. K., & Kalita, J. K. (2014). Network anomaly detection: Methods, systems, and tools. *IEEE Communications Surveys and Tutorials*, *16*(1), 303–336. DOI: 10.1109/SURV.2013.052213.00046

Biamonte, J., Wittek, P., Pancotti, N., Rebentrost, P., Wiebe, N., & Lloyd, S. (2017). Quantum machine learning. *Nature*, *549*(7671), 195–202. DOI: 10.1038/nature23474 PMID: 28905917

Bijone, M. (2016). A Survey on Secure Network: Intrusion Detection & Prevention Approaches. *American Journal of Information Systems*, *4*(3), 69–88. DOI: 10.12691/ajis-4-3-2

BJ, S., Seema, S., & Rohith, S. (2024). A Visual Computing Unified Application Using Deep Learning and Computer Vision Techniques. *International Journal of Interactive Mobile Technologies*, *18*, 1.

Bojarski, M., Testa, D. D., Dworakowski, D., Firner, B., Flepp, B., Goyal, P., . . . Zieba, K. (2016). End to end learning for self-driving cars. *arXiv preprint arXiv:1604.07316.*

Bonagiri, K., Marx, N., Gopalsamy, M., & Iyswariya, H. R., R. H., & S, S. (2024). AI-driven healthcare cybersecurity: Protecting patient data and medical devices. *2024 Second International Conference on Intelligent Cyber Physical Systems and Internet of Things*, 107–112. DOI: DOI: 10.1109/ICoICI62503.2024.10696183

Braber, F. Den, Lund, M. S., & Solberg, A. (n.d.). Sintef report.

Broklyn, P., Shad, R., & Egon, A. (2024). The Evolving Thread Landscape Pf Ai-Powered Cyberattacks:A Multi-Faceted Approach to Defense And Mitigate. SSRN Electronic Journal, 1-14 DOI: 10.2139/ssrn.4904878

Buczak, A. L., & Guven, E. (2016). A survey of data mining and machine learning methods for cyber security intrusion detection. *IEEE Communications Surveys and Tutorials*, *18*(2), 1153–1176. DOI: 10.1109/COMST.2015.2494502

Çakır, A. M. (2024). AI Driven Cybersecurity. *Human-Computer Interaction*, *8*(1), 119. DOI: 10.62802/jg7gge06

Callegari, C., Giordano, S., & Pagano, M. (2024). A Real Time Deep Learning Based Approach for Detecting Network Attacks. *Big Data Research*, *36*, 100446. DOI: 10.1016/j.bdr.2024.100446

Cartwright, A. J. (2023). The elephant in the room: Cybersecurity in healthcare. *Journal of Clinical Monitoring and Computing*, *37*(5), 1123–1132. DOI: 10.1007/s10877-023-01013-5 PMID: 37088852

Carver, C. A., Hill, J. M. D., Pooch, U. W., & Ieee, S. M. (2001). Limiting Uncertainty in Intrusion Response. February, 1–6. https://www.west-point.org/users/usma1982/39377/john/Publications/2001/2001-06_SMC-IAW/Limiting.pdf

Cazorla, L., Alcaraz, C., & Lopez, J. (2015). A three-stage analysis of IDS for critical infrastructures. *Computers & Security*, *55*, 235–250. DOI: 10.1016/j.cose.2015.07.005

Cheng, L., Liu, F., & Zhang, Y. (2021). A survey of zero trust security architecture in emerging networks. *IEEE Communications Surveys and Tutorials*, *23*(2), 165–190. DOI: 10.1109/COMST.2021.3051049

Chiriac, B.-N., Anton, F.-D., Ioni ă, A.-D., & Vasilică, B.-V. (2025). A modular AI-driven intrusion detection system for network traffic monitoring in Industry 4.0, using Nvidia Morpheus and generative adversarial networks. *Sensors (Basel)*, *25*(1), 130. DOI: 10.3390/s25010130 PMID: 39796921

Chong, B. (2021). K-means clustering algorithm: A brief review. *Academic Journal of Computing & Information Science*, *4*(5), 37–40. DOI: 10.25236/AJCIS.2021.040506

Chowdhury, F., & Khosla, R. (2019). Biometric authentication in autonomous vehicles: A comprehensive review. *Journal of Transportation Security*, *12*(1-2), 1–22.

Chukwunweike, J. N., Yussuf, M., Okusi, O., & Oluwatobi, T. (2024). The role of deep learning in ensuring privacy integrity and security: Applications in AI-driven cybersecurity solutions. *World Journal of Advanced Research and Reviews*, *23*(2), 2550.

Cooper, V. (2023, August 21). *Healthcare cybersecurity: Enhancing data security in healthcare*. Splashtop Inc. https://www.splashtop.com/blog/importance-of-cybersecurity-in-healthcare?

Croce, F., & Hein, M. (2020). Reliable evaluation of adversarial robustness with an ensemble of diverse parameter-free attacks. In *International Conference on Machine Learning* (pp. 2206–2216). PMLR.

Dacier, M., & Wespi, A. (1999). Towards a taxonomy of intrusion-detection systems.

Dam, D. T., Tran, T. H., Hoang, V. P., Pham, C. K., & Hoang, T. T. (2023). A survey of post-quantum cryptography: Start of a new race. *Cryptography*, *7*(3), 40. DOI: 10.3390/cryptography7030040

Danish, S. M., Nasir, A., Qureshi, H. K., Ashfaq, A. B., Mumtaz, S., & Rodriguez, J. (2018). Network Intrusion Detection System for Jamming Attack in LoRaWAN Join Procedure. IEEE International Conference on Communications, 2018-May(-December 2019). DOI: 10.1109/ICC.2018.8422721

Debenedetti, E., Sehwag, V., & Mittal, P. (2022). A light recipe to train robust vision transformers. arXiv preprint arXiv:2209.07399.

Dehghantanha, A., & Choo, K.-K. R. (2019). *Handbook of big data and IoT security*. Springer., DOI: 10.1007/978-3-030-10543-3

Dennstädt, F., Hastings, J., Putora, P. M., Schmerder, M., & Cihoric, N. (2025). Implementing large language models in healthcare while balancing control, collaboration, costs, and security. *NPJ Digital Medicine*, *8*(1), 143. Advance online publication. DOI: 10.1038/s41746-025-01476-7 PMID: 40050366

Dey, D., & Samanta, D. (2018). Biometric authentication in autonomous vehicles: Challenges and future directions. *International Journal of Biometrics*, *10*(3), 233–250.

Dhanushkodi, K., & Thejas, S. (2024). AI Enabled Threat Detection: Leveraging Artificial Intelligence for Advanced Security and Cyber Threat Mitigation. *IEEE Access : Practical Innovations, Open Solutions*, *12*, 173127–173136. DOI: 10.1109/ACCESS.2024.3493957

Ding, W., & Wang, Y. (2019). Driver identification using vehicle telematics data. *Transportation Research Part C, Emerging Technologies*, *104*, 159–174.

Dosovitskiy, A., Beyer, L., Kolesnikov, A., Weissenborn, D., Zhai, X., Unterthiner, T., Dehghani, M., Minderer, M., Heigold, G., Gelly, S., Uszkoreit, J., & Houlsby, N. (2020). An image is worth 16x16 words: Transformers for image recognition at scale. arXiv preprint arXiv:2010.11929.

Dwork, C., & Roth, A. (2014). The algorithmic foundations of differential privacy. *Foundations and Trends in Theoretical Computer Science*, *9*(3–4), 211–407. DOI: 10.1561/0400000042

Eid, A. M., Soudan, B., Nassif, A. B., & Injadat, M. (2024). Enhancing intrusion detection in IIoT: Optimized CNN model with multi-class SMOTE balancing. *Neural Computing & Applications*, *36*(24), 14643 ?"14659. DOI: 10.1007/s00521-024-09857-x

Ejeofobiri, C. K., Victor-Igun, O. O., & Okoye, C. (2024). AI-Driven Secure Intrusion Detection for Internet of Things (IOT) Networks. *Asian Journal of Mathematics and Computer Research*, *31*(4), 40–55. DOI: 10.56557/ajomcor/2024/v31i48971

Elamin, M. O. I., & Ismaiel, O. M. O. (2025). The AI Revolution in Cybersecurity: Transforming Threat Detection, Defense Mechanisms, and Risk Management in the Digital Era. *International Journal of Religion*, *6*(1), 228–246. DOI: 10.61707/1dmvn671

Elovici, Y., Shabtai, A., Rokach, L., & Braha, D. (2009). Collaborative attack on Internet users' anonymity. *Internet Research*, *19*(1), 60–77. DOI: 10.1108/10662240910927821

Emehin, O., Emeteveke, I., Adeyeye, O. J., & Akanbi, I. (2024). Securing artificial intelligence in data analytics: Strategies for mitigating risks in cloud computing environments. *International Research Journal of Modernization in Engineering Technology and Science*, *6*, 1978–1998.

European Commission. (2024). *Artificial Intelligence Act: Regulation of the European Parliament and of the Council laying down harmonised rules on artificial intelligence.* Official Journal of the European Union.

Eykholt, K., Evtimov, I., Fernandes, E., Li, B., Rahmati, A., Xiao, C., & Song, D. (2018). Robust physical-world attacks on deep learning visual classification. In *Proceedings of the IEEE Conference on Computer Vision and Pattern Recognition* (pp. 1625-1634). DOI: 10.1109/CVPR.2018.00175

Fagnant, D. J., & Kockelman, K. (2015). Preparing a nation for autonomous vehicles: Opportunities, barriers and policy recommendations. *Transportation Research Part A, Policy and Practice*, *77*, 167–181. DOI: 10.1016/j.tra.2015.04.003

Familoni, B.Babajide Tolulope Familoni. (2024). Cybersecurity Challenges in the Age of Ai: Theoretical Approaches and Practical Solutions. *Computer Science & IT Research Journal*, *5*(3), 703–724. DOI: 10.51594/csitrj.v5i3.930

Farzaan, M. A. M., Ghanem, M. C., El-Hajjar, A., & Ratnayake, D. N. (2024). AI-enabled system for efficient and effective cyber incident detection and response in cloud environments. arXiv preprint arXiv:2404.05602. https://arxiv.org/abs/2404.05602

Feng, S., Yan, X., Sun, H., & Li, L. (2020). A review of deep learning methods for vehicle detection in autonomous driving. *IEEE Transactions on Neural Networks and Learning Systems*, *32*(9), 3561–3578.

Flad, M., & Filippone, M. (2019). Safe and secure biometric authentication for autonomous vehicles. *IEEE Transactions on Intelligent Transportation Systems*, *20*(8), 3060–3069.

Flynn, A., Clough, J., & Cooke, T. (2021). Disrupting and preventing deepfake abuse: Exploring criminal law responses to AI-facilitated abuse. In *The Palgrave handbook of gendered violence and technology*, pp. 583–603.

Foret, P., Kleiner, A., Mobahi, H., & Neyshabur, B. (2020). Sharpness-aware minimization for efficiently improving generalization. arXiv preprint arXiv:2010.01412.

Gao, Z., Member, S., Cecati, C., Ieee, F., & Ding, S. X. (2015). IEEE TRANSACTIONS ON INDUSTRIAL ELECTRONICS A Survey of Fault Diagnosis and Fault - Tolerant Techniques Part I : Fault Diagnosis with Model - Based and Signal - Based Approaches. 62, 3757–3767.

Gao, Y. (2024). Cyber Attacks and Defense: AI-Driven Approaches and Techniques. *Academic Journal of Computing & Information Science*, *7*(7), 41–46. DOI: 10.25236/AJCIS.2024.070706

Garcia, S., Parmisano, A., & Erquiaga, M. J. (2020). *IoT-23: A labeled dataset with malicious and benign IoT network traffic (Version 1.0.0)* [Data set]. Zenodo. DOI: 10.5281/zenodo.4743746

Gera, M., & Goel, S. (2015). Data Mining - Techniques, Methods and Algorithms: A Review on Tools and their Validity. *International Journal of Computer Applications*, *113*(18), 22–29. DOI: 10.5120/19926-2042

Gogineni, V., & Kalyan, A. (2018). Biometric-based driver authentication in autonomous vehicles. *International Journal of Vehicle Autonomous Systems*, *14*(2), 123–138.

Goodfellow, I., Papernot, N., Huang, S., Duan, R., Abbeel, P., & Clark, J. (2017). *Attacking machine learning with adversarial examples*. OpenAI Blog.

Goodfellow, I., Pouget-Abadie, J., Mirza, M., Xu, B., Warde-Farley, D., Ozair, S., Courville, A., & Bengio, Y. (2014). Generative adversarial nets. *Advances in Neural Information Processing Systems*, •••, 2672–2680.

Guarnera, L., Giudice, O., Nießner, M., & Battiato, S. (2022). On the exploitation of deepfake model recognition. *In Proceedings of the IEEE/CVF Conference on Computer Vision and Pattern Recognition,* pp. 61–70. DOI: 10.1109/CVPRW56347.2022.00016

Gu, J., Tresp, V., & Qin, Y. (2022). Are vision transformers robust to patch perturbations? In *European Conference on Computer Vision* (pp. 404–421). Springer.

Gupta, A., & Gupta, P. (2019). Biometric security in autonomous vehicles: A survey. *International Journal of Computer Applications*, *177*(26), 1–7. DOI: 10.5120/ijca2019919451

Hafeez, Y., Memon, K., AL-Quraishi, M. S., Yahya, N., Elferik, S., & Ali, S. S. A. (2025). Explainable AI in Diagnostic Radiology for Neurological Disorders: A Systematic Review, and What Doctors Think About It. *Diagnostics (Basel)*, *15*(2), 168. DOI: 10.3390/diagnostics15020168 PMID: 39857052

Haleem, A., Javaid, M., & Khan, I. H. (2019). Current status and applications of artificial intelligence in the medical field: An overview. *Current Medicine Research and Practice*, *9*(6), 231–237. DOI: 10.1016/j.cmrp.2019.11.005

Hamid, R., & Brohi, S. (2024). A review of large language models in healthcare: Taxonomy, threats, vulnerabilities, and framework. *Big Data and Cognitive Computing*, *8*(11), 161. DOI: 10.3390/bdcc8110161

Hamza, A., Gharakheili, H. H., & Sivaraman, V. (2020). IoT network security: requirements, threats, and countermeasures. arXiv preprint arXiv:2008.09339.

Haque, M. A., & Nasir, M. A. (2019). Biometric authentication in autonomous vehicles: A comprehensive survey. *International Journal of Biometrics*, *11*(4), 357–375.

Harahsheh, K., Alzaqebah, M., & Chen, C.-H. (2024). An enhanced real-time intrusion detection framework using federated transfer learning in large-scale IoT networks. *International Journal of Advanced Computer Science and Applications*, *15*(12). Advance online publication. DOI: 10.14569/IJACSA.2024.0151204

Harris, D. (2018). Deepfakes: False pornography is here and the law cannot protect you. *Duke L. & Tech. Rev.*, *17*, 99.

Hasani, A., Rasheed, J., Alsubai, S., & Luma-Osmani, S. (2024, January). Personal rights and intellectual properties in the upcoming era: The rise of deepfake technologies. In *International Conference on Forthcoming Networks and Sustainability in the AIoT Era*, pp. 379–391. Cham: Springer Nature Switzerland. DOI: 10.1007/978-3-031-62881-8_32

He, K., Zhang, X., Ren, S., & Sun, J. (2016). Deep residual learning for image recognition. In *Proceedings of the IEEE Conference on Computer Vision and Pattern Recognition* (pp. 770-778).

Hengyu, Z. (2020, November). Improved SMOTE algorithm for imbalanced dataset. In *2020 Chinese Automation Congress (CAC)* (pp. 693 ?"697). IEEE. DOI: 10.1109/CAC51589.2020.9326603

He, Y., Aliyu, A., Evans, M., & Luo, C. (2021). Health care cybersecurity challenges and solutions under the climate of COVID-19: Scoping review. *Journal of Medical Internet Research*, *23*(4), e21747. DOI: 10.2196/21747 PMID: 33764885

Hoanca, B., & Mock, K. (2020). Artificial Intelligence-Based Cybercrime. Encyclopedia of Criminal Activities and the Deep Web, 1-16. DOI: 10.4018/978-1-5225-9715-5.ch003

Ho, J., Jain, A., & Abbeel, P. (2020). Denoising diffusion probabilistic models. *Advances in Neural Information Processing Systems*, •••, 6840–6851.

Huang, L., Joseph, A. D., Nelson, B., Rubinstein, B. I. P., & Tygar, J. D. (2011). Adversarial machine learning. In *Proceedings of the 4th ACM Workshop on Security and Artificial Intelligence (AISec '11)* (pp. 43–58). Association for Computing Machinery. DOI: 10.1145/2046684.2046692

Huang, X., Cheng, X., Geng, G., Cao, X., & Lu, H. (2019). The role of biometric authentication in autonomous vehicles: A survey. *IEEE Access : Practical Innovations, Open Solutions*, *7*, 177379–177392.

Humayed, A., Lin, J., Li, F., & Luo, B. (2017). Cyber-physical systems security—A survey. *IEEE Internet of Things Journal*, *4*(6), 1802–1831. DOI: 10.1109/JIOT.2017.2703172

Hussain, A. (2022). Deepfakes: A challenge to copyright law. *Jus Corpus Law Journal*, *3*, 249.

Hussain, R., & Zeadally, S. (2019). Autonomous cars: Research results, issues, and future challenges. *IEEE Communications Surveys and Tutorials*, *21*(2), 1275–1313. DOI: 10.1109/COMST.2018.2869360

Imam, R., Huzaifa, M., & Azz, M. E. A. (2023). On enhancing the robustness of vision transformers: Defensive diffusion. arXiv preprint arXiv:2305.08031.

Imamverdiyev, Y. N., & Abdullayeva, F. J. (2020). Deep learning in cybersecurity: Challenges and approaches. International Journal of Cyber Warfare and Terrorism (IJCWT, 10(2), 82–105.

Irvine, C., & Levin, T. (2000). Quality of security service. Proceedings New Security Paradigm Workshop, September, 91–99. DOI: 10.1145/366173.366195

Iturbe, E., Llorente-Vazquez, O., Rego, A., Rios, E., & Toledo, N. (2024). Unleashing offensive artificial intelligence: Automated attack technique code generation. *Computers & Security*, *147*, 104077. DOI: 10.1016/j.cose.2024.104077

Jain, A. K., & Ross, A. (2004). Multibiometric systems. *Communications of the ACM*, *47*(1), 34–40. DOI: 10.1145/962081.962102

Jain, S., Ashok, P., & Prabhu, S. (2024). Emerging technologies for cybersecurity in healthcare: Evaluating risks and implementing standards. *2024 International Conference on Cybernation and Computation (CYBERCOM)*, 725–731. DOI: 10.1109/CYBERCOM63683.2024.10803219

Jalali, M. S., & Kaiser, J. P. (2018). Cybersecurity in hospitals: A systematic, organizational perspective. *Journal of Medical Internet Research*, *20*(5), e10059. DOI: 10.2196/10059 PMID: 29807882

Javaid, M., Haleem, A., Singh, R. P., & Suman, R. (2023). Towards Insighting cybersecurity for healthcare domains: A comprehensive review of recent practices and trends. *Cyber Security and Applications*, *1*(100016), 100016. Advance online publication. DOI: 10.1016/j.csa.2023.100016

Jawhar, S., Miller, J., & Bitar, Z. (2024, February). AI-based cybersecurity policies and procedures. In 2024 IEEE 3rd International Conference on AI in Cybersecurity (ICAIC) (pp. 1-5). IEEE.

Jia, S., Lyu, R., Zhao, K., Chen, Y., Yan, Z., Ju, Y., Hu, C., Li, X., Wu, B., & Lyu, S. (2024). Can ChatGPT detect deepfakes? A study of using multimodal large language models for media forensics. In *Proceedings of the IEEE/CVF Conference on Computer Vision and Pattern Recognition*, pp. 4324–4333. DOI: 10.1109/CVPRW63382.2024.00436

Jobin, A., Ienca, M., & Vayena, E. (2019). The global landscape of AI ethics guidelines. *Nature Machine Intelligence*, *1*(9), 389–399. DOI: 10.1038/s42256-019-0088-2

Jung, H., Lee, J., Yim, J., Park, S., & Kim, J. (2016). Joint visual and thermal sequence alignment network for robust pedestrian detection. In *Proceedings of the IEEE Conference on Computer Vision and Pattern Recognition* (pp. 1420-1429).

Kabir, E., Hu, J., Wang, H., & Zhuo, G. (2018). A novel statistical technique for intrusion detection systems. *Future Generation Computer Systems*, *79*, 303–318. DOI: 10.1016/j.future.2017.01.029

Kairouz, P., McMahan, H. B., Avent, B., Bellet, A., Bennis, M., Bhagoji, A. N., Bonawitz, K., Charles, Z., Cormode, G., Cummings, R., D'Oliveira, R. G. L., Eichner, H., El Rouayheb, S., Evans, D., Gardner, J., Garrett, Z., Gascón, A., Ghazi, B., Gibbons, P. B., & Zhao, S. (2021). Advances and open problems in federated learning. *Foundations and Trends in Machine Learning*, *14*(1–2), 1–210. DOI: 10.1561/2200000083

Kaja, N., Shaout, A., & Ma, D. (2019). An intelligent intrusion detection system. *Applied Intelligence*, *49*(9), 3235–3247. DOI: 10.1007/s10489-019-01436-1

Kaloudi, N., & Li, J. (2020). The AI-Based Cyber Threat Landscape. *ACM Computing Surveys*, *53*(1), 1–34. DOI: 10.1145/3372823

Kang, L., & Wang, Y. (2019). Biometric authentication in autonomous vehicles: A survey. *IEEE Access : Practical Innovations, Open Solutions*, *7*, 177379–177392.

Kapil, D., Mehra, N., Mittal, V., & Gupta, A. (2024). Enhancing machine learning models for attack detection using SMOTE. In *2024 International Conference on Integrated Intelligence and Communication Systems (ICIICS)* (pp. 1 ?"6). IEEE. DOI: 10.1109/ICIICS63763.2024.10859848

Karras, T., Laine, S., & Aila, T. (2019). A style-based generator architecture for generative adversarial networks. *Proceedings of the IEEE/CVF Conference on Computer Vision and Pattern Recognition (CVPR)*, pp. 4401–4410. DOI: 10.1109/CVPR.2019.00453

Kaur, R., Gabrijelcic, D., & Klobučar, T. (2023). Artificial intelligence for cybersecurity: Literature review and future research directions. *Information Fusion*, *97*, 101804. DOI: 10.1016/j.inffus.2023.101804

Kazimierczak, M., Habib, N., Chan, J. H., & Thanapattheerakul, T. (2024). Impact of AI on the Cyber Kill Chain: A Systematic Review. *Heliyon*, *10*(24), e40699. DOI: 10.1016/j.heliyon.2024.e40699 PMID: 39720055

Keerthi, C. K., Jabbar, M. A., & Seetharamulu, B. (2017). Cyber-physical systems (CPS): Security issues, challenges, and solutions. In *2017 IEEE International Conference on Computational Intelligence and Computing Research (ICCIC)* (pp. 1–4). IEEE. DOI: 10.1109/ICCIC.2017.8524312

Khalaf, A., Mohamed, R., & Raziff, A. (2024). Detection model for ambiguous intrusion using SMOTE and LSTM for network security. *Journal of Advanced Research in Applied Sciences and Engineering Technology, 39*(2), 191 ?"203. DOI: 10.37934/araset.39.2.191203

Khan, M. A., & Salah, K. (2018). IoT security: Review, blockchain solutions, and open challenges. *Future Generation Computer Systems, 82*, 395–411. DOI: 10.1016/j.future.2017.11.022

Khan, N. W., Alshehri, M. S., Khan, M. A., Almakdi, S., Moradpoor, N., Alazeb, A., Ullah, S., Naz, N., & Ahmad, J. (2023). A hybrid deep learning-based intrusion detection system for IoT networks. *Mathematical Biosciences and Engineering, 20*(8), 13491 ?"13520. DOI: 10.3934/mbe.2023602 PMID: 37679099

Khedkar, S., Chandane, M., & Gawande, R. (2024). Integrated spatial and temporal features-based network intrusion detection system using SMOTE sampling. *International Journal of Computer Network and Information Security, 16*(2), 10 ?"18. DOI: 10.5815/ijcnis.2024.02.02

Korshunov, P., & Marcel, S. (2018). Deepfakes: A new threat to face recognition? Assessment and detection. arXiv preprint arXiv:1812.08685.

Korshunov, P., & Marcel, S., (2018). *Deepfakes: a new threat to face recognition? assessment and detection.* arXiv preprint arXiv:1812.08685.

Kumar, R., Anand, A., Singh, N., Singh, D., & Singh, P. J. (2023). An efficient machine learning approach for detecting malwares in IoT environment. *2023 3rd International Conference on Technological Advancements in Computational Sciences (ICTACS)*, 475 ?"481. DOI: 10.1109/ICTACS59847.2023.10390194

Kumar, N., & Sharma, S. (2019). Biometric authentication in autonomous vehicles: A review. *International Journal of Biometrics, 11*(4), 357–375.

Kumar, R., Jain, V., Leong, W. Y., & Prime, S. (2024). *Convergence of IoT, blockchain, and computational intelligence in smart cities.* CRC Press., DOI: 10.1201/9781032404240

Kuppusamy, P. (2024). A Digital Trust Architectural Model for Connected Medical Devices in the Healthcare Environment. In Hassan, A., Bhattacharya, P., Tikadar, S., Dutta, P., & Sagayam, M. (Eds.), *Lightweight Digital Trust Architectures in the Internet of Medical Things (IoMT)* (pp. 118–144). IGI Global Scientific Publishing., DOI: 10.4018/979-8-3693-2109-6.ch008

Kuppusamy, P., & Khang, A. (2024). An Advanced Cybersecurity Model for High-Tech Farming Using Machine Learning Approach. In Khang, A. (Ed.), *Agriculture and Aquaculture Applications of Biosensors and Bioelectronics* (pp. 461–495). IGI Global Scientific Publishing., DOI: 10.4018/979-8-3693-2069-3.ch026

Kuppusamy, P., & Suresh, J. K. (2023). Unified Cybersecurity Data Analytical Model for Smart Learning Operations. In Jimenez, R., & O'Neill, V. E. (Eds.), *Handbook of Research on Current Trends in Cybersecurity and Educational Technology* (pp. 92–120). IGI Global., DOI: 10.4018/978-1-6684-6092-4.ch006

Lees, D. (2024). Deepfakes in documentary film production: Images of deception in the representation of the real. *Studies in Documentary Film*, *18*(2), 108–129. DOI: 10.1080/17503280.2023.2284680

Le, M., Stavrou, A., & Kang, B. B. (2012). DoubleGuard: Detecting intrusions in multitier web applications. *IEEE Transactions on Dependable and Secure Computing*, *9*(4), 512–525. DOI: 10.1109/TDSC.2011.59

Liao, H.-J., Lin, C.-H. R., Lin, Y.-C., & Tung, K.-Y. (2013). Intrusion detection system: A comprehensive review. *Journal of Network and Computer Applications*, *36*(1), 16–24. DOI: 10.1016/j.jnca.2012.09.004

Li, H., Wu, J., Xu, H., Li, G., & Guizani, M. (2022). Explainable Intelligence-Driven Defense Mechanism Against Advanced Persistent Threats: A Joint Edge Game and AI Approach. *IEEE Transactions on Dependable and Secure Computing*, *19*, 757–775. DOI: 10.1109/TDSC.2021.3130944

Liu, Y., Yang, X., & Wang, P. (2019). Enhancing security in autonomous vehicles with AI-driven biometric systems. *IEEE Transactions on Vehicular Technology*, *68*(12), 11234–11245.

Liu, Z., Lin, Y., Cao, Y., Hu, H., Wei, Y., Zhang, Z., & Guo, B. (2021). Swin transformer: Hierarchical vision transformer using shifted windows. In *Proceedings of the IEEE/CVF International Conference on Computer Vision* (pp. 10012–10022).

Liu, Z., Mao, H., Wu, C. Y., Feichtenhofer, C., Darrell, T., & Xie, S. (2022). A ConvNet for the 2020s. In *Proceedings of the IEEE/CVF Conference on Computer Vision and Pattern Recognition* (pp. 11976–11986).

Li, Y., & Wang, X. (2020). Secure biometric authentication for self-driving vehicles. *Journal of Intelligent Transport Systems*, *24*(2), 89–103.

Lysenko, S., Verba, O., Kyrychenko, V., Gandziuk, V., & Odobetska, I. (2025). Managing Cybersecurity Risks in the Era of Digital Transformation. *Journal of Information Systems Engineering & Management*, *10*(2s), 416–429. DOI: 10.52783/jisem.v10i2s.330

Ma, Z., Wu, W., Zheng, Z., Guo, Y., Chen, Q., Zhang, S., & Chen, X. (2024, April). Leveraging speech PTM, text LLM, and emotional TTS for speech emotion recognition. In *ICASSP 2024—2024 IEEE International Conference on Acoustics, Speech and Signal Processing*, pp. 11146–11150. DOI: 10.1109/ICASSP48485.2024.10445906

Madry, A., Makelov, A., Schmidt, L., Tsipras, D., & Vladu, A. (2017). Towards deep learning models resistant to adversarial attacks. arXiv preprint arXiv:1706.06083.

Mahajan, R., & Sharma, K. (2018). Biometric-based vehicle access control: A survey. *International Journal of Automotive Technology*, *19*(4), 567–580.

Mahendrakhan, K., & Nagarathna, P. (2022). Cybersecurity in healthcare with artificial intelligence. *2022 IEEE 2nd Mysore Sub Section International Conference (MysuruCon)*, 1–8.

Mahmud, B. U., & Sharmin, A. (2021). Deep insights of deepfake technology: A review. *arXiv preprint*, arXiv:2105.00192.

Mao, X., Qi, G., Chen, Y., Li, X., Duan, R., Ye, S., & Xue, H. (2022). Towards robust vision transformer. In *Proceedings of the IEEE/CVF Conference on Computer Vision and Pattern Recognition* (pp. 12042–12051).

Marchette, D. J. (2012). Network intrusion detection. Handbook of Computational Statistics: Concepts and Methods: Second Edition, 1139–1165. DOI: 10.1007/978-3-642-21551-3_38

Martins, I., Resende, J. S., Sousa, P. R., Silva, S., Antunes, L., & Gama, J. (2022). Host-based IDS: A review and open issues of an anomaly detection system in IoT. Future Generation Computer Systems, 133(January 2021), 95–113. DOI: 10.1016/j.future.2022.03.001

Masood, M., Nawaz, M., Malik, K. M., Javed, A., Irtaza, A., & Malik, H. (2023). Deepfakes generation and detection: State-of-the-art, open challenges, countermeasures, and way forward. *Applied Intelligence*, *53*(4), 3974–4026. DOI: 10.1007/s10489-022-03766-z

Massaoudi, M., Refaat, S., & Abu-Rub, H. (2022). Intrusion detection method based on SMOTE transformation for smart grid cybersecurity. In *2022 3rd International Conference on Smart Grid and Renewable Energy (SGRE)* (pp. 1 ?"6). IEEE. DOI: 10.1109/SGRE53517.2022.9774070

Matsuo, T., & Yamashita, T. (2017). AI-powered facial recognition in autonomous vehicles. *IEEE Intelligent Transportation Systems Magazine*, *9*(3), 54–64.

Maurya, R. (2023). Analyzing the Role of AI in Cyber Security Threat Detection & Prevention. *International Journal for Research in Applied Science and Engineering Technology*, *11*(11), 514–519. DOI: 10.22214/ijraset.2023.56510

Ma, Z., & Zhang, H. (2021). Deep learning applications in biometric security for autonomous cars. *IEEE Access : Practical Innovations, Open Solutions*, *9*, 105678–105689.

Menghani, G. (2023). Efficient Deep Learning: A Survey on Making Deep Learning Models Smaller, Faster, and Better. *ACM Computing Surveys*, *55*(12), 1–37. Advance online publication. DOI: 10.1145/3578938

Meyer, P., & Fischer, S. (2019). Evaluating biometric authentication systems for self-driving cars. *Journal of Transportation Cybersecurity*, *5*(1), 27–42.

Mishra, N., Shivaji, G. B., Barekar, S. S., Dari, S. S., Dhabliya, D., & Patil, M. (2024). Artificial intelligence and machine learning in healthcare cybersecurity of current applications and future directions. *South Eastern European Journal of Public Health*, •••, 46–51. DOI: 10.70135/seejph.vi.750

Mo, B. (2024). Enhancing Cybersecurity in Healthcare: Machine Learning and Deep Learning Strategies for Intrusion Detection on the Internet of Medical Things, In Proc. of the 1st Int., Conf., on Engineering Management, Information Technology and Intelligence (EMITI 2024), 301–305. https://orcid.org/ 0009-0009-3413-2486.

Mohammed, S. Y., Aljanabi, M., & Mijwil, M. M. (2024). Detecting Denial-of-Service (DoS) Attacks with Edge Machine Learning. In Springer proceedings in business and economics, 119–127. DOI: 10.1007/978-3-031-67511-9_8

Mohammed, S. Y., Aljanabi, M., Mijwil, M. M., Ramadhan, A. J., Abotaleb, M., Alkattan, H., & Albadran, Z. (2024). A Two-Stage hybrid approach for phishing attack detection using URL and content analysis in IoT. BIO Web of Conferences, 97, 00059. DOI: 10.1051/bioconf/20249700059

Mohammed, F., & Hassan, R. (2020). Ethical challenges in biometric security for autonomous vehicles. *Ethics and Information Technology*, *22*(3), 243–257.

Mohammed, S. Y.Sahar Yousef Mohammed. (2023). Enhancing COVID-19 Patients Detection using Deep Transfer Learning Technique through X-Ray Chest Images. *Journal of Advanced Research in Applied Sciences and Engineering Technology*, *32*(1), 290–302. DOI: 10.37934/araset.32.1.290302

Monteiro, S. M., (2024). Detection of fake images generated by deep learning, *Master's thesis, Instituto Politecnico de Viseu, Portugal.*

Muneer, S., Farooq, U., Athar, A., Raza, M. A., Ghazal, T. M., & Sakib, S. (2024). A Critical Review of Artificial Intelligence Based Approaches in Intrusion Detection: A Comprehensive Analysis. *Journal of Engineering*, *2024*(1), 3909173. Advance online publication. DOI: 10.1155/2024/3909173

Nacheva, R., & Azeroual, O. (2024, November). Security of AI-Powered Systems: Threat Intelligence on the Edge. In 2024 8th International Symposium on Multidisciplinary Studies and Innovative Technologies (ISMSIT) (pp. 1-6). IEEE.

Nadella, G. S., Addula, S. R., Yadulla, A. R., Sajja, G. S., Meesala, M., Maturi, M. H., & Gonaygunta, H. (2025). Generative AI-Enhanced Cybersecurity Framework for Enterprise Data Privacy Management. *Computers*, *14*(2), 55. DOI: 10.3390/computers14020055

Nagaraja, N., & Bahsi, H. (2025). Cyber threat modeling of an LLM-based healthcare system. *Proceedings of the 11th International Conference on Information Systems Security and Privacy*, 325–336. DOI: 10.5220/0013289700003899

Nakamura, S., & Suzuki, Y. (2021). AI and biometric authentication: Securing the future of self-driving cars. *IEEE Transactions on Transportation Electrification*, *7*(2), 122–135.

Namgung, J., Son, S., & Moon, Y. S. (2021). Efficient deep learning models for DGA domain detection. *Security and Communication Networks*, *2021*, 1 ?"15. DOI: 10.1155/2021/8887881

Nandi, A., & Gupta, P. (2020). Risk assessment in biometric authentication for autonomous cars. *IEEE Access : Practical Innovations, Open Solutions*, *8*, 89765–89778.

Naseer, S., Saleem, Y., Khalid, S., Bashir, M., Han, J., Iqbal, M., & Han, K. (2018). Enhanced Network Anomaly Detection Based on Deep Neural Networks. *IEEE Access : Practical Innovations, Open Solutions*, *6*, 48231–48246. DOI: 10.1109/ACCESS.2018.2863036

National Institute of Standards and Technology. (2018). *Framework for Improving Critical Infrastructure Cybersecurity, Version 1.1.* DOI: 10.6028/NIST.CSWP.04162018

Nguyen, G., Dlugolinsky, S., Tran, V., & García, Á. (2020). Deep Learning for Proactive Network Monitoring and Security Protection. *IEEE Access : Practical Innovations, Open Solutions*, *8*, 19696–19716. DOI: 10.1109/ACCESS.2020.2968718

Nguyen, T. T., Nguyen, Q. V. H., Nguyen, D. T., Nguyen, D. T., Huynh-The, T., Nahavandi, S., Nguyen, T. T., Pham, Q. V., & Nguyen, C. M. (2022). Deep learning for deepfakes creation and detection: A survey. *Computer Vision and Image Understanding*, *223*, 103525. DOI: 10.1016/j.cviu.2022.103525

Nguyen, T., & Le, H. (2019). Biometric-enabled smart vehicle access control systems. *International Journal of Biometrics*, *12*(2), 123–140.

Othman, S. M., Alsohybe, N. T., Mutaher Ba-Alwi, F., & Zahary, A. T. (2018). Survey on Intrusion Detection System Types. *International Journal of Cyber-Security and Digital Forensics*, *7*(4), 444–462.

Othman, S. M., Ba-Alwi, F. M., Alsohybe, N. T., & Al-Hashida, A. Y. (2018). Intrusion detection model using machine learning algorithm on Big Data environment. *Journal of Big Data*, *5*(1), 34. Advance online publication. DOI: 10.1186/s40537-018-0145-4

Otoum, S., Kantarci, B., & Mouftah, H.SAFA OTOUM. (2021). A Comparative Study of AI-based Intrusion DetectionTechniques in Critical Infrastructures. *ACM Transactions on Internet Technology*, *21*(4), 1–22. DOI: 10.1145/3406093

Ouarda, L., Malika, B., Yousfi, N. E., & Brahim, B. (2022). Improving the efficiency of intrusion detection in information systems. *Journal of Intelligent Systems*, *31*(1), 835–854. DOI: 10.1515/jisys-2022-0059

Oyinloye, T. S., Arowolo, M. O., & Prasad, R. (2025). Enhancing cyber threat detection with an improved artificial neural network model. *Data Science and Management*, *8*(1), 107–115. DOI: 10.1016/j.dsm.2024.05.002

Patcha, A., & Park, J.-M. (2007). An overview of anomaly detection techniques: Existing solutions and latest technological trends. *Computer Networks*, *51*(12), 3448–3470. DOI: 10.1016/j.comnet.2007.02.001

Patel, A., & Desai, K. (2020). Machine learning in biometric security for autonomous vehicles. *Machine Learning Applications in Automotive Systems*, *32*(4), 205–218.

Peddabachigari, S., Abraham, A., Grosan, C., & Thomas, J. (2007). Modeling intrusion detection system using hybrid intelligent systems. *Journal of Network and Computer Applications*, *30*(1), 114–132. DOI: 10.1016/j.jnca.2005.06.003

Perov, I., Gao, D., Chervoniy, N., Liu, K., Marangonda, S., Umé, C., & Facenheim, C. S. RP, L., Jiang, J., Zhang, S., & Wu, P., (2020). DeepFaceLab: Integrated, flexible and extensible face-swapping framework. *arXiv preprint*, arXiv:2005.05535.

Petit, J., & Shladover, S. E. (2015). Potential cyberattacks on automated vehicles. *IEEE Transactions on Intelligent Transportation Systems*, *16*(2), 546–556. DOI: 10.1109/TITS.2014.2342271

Podder, P., Bharati, S., Mondal, M. R. H., Paul, P. K., & Kose, U. (2021). Artificial neural network for cybersecurity: A comprehensive review. *arXiv [Cs.CR]*. DOI: 10.48550/ARXIV.2107.01185

Ponmalar, A., & Dhanakoti, V. (2021). An Efficient Classification of Intrusion in Bigdata based on Chaos Game Optimization and Ensemble SVM. DOI: 10.21203/rs.3.rs-385392/v1

Popoola, S. I., Adebisi, B., Ande, R., Hammoudeh, M., Anoh, K., & Atayero, A. A. (2021). SMOTE-DRNN: A deep learning algorithm for botnet detection in the internet-of-things networks. *Sensors (Basel)*, *21*(9), 2985. DOI: 10.3390/s21092985 PMID: 33923151

Pradipta, G. A., Wardoyo, R., Musdholifah, A., Sanjaya, I. N. H., & Ismail, M. (2021, November). SMOTE for handling imbalanced data problem: A review. In *2021 Sixth International Conference on Informatics and Computing (ICIC)* (pp. 1 ?"8). IEEE. DOI: 10.1109/ICIC54025.2021.9632912

Putty, C. (2025, March 12). Cybersecurity in healthcare: AI as a guard against threats. *Thoughtful.Ai*. https://www.thoughtful.ai/blog/cybersecurity-in-healthcare-ai-as-a-guard-against-threats

Qaddos, A., Yaseen, M. U., Al-Shamayleh, A. S., Imran, M., Akhunzada, A., & Alharthi, S. Z. (2024). A novel intrusion detection framework for optimizing IoT security. *Scientific Reports*, *14*(1), 21789. DOI: 10.1038/s41598-024-72049-z PMID: 39294195

Rahbari, H., & Krunz, M. (2017). Rolling preambles: Mitigating stealthy FO estimation attacks in OFDM-based 802.11 systems. *2016 IEEE Conference on Communications and Network Security, CNS 2016*, 118–126. DOI: 10.1109/CNS.2016.7860477

Rajan, V., & Natarajan, P. (2018). Fingerprint authentication for self-driving vehicle security. *International Journal of Intelligent Transportation Systems Research*, *16*(2), 135–148.

Ramesh, S., & Kumar, R. (2019). Multimodal biometrics in autonomous driving. *Advances in Intelligent Transportation Systems*, *18*(4), 245–258.

Rana, M. S., Nobi, M. N., Murali, B., & Sung, A. H. (2022). Deepfake detection: A systematic literature review. *IEEE Access : Practical Innovations, Open Solutions*, *10*, 25494–25513. DOI: 10.1109/ACCESS.2022.3154404

Rana, P., & Mehta, S. (2021). Secure facial recognition for autonomous vehicle authentication. *IEEE Transactions on Intelligent Vehicles*, *6*(3), 420–435.

Rana, R., & Kumar, R. (2019). Performance analysis of AODV in presence of malicious node. *Acta Electronica Malaysia*, *3*(1), 1 ?"5. DOI: 10.26480/aem.01.2019.01.05

Rangaraju, S. (2023). Secure by intelligence: Enhancing products with AI-driven security measures. *EPH-International Journal of Science and Engineering*, *9*(3), 36–41.

Rani, S., Kumar, N., Srivastva, A., & Sharma, A. (2024, October). Leveraging artificial intelligence and machine learning for enhanced privacy and security. In *2024 IEEE International Conference on Blockchain and Distributed Systems Security (ICBDS)* (pp. 1-6). IEEE. DOI: 10.1109/ICBDS61829.2024.10837569

Ravindar, G., M., Abdul-Zahra, D. S., Subhashini, K., M., N., & Chawla, R. (2023). Healthcare chatbots with NLP and cybersecurity: Safeguarding patient data in the cloud. *2023 International Conference on Artificial Intelligence for Innovations in Healthcare Industries (ICAIIHI)*, 1–7.

Ricks, B. E. (2014). Intrusion detection systems. Physical Security and Safety: A Field Guide for the Practitioner, 101–108. DOI: 10.48175/IJARSCT-17606

Roe, J., Perkins, M., & Furze, L. (2024). Deepfakes and higher education: A research agenda and scoping review of synthetic media. *Journal of University Teaching & Learning Practice*, *21*(10), 1–22. DOI: 10.53761/2y2np178

Sadaram, G., Karaka, L. M., Maka, S. R., Sakuru, M., Boppana, S. B., & Katnapally, N. (2024). AI-Powered Cyber Threat Detection: Leveraging Machine Learning for Real-Time Anomaly Identification and Threat Mitigation. *MSW Management Journal*, *34*(2), 788–803.

Sadia, H., Farhan, S., Haq, Y. U., Sana, R., Mahmood, T., Bahaj, S. A. O., & Khan, A. R. (2024). Intrusion Detection System for Wireless Sensor Networks: A Machine Learning Based Approach. *IEEE Access : Practical Innovations, Open Solutions*, *12*(April), 52565–52582. DOI: 10.1109/ACCESS.2024.3380014

Saeed, S., Altamimi, S. A., Alkayyal, N. A., Alshehri, E., & Alabbad, D. A. (2023). Digital Transformation and Cybersecurity Challenges for Businesses Resilience: Issues and Recommendations. *Sensors (Basel)*, *23*(15), 6666. DOI: 10.3390/s23156666 PMID: 37571451

Sahu, C. K., Young, C., & Rai, R. (2021). Artificial intelligence in augmented reality-assisted manufacturing applications: A review. *International Journal of Production Research*, *59*(16), 4903–4959. DOI: 10.1080/00207543.2020.1859636

Salman, H., Li, J., Razenshteyn, I., Zhang, P., Zhang, H., Bubeck, S., & Yang, G. (2020). Provably robust deep learning via adversarially trained smoothed classifiers. *Advances in Neural Information Processing Systems*, *33*, 11292–11303.

Sameer, T., Rashmi, J., Khushi, B., Khushi, M., Rahul, R., & Prachi, J. (2024). Enhanced intrusion detection framework: Integrating SMOTE-ENN with random forest and XGBoost. *i-manager ?(tm)s. Journal of Information Technology*, *13*(3), 1 ?"10. DOI: 10.26634/jit.13.3.21454

Sandhu, K. (2021). Advancing Cybersecurity for Digital Transformation. Handbook of Research on Advancing Cybersecurity for Digital Transformation, 1-17. DOI: 10.4018/978-1-7998-6975-7.ch001

Sarker, I. H. (2024). AI-Enabled Cybersecurity for IoT and Smart City Applications. In *AI-Driven Cybersecurity and Threat Intelligence: Cyber Automation, Intelligent Decision-Making and Explainability* (pp. 121–136). Springer Nature Switzerland. DOI: 10.1007/978-3-031-54497-2_7

Satilmis, H., Akleylek, S., & Tok, Z. Y. (2024). A Systematic Literature Review on Host-Based Intrusion Detection Systems. *IEEE Access : Practical Innovations, Open Solutions*, *12*(January), 27237–27266. DOI: 10.1109/ACCESS.2024.3367004

Sato, H., & Tanaka, M. (2020). AI-based voice authentication for autonomous vehicle security. *IEEE Transactions on Intelligent Transportation Systems*, *21*(11), 5512–5525.

Sayegh, H., Dong, W., & Al-Madani, A. (2024). Enhanced intrusion detection with LSTM-based model, feature selection, and SMOTE for imbalanced data. *Applied Sciences (Basel, Switzerland)*, *14*(2), 479. DOI: 10.3390/app14020479

Sayyed, T., Kodwani, S., Dodake, K., & Adhayage, M. (2011)... *Intrusion Detection System.*, *14*(01), 39–57. DOI: 10.1142/9781848164482_0004

Schuster, M., & Lang, D. (2018). Biometric security risks in self-driving cars. *Cybersecurity Journal*, *9*(1), 77–89.

Sendjaja, T., Irwandi, , Prastiawan, E., Suryani, Y., & Fatmawati, E. (2024). Cybersecurity In The Digital Age: Developing Robust Strategies To Protect Against Evolving Global Digital Threats And Cyber Attacks. *The International Journal of Science in Society*, *6*(1), 1008–1019. DOI: 10.54783/ijsoc.v6i1.1098

Serac, C. A. (2023). Digital Transformation Vulnerabilities: Assessing The Risks And Strengthening Cyber Security. Annals of Faculty of Economics, University of Oradea. *Faculty of Economics*, *32*(1), 771–781.

Sethuraman, S. C., Dhamodara, S., & Vijayakumar, V. (2019). Intrusion detection system for detecting wireless attacks in IEEE 802.11 networks. *IET Networks*, *8*(4), 219–232. DOI: 10.1049/iet-net.2018.5050

Shafiullah, M. (2025). The FCM-guided deep learning model for low-frequency oscillation damping for electric power networks. *Neural Computing & Applications*, *37*(1), 105–121. DOI: 10.1007/s00521-024-10377-x

Shahana, A., Hasan, R., Farabi, S. F., Akter, J., Mahmud, M. A. A., Johora, F. T., & Suzer, G. (2024). AI-driven cybersecurity: Balancing advancements and safeguards. *Journal of Computer Science and Technology Studies*, *6*(2), 76–85. DOI: 10.32996/jcsts.2024.6.2.9

Shang, L., Guo, D., Ji, Y., & Li, Q. (2021). Discovering unknown advanced persistent threat using shared features mined by neural networks. *Computer Networks*, *189*, 107937. DOI: 10.1016/j.comnet.2021.107937

Shao, R., Shi, Z., Yi, J., Chen, P. Y., & Hsieh, C. J. (2022). On the adversarial robustness of vision transformers. *Transactions on Machine Learning Research*. arXiv2103.15670

Sharma, R., Sharma, V., Vashishth, T. K., Kumar, B., Sharma, B. K., & Chaudhary, S. (2025, February). Implementation of adaptive cloud security framework for cloud computing monitoring system applications. In AIP Conference Proceedings (Vol. 3224, No. 1). AIP Publishing. DOI: 10.1063/5.0246104

Sharma, B., Kumar, R., Kumar, A., Chhabra, M., & Chaturvedi, S. (2023). *A systematic review of IoT malware detection using machine learning*. In *Proceedings of the 10th International Conference on Computing for Sustainable Global Development (INDIACom)*, IEEE, pp. 91-96.

Sharma, M. (2024). Cybersecurity Platforms: Tackling Challenges in a Digital Age. [IJSREM]. *International Journal of Scientific Research in Engineering and Management*, *6*(4), 1–8. DOI: 10.55041/IJSREM12257

Sharma, R. (2020). Study of Supervised Learning and Unsupervised Learning. *International Journal for Research in Applied Science and Engineering Technology*, *8*(6), 588–593. DOI: 10.22214/ijraset.2020.6095

Siam, A., Alazab, M., Awajan, A., & Faruqui, N. (2025). A Comprehensive Review of AI's Current Impact and Future Prospects in Cybersecurity. *IEEE Access : Practical Innovations, Open Solutions*, *13*, 14029–14050. DOI: 10.1109/ACCESS.2025.3528114

Sigma Solve, I. N. C. (2024, September 12). Future of AI in cybersecurity: Key technologies and trends. Sigma Solve INC. https://www.sigmasolve.com/blog/the-future-of-ai-in-cybersecurity-emerging-technologies-and-trends/

Silvestri, S., Islam, S., Papastergiou, S., Tzagkarakis, C., & Ciampi, M. (2023). A Machine Learning approach for the NLP-based analysis of cyber threats and vulnerabilities of the healthcare ecosystem. *Sensors (Basel)*, *23*(2), 651. DOI: 10.3390/s23020651 PMID: 36679446

Singh, A., & Patel, V. (2019). Keystroke dynamics as a biometric authentication method for autonomous vehicles. *International Journal of Vehicular Biometric Systems*, *15*(3), 199–213.

Sowmya, T., & Mary Anita, E. A. (2023a). A comprehensive review of AI based intrusion detection system. Measurement: Sensors, 28(October 2022). DOI: 10.1016/j.measen.2023.100827

Srivastava, S. (2024, October 24). Healthcare cybersecurity – key strategies and best practices to protect patient data. *Appinventiv*. https://appinventiv.com/blog/cybersecurity-in-healthcare/

Subba, B., Biswas, S., & Karmakar, S. (2016). Intrusion Detection Systems using Linear Discriminant Analysis and Logistic Regression. 12th IEEE International Conference Electronics, Energy, Environment, Communication, Computer, Control: (E3-C3), INDICON 2015, June. DOI: 10.1109/INDICON.2015.7443533

Subramanya, A., Koohpayegani, S. A., Saha, A., Tejankar, A., & Pirsiavash, H. (2024). A closer look at robustness of vision transformers to backdoor attacks. In *Proceedings of the IEEE/CVF Winter Conference on Applications of Computer Vision* (pp. 3874–3883).

SuhanaSulaiman, N. (2020). Overview of Network Dataset and Data Mining Technique. International Journal of Advanced Trends in Computer Science and Engineering, 9(1.3), 287–290. DOI: 10.30534/ijatcse/2020/4391.32020

Sulaiman, N. S., Nasir, A., Othman, W. R. W., Wahab, S. F. A., Aziz, N. S., Yacob, A., & Samsudin, N. (2021). Intrusion Detection System Techniques : A Review. *Journal of Physics: Conference Series*, *1874*(1), 012042. Advance online publication. DOI: 10.1088/1742-6596/1874/1/012042

Sundaram, A. (1996). An introduction to intrusion detection. XRDS: Crossroads. *The ACM Magazine for Students*, *2*(4), 3–7. DOI: 10.1145/332159.332161

Sundaram, A. (2006). An Introduction to Intrusion Detection The need for Intrusion Detection Systems. *Computers & Security*, *1*(1), 10.

Sun, L., & Zhang, T. (2020). Deep learning in facial recognition for autonomous vehicle entry systems. *IEEE Transactions on Cybernetics*, *50*(8), 3754–3766.

Swords, J., & Willment, N. (2024). "It used to be fix-it in post production! Now it's fix-it in pre-production": How virtual production is changing production networks in film and television. *Creative Industries Journal*, •••, 1–17. DOI: 10.1080/17510694.2024.2430025

Tannenbaum, Y. (2024, April 2). AI, cybersecurity, and the rise of large language models. *Palo Alto Networks Blog*. https://www.paloaltonetworks.com/blog/2024/04/ai-cybersecurity-and-large-language-models/

Tan, R., & Huang, W. (2019). Challenges in biometric authentication for autonomous vehicle security. *IEEE Access : Practical Innovations, Open Solutions*, *7*, 99112–99125.

Tao, W., Honghui, F., & Hongjin, Z. CongZhe, Y., Hongyan, Z., & Xianzhen, H. (2021). Intrusion detection system combined enhanced random forest with SMOTE algorithm. Research Square. DOI: 10.21203/rs.3.rs-270201/v1

Thapa, N., Liu, Z., Kc, D. B., Gokaraju, B., & Roy, K. (2020). Comparison of machine learning and deep learning models for network intrusion detection systems. *Future Internet*, *12*(10), 1–16. DOI: 10.3390/fi12100167

Thompson, J., & Williams, C. (2018). Biometric data privacy in autonomous vehicles. *Journal of Privacy and Security*, *14*(2), 88–102.

Tolstikhin, I. O., Houlsby, N., Kolesnikov, A., Beyer, L., Zhai, X., Unterthiner, T., & Dosovitskiy, A. (2021). MLP-mixer: An all-MLP architecture for vision. *Advances in Neural Information Processing Systems*, *34*, 24261–24272.

Toth, T., & Kruegel, C. (2002). Evaluating the impact of automated intrusion response mechanisms. Proceedings - Annual Computer Security Applications Conference, ACSAC, 2002-January, 301–310. DOI: 10.1109/CSAC.2002.1176302

Tucci, V., Saary, J., & Doyle, T. E. (2022). Factors influencing trust in medical artificial intelligence for healthcare professionals: A narrative review. *Journal of Medical Artificial Intelligence*, *5*, 4–4. DOI: 10.21037/jmai-21-25

Unal, D., Bennbaia, S., & Catak, F. O. (2022). Machine learning for the Security of Healthcare systems based on the Internet of Things and edge computing. In *Cybersecurity and Cognitive Science* (pp. 299–320). Elsevier., DOI: 10.1016/B978-0-323-90570-1.00007-3

Valiathan, P. (2002). Blended Learning Models. Learning Circuits. Astd, 2000–2003. https://purnima-valiathan.com/wp-content/uploads/2015/09/Blended-Learning-Models-2002-ASTD.pdf

Vashishth, T. K., Sharma, V., Samania, B., Sharma, R., Singh, S., & Jajoria, P. (2025). Ethical and Legal Implications of AI in Cybersecurity. In Machine Intelligence Applications in Cyber-Risk Management (pp. 387-414). IGI Global Scientific Publishing.

Vashishth, T. K., Sharma, V., Sharma, K. K., Kumar, B., Chaudhary, S., & Panwar, R. (2024). Enhancing Cloud Security: The Role of Artificial Intelligence and Machine Learning. In Improving Security, Privacy, and Trust in Cloud Computing (pp. 85-112). IGI Global.

Vaswani, A., Shazeer, N., Parmar, N., Uszkoreit, J., Jones, L., Gomez, A. N., Kaiser, Ł., & Polosukhin, I. (2017). Attention is all you need. *Advances in Neural Information Processing Systems*, •••, 5998–6008.

Verma, N. (2023). *Deepfake technology and the future of public trust in video*, Doctoral dissertation.

Vijay Prabhu, K, V. P. & Lakshmi, C. (2024). A Study on Cybersecurity Challenges and Strategies in a Digitally Transformed Business Environment. [IJSREM]. *International Journal of Scientific Research in Engineering and Management*, *8*(10), 1–11.

Vinayakumar, R., Alazab, M., Soman, K. P., Poornachandran, P., Al-Nemrat, A., & Venkatraman, S. (2019). Deep Learning Approach for Intelligent Intrusion Detection System. *IEEE Access : Practical Innovations, Open Solutions*, *7*, 41525–41550. DOI: 10.1109/ACCESS.2019.2895334

Wang, J., & Liu, Z. (2020). Using AI to enhance biometric security in self-driving cars. *IEEE Transactions on Artificial Intelligence*, *2*(4), 320–335.

Wang, W., Xu, H., Wan, Y., Ren, J., & Tang, J. (2022). Towards Adversarial Learning: From Evasion Attacks to Poisoning Attacks. *Proceedings of the 28th ACM SIGKDD Conference on Knowledge Discovery and Data Mining*, 4830 - 483. DOI: 10.1145/3534678.3542608

Wang, X., Ji, Z., Ma, P., Li, Z., & Wang, S. (2023). InstructTA: Instruction-tuned targeted attack for large vision-language models. arXiv. https://arxiv.org/abs/2312.01886

Wang, Y., Tan, Y., Baker, T., Kumar, N., & Zhang, Q. (2023). Deep Fusion: Crafting Transferable Adversarial Examples and Improving Robustness of Industrial Artificial Intelligence of Things. *IEEE Transactions on Industrial Informatics*, *19*(6), 7480–7488. DOI: 10.1109/TII.2022.3168874

Westerlund, M. (2019). The emergence of deepfake technology: A review. *Technology Innovation Management Review*, *9*(11), 11. DOI: 10.22215/timreview/1282

Widodo, A., Setiawan, B., & Indraswari, R. (2024). Machine learning-based intrusion detection on multi-class imbalanced dataset using SMOTE. *Procedia Computer Science*, *213*, 1096 ?"1103. DOI: 10.1016/j.procs.2024.03.042

Wilson, H., & Campbell, D. (2019). Securing autonomous vehicles with biometric encryption. *Journal of Automotive Cybersecurity*, *5*(2), 110–123.

Wu, Y. S., Foo, B., Mei, Y., & Bagchi, S. (2003). Collaborative intrusion detection system (CIDS): A framework for accurate and efficient IDS. Proceedings - Annual Computer Security Applications Conference, ACSAC, 2003-January(Acsac), 234–244. DOI: 10.1109/CSAC.2003.1254328

Wu, B., Gu, J., Li, Z., Cai, D., He, X., & Liu, W. (2022). Towards efficient adversarial training on vision transformers. In *European Conference on Computer Vision* (pp. 307–325). Springer.

Xie, F., & Yu, L. (2021). Driver monitoring systems using biometric data: An AI approach. *IEEE Transactions on Intelligent Vehicles*, *7*(1), 56–72.

Xie, J. (2024). Application Study on the Reinforcement Learning Strategies in the Network Awareness Risk Perception and Prevention. *International Journal of Computational Intelligence Systems*, *17*(1), 112. Advance online publication. DOI: 10.1007/s44196-024-00492-x

Yamin, M. M., Ullah, M., Ullah, H., & Katt, B. (2021). Weaponized AI for cyber attacks. *Journal of Information Security and Applications*, *57*, 102722. DOI: 10.1016/j.jisa.2020.102722

Yan, Y. (2022). Deep Dive into Deepfakes-Safeguarding Our Digital Identity. *Brook. J. Int'l L.*, *48*, 767.

Yellepeddi, S. M., Advisor, S. T., & Researcher, I. (n.d.). AI-Powered Intrusion Detection Systems : Real-World Performance Analysis. 4(1).

Yeng, P. K., Nweke, L. O., Yang, B., Ali Fauzi, M., & Snekkenes, E. A. (2020). Artificial intelligence–based framework for analyzing health care staff security practice: Mapping review and simulation study (Preprint). DOI: 10.2196/preprints.19250

Yin, D., Lopes, R. G., Shlens, J., Cubuk, E. D., & Gilmer, J. (2019). A Fourier perspective on model robustness in computer vision. *Advances in Neural Information Processing Systems*, •••, 32.

Yodha, V. (2024). Leveraging Federated Learning for Privacy-Preserving Cybersecurity in Decentralized AI Systems. *Eastern European Journal for Multidisciplinary Research*, *1*(1), 89–106.

Yuan, L., Chen, Y., Wang, T., Yu, W., Shi, Y., Jiang, Z. H., & Feng, J. (2021). Tokens-to-token ViT: Training vision transformers from scratch on ImageNet. In *Proceedings of the IEEE/CVF International Conference on Computer Vision* (pp. 558–567).

Yu, P., Xia, Z., Fei, J., & Lu, Y. (2021). A survey on deepfake video detection. *IET Biometrics*, *10*(6), 607–624. DOI: 10.1049/bme2.12031

Zhang, F., Chan, P., Biggio, B., Yeung, D., & Roli, F. (2016). Adversarial Feature Selection Against Evasion Attacks. *IEEE Transactions on Cybernetics*, *46*(3), 766–777. DOI: 10.1109/TCYB.2015.2415032 PMID: 25910268

Zhang, Z., & Krunz, M. (2024). Preamble Forgery and Injection in Wi-Fi Networks: Attacks and Defenses. *IEEE Transactions on Mobile Computing*, *X*(X), 10752–10769. Advance online publication. DOI: 10.1109/TMC.2024.3383065

Zhao, Q., & Chen, M. (2020). Enhancing security in self-driving cars using biometrics. *IEEE Transactions on Neural Networks and Learning Systems*, *31*(12), 5124–5135. PMID: 32011269

Zhou, Y., & Li, J. (2019). AI-driven multimodal biometric authentication for autonomous vehicles. *IEEE Access : Practical Innovations, Open Solutions*, *7*, 123451–123465.

Zuech, R., Khoshgoftaar, T. M., & Wald, R. (2015). Intrusion detection and Big Heterogeneous Data: A Survey. *Journal of Big Data*, *2*(1), 3. Advance online publication. DOI: 10.1186/s40537-015-0013-4

About the Contributors

Toufik Mzili is a professor and researcher in Artificial Intelligence and Optimization at Chouaib Doukkali University, Morocco. He holds a Ph.D. in computer science and specializes in combinatorial optimization and computational intelligence. His research focuses on hybrid metaheuristic and machine learning approaches for solving large-scale NP-hard problems, including QAP and scheduling. He has published in high-impact journals and serves as an Associate Editor and reviewer for leading scientific venues. His interests include hybrid AI–optimization systems, swarm intelligence, fuzzy optimization, and intelligent applications in healthcare and industry.

Zahra Oughannou an Assistant Professor at Ibn Zohr University. Received her Professional Degree in Mobile Application Engineering from Higher School of Technology, Salé, and her Master's in Information Systems Security from Ibn Tofail University, Kenitra. She completed her Ph.D. in Computer Science at Ibn Tofail University in 2023. Her research focuses on IoT security, real-time data analysis, and smart university systems. Dr. Oughannou has published several papers in international conferences and journals and has served as a reviewer for scientific articles.

Nebojsa Bacanin received his Ph.D. degree from the Faculty of Mathematics, University of Belgrade, in 2015 (study program Computer Science, average grade 10,00). He started his university career in Serbia 18 years ago at the Graduate School of Computer Science in Belgrade. He currently works as Full Professor, Vice-Rector for Scientific Research and Head of Applied Artificial Intelligence study program at Singidunum University, Belgrade, Serbia. He is involved in scientific research in the field of computer science, and his specialty includes stochastic optimization algorithms, swarm intelligence, soft-computing, optimization, and modeling, as well as artificial intelligence algorithms, swarm intelligence, machine learning, image processing, and cloud and distributed computing. He has published more than 430 scientific papers (more than 180 SCIE papers) in high-quality journals and international conferences indexed in Clarivate Analytics JCR, Scopus, WoS, IEEExplore, and other scientific databases. As member of numerous Editorial boards in cutting-edge international journals and Committee boards of international conferences, he regularly edit and perform review activities. He has also been included in the prestigious Stanford University list of the 2% best world researchers, when the whole career is considered, in the field of Artificial Intelligence. Also, according to AD scientific index, he is currently listed as the best researcher from Computer Science area in Serbia.

Widi Aribowo as an Assistant Professor in the Department of Electrical Engineering at the Faculty of Vocational Studies, Surabaya State University. Known as a leading researcher, he has made significant contributions in the fields of metaheuristics, optimization, artificial intelligence, power systems and Microgrid. His scientific impact is evident through various publications in leading journals. In addition, Widi Aribowo has demonstrated his expertise as a peer reviewer for several prestigious Q1 journals, demonstrating his commitment to advancing academic discourse in the fields of metaheuristics, optimization, artificial intelligence, power systems and Microgrid.

***

Praveen is presently working as Assistant Professor in Department of Computer Science and Engineering, ITS Engineering college, Greater Noida. He completed his M. Tech in Artificial Intelligence and Robotics from Gautam Buddha University, Greater Noida, India. He has broad research interests in Networking, Artificial Intelligence and Natural language processing. He has published more than 3 papers in reputed journals and conferences.

Sherly Alphonse has received her B.E degree from Manonmaniam Sundaranar university, India and M.E from Anna University, India. She has five years teaching experience in various prestigious institutions. She is a reviewer of various international journals. She completed her full time Ph.D at Anna University, Chennai, India. Her research interest includes image processing and facial expression analysis.

Aman Anand is presently working as Assistant Professor in Department of Computer Science and Engineering, ITS Engineering college, Greater Noida. He pursuing his Ph.D in Computer Science and Engineering from Indian Institute of Information Technology Pune, Maharashtra, India. He has broad research interests in Networking, IoT, Software Engineering, Artificial Intelligence and Natural language processing. He has published more than 10 papers in reputed journals and conferences.

Manasab Balaji is a second year student doing her bachelors in Computer Science with specialization in Data Science at VIT Chennai.She has a strong interest in the field of data science and artificial intelligence,with a passion for exploring how data-driven insights can solve real-world problems. Apart from academics,she actively participates in event management roles for numerous clubs and events in her college and has a keen interest in taking up roles that test her creativity and organsational abilities.She aspires to become a data scientist that will allow her to create data driven solutions for real world problems.

Ankit Bansal has 20 years experience in applying AI in multiple domains like, Artificial intelligence, Apply Generative AI into more robust areas to solve business problem Encode -decoder, transformer optimization to apply Gen AI for image based PDFs. He has published many papers in journals, chapters in the edited books and presented papers in conferences.

Sandeep C. S is an accomplished academician and researcher with over 16 years of experience in teaching, research, and administration in Electronics and Communication Engineering. He serves as Associate Professor and Head of the ECE Department at Jawaharlal College of Engineering and Technology, Kerala. He is also engaged in postdoctoral research at the University of Louisiana, USA, focusing on AI, machine learning, and biomedical signal processing. He holds a Ph.D. from the University of Kerala, with research on advanced biomedical imaging. He earned his M.E. and B.E. from Anna University, Chennai, and an MBA in HRM from IGNOU. A Senior Member of IEEE and a recognized research supervisor under APJ Abdul Kalam Technological University, he has authored over 60 research papers and contributed to books, chapters, and patents. His interdisciplinary projects span healthcare, computing, and intelligent systems. He continues to contribute actively to academic innovation and global research collaborations.

Puneet Chauhan is a dedicated research scholar in the Department of Computer Applications at Subharti University, Meerut. With a strong academic foundation and a passion for cybersecurity, he has transitioned to an impactful professional role as a Ransomware Analyst in the United Kingdom. His work focuses on identifying, analyzing, and mitigating ransomware threats, contributing significantly to enhancing organizational security frameworks. Mr. Chauhan's expertise bridges academic research and practical applications, making him a valuable contributor to the evolving field of cybersecurity.

G. Saravanan, currently working as Professor in the Department of Electrical and Electronics Engineering at V.S.B. Engineering College, Karur with 4 years of teaching experience.His Research area includes electro mechanical in Micxro turbine generation system. He has published research papers in various National and International journals in WoS, Scopus, SCI Indexed Journals and various IEEE Explore conferences. He also published various Scopus indexed Book Chapters in IG Global.

Mayur Jariwala is an experienced IT professional with over 15 years of expertise in managing complex technology-driven projects. His background spans product design, system integration, and IT infrastructure management, with a strong focus on delivering solutions that meet both business and technical requirements. Mayur has a deep understanding of both traditional Waterfall and Agile methodologies, making him adept at leading cross-functional teams through all phases of the project lifecycle. Currently pursuing a PhD in Information Technology at the University of the Cumberlands, Mayur's academic and professional journey is rooted in the intersection of technology and project management. He holds master's degrees in Information Technology and Project Management, as well as Business Administration, and is certified as a Project Management Professional (PMP)®, Lean Six Sigma Green Belt, and SAFe® 5 Scrum Master. Mayur's contributions to the field extend beyond project management. He is an active researcher and author, with a focus on the integration of AI and cybersecurity in IT frameworks. His publications include "The Cyber Security Roadmap: A Comprehensive Guide to Cyber Threats, Cyber Laws, and Cyber Security Training for a Safer Digital World," as well as numerous research articles on cutting-edge topics like blockchain's potential in space missions and AI's role in enhancing IT project management. Mayur also serves as a reviewer for several IT journals and contributes to the Project Management Institute's AI content, reflecting his commitment to advancing the fields of information technology, AI, and cybersecurity.

Robinson Joel received the Doctorate Ph.D degree in Computer and Information Technology from the Manonmaniam Sundaranar University, Tirunelveli in March 2019. He completed his M.Tech and MCA from the same university year 2008 and 2002 respectively. He is currently working as an Associate Professor in the Department of Computer Science and Engineering at KCG College of Technology, Chennai. He has 16 years of teaching experience.

Suresh Joesph Kanagarai received his Bachelor's Degree in Computer Science & Engineering from Bharathiar University and a Master's in Computer Science & Engineering from the University of Madras in 1999 and 2003, respectively.

He received his Doctoral Computer Science & Engineering degree from Anna University in 2013. Presently, he is working as an Associate Professor in the Department of Computer Science at Pondicherry University. His areas of research interest include Services Computing and Image Processing. He has more than 50 research publications in reputed and peer-reviewed journals.

Daniel Raj K is a faculty member in the Department of Computer Science and Engineering (AI & ML) at Kalaignar Karunanidhi Institute of Technology, Coimbatore. He holds a B.Tech in Information Technology and an M.E in Computer Science Engineering. His work includes journal publications on neuromorphic computing and intelligent systems, as well as reviewing contributions for IEEE, IGI Global, and other SCOPUS-indexed venues. He has authored book chapters and continues to work on applied projects in machine learning and resilient communication systems.

Rajendra Kumar is Associate Professor in Computer Science & Engineering Department School of Engineering and Technology, Sharda University, Greater Noida, India. His research are includes Blockchain, IoT, Biometrics, Human Computer Interaction, and Theoretical Computer Science.

Palanivel Kuppusamy holds a Ph.D. in Computer Science & Engineering (2023) from Pondicherry University (A Central University), Puducherry, India. He is a graduate of Engineering (1994) from Bharathiar University, Tamil Nadu, India, and a Post Graduate of Engineering (1998) from Pondicherry University, Puducherry, India. He has over 20 years of diverse professional and teaching experience at Pondicherry University. His research interests include smart education, software architecture, network management & analytics, and technological applications in the higher education sector.

Bikender Kushwaha is an academic and researcher with over 3.5 years of teaching experience along with 1 year of professional experience in the IT industry. He is currently serving as an Assistant Professor in the Department of Computer Science and Engineering at Galgotias University, a position he has held for the past 14 months. He completed his B.Tech in Computer Science and Engineering and M.Tech in Artificial Intelligence and Robotics from Gautam Buddha University. His research contributions include three international conference papers, one published in IEEE Xplore (2024) and two through Springer Nature. His primary areas of specialization are Artificial Intelligence and Machine Learning, with ongoing interests in advanced computational models and emerging technologies.

Bhavana M is an innovative and driven individual currently pursuing an MBA in Business Analytics and Operations at Dayananda Sagar College of Engineering. With a background in Computer Science, she has channeled her skills into impactful mini projects that showcase her technical and analytical abilities. Among her notable works are a sentiment analysis tool developed using Python to evaluate social media trends, a personal finance tracker built with basic web technologies for efficient budget management, and a data visualization dashboard created with R to simplify complex datasets. These projects highlight her knack for blending programming, analytics, and practical problem-solving. Areas of Expertise Business Analytics and Operations. Python and R for data analysis and visualization. Web development for functional applications. Creative solutions through mini project development. Bhavana M's hands-on approach to mini projects reflects her passion for leveraging technology to address real-world challenges, marking her as a promising talent in analytics and beyond.

Maad M. Mijwilis is an Iraqi Academician; he was born in Baghdad, Iraq, in 1987. He received his B.Sc. degree in software engineering from Baghdad College of Economic Sciences University, Iraq, in 2009. He received a M.Sc. degree in 2015 from the computer science department, University of Baghdad, in the field of wireless sensor networks, Iraq. Currently, he is a director of the Division of Quality Assurance and Performance at the College of Administration and Economics, Al-Iraqia University. He is working as an Assistant Professor and an academic member of staff in the Computer Techniques Engineering Department at Baghdad College of Economic Sciences University, Iraq. He has over ten years of experience in teaching, guiding projects for undergraduates, and laboratory sessions. He has published 218 works, including research papers, review articles, book chapters, and preprints in national and international journals and conferences. He is also an editor in more than 10 international/national journals and a reviewer in more than 100 international/national journals. He has served on technical program committees for many prestigious conferences. Also, he graduated from Publons Academy as a peer reviewer. According to his Google Scholar profile, he has amassed over 5,600 citations, reflecting the high visibility of his research in the global scientific community.

P. K. Poonguzhali, currently working as Associate Professor in the Department of Electronics and Communication Engineering at Sri Krishna College of Engineering and Technology, Coimbatore with 22 years of teaching experienceHer Research area includes Energy Efficiency in Wireless sensor Network, Data Analysis, Cluster/Cloud Computing and Computer Networking. She has published research papers in various National and International journals in WoS, Scopus, SCI Indexed

Journals and various IEEE Explore conferences. She also published various Book Chapters in CRC Taylor &Francis.

Anshad A. S. is dedicated to fostering a culture of innovation and excellence in engineering education. With his extensive experience in academia and administration, he has been instrumental in driving research and development in cutting-edge areas such as WSNs, AI, Medical Imaging, BME, and Deep Learning. As the Principal of John Cox Memorial CSI Institute of Technology, he has been instrumental in promoting OBE skills and has guided numerous research projects, leading to publications in reputed SCIE, SCOPUS, and Google-indexed journals. Dr. Anshad's research focus is complemented by his commitment to lifelong learning, as evident from his participation in various FDPs, workshops, seminars, and MOOCs. He is a recognized research supervisor, author, and inventor, with memberships in prestigious professional institutions. As a reviewer for reputed journals and a contributor to funded projects, Dr. Anshad's work embodies his passion for promoting innovation, research, and academic excellence in engineering education.

Vikas Sharma is an active academician and researcher in the field of computer science with 7 years of experience. He earned M. Tech degree specialized in Computer Science. He is involved in academic development and scholarly activities. He is member of International Association of Engineers, The Society of Digital Information and Wireless Communications, Global Professors Welfare Association, International Association of Academic plus Corporate (IAAC), Computer Science Teachers Association and Internet Society. His research interest includes Cloud Computing, Artificial Intelligence, Machine Learning; published more than 55 research articles with 4 books and 75 book chapters in edited books. He is contributing as member of editorial and reviewers' boards in conferences and various computer journals and edited books published by Elsevier, CRC Press, Taylor and Francis, Springer, IGI global, Wiley Publication, IET Publication, De Gruyter, River Publication etc.

Sanjay Srivastava is currently an Associate Professor in the Department of Computer Science & Engineering, Raj Kumar Goel Institute of Technology, Ghaziabad, U.P. Prior to his recent appointment at the RKGIT; he was an Associate Professor in Department of Computer Science & Engineering, MGMCOET, Noida. Mr. Srivastava received his undergraduate & Master degrees in CSE. He had published a number of papers in preferred Journals and chapters in books, and participated in many Conferences as reviewer and session chair. He also presented various academic as well as research-based papers at several national and international conferences. Mr. Srivastava had published books in domain of

Computer Organization, Computer Networks & Programming in "C". His research activities are currently twofold: while the first research activity is set to explore the developmental role that entrepreneurship – as a developmental alternative – which could play in advancing the well-being of Indian Students; the second major research theme that he is pursuing is focused on the IoT, Machine learning, Artificial Intelligence, Computer Vision & design of advance Computer Architecture.

Roopa Udupi is an esteemed Assistant Professor at Dayananda Sagar College of Engineering, bringing over two decades of dedicated teaching experience in academia. Her academic journey includes the attainment of an M.Sc. and M.Phil. in Statistics, coupled with an MBA in Marketing. She is pursuing her Ph.D. from Visvesvaraya Technological University in the field of exploring the transformative impact of social media applications on higher education further enhancing her expertise and contributions to the field. Areas of Expertise • Business Analytics using Python, R, Excel, and SPSS tools. • Machine Learning, Quantitative Techniques, Operations Research, Business Mathematics. • Research Methodology and Statistical Analysis for interdisciplinary applications. • Curriculum design and facilitation of innovative teaching methods.

Varadharajan Bhoopathy is a Professor at Sree Rama Engineering College. He holds a Ph.D. in Information and Communication Engineering from Anna University and has over 16 years of academic experience. Specializing in wireless sensor networks and IoT, he has published numerous research papers and holds several international patents. Dr. Bhoopathy is a recipient of prestigious awards for his contributions to education and research. His commitment to academia continues to drive innovation and excellence in the field of computer science.

Tarun Kumar Vashishth is an active academician and researcher in the field of computer science with 21 years of experience. He earned Ph.D. Mathematics degree specialized in Operations Research; served several academic positions such as HoD, Dy. Director, Academic Coordinator, Member Secretary of Department Research Committee, Assistant Center superintendent and Head Examiner in university examinations. He is involved in academic development and scholarly activities. He is member of International Association of Engineers, The Society of Digital Information and Wireless Communications, Global Professors Welfare Association, International Association of Academic plus Corporate (IAAC), Computer Science Teachers Association and Internet Society . His research interest includes Cloud Computing, Artificial Intelligence, Machine Learning and Operations Research; published more than 50 research articles with 2 book and 75 book chapters. He is contributing as member of editorial and reviewers boards in conferences and various computer journals published by CRC Press, Taylor and Francis, Springer, IGI global and other universities.

Pushpendra Verma is an Associate Professor, School of Computer Science and Applications, IIMT University, Meerut, UP, India. He has done MCA, MTech-CSE. MPhil (CS) and Doctorate in Computer Science. His area of research is in Cryptography and Network and Security/ Cyber Security, and his other areas of specialization include Artificial Intelligence, Deep Learning and Machine Learning. He has Convener, Keynote Speakers and participated in several high-profile conferences, seminars and workshops. The author has many research papers in international journals, review articles in various Scopus Indexed Journals, international journals and interested in academics and research. He has !9+ years extensive teaching and research experience in various Universities as well as colleges across India. He also reviewed the Reputed International Journal Papers. He is member of Vidwan, Springer, International Association of Engineers (IAENG), Society of Digital Information and Wireless Communications (SDIWC). IEEE, etc.

Vidhya Rathinasamy serves as Professor and Head of the Department of Artificial Intelligence and Machine Learning at Hindusthan College of Engineering and Technology,Coimbatore. She has over 22 years of experience in teaching and administrative leadership in engineering education, she brings extensive expertise to her role. Her educational background includes a Bachelor of Engineering in Electrical and Electronics Engineering from Bharathiar University, a Master of Technology in Information Technology from Anna University, Coimbatore, and a Doctor of Philosophy in Information and Communication Engineering from Anna University, Chennai. Dr. Vidhya has authored 20 papers in refereed international journals, 10 papers in international conferences and authored 3 books. Her research interests and specialization encompass Wireless Sensor Networks,Artificial intelligence, Machine learning,Cloud computing and data analytics.

Index

F

H

I

P

R

www.ingramcontent.com/pod-product-compliance
Ingram Content Group UK Ltd.
Pitfield, Milton Keynes, MK11 3LW, UK
UKHW052003051026
15624UKWH00003B/536

9 798337 329222